CONTENTS

INTRODUCTION

SECTION 1 : NAMIBIA   9

BACKGROUND INFORMATION   11

Introduction   11

Travel Facts   11
Entry requirements 12 / Quick facts 13 / Customs regulations 13
Currency 14 / Getting there 14 / Getting around 15 / Climate 17
Health 18 / What to pack 18 / National parks 19
Tourist information 19 / Adventure safaris 19 / Tour operators 20
Accommodation 20 / Food 21 / Tipping 22 / Security 22

Country File   23
History 23 / Geology, flora and fauna 31 / The economy 33
The people 34 / Recommended reading 37

AROUND NAMIBIA   38

Windhoek   38
Swakopmund   50
The Skeleton Coast   62
Etosha National Park   64
Damaraland   71
Caprivi   75
Luderitz   80
Fish River Canyon   87

SECTION 2 : BOTSWANA   91

BACKGROUND INFORMATION   92

Introduction   92

Travel Facts   92
Entry requirements 92 / Quick facts 93 / Customs regulations 93
Currency 93 / Getting there 94 / Getting around 95 / Climate 97
Health 98 / What to pack 98 / National parks 99
Tourist information 99 / Accommodation 102 / Food 102
Tipping 103 / Arts and crafts 103

Country File	104
History 104 / Geology, flora and fauna 108 / The economy 109 Recommended reading 112	
AROUND BOTSWANA	**113**
Maun	113
Okavango Delta	121
Chobe National Park	133
The Panhandle	142
Tsodilo Hills	144
Other National Parks and Game Reserves	146
Gaborone	153
Francistown	158
SECTION 3 : SOUTH AFRICA	**161**
BACKGROUND INFORMATION	**165**
Introduction	165
Travel Facts	166
Entry requirements 166 / Quick facts 166 / Customs regulations 167 Currency 167 / Taxes 167 / Getting there 167 / Getting around 167 Climate 170 / Health 171 / What to pack 172 / Shopping 172 National parks 172 / Tourist information 173 / Activities 174 Adventure safaris 175 / Accommodation 175 / Food 176 Tipping 177	
Country File	178
History 178 / Geology, flora and fauna 191 / The people 194 Recommended reading 195	
AROUND SOUTH AFRICA	**197**
Johannesburg	197
Sun City	210
Eastern Transvaal: The Panorama Route	211
Kruger National Park	221
The Drakensberg	233
Durban	239
The Game Reserves of Zululand	255
Capetown	259
The Winelands	284
The Garden Route	299

Discovery Guide to Southern Africa

SECTION 4 : SWAZILAND   327

BACKGROUND INFORMATION   328

Introduction   328

Travel Facts   328
Entry requirements 328 / Customs regulations 328 / Currency 328
Quick facts 329 / Getting there and getting around 329
Car hire 331 / Taxes 331 / Climate 331 / Health 331
Shopping 331 / Accommodation 332 / Tourist information 332
Food 332

Country File   333
History 333 / The economy 334 / The people 334

AROUND SWAZILAND   335

Ezulwini Valley   335
Mbabane   337
Pig's Peak   342

Discovery Guide to Southern Africa

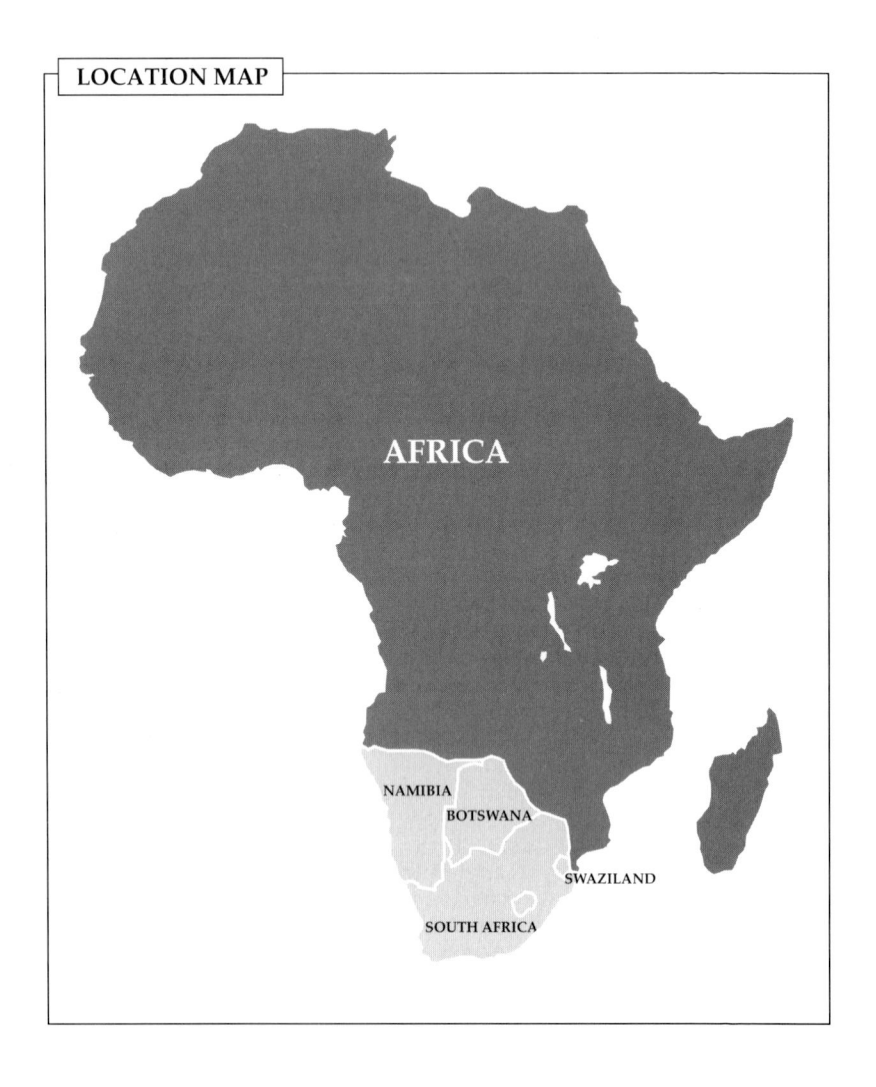

LOCATION MAP

AFRICA

NAMIBIA
BOTSWANA
SWAZILAND
SOUTH AFRICA

INTRODUCTION

I had roamed the world for a decade before I turned my attention to Africa. I suppose it was a bit like Antarctica for me: somewhere I wanted to visit after I had been everywhere else. I had no inkling then that Africa was going to cast her spell on me. And yet, all it took was that one quick visit to change my perceptions and my interests for ever. Back at home, far from the bushveld and savannah, I discovered that images and thoughts of Africa dominated my mind. Somehow, I had been transfixed and bewitched by the light, the sounds, the very smell of her lands. That first journey marked the beginning of my obsession with Africa; since then I have travelled the continent extensively and exclusively, to the neglect of Antarctica and other places in the world.

Although there is much I like about each of the countries of Africa, it is in Southern Africa that my passion has found its home. The land is vast and ancient and the face of old Africa still lurks in unexpected places. Striking contrasts of terrain, wild extravagances of beauty, the subtle power of the desert and magnificent concentrations of game characterize this long overlooked region. As travel destinations, the countries of Southern Africa under discussion in this guide – Namibia, Botswana, South Africa and Swaziland – are relatively unheralded and unknown. Political problems in concert with distance and scant tourist information have conspired to keep visitors to a minimum. For the past three decades Kenya has capitalized on the safari industry in Africa; times have changed however, and Kenya's charms have begun to pall. Mass tourism and excessive commercialization now characterize most of the safari destinations there. Once the success story of post-colonial Africa, Kenya is currently reeling from massive unemployment, a rocketing birth rate and serious political disenchantment. Meanwhile, the situation has taken a turn for the better in Southern Africa. The war for independence has been won in Namibia and the demise of apartheid and white rule in South Africa is imminent. Neighbouring Angola and Mozambique, racked by civil war for years, are now on the verge of peace, and stability has returned to the region as a whole.

I am often asked why I have chosen to lead safaris and to spend so much of my time in Southern Africa. The response is simple: in combination, these countries have a greater diversity of wildlife, flora, habitat, culture, history, activities and attractions than any other region on the continent. Equally important from a safari perspective, large-scale group tourism has not run rampant here and it is still possible to experience untrammeled wilderness, the solitude of the desert and the timeless, primeval magic of the bush.

A more multi-faceted landscape is difficult to imagine. From Namibia's Etosha Pans and Namib dunes, to Botswana's unique, labyrinthine Okavango Delta, to the vast savannahs, rugged mountains and pristine beaches of South Africa, the underlying theme is dramatic contrast. Whatever preconceptions you may have, few travellers are prepared for the raw beauty, diversity and power of this land. As an added bonus, these countries also offer some of the finest and best-managed game parks in the world and for many that is reason enough to visit. Lastly, in practical terms, Southern Africa is easy to access, the infrastructure and tourist facilities are consistently excellent and the people are honest and friendly. Nowhere on the continent will you discover a more felicitous combination of factors to ensure an unparalleled safari experience.

In the course of researching and writing this book, I have seen more of Namibia, Botswana, South Africa and Swaziland than most of their inhabitants. Far from satisfying my yearning for this land, it has only reinforced my sense that this is the world's last Eden, a place where the rhythm of nature is still heedless of man. The imagery of Africa has etched itself on my mind: the haunting lament of the fish eagle, the pungent sage perfume of the bush, the silhouette of giraffes caught in the red glare of the setting sun, the wind warm on my face as I camp under the roof of a starry black sky. How much longer these quintessentially African pleasures can exist is uncertain; the pressures of modern civilization, of a burgeoning population dependent on land, water and food do not bode well for the future. Go soon then, before it is too late. The pages that follow contain practicalities and recommendations to advise you how and where to travel. I am hopeful that this guide will be of particular interest and assistance to those individuals who like to plan their own itinerary and travel without benefit of guide or tour group, as well as to those who seek adventure and off-the-beaten-path destinations. In tandem with my own interests I have made a point of including unusual and challenging activities whenever possible, such as elephant safaris, wilderness treks, ATV and balloon adventures, even spelunking. Above all I hope my enthusiasm and love of Africa will be contagious and that you too will be captivated by one of the most exhilarating and memorable destinations in the world.

SECTION 1: NAMIBIA

BACKGROUND INFORMATION
Travel Facts

Country File
AROUND NAMIBIA
Windhoek

Swakopmund

The Skeleton Coast

Etosha National Park

Damaraland

Caprivi

Luderitz

Fish River Canyon

Namibia

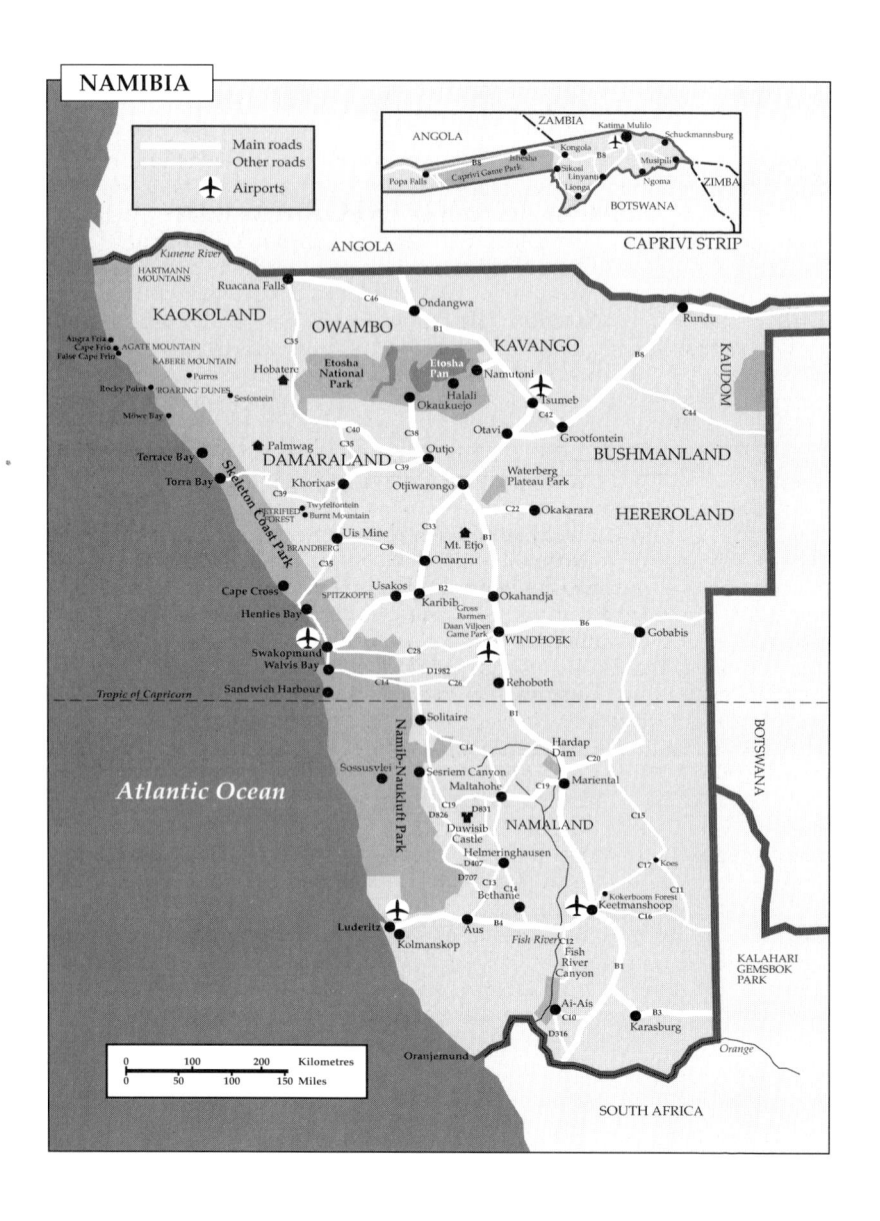

BACKGROUND INFORMATION

INTRODUCTION

Namibia is Africa's newest nation, having gained its independence in 1990 after 35 years of bitter conflict. It is a fascinating country abounding with natural wonders, diverse habitats, remote wilderness areas and desert-adapted wildlife. Travel here is easy and safe. Accommodation is spotless, the people are friendly and the infrastructure is sophisticated. Namibia occupies a large, sparsely populated territory and tourist destinations are far flung. For this reason I recommend a minimum of two weeks for exploring the major attractions: Windhoek, Swakopmund, The Namib Desert, Etosha and the Skeleton Coast. If you like off-the-beaten-path travelling, Namibia is ideal. The road system is excellent and there is an impressive network of government rest camps. If you prefer to leave the travel details to someone else, a number of tour operators cover the countryside.

The bleak and inhospitable Namib Desert forms the centrepiece of the country; its vast reaches are compelling and unforgettable. No traveller to Namibia should miss an opportunity to venture into this hinterland for there is an astounding array of hidden life and beauty lurking beneath its desolate exterior. The two major cities, Windhoek and Swakopmund, are delightful places to spend a few days. Although incongruously European in appearance, there is charming colonial architecture, excellent shopping and dining, as well as a number of destinations to explore within a short radius. Further afield, the Etosha National Park offers superb game viewing. The blinding white salt pans which characterize Etosha form a dramatic backdrop for the herds of plains game which roam the enormous expanses of the park. A number of desert-adapted animal species not commonly seen elsewhere in Africa are found here.

Personally, the highlight of a journey to Namibia is a safari to the Skeleton Coast. Few places on earth can rival it for spectacular scenery. It is one of the truly wild, untouched places left on the continent. Man is the intruder here and he is no match for nature in her raw, unadulterated state.

Namibia is a land of contrasts, at once austere and extravagant, subtle yet dramatic. If, like me, you were raised far from the desert and could never understand or imagine its appeal, a journey to Namibia will be a revelation. This is an Africa far from game-dotted savannahs and verdant forests, but it is enthralling and magnificent all the same.

TRAVEL FACTS

Namibia is one of the largest countries in sub-Saharan Africa and it is also the least populated. A land of compelling harsh beauty, it offers the tourist a kaleidoscope of unspoilt landscapes. The sense of untrammelled space, of wide horizons and solitude is unequalled in Africa. Conservation is a high priority, and already 12.3 per cent of the land has been set aside for wildlife sanctuaries. The tourist infrastructure is very good and the future growth of this industry is being carefully guided. The Government views tourism as a renewable resource and a potential generator of significant economic activity. Fortunately there is a great desire to ensure the protection of the environment in addition to promoting tourism. The mixture of wilderness and modern amenities that is found in Namibia make this country a pleasure for the traveller.

The scenic splendour is far-flung and this means that the average traveller with a two- or three-week holiday will not be able to see the country in its entirety. Although this guide canvasses most regions, not every locale needs to be visited in order to experience Namibia. Making the assumption that the majority of readers are not anthropologists, geologists or art historians, I would recommend the following itinerary:

> Windhoek - 2 nights
> Swakopmund (Namib-Naukluft Park) - 3-5 nights
> Etosha National Park - 2 or 3 nights
> Skeleton Coast Fly-In Safari - 5 or 6 nights

As I have said elsewhere, a fly-in safari to the wilderness area of the Skeleton Coast is my number one recommendation. Although this is not a game viewing trip it is the very best way to discover the pristine beauty and the power of the vast landscape that is Namibia. If this trip is not feasible, the second best option is to set aside a few days to explore the dunes, coastline and desolate plains of the Namib Desert in the Namib-Naukluft Park just outside Swakopmund.

Overall, the standard of accommodation and food is excellent in Namibia. The communication and transport systems are some of the best in Africa. It is a very clean country and its diverse peoples are cheerful and friendly. It offers the tourist fascinating geology, magnificent and unique landscapes, and terrific, easily accessible game viewing without the crowds of tourists and proliferation of vehicles and lodges which has plagued other areas of Africa.

ENTRY REQUIREMENTS

All visitors to Namibia must possess a valid passport. In addition to this, proof of exit date is often requested, a requirement which can be satisfied with a return plane ticket. No visas are required of tourists from the United Kingdom, Ireland, Austria, Italy, France, the United States, Norway, Finland, West Germany, Lichtenstein, Canada, Japan, Sweden, Denmark, Switzerland, the Netherlands and other Southern African countries. Citizens of all other countries do need to obtain visas. An entry permit is issued to all visitors upon arrival and the length of stay granted will depend on your travel plans. For additional information on entry requirements contact your nearest South African embassy or consulate.

Travel Facts

QUICK FACTS

TOTAL AREA: 823,144 sq km; for comparative purposes about 1½ times the size of France.

NEIGHBOURS: Angola to the north, Zambia to the extreme north-east, Botswana and Zimbabwe to the east and South Africa to the south. The Atlantic Ocean forms a 1,350 km coastline and defines the western border.

POPULATION: With roughly 1.3 million inhabitants, Namibia has one of the lowest population densities in the world. This works out to be a little more than one person per square kilometre. 26 per cent of the population is concentrated in urban areas.

ETHNIC GROUPS: 86 per cent of the populace is black, 7 per cent white and 7 per cent of mixed descent. The Ovambo is the largest ethnic group and is comprised of eight different tribes, each with its own dialect and territory. Then in descending numerical order are the Kavango, Herero, Damara, White, Nama, Coloured (mixed race), East Caprivian, Kaokolander, Bushman, Rehoboth Baster and Tswana communities.

CAPITAL: Windhoek.

LANGUAGES: English and Afrikaans are the official languages, although German is also widely spoken, a legacy of German rule here from 1884 to 1915. There are numerous indigenous African languages, all of which are derived from either Bantu or Khoisan tongues.

RELIGION: 75 per cent of the populace is Christian with roughly half of this group Lutheran.

INDEPENDENCE: Namibia severed its ties with South Africa on 21 March, 1990 and in so doing, became the last country on the African continent to gain independence.

ELECTRICITY: 220/240 volts; outlets are of the three-pin, 15 amp type.

TIME: GMT plus 2 hours.

CURRENCY: At the time of writing the monetary unit remains the South African rand. The rate of exchange as of November 1991 is $1.00 = R2.80; £1.00 = R4.80. Credit cards are widely accepted at hotels, restaurants and shops.

CUSTOMS REGULATIONS

In addition to personal effects the following items and quantitites may be imported into Namibia duty free: 1 litre of spirits including liqueurs and cordials; 2 litres of wine; 50 ml of perfume; 250 ml of toilet water; 400 cigarettes, 50 cigars and 250 g of tobacco. Firearms are not allowed into the country without a permit; such permits will be issued by a customs official at the point of entry.

Hunters are allowed to bring their personal rifles into Namibia provided that they are declared upon arrival. It should be noted that it is an offence to be in the possession of an unlicensed firearm.

CURRENCY

At the present time the monetary unit of Namibia remains the South African rand. There is currently some political discussion as to the advisability of establishing a Namibian currency independent of the rand. This is certain to occur eventually but for now it appears that Namibians are going to live with the rand for a while longer. There is no limit to the amount of foreign currency a visitor is allowed to bring into the country. However, you may only legally import or export 200 rand per person.

GETTING THERE

Air: At the time of writing, the only direct flight to Namibia from overseas is offered by *Namib Air* from Frankfurt to Windhoek, twice weekly. The airline is hoping to secure a slot at JFK Airport in New York to establish a non-stop service. If you are coming from overseas, it is generally necessary to fly to Johannesburg or Cape Town and then transfer to a connecting *South African Airways* or *Namib Air* flight, of which there are several daily. Alternatively, direct flights are available from London to Harare and New York to Lusaka several times a week. There is a service connecting Windhoek with these cities, although not on a daily basis.

Both *Namib Air* and *Air Botswana* offer direct flights to Windhoek from Maun. Connections to other destinations in Botswana may be made through Maun. There is also direct service from Lusaka to Windhoek twice a week by *Zambia Air* and *Royal Swazi Air*. *Namib Air* has scheduled service to Harare once weekly.

Road: Road access to Namibia from South Africa is excellent. The two main entry points are at Vioolsdrif on the N7 from Cape Town and at Nakop on the R32 from Upington. Both of these routes are fully tarred. Other border control monitoring posts are located at Alexander Bay (N6), Onseepkans (N9), Noenieput (M10) and Rietfontein (L10). The posts are operated 24 hours a day and a passport must be produced for entry into Namibia.

Overland travel from Botswana can only be accomplished on sand and gravel roads. Entry to Namibia is via the border posts at Buitepos/Mamuno, Mohembo/Shakawe or Ngoma Bridge (Caprivi). There is no official border post at Mohembo or Ngoma Bridge so you must report to the nearest police station immediately. A four-wheel drive vehicle is essential if you are approaching from Mamuno or Mohembo. An ordinary car can be used to cross into East Caprivi at Ngoma if there hasn't been heavy rain. If you are planning to drive from Botswana to Namibia, it is absolutely critical to research your route in advance of your trip. The roads that traverse the Kalahari desert and the Caprivi Strip are notoriously bad and road conditions change frequently.

The political situation in Angola is unstable and volatile at the moment, making overland travel from there both dangerous and impractable. Entry to Namibia from Zambia by road is only possible at Katima Mulilo in East Caprivi. A four wheel drive vehicle is helpful but not essential to complete the trip to Windhoek.

Travel Facts

To drive from Zimbabwe to Namibia one must enter Botswana at Kazungula and then complete exit formalities at Kasane before entering East Caprivi at Ngoma Bridge.

Rail: There is an international rail service between Namibia and Johannesburg or Cape Town three times weekly. It should be noted that it takes four days as the train carries freight as well as passengers.

Coach: The F.P. du Toit Transport Company provides a luxury Mainliner service between Windhoek and Johannesburg or Cape Town twice a week. The trip takes 20 hours to Johannesburg and 18 to Cape Town.

GETTING AROUND

Air: *Namib Air* is the domestic carrier and services Windhoek, Swakopmund, Luderitz, Keetmanshoop, Oranjemund, Tsumeb, Oshakati, Rundu and Katima Mulilo on a regular scheduled basis. As distances are great and attractions are far flung, air travel is very practical and is sometimes more economical than car hire. In addition to the scheduled services of *Namib Air*, charter flights are available to many off-the-beaten path destinations that do not have suitable runways for scheduled planes. There is an excellent network of bush pilots in Namibia and charter flights can help you to get to some of the most spectacular areas of this country.

Road: Namibia has an excellent network of roads, a legacy of the South African government. Actually, the country has more kilometres of road per person than any other African nation, a statistic it is particularly proud of. All main roads radiating from Windhoek are tarred which makes travel easy and possible in all weathers. Motoring is on the left-hand side of the road and there is a general speed limit of 120 kph on open roads. On Namibia's gravelled roads, of which there are many, it is advisable to travel at lower speeds, despite the fact that they are generally well graded and maintained. Animals roam freely over most of the countryside and although there are signposts advising of animal crossings, it is easy to become complacent. Extra caution should be exercised when driving at night as animals on the road can be a real hazard in the dark.

Seat belts are required by law and overseas visitors should be in possession of a valid International Driving Permit. Road signs are international and the signposting is adequate. Petrol is available in settled areas with prices comparable to Europe. It is essential to remember that in Namibia, petrol stations, road services and even towns are few and far between.

Before you set out on a trip by road it would be advisable to invest in a small cool box so that you can carry water, cold drinks and fruit with you. This is a hot and dusty country and once *en route* I guarantee you will welcome this advance preparation. Check to make sure that your vehicle has a good spare tyre and consider packing a shovel, tow rope and a basic tool kit if you are planning to undertake excursions to the remote and little-visited regions of Namibia. It is also wise to investigate in advance the

Namibia

availability of petrol, food and water supplies both en route and at your destination.

The *Automobile Association*, (AA) of South Africa maintains a branch office in Windhoek, which can be of great assistance to the tourist. In addition to excellent maps which are available to international members free of charge, the people at the AA have up-to-date information on road conditions across Namibia.

A brief explanation of the road designations in Namibia will help you plan your driving. A B route is a tarred highway and a C route is a gravelled road, well maintained and generally suitable for all-weather travel. I found that you can average 100 kph on a C road. Roads designated with a D are also gravel surfaced; the condition of these roads can vary from excellent to poor but they are usually easily negotiable in a car. D routes do not have any bridges, which means that wherever there is a wash (water run-off course) the road will dip. This is no problem except in the event of a fierce rainstorm. At such times the water could rush down from the mountains and briefly flood the low-lying sections of the road. In the unlikely event that it is raining in earnest during your travels to Namibia, avoid the D routes that would be affected. The best speed on this class of road is about 70 kph. Please note that it is not unusual to have to open and close cattle gates on some of these roads, especially in Damaraland.

Unless you are joining a coach tour or a guided private safari, motoring is the best way to experience this country. Four-wheel drive vehicles are not necessary except in the Namib and Kalahari Desert regions. All permanent roads are quite drivable as long as one exercises common sense, and a little advance planning will assure you of a safe and enjoyable trip.

Rail: The Namibian railway system is probably the least desirable means of transport for the tourist. Trains carry freight as well as passengers, which results in long journeys with innumerable stops. This said however, the rail network currently connects Windhoek, Swakopmund, Keetmanshoop, Luderitz, Tsumeb and Grootfontein, and it is an option.

Coach: A good coach service links Windhoek, Swakopmund/Walvis Bay, Keetsmanhoop, Rehoboth, Mariental, Okahandja and many small towns *en route*.

Car Hire: The major international car hire firms are all represented in Namibia. Cars are available in Windhoek at the international airport and at Eros Airport, which serves charter aircraft and domestic flights and is located just a few kilometres from the capital. Cars may also be hired at Keetmanshoop, Walvis Bay, Swakopmund, Luderitz, Tsumeb, Okaukuejo and Katima Mulilo. *Avis* is represented at each of these locations and *Budget Rent-A-Car* and *Hertz/Imperial* service at some of them.

I have found that almost without exception the cars for hire are quite new, clean and in good condition. If you book a car before you leave home, you will save money because the international rate allows for unlimited mileage without a kilometre charge.

The car hire firms do not offer 100 per cent collision damage coverage in

Namibia. The collision damage waiver only covers 80 per cent and this amount drops to 70 per cent if you have an accident on a gravel road. A hired car does not have to be returned to the town of origin - it can be left at another location serviced by the company. *Avis* allows its vehicles to be hired in Namibia and dropped in South Africa, or vice versa, but there is a significant charge for this option. Generally speaking it is not possible to drop a car hired in Namibia at a location in Botswana or Zimbabwe, but with some perseverance and luck you may be able to make such arrangements. None of the agencies allows vehicles to be driven into Zambia for the very good reason that they generally do not reappear!

Four-wheel drive vehicles are available from *Kessler Car Hire* in Windhoek and *Avis* in Windhoek and Etosha. Fully equipped caravans may be hired for a minimum period of one week. It is also possible to hire a camper van in Windhoek and return it to Cape Town or Johannesburg, although there is a surcharge for this option. Bookings should be made well in advance through *Capricorn Tours and Campers,* 39 Elsenham Avenue, PO Box 1530, Somerset West 7130, South Africa. Tel. (025) 55-2331; fax (024) 55-4062.

Taxis: Taxis are equipped with meters and generally must be hired by telephone. There is a taxi rank in Windhoek at the bus terminal on Independence Avenue, but please note that taxis do not queue at the airport, at least not at the time of writing. There is, however, a handy bus service that plies the 42 km from the international airport to the centre of Windhoek on a regular schedule conforming to airline arrivals. Tickets cost R10,00 per person.

CLIMATE

The climate of Namibia is characterized by hot days and cool nights, typical of a semi-desert environment. Dry and cloudless conditions are the norm for the majority of the year; Namibia enjoys a remarkable average of 300 days of sunshine each year.

There are four distinct topographical regions in the country. The coastal belt, which includes the 80-120 km wide strip of Namib Desert, is affected by the ice-cold Benguela current which flows from Antarctica. Temperatures are cool all year round here and rainfall typically does not exceed 25mm annually. The more or less constant temperature of the ocean (12-15°C) is a moderating influence on the heat of the desert, inhibiting rainfall and causing dense fog along this coastal stretch. The fog belt frequently extends 50 km inland, bringing with it much needed moisture which in turn supports a myriad of life forms in this most inhospitable of terrains.

The central interior of the country around Windhoek is a semi-arid mountainous plateau varying in altitude from 1000 to 2000m. Temperatures in this region are more moderate than in other parts of Namibia, although it can drop below freezing in the early hours before dawn during the winter months. Rainfall averages about 300mm a year in the central highland.

The north-eastern and south-eastern areas of the country are arid and are largely extensions of the Kalahari Desert in Botswana and the Karoo region of South Africa. Temperatures here often exceed 40°C in the summer. Rainfall is virtually nil.

The fourth region of Namibia is the bushveld area north of the Etosha Pan, which includes the Caprivi Strip. This is the area of highest rainfall, although accumulations only range between 400 and 500mm per year. The short rains occur between October and December and the main rains fall in the winter, between January and April. Daytime temperatures range between 20 and 30°C in the winter and 30 and 40°C in the summer.

With its generally dry climate any time of the year is a good time to visit Namibia. May-September is the best time to visit the interior of the country as daytime temperatures are pleasant and evenings are cool. Large concentrations of wildlife congregate at the waterholes in the Etosha National Park just before the advent of the winter rains, making August, September and October the best months for game viewing. Travellers should note that the Ai-Ais Hot Springs Resort is closed during the summer months, from 1 November to mid-March due to the extreme temperatures and the danger of flash floods.

HEALTH

The standard of hygiene in Namibia is very high, higher than one would generally find in the rest of Africa. This is in large part due to the long period of South African administration here. No vaccinations of any kind are presently required for a visit to Namibia and it is safe to drink the tap water anywhere in the country. There are however, two major health concerns which travellers should note: malaria and bilharzia. In many areas of Namibia there is absolutely no risk of contracting either disease due to the extreme aridity of the land. However, if you are planning to visit the Caprivi Strip or the Etosha National Park, you should take anti-malarial precautions. Bilharzia is only a risk to travellers visiting the Okavango and Caprivi regions.

WHAT TO PACK

Dress is casual, so pack accordingly! If you are spending much time in Windhoek you might consider including a lightweight suit or dress with appropriate footwear. However, unless you are on business it really isn't necessary to pack formal or dress clothes. The key to successful travelling is a wardrobe of colour-coordinated, comfortable cotton clothing that is not tight-fitting. Layering is an important concept given the temperature fluctuations that occur in a semi-desert environment. Early mornings and evenings tend to be cool and sometimes downright cold, so it is essential to include a sweater or jacket. If you are journeying to the Skeleton Coast, long trousers and a warm jacket are mandatory as the dampness and ubiquitous wind can chill you to the bone. Visitors to the Etosha region can anticipate hot, dusty days. If you intend to do some game viewing, bring a hat or scarf, sunglasses, lip emollient and a bathing costume and remember to wear neutral colours.

NATIONAL PARKS

Namibia maintains 13 recreation resorts and reserves which fall under the jurisdiction of the Directorate of Nature Conservation (DNC). Accommodation is available at all of the parks and recreation areas with the exception of the wilderness area of the Skeleton Coast Park (north of Terrace Bay) and the Mahango and Caprivi Game Reserves. There is a small entrance fee per person and vehicle at most of the parks and recreation areas. Bookings for the rest camps and caravan and camping sites are accepted by the DNC in Windhoek up to 11 months in advance of the desired reservation date. The DNC has recently recommended that advance bookings also be made for day visits to the resorts, at least during the peak holiday periods. For full particulars on each of the parks and resorts, write to the DNC, Private Bag 13267, Windhoek 9000.

TOURIST INFORMATION

Namibia Trade & Tourism, Private Bag 13297, Windhoek 9000, Tel. (061) 22-6571

Windhoek Publicity Association, PO Box 1868, Windhoek 9000, Tel. (061) 22-8160

Automobile Association, PO Box 61, Windhoek 9000, Tel. (061) 22-4201

ADVENTURE SAFARIS

Increasingly, travellers are combining sightseeing holidays with adventure or physical activities. There are several exciting outdoor holiday possibilities available in Namibia. If you are looking for something different or daring, contact one of the operators listed below for information on the adventure trips they offer.

Orange River Canoe Trips
River Runners, PO Box 583, Constantia 7848, South Africa, Tel. (021) 73-5111

Fish River Canyon Hike
Hikers Africa, PO Box 84262, Greenside 2034, South Africa, Tel. or fax (011) 782-2565

Fish River Canyon Cycling/Hiking Trip
Drifters, PO Box 48434, Roosevelt Park 2129, South Africa, Tel. (011) 486-1224; fax (011) 486-1237

Namibia Rock and Surf Fishing Adventure
African Fishing Safaris, PO Box 124, Bergvliet 7945, South Africa, Tel. (021) 72-1272 ; fax (021) 75-3283

Wilderness Safari
Overland Safaris, PO Box 82, Warden 9890, South Africa, Tel. 013342 and ask for Roadside 7330

Trans-Kalahari Safari (includes Botswana)
Africa Calls!, Private Bag 83, Maun, Botswana, Tel. (09267) 26-0351; fax (09267) 26-0671

Naukluft Hiking Trail or Ugab Hiking Trail
Directorate of Conservation and Recreational Resorts, Private Bag 13267, Windhoek 9000

Kalizo Fishing and Canoe Safaris
Kalizo (Pty) Ltd. Namibia, PO Box 343, Randburg 2125, South Africa, Tel. (011) 886-4067; fax (011) 886-3576

TOUR OPERATORS

The following operators offer scheduled, countrywide tours. Other companies specializing in regional safaris are mentioned in the sections on those areas.

Namib Wilderness Safaris (Coach), PO Box 6850, Windhoek 9000, Tel. (061) 22-5178

Springbok-Atlas Safaris (Coach), PO Box 2058, Windhoek 9000, Tel. (061) 22-4252/3

Desert Rose Tours (Coach), PO Box 41032, Craighall 2024, South Africa, Tel. (061) 788-0825 ; fax (061) 788-2664

Fly-In Tours (Air), Namib Air, PO Box 731, Windhoek 9000, Tel. (061) 3-8220; fax (061) 36-460

ACCOMMODATION

It is important to bear in mind that tourism is not yet a major industry in Namibia and as a result accommodation is not as easy to find as one might expect. Each of the larger towns has several hotels which I would rank as equivalent to three star European hostelries. Amenities such as air conditioning, telephone, television and private baths are usually offered. There is a high standard of cleanliness and the service is almost always efficient and friendly. Rooms tend to be good-sized and adequately, if unimaginatively, furnished or decorated. The Trade and Tourism Department publishes a list of Namibian accommodation and explains their rating system as follows: one star denotes a 'standard' hotel, two a 'good' hotel and three a 'really good' hotel. There is currently only one four star hotel in Namibia and no five star establishments.

Away from the urban areas, accommodation generally falls into the guest or holiday farm category. Amenities will vary, but again, rooms are characteristically spotless and the hospitality is grand. Grading awards are given on the same basis as for hotels. A few nights stay at a guest farm is a wonderful way to experience the pulse of Namibia and to meet some of her people. The guest farms are typically located near a geographical wonder or curiosity, miles from any town. Many farms offer swimming pools and licenced restaurants with liquor, and some are run exclusively for hunters.

The final category of accommodation is rest camps and caravan parks. Namibia has an excellent network of campsites for those tourists who wish to self-cater. Most of these facilities have swimming pools, restaurants or barbecue areas and ablution blocks with hot and cold water. Power points are available at some of the rest camps. Prices are extremely reasonable, averaging R10.00 per site. Many rest camps also offer bungalows or rondavels at modest prices. In most cases, you must bring your own food, supplies and linen, although fully equipped bungalows are very common in those camps where tourism is thriving. In general, facilities at rest camps and caravan parks are more than adequate and always clean.

Destinations are far-flung in Namibia and self-catering is about the only way to overnight in certain regions. It is also a way to commune with the vast spaces of this country and experience a romance that is uniquely African. Miles from civilization under a black velvet sky twinkling with the fire of a trillion stars, you can truly savour the sights and sounds of the African bush.

An *Accommodation Guide for Tourists* is published annually by the Government, which lists and grades all hotels, guest farms and rest camps in Namibia. It is available from the *Trade and Tourism Department*, Private Bag 13297, Windhoek 9000; fax (061) 3-8643.

FOOD

The cuisine of Namibia is a blend of German and British styles, a traditional kind of cooking that rarely approaches the gourmet level. Fresh fish is available throughout most of the country except in the most remote areas where refrigeration is impossible. The cold waters of the Atlantic Ocean yield rock lobsters, oysters, kingklip kabeljou, yellowtail and other delicious fish indigenous to the region. Fresh water fish such as black bass, bream and barbel are also available.

As in most African countries, however, meat is the primary dietary staple. Quality is good and portions are ample. Beef and lamb are common, as cattle and sheep ranching are big businesses in Namibia. Chicken is less frequently encountered on restaurant menus. The Southern African barbecue, called a *braaivlei*, is a popular tradition in Namibia. Great quantities of beer, sausages and meat are consumed at these very social occasions. Another local favourite is *biltong* - salt-cured and sun-dried meat most commonly eaten as a snack food. The very tastiest is made from ostrich meat but *biltong* is also made from beef or other game. Every food store in Namibia sells *biltong* and as it requires no refrigeration, preparation or cooking, it is an excellent item to take along if you are travelling to remote areas. In the urban areas you will find a large selection of fresh fruit and vegetables as well as all the usual staples. Food prices are reasonable although imported produce will be considerably more expensive than locally (South African) grown items.

Restaurants in Namibia maintain, for the most part, very high standards. Prices are extremely reasonable in comparison to countries abroad and dinner for two with a bottle of wine rarely exceeds R50. Many dining establishments specialize in German dishes, notably in the Windhoek area. International cuisine is available in urban restaurants but out in the bush, food tends to be less exciting with a heavy and sometimes monotonous emphasis on beef and mutton.

Namibia brews two terrific lager beers, Hansa and Windhoek, considered by many to be the best in Africa. It does not distil any spirits nor does it produce any wines, not surprisingly in view of the climate. However, excellent South African wines are readily available and the prices are very reasonable. South African vineyards were established early in the seventeenth century and many of the wines can hold their own against French or German products. With the rand in its current state of weakness against most foreign currencies, South African wines are an exceptional bargain.

A full spectrum of imported spirits and liqueurs may be purchased although the selection may not be complete in out-of-the-way places. Alcoholic beverage prices are reasonable in comparison with many African countries, averaging R7.00 per cocktail.

TIPPING

In many establishments a 10 per cent service charge is automatically added to the bill. If service is not included then the matter is left to your discretion. Although tipping is not mandatory nor generally expected outside of the better hotels and restaurants, it will most certainly be appreciated. It is important to remember that the wage scale in Namibia is far below that of Western countries. It is my personal opinion that service is better the world around when a gratuity for services rendered is anticipated.

In general, plan on tipping porters about 50 cents per bag. Safari guides and drivers often receive tips for their services but there are no hard and fast rules on this subject. From my experience I would generalize by saying that Americans always seem to tip while only some Europeans do.

SECURITY

In a world fraught with global problems, it is inevitable that travellers have concerns about the potential for crime, terrorism or political violence. Unlike so many African countries, crime and street violence are almost non-existent here at present. Windhoek must be one of the only cities in the world where it is safe to walk the streets after dark. Since independence there has been remarkable co-operation among all political groups. Furthermore, as a white person travelling in a black land, I can categorically say that I have never experienced racial antagonism anywhere in this country.

COUNTRY FILE

HISTORY

The Pre-Colonial Era

The earliest inhabitants of this land were the San people, popularly known as Bushmen. It is thought that as many as 3,000 years ago they roamed this region as hunters and gatherers. By today's standards it would appear to have been a bleak existence, for the same climatic conditions, parsimonious nature of the land, and lack of easily accessible water would have existed in that era. However, one must remember that game was abundant and there would have been little or no competition for such sustenance as the desert could provide. The San were a migratory people and they lived in loosely structured family groups. They built no permanent homes or villages, raised no crops, tended no livestock. Personal possessions were minimal, amounting to a bow and arrows, a quiver, and possibly some ostrich-shell beadwork or musical instruments. Much has been made of their ability to live in total harmony with nature and their environment. There is no doubt that these were a peaceful, self-sustained people who were at home in this most inhospitable of lands. They killed game only as needed for food, not for sport. Bushman rock art exists all over Namibia, testimony to a creative and joyous collective spirit which flourished despite the rigours of their daily life.

By 500 AD, Nama herders had moved into the southern central plateau region. The Nama, often called Hottentots, were a Khoisan speaking group of people like the San, but although nomadic, they raised livestock (sheep and goats). In the sixteenth or seventeenth century these indigenous inhabitants were joined by the Bantu-speaking Herero tribe who came from the Zambezi River area. Settling primarily in the north-western and central regions of Namibia, the Herero were herders like the Nama, but with a history of tribal structure and tradition. The Herero settled in semi-permanent villages and migrated only as necessary for their cattle. At about the same time an influx of Ovambo people from the region now known as Angola occurred. They established settlements along the northern flood plain of the Okavango River where both cultivation of the land and herding of livestock were possible. The Ovambo people were not nomadic and as a result a strong tribal society developed.

The first European to set foot in Namibia was the Portuguese knight and renowned navigator, Diego Cão. Commissioned in 1485 by King John II of Portugal to find a route around Africa to the Indian Ocean, Diego Cão landed at what is now known as Cape Cross in January 1486. Here he erected a stone pillar proclaiming the territory for Portugal. Although Diego Cao was unable to complete his mission, in 1487 another Portuguese navigator, Bartholomew Dias, landed at Luderitz *en route* to a successful circumnavigation of the Cape of Good Hope. After this however, almost two centuries were to pass before the white man surfaced in Namibia again. In 1670, and again in 1677, the Dutch undertook explorations of this region by sea. Several overland expeditions were mounted from the Cape Province in the mid-eighteenth century. Although European settlements were

Namibia

established in other areas of Africa as early as the fifteenth and sixteenth centuries, the harsh terrain and forbidding coastline of Namibia discouraged exploration and colonisation.

The first influx of immigration to this region occurred around 1800, well after the settlement of Cape Town by the Dutch East India Company. Racial tensions prompted a group of Hottentot people known as the Orlams to flee across the Orange River and settle in the southern region of Namibia. By this time there was large scale fighting between the Bushmen, the Nama and the Herero. The Nama and Herero people were stock breeders and disputes over grazing land and water holes were inevitable as overcrowding occurred. The Bushmen possessed no livestock but they pursued a policy of hunting cattle they deemed to be in their territory. Naturally this incurred the wrath of both Namas and Hereros. The arrival of the Orlams, another cattle-oriented tribe related to the Nama, only served to exacerbate an already volatile situation. The Orlams entered the fray and were successful in defeating the Herero, largely because they possessed firearms. The area from Windhoek south to the Orange River fell under the rule and command of one Jonker Afrikaner. He was able to control this region for about thirty years, from 1830 to 1860. By 1880 the Herero were once again a formidable power and in this year a decade-long war broke out between the Herero and Hottentots.

The Colonial Era

By the late nineteenth century, colonialism was in full flower in this region. Whales and guano were being harvested commercially along the coast between Luderitz and Walvis Bay. Traders had ventured into the interior and a market for cattle and copper was developed.

Missionaries flocked to southern Africa and by 1867 at least eight mission stations had been established throughout the country. The Germans and British were also well into their dispute over territory in this region. One hundred years earlier they had begun laying claim to various parts of the coastline. During the latter half of the nineteenth century the British government was petitioned several times by both tribal chiefs and the German government to place the region under its protection and control. The British did not want to assume financial and military responsibility for the territory, however, and only annexed Walvis Bay (1878) and some coastal islands in that vicinity.

In 1890 the imperial powers agreed upon international borders to define a territory they named South West Africa; these borders remain the same today. The German chancellor, Bismarck, then declared South West Africa a protectorate and colonial troops (*Schutztruppe*) were sent from Europe to maintain law and order. This coincided with the outbreak of Herero-Hottentot hostilities and Windhoek was founded as a military and administrative headquarters midway between the two warring tribal regions.

As happened elsewhere on the continent, conflict between the indigenous population and the Europeans was inevitable. In such a harsh and unremitting land, overpopulation and loss of grazing lands to the white

Country File

Originally built as a colonial German garrison, Fort Namutoni now provides accommodation for tourists within the Etosha National Park.

population meant certain starvation for the native peoples. The German governor, intent on attracting European settlers to South West Africa, appropriated or bought land from the natives. Specific areas were then set aside for tribal habitation. As the indigenous peoples lost their homes and grazing lands to the white man, rebellion was quick to surface. The white settlers' farms were repeatedly attacked and cattle are stolen. In 1903 the Nama revolted against the German government and in 1904 the Herero followed suit. The superior military skill and sophisticated armaments of the German troops assured their victory. Four years of brutal military reprisals against the native tribes resulted in the death of an estimated 84,000 black Africans. The Herero tribe was particularly devastated, losing approximately 54,000 members out of a total population of 70,000. The Germans then appropriated all of the Herero and Hottentot land for the crown, totally destroying tribal structures and an independent way of life. The natives were no longer allowed to possess cattle and so for survival they were forced to turn to the whites for employment. A ready market for their labour existed in the mines and diamond fields as well as on white farms. During this period only a few tribes escaped the genocide and dispossession of their tribal lands, among them the Ovambo, who claimed neutrality and were successful in manipulating the Germans' aspirations against the Portuguese. However, even their autonomy was short-lived. The First World War was just around the corner and a new era in South West African history was about to begin.

South African Rule
During the First World War, South African troops invaded German South West Africa on behalf of the British government. By July 1915 the Germans were forced to surrender to the superior South African forces. Following the Treaty of Versailles and a League of Nations decision, administration of South West Africa was mandated to the new Union of South Africa government in 1920. This government quickly settled additional white farmers in the territory and continued exploitation of the vast mineral resources of the land. Despite South Africa's lofty promises to promote the well-being and social progress of the native inhabitants, rather the opposite was to occur. To the indigenous tribes of South West Africa the new colonial power was merely a different face on the same problem. In 1921 and 1922 a group of Nama people revolted against South African rule but government forces easily defeated them. For the next 40 years, tribal leaders persisted in a policy of passive resistance in defiance of colonial rule. During this time the South Africans expanded the system of native land reserves originally begun by the German colonial government. Under this plan tribal groups were given land and permitted to raise cattle within those areas. However, only an estimated one quarter of the native population elected to resettle in these reserves, as the land set aside for them was arid and could not sustain many people. It is not surprising that this policy was identical to the apartheid concept of homelands being implemented during the same period in South Africa.

In 1946 the League of Nations was dissolved and the United Nations was formed. In this same year South Africa attempted to annex South West Africa despite objections from some tribal leaders. The General Assembly of the UN unanimously rejected this incorporation proposal and established a Trusteeship Committee to oversee South African administration of the territory. Twenty years of harassment, suppression and exploitation concurrent with steadily deteriorating living and working conditions were to follow before the UN General Assembly formally terminated South Africa's mandate over South West Africa in 1966. The next important international censure came in 1971 when the International Court in The Hague ruled that South Africa's occupation of Namibia was illegal and ordered her departure. Sadly, South Africa took no heed of this decree and nearly two decades of bloodshed followed.

The War for Independence
By the 1960s the winds of change were blowing across the African continent and with them came the first stirrings of organized social and political action among the blacks of South West Africa. Two groups were formed, SWANU (South West African National Union) and OPO (Ovamboland People's Organization). SWANU was a Herero movement comprised of students, white-collar workers, and urban youth from the south whereas OPO was an organization originally founded by the Ovambo as a means of ending the despised contract- labour system. Eventually, OPO became a national liberation movement and was renamed SWAPO, an acronym for South West Africa People's Organization.

In 1960 Sam Nujoma was elected president of the SWAPO party and the resistance movement gained momentum, especially in the villages of the north. In 1962, with Nujoma and many of his comrades in exile, the decision to undertake an armed struggle was made, launching what was to become one of the longest wars on the African continent. SWAPO's headquarters were established in Dar es Salaam, Tanzania, and the liberation movement looked to the Eastern Bloc nations for arms and guerrilla training. In 1965 the Organization of African Unity (OAU) lent financial support to the struggle. Meanwhile, the SWANU party declined to take up arms and this led to its disappearance on the international scene.

SWAPO noted 26 August 1966 as the official commencement of their 'revolutionary armed struggle' after a military encounter with South African forces at a guerrilla recruitment camp in the north. As the military skirmishes, the violence against civilians and the number of political detainees continued to multiply, the UN could not help but take note. Finally in 1968 the it passed a resolution renaming the territory Namibia and established the Council for Namibia. The UN Security Council jumped on the bandwagon in 1969 and endorsed the General Assembly's 1966 decision to rescind South Africa's mandate over the region. It went a step further and set a deadline of October 1969 for that country's formal withdrawl from the territory.

In response, the South African government refused to recognize UN authority and subsequently implemented the Odendaal Plan. The Odendaal Commission undertook to transform Namibia into ten tribally segregated homelands or *bantustans.* In part, the rationale of the South African government was to reduce Namibia to the status of a fifth province. In essence the Odendaal Plan was a means of introducing separate development, a euphemism for apartheid, to the country. As I have said, this process of relocating blacks to tribal reserves had its origin in German colonial days and was expanded after the Second World War by the South Africans. The programme was now launched in earnest and about 40 per cent of the country's area was divided into homelands. As was the case in South Africa itself, most of the arable land was demarcated as a white zone with the majority of the population consigned to a smaller, less desirable portion of the territory. The stage for further political struggle and a prolonged international dispute was now set and 20 long years was to pass before Namibia would gain its independence.

1970 ushered in a decade of popular resistance to South African rule manifested by striking workers, bantustan election boycotts, strident criticism from the churches and a state of emergency in Ovamboland. The fall of the Portuguese colonial governments in Angola and Mozambique brought with it a Marxist threat. Already paranoid about Communism and Soviet support of SWAPO, South Africans perceived that the 'red menace' was now in their midst and this galvanized them into military action. Angola, furthermore, was seen as an ally and haven for SWAPO insurgents, and as such was drawn into the rapidly escalating war. South African invasions of southern Angola became routine as they pursued SWAPO guerrillas across the Kunene River. In response, Cuba sent a large army to Angola to counter the attacks. The presence of the Cuban military then brought the United States running. The US were only too willing to supply arms, money and advisors to combat its enemy, Fidel Castro. In the long run, the Cuban military presence in Angola served as a pretext to delay Namibia's independence from Pretoria.

The conflict quickly intensified as South Africa increased its weaponry and manpower to unprecedented levels, eventually making Namibia the most militarized country in the world. Police and army brutality were rife, and torture and massacre of unarmed civilians were not uncommon. And where was the UN during this turmoil? Mandates without muscle had paralysed the General Assembly so that no effective action was possible on behalf of Namibia. Even when economic sanctions were promulgated, Britain, France or the United States always managed to veto the proposal. Their argument was that economic sanctions would not work and would jeopardize Western strategic and investment interests in South Africa.

In the meantime, the war dragged on and Western nations continued to reap a profit from the expanding South African economy. Only too aware of world condemnation of its actions, South Africa stated in 1972 that it was willing to consider independence for Namibia after a transitional period. To counter international pressure and disapproval, South Africa convened what came to be called the Turnhalle Conference. In 1975, 11 ethnic delegations met in Windhoek to formulate a constitution. Although they succeeded in this mission and set independence for December 1978, the UN was not satisfied. First, the Turnhalle plan, which revolved around the creation of three tiers of government, was really changing very little. All financial and political powers were to remain in white hands. Secondly, the delegations sent to the Turnhalle Conference consisted of tribal appointees hand-picked by the South African authorities and were not seen to represent the majority of the Namibian people. Even more importantly, no opposition parties, notably SWAPO, were invited to attend the constitutional convention. This was especially galling as the UN had taken steps in 1973 to recognize SWAPO officially as the 'sole authentic representative' of the Namibian people – a move, it should be noted , that some thought was premature and unwarranted.

Thus, South Africa's first step toward relinquishing control was largely ineffectual because it was not internationally recognized. It did accomplish something, however. For the first time the principle of one man one vote was recognised in the election of the Constituent Assembly in 1978. The turnout was good (80 per cent) and the Democratic Turnhalle Alliance (DTA), a coalition of 11 independent parties in Namibia representing 11 population groups, won the day by an overwhelming margin. The DTA was founded in 1977 in response to the Turnhalle Conference and it exists today as a moderate democratic party with wide support among the whites.

In 1977 the UN Security Council took the unprecedented step of initiating an arms embargo against South Africa. Steve Biko's death in South Africa as a result of police brutality precipitated this action. In the long run the embargo proved to be a contributing factor to South Africa's defeat in Namibia. Following this action a UN contact group was established with the goal of negotiating Pretoria's withdrawl from Namibia. This group spent 18 months mediating between SWAPO and the South African government in an effort to devise an independence formula acceptable to all sides. A particularly thorny point of dissension was the question of Walvis Bay. The UN contact group proposed that it be reintegrated with Namibia. South Africa's territorial claim to Walvis Bay dates back to 1878 when it was made part of the British Cape Colony. As the country's only deep-water port, a major railhead and the centre of the fishing industry, Walvis Bay was of paramount importance to the future of an independent Namibia. To further complicate the issue South Africa maintained large army and naval bases in Walvis Bay, of strategic concern to both countries. However, the UN proposal of 1978 awarded Walvis Bay to Namibia and warned South Africa not to interfere.

Hope flared and peace seemed imminent when Security Council Resolution 435 was ratified by the UN as well as SWAPO and South Africa in July of 1978. Although UN-supervised elections were planned they never materialized. Agreement could not be reached on crucial issues such as the composition of UN troops for the supervision of SWAPO bases and the electoral process. In the meantime, the South Africans proceeded with their own elections in 1979 to replace the Constituent Assembly with a National Assembly that would have legislative powers. One of the first steps this new body undertook was to pass an anti-discrimination bill which forbade racial segregation on the basis of colour in public places and residential areas. Although the war was far from over, some limited human-rights progress was being made.

In January 1981 with Resolution 435 still not enacted and independence seemingly no closer, an international conference was held in Geneva in one more effort to negotiate an acceptable peace plan. Pretoria however, continued to stall and nit-pick, maintaining that the UN proposal was biased toward SWAPO, and as such was unacceptable. Despite the granting of a number of concessions to the South Africans such as allowing it to retain Walvis Bay, Pretoria's position remained unchanged. It is interesting to note that South African opposition to resolution 435 also coincided with the election of the Thatcher and Reagan administrations in Britain and the United States. Both of these administrations looked favourably upon the white South African government and with this the tide began to turn. Reagan's African policy was one of 'constructive engagement' and South Africa was viewed as a 'friendly' nation. In 1981 the United States decided that a SWAPO government in Namibia would not be advantageous to their interests, noting also that Resolution 435 was no longer a viable proposal because South Africa was opposed to it. The United States then went one step further and made Cuban withdrawal from Angola a condition for Namibian independence. The South Africans were eager to agree. At this point, four years after its enactment, resolution 435 was dead.

And so, the war continued as the stalemate persisted. Cuba vowed to stay in Angola until the South Africans left and South Africa pledged to fight until the Cubans withdrew. This attitude resulted in an inevitable escalation of the war on both the Namibian and the Angolan fronts. To make matters worse the United States began arming and supporting Jonas

Savimbi, a rebel Angolan who headed a freedom fighting group called UNITA. Under US-South African guidance Savimbi began a campaign of destabilization within Angola. From 1983 to 1987 no real progress toward independence was made although the West sporadically continued efforts to negotiate a peace, predicated on the withdrawal of Cuban troops. Meanwhile, frustrated by the impasse on political, military and diplomatic levels, the Namibian blacks turned to more radical measures. Trade union, church and student activism became the order of the day. If the war couldn't liberate the Namibian people perhaps disruption of the work force, especially in the mines, could effect some change. The townships of South Africa were also in revolt. The uncensored scenes of repression, chaos and violence broadcast on the nightly news finally prompted world-wide outrage. Responding to public pressure, the United States Congress voted in 1986 to impose economic sanctions on South Africa and Namibia. At the same time American corporations began reacting to investors' demands for divestiture and disinvestment.

SWAPO's popularity continued to grow both at home and abroad. Despite the might of the South African military machine abetted by the CIA-funded UNITA forces in Angola, SWAPO was surviving and South Africans increasingly began to view Namibia as their Vietnam. When the Soviet Union stepped up shipments of sophisticated weaponry accompanied by military personnel to Angola, the South Africans began suffering greater casualties and strategic setbacks. The bite of economic and arms sanctions, the enormous financial costs of waging war, and the increasing public opposition to the fighting were crucial factors that led to a turning point in this 30 year conflict. In May 1988 South Africa was finally ready to talk about ending its occupation of Namibia. Cuban and Angolan troops were also eager to end a war in which they deemed themselves to be the victors. Talks took place in London between Angola, Cuba, South Africa, the United States and the Soviet Union. SWAPO was not represented. Initial progress was slow but by the end of the year a peace agreement was signed at the UN. Resolution 435 was to be implemented on 1 April, 1989, culminating in elections for a constituent assembly in October. Formal independence was scheduled for some-time in early 1990.

South Africa had lost the war and none of its major aims were realized in the peace settlement. Despite seven years of rhetoric about Cuban withdrawal as a precondition for a negotiated peace, in the final analysis South Africa agreed to a phased pull-out that would continue well after the official independence date. UNITA was not awarded a role in the Angolan government as hoped and Namibia was going to 'go black'. Tens of thousands of lives had been lost and billions of dollars in property damage had occurred. The people of Namibia were not all SWAPO supporters but what they did share was a common hatred of South Africa. Despite the years of suffering and frustration, however, in the long run their armed struggle had succeeded in vanquishing the enemy.

Although the road to independence seemed assured now, Resolution 435 was fraught with problems, some stemming from the concessions granted to Pretoria back in the late seventies and early eighties. The most serious flaw involved the disposition of SWAPO guerrillas within Namibia at the time of the ceasefire. One last, unnecessary tragedy unfolded in April 1989 as guerrillas returning to Namibia to surrender to UN forces were attacked by South African troops. Pretoria had maintained that all guerrillas were to remain above the sixteenth parallel, 150 km north of the border, until South African troops had withdrawn from Namibia. Lack of clarity during a decade of negotiations had left this issue unresolved and thus open to varying interpretations. As a result of the renewed violence, the UN peace plan was put on hold until 19 May 1989 when the war was officially declared over.

Post Independence

The guns were finally silenced. Independence was set for the following Spring, following a ten month UN-supervised transition period. On 21 March 1990, Africa's last colony was liberated and the world's youngest independent nation was born. Sam Nujoma, the leader of SWAPO for 24 years, was sworn in as Namibia's first president. He had been elected unanimously for a five-year term by the Namibian Constituent Assembly. In addressing the jubilant crowd which attended the independence ceremony he proclaimed: 'In the name of our people, I declare that Namibia is forever free, sovereign and independent. The destiny of our country is now in our own hands'.

Today, the euphoria of independence has faded and Namibia's new leaders have settled down to face the daunting task of nation-building. The Government is committed to a mixed economy and is encouraging private enterprise. In the light of SWAPO's traditional preference for socialism, many found this surprising. Mass unemployment, housing shortages, a lopsided economy and economic dependence on South Africa are some of the major issues which face the new administration. Fortunately, the country is blessed with rich natural resources and there is a sound infrastructure on which to build. Despite this, Namibia will need significant external assistance. Financial support has been promised from all over the world and the UN and the World Bank have already begun lending their expertise and resources. Given time and suppport the prognosis for the future is hopeful.

GEOLOGY, FLORA AND FAUNA

The topography of Namibia is as diverse as its peoples, although in general the country is characterized by semi-arid desert terrai n and climate. Geologically speaking, Namibia is part of an extremely ancient region at least two billion years old. The continent split during the Mesozoic Era, and the land mass which drifted away formed the continent of South America. Evidence of this wrenching apart, called the Mid-Atlantic Rift, is quite easy to see in the area along the Atlantic coastline north of Swakopmund.

The coastal plain that defines the western edge of Namibia gradually gives rise to an escarpment forming the central plateau of the country. This escarpment is basically a chain of mountains that runs roughly north-south, bisecting the land. On the eastern side of this plateau the high ground gently descends to the flat bushveld of the Kalahari Desert. The vast plains of Namibia are broken occasionally by granite mountains and solitary buttes rising like sentinels from the earth. These are believed to be the remnants of much larger massifs which were eroded by wind and water over the eons.

Although a land of great contrasts, Namibia hardly qualifies as a botanist's paradise. The vegetation of the Namib Desert is of interest, however, because a fascinating plant community has adapted in this oldest and driest of deserts as a result of the almost daily coastal fog. This is particularly apparent when one contrasts the amount of vegetation on the western (coastal) side of a dune or ridge with that on the eastern slope. An entire ecosystem has evolved in this most inhospitable of places and the moisture of the fog is crucial to its survival. The Namib Desert is home to three species of Euphorbiaceae, lichen fields, lithops, dune lucerne, commiphora trees, brack bush and the narra plant, to name a few. Of special note is the *Welwitschia mirabilis* plant, thought to be the oldest in the world. Actually a tree, it takes hundreds of years for the *welwitschia* to grow a mere 300 cm. In a classic example of adaptation, the tree became stunted into a shrub in order to adjust to its desert habitat.

As one moves inland from the coast dry woodlands, savannah grasslands and bushveld predominate. Wherever there is a river bed, groves of camel thorn acacia trees flourish, a welcome note of bright green in the otherwise monochromatic landscape. Although there is rarely water flowing in these courses, the trees tap the perennial subterranean flow. In the south semi-desert vegetation prevails, characterized by low shrubs and sparse grass. As one moves northward mopane forests occur in the central region of the country. Only in the northernmost reaches, along the banks of the great rivers which flow all year round (the Kunene, Okavango, Zambezi, Kwando and Chobe), will one find lush flood plains and riverine vegetation.

If you are coming to Namibia to see African wildlife I doubt whether you will be disappointed. There are few places left on the continent where one can see game in such abundance as at the Etosha National Park. Indeed, Etosha is Namibia's most popular tourist attraction. Vast herds of zebra and springbok roam the grasslands and salt pans. Healthy populations of giraffe, gemsbok, lion, elephant, kudu, eland, black rhino, cheetah, hyena and other species too numerous to mention flourish here. Just about the only common species you won't encounter in Namibia is the African (Cape) buffalo.

Bird life is also prolific, a fact that surprises many who erroneously assume that a lush, wet environment is essential for bird-watching. Over 630 species have been recorded in Namibia to date, including migratory birds. Of this number, approximately 130 are found only in the Caprivi and eastern Kavango where the climate and vegetation are more tropical. The birding is very good in the north as well as in the Windhoek vicinity, Swakopmund-Walvis Bay, Hardap Dam, Waterberg Plateau and of course, Etosha. In the desert itself about 50 species of birds occur. Birds especially associated with Namibia are the herero chat, the crimson-breasted shrike

Herero women in colourful traditional dress.

An ovaHimba settlement in Damaraland.

Elephants en route to the river.

The desert-adapted springbok browse near a fresh-water oasis.

Cascading streams of sand simulate a waterfall in the Hoarusib River canyon.

King of the beasts.

Country File

Welwitschia mirabilis *plants are indigenous to the Namib desert and can live 2,000 years.*

(Namibia's emblematic bird), the rosy-faced lovebird, the rockrunner, Monteiro's hornbill, Bradfield's swift and the Namaqua sand grouse. The bird watching is best from November to April because there is an influx of migratory birds to Southern Africa during the northern hemisphere winter. This is especially true in the Etosha Pan if the rains have been good.

THE ECONOMY

Namibia is an economically advanced country in comparison to other African nations. South Africa's long administration of the region resulted in the development of a number of industries as well as modern communication and transport systems. Today Namibian citizens enjoy the highest per capita income of any country in Southern Africa with the exception of South Africa. The Namibian economy is based on three sectors: mining, agriculture and fishing. In terms of the gross domestic product, the contribution from the mining industry is the most significant ($600 million). In 1990 there were 39 mines in operation in Namibia and mining has consistently been the largest taxpayer in the country. The great majority of the minerals mined here are exported with diamonds, copper ore, lead and uranium dominating the list.

Namibia is the world's leading producer of diamonds and CDM

(Consolidated Diamond Mines) is the largest employer in the country, contributing between 10 and 16 per cent of the gross domestic product annually. The uranium mine at Rossing is the largest in the world and that company has the stated objective of creating a completely indigenous workforce to operate the mine. In addition to diamonds and uranium, the major minerals mined are refined lead, concentrated pyrite, coarse salt and zinc. Gold and precious and semi-precious stones are also well-represented. In the Tsumeb region alone, over 200 different minerals and stones have been removed from one mine.

Agriculture provides work for more than 50 per cent of the labour force, although much of this is in the form of subsistence farming. 41 per cent of the total land surface of the country is used for agricultural purposes and farming contributes 10.2 per cent of the gross domestic product (1990). As with any developing country, expanding the agricultural potential of Namibia is of paramount importance. Unfortunately, due to the almost chronic shortage of water, crop farming is virtually impossible except in certain areas of the north and north-east. Stock raising is a much more viable industry as there are abundant savannah grasslands. Karakul lambs, often referred to as 'black diamonds', form the basis of the economy in the southern region. Karakul pelts are highly prized in the fur industry and this has been a small but lucrative business for decades. The mutton industry also has great potential and this may be capitalized upon in the future. Namibia is a net exporter of beef with South Africa forming the primary market. Beef cattle are raised primarily in the northern and eastern regions. A total of 51 per cent of the land in Namibia is suitable for cattle farming and in 1990, beef farming represented 87 per cent of the total agricultural income.

Of the three pillars of the economy, fishing is the industry experiencing the most difficult times. The coastal waters of Namibia are considered some of the world's richest fishing grounds. Pelagic species such as anchovy, mackerel and pilchard form enormous schools on the surface of the sea while white fish populate the deeper waters. Until just recently the 200-nautical-mile fishing zone that exists almost everywhere in the world was not recognized nor adhered to by many foreign fishing fleets. As a result there has been devastating exploitation of these coastal waters and the fishing industry of Namibia has inevitably suffered. Namibia now has jurisdiction over her coastal waters but patrolling the 200-mile zone is a problem. Police boats and aircraft are needed and the price of such a scheme has been estimated at a minimum of $15 million. Although the potential for expansion and growth of the fishing industry is excellent it will require a tremendous financial outlay. The World Bank has been studying the multifaceted needs of Namibia and it is certain to concentrate some of its energies and expertise on the fishing industry.

THE PEOPLE

Namibia has an estimated 1.3 million inhabitants. This represents one of the lowest population densities in the world with just over one inhabitant per square kilometre. There are 11 ethnic groups. The largest is the Ovambo, followed by the Kavango, Herero, Damara, Whites, Nama, Coloureds, Caprivians, Bushmen, Basters and Tswanas. Seventy percent of the population live in the north where the rainfall is highest and agriculture is feasible.

If you look at a map of Namibia you will see that it is divided into ethnic territories, a practice begun by the Germans in the colonial era and perfected by the South African administration. (see History). Although many of these regions are inhabited predominantly by the ethnic groups which lend their name, numerous Namibians live outside their traditional lands because of personal choice or employment demands.

It would need a book in itself to discuss each of Namibia's ethnic groups, but the following synopsis will hopefully help you.

Ovambo
Over 51 per cent of the total population of Namibia belongs to the Ovambo group. This ethnic group sub-divides into seven distinct tribes, each with its own language. Ovamboland is situated in the north along the Angolan border and was settled by these peoples in the sixteenth century. The land is uniformly flat and the rainfall is heavy, at least by Namibian standards. The Ovambo women tend to the traditional crop raising and the men are stock breeders. Unfortunately the high population density in Ovamboland has contributed to soil erosion, deterioration of grazing lands and large scale unemployment.

Kavango
Kavangoland borders Angola and the Okavango River. The Kavango people, many of whom are Angolan refugees, are predominantly crop farmers and fishermen, although there is some stock raising.

Caprivans
The Caprivi Strip is home to approximately 40,000 people. This is the most fertile region of Namibia and agricultural potential is high; the tsetse fly has kept livestock farming in this area to a minimum. The Caprivi Strip was especially hard-hit during the war for independence because of its proximity to Angola; unemployment is high and morale is low in this region at the present time.

Herero
The original home of the Herero is unknown but these people eventually immigrated to Botswana and then moved west into Namibia in search of grazing land. They were evidently quite proficient at cattle raiding because their history is one of conflict with other tribes. Today the Herero live mainly in Hereroland West and Hereroland East. They are strictly pastoralists and as is the case in many parts of Africa, their cattle represent wealth and social prestige, so are rarely slaughtered. It is easy to recognize the Herero women in Namibia because they wear a traditional style of dress which is distinctively Victorian. These dresses were introduced by the German missionaries and no less than 12 metres of cloth are used to make the cumbersome outfits.

Himba
The Himba or Ova-Himba share a common ethnic origin with the Herero and as such are considered a sub-group. About 8,000 Himba reside in Kaokoland in the far north-western corner of the country. This region is mountainous with minimal vegetation and very little water. The Himba are cattle breeders although for status rather than commercial purposes. If you are planning a fly-in safari to the Skeleton Coast it is quite possible that you will visit some Ova-Himba just outside the wilderness area in Purros. There you will encounter a people virtually untouched by modern civilization. Of especial interest is the traditional adornments of some of this group. The women smear their bodies with a mixture of red clay and butter. Their hair is plaited into hundreds of small braids and these are also coated with mud. Body adornments include copper wire, shells, pieces of goat skin and crude metal beads.

Damara
The origin of these people is unknown but their totally black colour and their early knowledge of metallurgy suggests to many that they may have migrated from the Sudan. Whatever their origins, today they speak the Nama language and the hunter-gatherer lifestyle they practised for centuries has given way to small scale stock breeding. The majority of the Damara people do not live in Damaraland as there is no work for them in that region.

Nama
The Nama people are a Hottentot (Khoikhoi) people, and are considered to be one of the indigenous peoples of Southern Africa. Like the Bushmen they were hunter-gatherers but the Nama also bred some livestock for milk, skins and meat. Today, the Nama population numbers about 50,000. Their nomadic style of life has disappeared and the majority are employed on white farms.

Rehoboth Baster
The Baster people are the descendants of Hottentot women and white Boers from the Cape Colony. The name Baster is their choice of wording, for they find the term 'coloured', used to denote people of mixed race in South Africa, offensive. They migrated north to Namibia in the mid-nineteenth century to escape racial persecution and settled in Rehoboth. This area is endowed with excellent grasslands for the grazing of sheep and cattle.

Bushman (San)
The traditional home of the Bushman is sandwiched between Kavangoland and Hereroland East. Since Sir Laurens van der Post's amazing 'rediscovery' of the Bushmen, there has been extensive discussion and research centring on their culture and history. Of these fascinating people who roamed Southern Africa for thousands of years, today approximately 33,000 exist in Namibia. The largest group is the Kung! and fewer than 2,000 of them, if that, maintain a traditional lifestyle. The romanticized view of the Bushmen as portrayed in the popular James Uys film, *The Gods Must Be*

Crazy is out of date today. The majority of the San people earn a living as squatters or by working for white and black farmers, their centuries-old survival skills and unique customs long gone.

The Bushmen are considered to be one of the indigenous people of Southern Africa, a hardy group who forged a way of life suited to the harsh and arid environment of much of this region. They were stone-age hunter-gatherers who possessed no livestock, built no homes, tended no crops. The Bushmen had an intimate knowledge of their land and could find sustenance and water where none seemingly existed. Unlike modern man the Bushman lived in harmony with his environment, his nomadic lifestyle perfectly suited to the resources of the land and the changing of the seasons. With the advent of other tribes such as the Nama and Herero, followed by the intensive colonization of the whites, the Bushman's life changed from one of freedom to one of persecution and pursuit. The Bushmen were all but decimated by the early twentieth century. Those who did not perish at the hands of white and black alike were assimilated into 'modern' society, their ancient ways gradually forgotten, their bloodlines mingled with other peoples.

RECOMMENDED READING

Bannister, A. and Johnson, P., *Namibia, Africa's Harsh Paradise*, New Holland, London, 1990

Bristow, David, *Namibia, the Beautiful Land*, Struik Publishers, Cape Town, 1990

Coulson, David, *Namib*, Sidgwick & Jackson, London, 1990

Herbstein, D. and Evenson, J., *The Devils Are Among Us; The War For Namibia*, Zed Books Ltd, London & New Jersey, 1989

Iwanowski, Michael, *Deserts, Paths and Elephants: Travel Guide Southwest Africa /Namibia*, V&S Verlag Publishers, Dormagen, Germany, 1986

Lambrechts, H., *Namibia-A Thirst Wilderness*, Struik Publishers, Cape Town, 1985

Marsh, John, *Skeleton Coast*, Hodder & Stoughton, London, 1944

Martin, Henno, *The Sheltering Desert*, Ad Donker (Pty) Ltd, Craighall, South Africa 1983

Oliver, Willie and Sandra, *Visitor's Guide to Namibia*, Southern Book Publishers, Johannesburg, 1989

Reardon, Mitch and Margot, *Etosha: Life and Death on an African Plain*, New Holland, London, 1988

Schoeman, Amy, *Skeleton Coast*, Southern Book Publishers, Johannesburg, 1984

Walkden-Davis, Allan, *Shell Tourist Guide*, Shell Oil SWA Ltd, Windhoek, 1985

White, Jon M., *The Land God Made in Anger*, Rand McNally & Co. Chicago, 1969

AROUND NAMIBIA

WINDHOEK

INTRODUCTION

Windhoek is situated in the central highlands of Namibia at 1,650 metres above sea level. Long before a town was established here, this area was frequented by tribal settlements of Hereros and Namas because of the hot springs nearby. In 1840 it became a place of settlement for the Orlam tribe of Namas under the leadership of Jonker Afrikaner. Originally called Winterhoek, over time the name was corrupted to Windhoek, an Afrikaans word meaning windy corner. In 1890 Imperial Germany, in the person of Curt von Francois, occupied Windhoek and established a colony here. A fort called Alte Feste was built to serve as administrative headquarters for all of German South West Africa.

German colonialism

Today Windhoek is a delightful, bustling town of about 130,000 people. As capital of Namibia it is the seat of the judicial, legislative and executive branches of government. Since independence an enormous building boom has been underway. Urban renewal in the form of wide pavements, pedestrian malls and several architectuarally stunning buildings has given Windhoek a prosperous, dynamic look. Good town planning has resulted in a nice blending of German colonial architecture with the newer, modern structures to a favourable effect. Clean and neat with lovely flowers and trees, Windhoek is a pleasure to visit, a rarity among African cities.

GETTING THERE

Namib Air is the national carrier and offers a scheduled domestic and international service. Domestic flights depart from Eros Airport, 3 km from the city centre, connecting Windhoek with Swakopmund, Luderitz, Keetmanshoop, Tsumeb, Oshakati, Rundu and Katima Mulilo.

Airport transfers

The international airport is located 42 km from the city centre. A deluxe airport bus meets every plane and ferries passengers to the terminal on Independence Avenue, a journey of about 45 minutes. The bus will also go to Eros Airport on request. The charge is R10.00 per person and

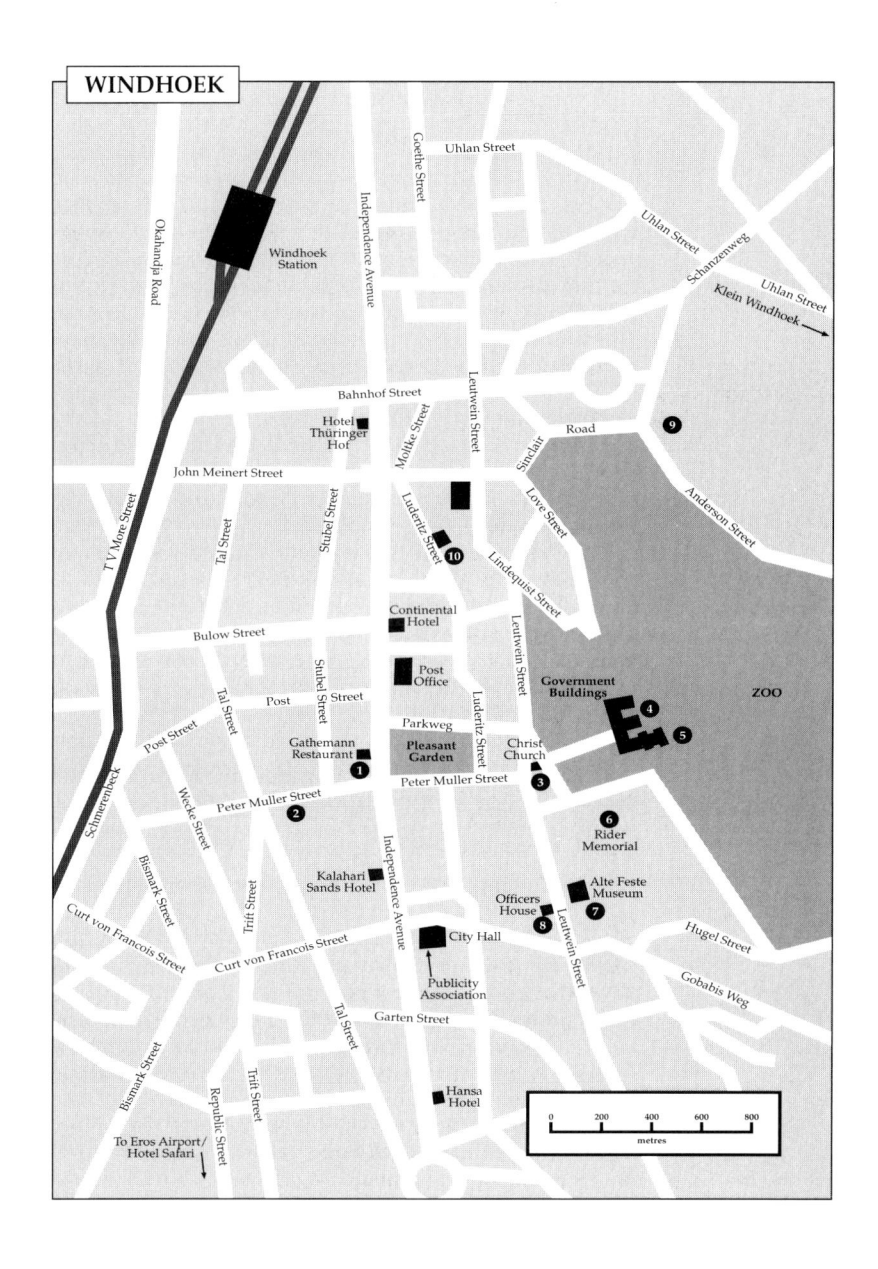

Windhoek

WINDHOEK

Airport services

you purchase your ticket on the bus. A return schedule is posted at the bus terminal. If you want a taxi from the airport you must telephone and then wait for the taxi to drive from Windhoek to collect you.

There is a restaurant and small shop at the new airport terminal. A bank operates in conjunction with international flights. Please note that there are no long term luggage storage facilities at this airport; outside the terminal there are a limited number of small lockers that are adequate for storing odds and ends. The lockers operate with a 20 cent coin and there is no time limit at the time of writing. *Mainliner* provides a coach service to Windhoek from Swakopmund, Walvis Bay and Keetmanshoop with numerous stops at small towns *en route*. Three times a week there is a super luxury coach which runs non-stop between Windhoek and Swakopmund.

Mainliner also offers scheduled service to and from Cape Town and Johannesburg, a trip of 18 and 20 hours respectively. Reservations can be made through Trip Travel, telephone (061) 3-6880.

The Namibian railway system connects Windhoek with Swakopmund, Walvis Bay, Keetmanshoop, Luderitz, Tsumeb and Grootfontein, but trains are very basic and journey times are long as the trains carry freight as well as passengers. The International service to Cape Town or Johannesburg takes 4 days.

ACCOMMODATION

Best in town

Kalahari Sands Hotel****. Independence Ave. Tel. (061) 3-6900. Situated in the heart of the city, this is Namibia's premier hotel. There are 187 standard and de luxe rooms with mini bar, TV, telephone, 24-hour room service and air conditioning. The only difference between a standard and a de luxe room is that the de luxe has a king size bed rather than 2 doubles. Rooms are good-sized, clean and attractively furnished. Although this is the best hotel in town, the service does not reflect this distinction.

Hotel Safari and Safari Court****. Tel. (061) 3-8560. This hotel is located 3 km from the city centre next to Eros Airport, not a particularly convenient position for those without a car who would like to explore, shop and dine in Windhoek. The Safari Hotel complex is really two hotels in one: the original two-storeyd structure has 200 rooms and is now augmented by the Safari Court, a new luxury tower with 252 additional rooms. Not surprisingly, the rooms in the Safari Court are more

Colonial and modern architecture blend harmoniously in Windhoek.

Swimming
pool

expensive. All accommodation has air conditioning, TV, and telephone. There is a lovely pool, two restaurants and 24-hour room service; the hotel also offers a complimentary shuttle service to and from the city centre every 30 minutes. I have difficulty recommending this establishment because on the several occasions that I have stayed here the level of service and the indifference and unfriendliness of the personnel have been shocking. Hopefully this will improve with time!

Furstenhof Hotel**. 4 Romberg St. Tel. (061) 3-7380. The Furstenhof offers 18 rooms with private bath, telephone and TV. The hotel is located about four blocks from the city centre; it has become the victim of recent highway construction with the result that a new access ramp is now very close to the building. The hotel has an excellent a la carte restaurant.

Continental Hotel**. Independence Ave. Tel. (061) 3-7293; fax (061) 3-1539. This hotel has 70 recently refurbished rooms, most with private bath and all with

TV, telephone and air conditioning. There is a restaurant, nightclub and bar but no swimming pool
Hotel Thuringer Hof. Independence Ave. Tel. (061) 22-6031. A Namib Sun hotel just five minutes from the city centre with 40 double rooms all with private bath, air conditioning, telephone and TV. There is a courtyard restaurant and bar on the premises, but no pool.
Hansa Hotel*, Independence Ave. Tel. (061) 22-3249. Located just a few blocks from the central city centre, the Hansa is a small ten room hostelry that is basic but clean. All rooms have air conditioning, telephone and radio but only six have private bathrooms. There is a TV lounge and a restaurant and bar on the premises.

DINING

Kaiserkrone. Post Street Mall. Tel (061) 22-2779. The Kaiserkrone is really two restaurants in one: a fancy indoor dining room for dinner and an outdoor café for daytime service. The café serves light breakfasts and lunches with the emphasis on a daily selection of fresh salads. The patio is shaded by eight giant palm trees and is a lovely place to relax. The service here is slow and indifferent but as long as you are in no hurry this is tolerable. Dinner in the main building is consistently excellent with an ambitious menu featuring fresh fish, game and German specialities. The service is quite professional in the dining room and there is a very good selection of wines. Open daily except Sunday.

German cuisine

Gathemann's Restaurant. Independence Ave. Tel. (061) 22-3853. This restaurant is housed in an historic German colonial building one floor above ground level. The outdoor terrace is very popular as is the dining room which features continental cuisine. Gathemann's is open daily from 9 a.m. till late.

Grand Canyon Spur. Independence Ave. Tel. (061) 3-1003. One of the popular Spur steakhouses with an upbeat atmosphere serving good steaks, ribs, pizzas, sandwiches and vegetarian dishes. Prices are reasonable and there is always a crowd. Open seven days a week for lunch and dinner, 10 a.m. to midnight.

Always a crowd

Le Tamarisk Room. Kalahari Sands Hotel. Tel. (061) 3-6900. This is an elegant restaurant with an ambitious menu that features dishes from famous restaurants around the world. The food and presentation are laudable and the desserts are outstanding. Open for dinner daily except Sunday.

Windhoek

Le Bistro Corner of Independence Ave. and Post St. Tel. (061) 22-8742. A small but immensely popular café that serves soups, salads, waffles, stuffed potatoes, pizzas and pastries throughout the day from 7.30 a.m. to 9 p.m. Fresh juices and cappuccino are also available.

Homemade ice cream

Sardinia. Independence Ave. Tel. (061) 22-5600. A charming ice-cream parlour and pizzeria which is open from Monday to Saturday until 18h00. The ice cream is home-made and there are basic pasta dishes in addition to pizza.

SHOPPING

You should be able to find just about anything you need in Windhoek. Urban renewal precipitated the development of several fountain and tree-lined walking malls, adding about 100 new shops to the central area. The selection of goods is amazingly complete and there is a wide array of clothing, shoes, accessories, jewellery, minerals and curios available.

Namibian ranchers raise a special breed of sheep for the production of karakul pelts. These skins are marketed under the brand name of Swakara, an acronym for South West Africa karakul. The pelts are dyed in a myriad of colours and fashioned into beautiful coats. Windhoek is an excellent place to buy a karakul product: the selection is large and the prices are as low as can be found anywhere.

Given its vast mineral resources, it should come as no surprise that gems, semi-precious stones, mineral samples and jewellery are good buys in Namibia. Amethyst, garnet, topaz, malachite, sodalite and hematite are all mined here and prices are reasonable. Additionally, Namibia has the finest tourmalines in the world so if you are an admirerer or connoisseur you might want to do some investigating!

Duty-free

Bona-fide foreign tourists are exempt from tax and duty on purchases of jewellery and furs. There is ample shopping for items other than luxury goods: native handicrafts such as basketry, wood and stone carvings and beadwork are well represented in the city's curio shops. It is important to note that shops are closed in Windhoek after 1p.m. on Saturdays and all day on Sundays.

Shopping Centres
Gustav Voights Centre. Independence Ave. at the Kalahari Sands Hotel
Levinson Arcade. Off Independence Ave.
Post Street Arcade. A pedestrian mall lined with fountains and boutiques that connects to the Wernhill Park Galleria
Wernhill Park. A new complex with 40 shops on two levels of shopping

Department Stores (clothing)
Foschini. Independence Ave.
Truworth. Levinson Arcade
Markhams. Independence Ave.
Edgars. Levinson Arcade

Crafts and Curios
Capricorn Gems and Souvenirs. 165 Independence Ave. Excellent jewellery, stone and wood carvings and assorted curios
Bushman Art. 187 Independence Ave. A large selection of genuine Bushman artefacts and Ovahimba jewellery
Cheetah Souvenirs. 242 Independence Ave.
Namibia Crafts Centre. 40 Tal St. A showcase for indigenous crafts, pottery, wood carvings, leather articles, baskets and jewellery
Masters Weavers. Wernhill Park. Handwoven tapestries and rugs and gorgeous raku pottery

Rocks and Minerals
Rocks and Gems. Independence Ave.
African Gemstone Exchange. Wernhill Park
Capricorn Gems and Souvenirs. Independence Ave.

Furs
Hamm Pelze. Gustav Voights Centre, Independence Ave.
Pelzhaus Huber. Independence Ave.

Jewellery
Adrian. Levinson Arcade
G.W. Leitner. Gustav Voights Centre, Independence Ave.
H. Knop. Stubel Strasse

Photo Supplies
Nitzsche-Reiter: two locations, Gustav Voights Centre and Independence Avenue next to Markhams

Boutiques
Alma Mode. Stubel (women)
Otto Muhr and Co. Independence Ave. (men)
Inge's Boutique. Levinson Arcade (women)
Ernst Holtz. Gustav Voights Centre (safari outfitter)

Windhoek

SIGHTSEEING

A one-hour walk around town will acquaint you with historic Windhoek. The highlights of such a stroll include:

1. Several **German colonial facades** that are still visible on Independence Avenue across from Pleasant Garden. Note the unusually steep roofs, a European feature designed to prevent snow from collecting!

2. **Pleasant Garden** (formerly Zoo Park), in Independence Avenue, a lovely oasis of flowers, trees, fountains and lawn. The zoo has been moved to an area behind Tintenpalast and there are a small number of ostrich, antelope, zebra and giraffe on display.

Zoo

3. **Christ Church** at the top of Peter Muller Street is a beautiful sandstone German Lutheran church dating from 1910; the stained glass windows were a gift from Kaiser Wilhelm II.

4. **Tintenpalast** was built in 1912 to house the administrative offices of the German colonial government. It was named the Ink Palace in reference to the large volume of writing that occurred there. The edifice is surrounded by gorgeous gardens and verdant bowling greens and over 100 olive trees grace the grounds. Today the building is used by the government of independent Namibia.

5. The **Legislative Assembly** is a modern building to the right of Tintenpalast. Murals and works of art in indigenous materials depict the economy, industry, history and nature of Namibia. Guided tours of 45 minutes are given Monday-Friday at 11 a.m. and 3 p.m. except when the assembly is in session.

6. The bronze **Rider Memorial** commemorates the German troops killed in the Nama and Herero wars of 1904-08.

7. **Alte Feste Museum** is the oldest structure in Windhoek, dating from 1890. Built as a headquarters and military fort for the first German colonial troop contingency, it is now a historical museum. It is open to the public on Monday-Friday from 8 a.m.-6 p.m. Saturday from 10 a.m.-12.45 p.m. and 3 p.m.-6 p.m. Sundays and public holidays from 11 a.m.-12.30 p.m. and 3 p.m.–6p.m. Of special interest are the Gibeon meteorites displayed in the courtyard. This collection is part of the world-famous Gibeon Shower believed to be one of the most extensive meteorite showers in the world, covering

Gibeon meteorites

approximately 2,500 sq km in the southern region of Namibia. A total of 77 meteorites with a combined weight of 21 tonnes have been recovered to date, and many of these are in museums throughout the world.

8. The **Officers' House**, located across the street from Alte Feste is a beautifully preserved example of the German architectural style fashionable in the first decade of this century. This building originally served as dormitory and stables for the colonial troops. Today it is used for the offices of the Ombudsman.

An interesting walk

9. If you have the time and energy there is a lovely trail called the **Hofmeyer Walk** that entails an hour of easy strolling. There are nice views of the surrounding valley and a leisurely pace will afford ample opportunity to examine the native vegetation and bird life. The Hofmeyer Walk is located in the area behind Alte Feste and Tintenpalast; it may be reached from Orban or Sinclair Roads.

10. The **State Museum** is also worth a visit for those interested in the natural history of Namibia. The museum is located on Luderitz Street. Visiting hours are 9 a.m.-6 p.m. Monday-Friday; 10 a.m.-12.45 p.m. and 3 p.m.-6 p.m. on Saturday; 11 a.m.-12.30 p.m. and 3 p.m.-6 p.m. on Sunday and public holidays.

EXCURSIONS

In my opinion the following resorts are not of particular interest to the overseas visitor but if you are curious or in need of a swim, any one of them can satisfy those urges.

The Daan Viljoen Game Park

Located 24 km north of Windhoek off the C28, a scenic route through the Khomas Hochland that eventually leads to Swakopmund on the coast. There are no predators in the park so walking is a delight. It boasts 200 species of animals and birds. There is a rest-camp offering bungalows, camping and caravan sites, a restaurant and a swimming pool.

Von Bach Dam and Recreation Resort

Camping

Situated 72 km north of Windhoek near the town of Okahandja. This resort offers angling and swimming. There are camp sites and 22 basic huts for hire. You must provide all your own food, linen and equipment as there are no shops or facilities here other than braai pits and ablution blocks. Day use of the facilities is welcomed and there is a small entrance fee.

Gross Barmen
This is a hot springs resort only 100 km from Windhoek. The bird life is prolific here and facilities include a large indoor thermal bath and an open-air swimming pool, both of which are fed by the warm, mineral-rich water of the springs. Accommodation runs the gamut from caravan and camp sites to luxury air-conditioned units. There is a restaurant that serves three meals a day, a kiosk, shop and petrol pumps. Day use of the outdoor swimming pool is allowed for a small charge. Book for accommodation through the DNC in Windhoek.

Thermal baths

Hardap Dam and Recreation Resort
A two hour drive south from Windhoek. This is Namibia's largest dam and aquatic sports and fishing are favourite pastimes here. Facilities include one- or two-bedroomed bungalows with en-suite bathrooms as well as simple rooms and dormitory space with communal ablution blocks. Tent and caravan sites are also available. Day visitors are welcome and there is a restaurant, a large swimming pool, tennis courts and hiking trails for the visitor's enjoyment. Once again, for overnight accommodation, book with the DNC.

PHOTOGRAPHIC AND HUNTING SAFARIS

Not too far from Windhoek there are several excellent private game ranches that offer visitors the opportunity to partake in photographic or hunting safaris, or both.

Mt Etjo Safari Lodge***. This is my favourite, easily accessible from the capital by car in under three hours. Transport to and from Windhoek can be arranged by the staff at the Lodge for those who do not wish to drive themselves.

A personal favourite

Mt Etjo is a privately owned 30,000 acre farm and is one of the most beautifully maintained and professionally run operations in Namibia. Guests are accommodated in spacious rooms, each with two queen-sized beds and tiled bathrooms. The swimming pool and grounds are impeccable and you won't see a larger expanse of green lawn anywhere in the country. The daily rate includes full board and two game drives. The entire perimeter of the property is fenced so game viewing is very good. Elephant, white rhino, lion, leopard, cheetah, giraffe, black wildebeest and all manner of antelope are represented. The scenery in this part of Namibia is very beautiful, ranging from rugged savannah to stone mountains to areas of lush riverine vegetation.

Namibia

Treetop hides — Open vehicles are used for the game drives and a special feature of Mt Etjo is the very clever hide from which one can observe lions feeding. Walking safaris and overnights in a comfortable treetop hide are possible also. This lodge represents excellent value for money and if you are unable to travel to Etosha, this is a convenient and far more luxurious game camp. Tel. (06532) 1602.

Immenof Guest Farm**. Tel. (06532) 1803; fax (061) 22-8207. Near Omaruru, is a few hours drive from Windhoek or Swakopmund. Accommodation consists of six double rooms, three of which have private bathrooms. Horseback riding, game drives, tours to Etosha and visits to nearby rock paintings and engravings are some of the attractions offered. The owners also operate a hunting safari farm.

Otjisazu Hunting and Guest Farm***. Tel. (06228) 8-1640; Fax. (061) 22-8207. Located just east of Okahandja, about an hour's drive from Windhoek. Accommodation consists of five double rooms, two of which have en-suite facilities. Full board is included in the reasonable daily rate and there is a swimming pool on the grounds. Photographic safaris are available year round and trophy hunting is offered from February to November.

Professional hunter — **Jan Oelofse Wild Hunting Safaris.** Operated by the well known conservationist, Jan Oelofse, owner of the Mt Etjo Safari Lodge. The hunting camp is a separate entity from the game viewing ranch but the same excellence of service and facilities prevails. Trophy fees and licenses are expensive and the daily rate per person starts at US $350.00, inclusive of full board, accommodation and the services of a professional hunter. The minimum booking is for a ten-day period. For full details write PO Box 81, Kalkfeld or ring (06532) 1602.

SERVICES

TOURIST INFORMATION

Windhoek Publicity Association, Municipal Bldg., East Entrance, Neser St., Tel. (061) 22-8160

The Ministry of Wildlife, Conservation & Tourism, Private Bag 13346, Windhoek 9000, Tel. (061) 22-0241.

Directorate of Nature Conservation (DNC), Independence Ave. (Next to the Post Office), Postal address: Private Bag 13267, Windhoek 9000., Tel.(061) 3-6975 Hours of operation for bookings and permits are Monday to Friday from 8 a.m.-1 p.m. and 2 p.m.-3 p.m.

GETTING AROUND

Car Hire

Avis, Budget and Imperial(Hertz) all have offices at the International Airport, as well as in the city centre and at Eros

Airport.
Avis. Tel. (061) 3-3166
Budget. Tel. (061) 22-8720
Imperial. Tel. (061) 22-7103
   There is an independent car hire company in Windhoek called *Kessler Car Hire*, 42 Tal Street. This agency leases all types of cars including four-wheel drive vehicles and camping equipment. Tel. (061) 3-3451.

Taxis
At the time of writing taxis are in short supply in Windhoek. However, there is a taxi rank on the corner of Independence Avenue and Peter Muller St. at the bus terminal. In most cases it is necessary to ring for a taxi, even from the International Airport. Tel. (061) 3-7070 or 22-3220.

Bus Service
Mainliner. Tel. (061) 6-3211.

Airlines
Namib Air, Post Street Arcade, Tel. (061) 3-8220

South African Airways, Independence Ave., Tel. (061) 3-1118 or 3-1179

Air Charter
Namib Commercial Aviation, Eros Airport, Tel. (061) 22-3562/3

Motoring Organisation
Automobile Association, 15 Carl List Building, Independence Ave., Tel. (061) 22-4201
8.30 a.m.-5 p.m. Monday-Friday, 8.30 a.m.-12.30 p.m. Saturday. If you are planning a road trip be sure to call here for advice and an update on the latest road conditions and construction projects. Visitors who are members of the AA in their own country are entitled to complimentary maps upon presentation of a membership card.

TRAVEL AGENCY
Trip Travel Office, Independence Ave., Tel. (061) 3-6880

POST OFFICE
Independence Ave.

PUBLIC LIBRARY
18 Luderitz Street
8 a.m.-1 p.m. and 2 p.m.-5 p.m. Monday-Friday.

CAMPING EQUIPMENT HIRE
Gav's Camping Hire, 11 Sydney Atkinson Street, Olympia, Tel. (061) 5-1526
Has everything you need for camping from tents to teaspoons. If you want to explore the less frequented regions of Namibia, camping is a practical and inexpensive way to do so. Rather than bring your own equipment to Africa you might consider renting a complete outfit from this company.

TOUR COMPANIES
There are a number of reputable operators based in Windhoek that offer coach tours to Etosha, Waterberg, Swakopmund, Twyfelfontein, Luderitz, Sossusvlei and the Fish River Canyon on a scheduled daily or weekly basis. All of these companies can also tailor private tours to your needs.
Oryx Tours. Tel. (061) 22-4254; fax (061) 3-5604
Namib Wilderness Safaris & Travel Shop. Tel. (061) 22-5178; fax (061) 3-3332
SWA Safaris. Tel. (061) 3-7567; fax (061) 22-5387

HUNTING COMPANIES
Hunt Africa welcomes big game hunters and photography enthusiasts alike to partake in one of their specially organized excursions. Professional hunters or guides will meet you at the airport in Windhoek and will accompany you throughout your stay. Accommodation is in three star lodges and full board, transport, laundry, guide service and field preparation of trophies are included in the daily rate. Tel. (06228) 5313; (061) 3-5936.

SWAKOPMUND

INTRODUCTION

Swakopmund is most people's favourite town in Namibia. Located 363 km due west of Windhoek on the Atlantic Ocean, it enjoys pleasant temperatures and sea breezes while the interior of the country is baking under the summer sun. Swakopmund was established in 1892 by the German colonial government as a port facility. An artificial harbour was created and a railway line was built to Windhoek. By 1915, however, South African had replaced German rule and all port activities were moved to Walvis Bay, a natural deep-water harbour. Today the remains of the German-built harbour at Swakopmund form the Mole Basin which is the town's safe bathing beach. Although the cold Benguela Current affects the temperature of the sea water so that it rarely exceeds 20°C, Swakopmund is Namibia's premier beach resort. Swimming, surfing, sunbathing and angling, in addition to a full range of sporting activities, make this is very popular holiday spot.

Namibia's beach resort

The town is characterised by lovely colonial German architecture and is an oasis of palm trees, flowers and green lawns. This profusion of plants and grass is all the more remarkable when one looks just beyond the periphery of the town. The sand sea of the Namib Desert completely surrounds Swakopmund and where the watering stops, the dunes begin.

Sea of sand

Swakopmund offers the visitor much to see and do and is the departure point for fascinating trips into the Namib-Naukluft Park and the Skeleton Coast.

GETTING THERE

There are several choices of road from Windhoek. The fastest and easiest is the B2, a fully tarred road of 363 km. The most direct route is via the C28 and the Bosua Pass. The gravel surface of this road is in good condition but the gradient is very steep so it is not an advisable choice if you are towing a caravan. The most scenic route is the C26, a gravel road which traverses the Khomas Hochland plateau via the Gamsberg and Kuiseb Passes. The road is in excellent shape and the scenery through the mountains is spectacular. After negotiating the Kuiseb Pass the road descends to the flat sand plains of the Namib Desert. The C26 ends 175 km out of Windhoek where it joins the C14. Turn right following the signpost for Walvis Bay. The

Swakopmund

Walvis Bay remaining 145 km until you reach Walvis Bay crosses the Namib-Naukluft Park (no permit is required on this road). If you choose this route you will need to show a passport, preferably with a South African visa, to enter Walvis Bay. If you do not have a visa, you might be asked to fill out a minor bit of paperwork to obtain a temporary entry permit. On the other hand, you could very possibly just be waved through the border post.

Travellers choosing either of the gravelled routes to Swakopmund should note that almost a full day's drive is entailed. Temperatures do soar in the desert so it is prudent to get an early start. No services or provisions of any kind are available on these roads, so bring a picnic lunch and plenty of liquid refreshments!

Public transport includes luxury coach service provided by *Mainliner* to and from Windhoek three times a week, a passenger train every other day from the interior, and *Namib Air's* four-times-a-week air service from Eros Airport in Windhoek.

ACCOMMODATION

Best hotel in town   **Hansa Hotel*****. Roon St. Tel. (0641) 311; fax (0641) 2732. This centrally located hotel is the best in town. The 63 spacious rooms all have private bath, telephone and radio. The hotel has a new wing and the rooms in it are slightly more luxurious as a result of the new carpeting and furnishings.

Hotel Garni Adler. 3 Strand St. Tel. or fax (0641) 42060. Three blocks south of the pier is a brand new pension on the beach. There are ten beautiful rooms all with private bath, telephone and radio. TV is also available in your room upon request. The hotel has an indoor heated swimming pool and sauna, the only hotel in town with this distinction.

Strand Hotel**. Tel. (0641) 315. A beachfront hotel adjacent to the jetty operated by the Namib Sun chain. There are 42 rooms, all with private bath, telephone and radio, and many have sea-facing balconies.

Pension Schweizerhaus*. Am Zoll St. Tel. (0641) 2419; fax (0641) 5850. This bed and breakfast establishment has 22 nicely furnished, immaculately clean rooms all with private bath. There is also an excellent *konditerei* on the premises which serves the best pastries in town. The hotel is very close to the beach and municipal garden.

Kobo Kobo Lodge. Tel. (0641) 4710. This lodge is quite a distance from Swakopmund, located on the edge of the Namib-Naukluft Park halfway between Windhoek and

Namibia

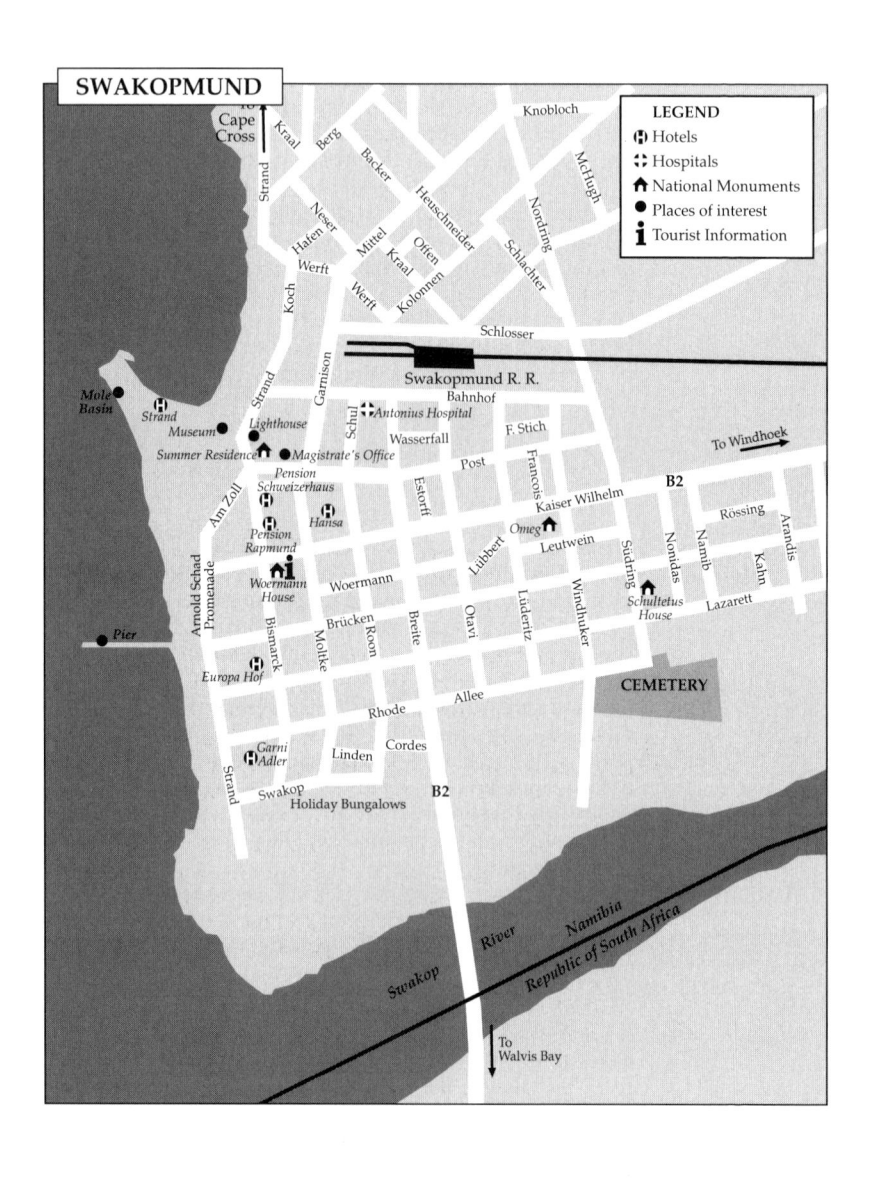

SWAKOPMUND

LEGEND
- Hotels
- Hospitals
- National Monuments
- Places of interest
- Tourist Information

the coast. It is a very special spot however, with beautiful thatched and stone cottages, a lovely pool and waterholes that attract game. Landrover tours, horseback riding and hiking are offered to explore the surrounding desert. Access is via the C28 to the D1985.

Mile 4. This is one of the best-equipped caravan and campsites in the country and it is located 7 km north of Swakopmund. It accommodates 360 tents or caravans and each site has a braaipit and electrical hookups. The spotlessly clean ablution blocks have hot water, baths, showers and toilets. Book with the DNC in Windhoek.

DINING

Erich's Restaurant. Post St. Tel. (0641) 5141. This restaurant specializes in fresh fish and international dishes. The food and service are excellent. Try the fresh Swakop asparagus in butter sauce when it is in season. This establishment is very popular with the locals so book in advance. Open for lunch and dinner daily except Sunday.

Excellent seafood

Western Saloon. 8 Moltke St. Tel. (0641) 5398. This restaurant is known for fresh seafood and steaks served in a rustic, publike setting. It is one of the few restaurants in Swakopmund that is open on Sundays. Open daily from 5p.m.

Napolitana Restaurant. Breite St. Tel. (0641) 2773. Serves pizzas, pasta and calzones as well as a complete menu of fish and meat dishes all prepared in an Italian manner. The atmosphere is casual and the food is decent. Open for lunch and dinner every day except Tuesday.

Café Anton at the Pension Schweizerhaus. Corner of Bismarck and Post St. There is a lovely outdoor terrace here where exquisite homemade pastries and cakes are served from 7a.m. to 8p.m. daily. Lunch service is limited to *soup du jour* and light sandwiches. Dinner is served from Tuesday to Sunday in the indoor dining room; the menu is limited to five or six items but is very reasonably priced.

Kucki's Pub. Moltke St. Tel. (0641) 2407. Kucki's offers a large selection of fish and seafood with steak and lamb also making the requisite appearance. Reasonable prices in a plain setting characterize this establishment. Lunch is served weekdays and dinner daily except Sunday.

Outstanding food

Lalainya's Restaurant. 7 DE Street, Walvis Bay. Tel. (0642) 2574. Although this restaurant is not in Swakopmund, I am including it in this listing because the food, service and ambiance are outstanding. If you want delicious French food in a beautiful setting at surprisingly reasonable prices, Lalainya's is the place to go. Lunch is served from Monday to Friday; dinner from Monday to Saturday.

SHOPPING
Jewellers
Immo Bohlke Goldsmith, Kaiser Wilhelm St. Unique handmade jewellery which is tax and duty free to bona fide overseas visitors

African Art Jewellers, Roon St. at the Hansa Hotel. Exquisite African-styled creations duty and tax free to the foreign tourist

Desert Gems, 2 Roon St. Minerals, gems, curios, stonecraft and jewellery

Art and Antiques
Peter's Antiques, 24 Moltke St. A large shop with an extensive selection including many African pieces

Reflections, Post St. A small shop with lovely paintings, unusual cards, photographs and carvings.

Karakulia, Knobloch St. The public is welcome to watch the spinning and weaving of karakul carpets, rugs and wallhangings. Custom designs and orders are possible.

Die Muschel, 32 Breite St. An art gallery and bookshop.

SIGHTSEEING

A walking tour A walking tour of Swakopmund should be one of your first priorities upon arrival. The town is easily negotiated on foot and there are many historic buildings dating from the colonial era that are worthy of attention. For an exhaustive list consult the tourist information booklet entitled, *Swakopmund.* Otherwise, walk the length of Post Street, then turn left onto Moltke Street and continue until it intersects with Lazarett Street. Turn right, then turn right again at Bismarck Street. Follow Bismarck Street back to the Am Zoll and then cross the car park and municipal garden to the beach. The most noteworthy examples of German architectural style will be encompassed on this walk which can easily be accomplished in less than two hours. On foot one has the opportunity to take note of the delightful profusion of flowers in Swakopmund that forms a wonderful counterpoint to the ubiquitous sand which surrounds this oasis town.

Guided historical tours of the town are given daily, usually in the afternoon by Mrs Hamm, tel. 61647. Interested visitors should ring direct or check with either the museum or the Tourist Bureau to ascertain the departure time.

The Woermann House in Bismarck Street houses the Tourist Information Bureau, the public library and an art gallery. This historic building is the pride of Swakopmund. For an excellent bird's-eye perspective of the town, be sure to climb the tower.

The museum can be found next to the public beach and is open daily from 10 a.m. to 12.30 p.m. and 3 p.m. to 5.30 p.m. It displays a fascinating collection of tribal artefacts, minerals, flora, fauna and memorabilia. The dioramas of marine and desert-adapted animal life are excellent. For those who are unable to schedule a visit to Rossing, don't miss the brilliant series of exhibits which portray all aspects of this mining operation.

Salt factory

Just 7 km north of Swakopmund there is a company involved in the commercial harvesting of salt. Great mounds of pure white crystallized salt decorate the landscape and interested visitors can arrange to view the salt works. The *Richwater Oyster Company*, an ancillary concern, is located at the same premises. Seed oysters are imported monthly from Guernsey and are planted in the nutrient rich beds. To arrange a visit to either operation, ring (0641) -2611 or visit the *Salt Company* offices at 23 Schlosser Street.

EXCURSIONS

The Cape Cross Seal Reserve

Seals galore

This reserve, 125 km north of the town is home to approximately 100,000 Cape fur seals. The public is welcome to visit but it is essential to check with the Tourist Information Office before you make this journey to ascertain which days of the week the reserve is open. The schedule keeps changing. If you do not want to drive yourself, all the tour companies offer an excursion to Cape Cross. There is an entrance fee of R5.00 per person and per vehicle. A fence separates the public from the seals but photographic opportunities abound. Be forewarned: the seals are highly odoriferous!

The Rossing Mine

Uranium mining

Located 40 km from Swakopmund, this is the world's largest open-cast uranium mine. Very informative guided tours are given every Friday. The luxury bus departs at 8 a.m. from the car park below the Café Anton, and

Namibia

returns at 1.30 p.m. There is a small fee for this tour which is donated to the *Swakopmund Museum*. For information and reservations, check with the museum or ring (0641) 2246.

Walvis Bay and Sandwich Harbour

Significance of Walvis Bay

Walvis Bay, which means 'whale bay' in English, is the only natural harbour of any importance in Namibia. It was used as a refuge as early as 1487 when Bartholemew Dias sailed the coastline. It wasn't until the 1780's however, when American and British seamen noted the large populations of whales, that attention was focused here. The Dutch and the British both claimed sovereignty of Walvis Bay in the last years of the eighteenth century but lack of fresh water made settlement difficult. One hundred years later, the British, alarmed by increasing German involvement in South West Africa, officially proclaimed the area as part of the Cape Colony. Although Namibia is now an independent country, Walvis Bay has remained an enclave of the Republic of South Africa, although this situation could change in the future. As Namibia's only significant deep-water port it represents a crucial link with the outside world. Also, Walvis Bay is the centre of Namibia's fishing and fish processing industry, and a major contributor to the economy.

For the bird watching enthusiast a trip to Walvis Bay and Sandwich Harbour is a must. The Walvis Bay wetland area and lagoon is the most important in Southern Africa and the second most important on the contintent. This coastal region supports 42 per cent of the total population of greater flamingos and 60 per cent of the lesser flamingos found on the sub-continent. It also supports 50 per cent of the world population of chestnut banded plovers. If you are interested in flamingo photographs, just drive along the beachfront south of the Walvis Bay business district and you will see thousands of birds feeding in the shallow water.

Flamingos

For a more in-depth look at the teeming birdlife and ecology of this region, contact *Charly's Desert Tour Company* in Swakopmund, who offer an excellent full-day excursion to Sandwich Harbour. The fresh water lagoon here attracts migrating and breeding birds by the thousands. Towering sand dunes provide a stunning backdrop for the reed-fringed pools and barely 15 metres away the Atlantic Ocean pounds the shore. Unfortunately, a tremendous amount of erosion has seriously jeopardized the Sandwich Harbour lagoon and salt water contamination is a real possibility if the beach barrier continues to erode. Charly's Desert Tours is the only company offering this trip so check with the owner, Mike Heroldt, for the latest update on the situation. Sandwich Harbour is located 40 km south of Walvis Bay and is only accessible by four-wheel drive vehicle; a permit is required for entry to this area. There is a 2 km walk involved in viewing the lagoon so wear proper shoes.

Namib Desert Tour

The fascinating desert

If you only do one thing in Swakopmund, take a desert tour - unless you are *en route* to the Skeleton Coast with Loew Schoeman. The various safari companies based in town all offer half or full day tours into the Namib. It is impossible to appreciate the geology and complexity of life in this desert without a knowledgeable guide. Your visit will encompass the Swakop and Khan canyons, the Goanikontes oasis, 'moonscape' dunes, *Welwitschia mirabilis* and lichen plains. In just a matter of 100 km you will experience the incredible diversity that characterizes the Namib. This excursion will introduce you to the three types of desert which co-exist here: the shifting sand dune sea, the rocky canyon desert and the flat gravel plains. The tour is informative as well as fascinating and it will change your perception of the desert forever. If you want to venture into the Namib-Naukluft Park on your own, call at the *Swakopmund Tourist Information Office* or the *DNC* for a permit to visit the area. Be sure to ask for the pamphlet which corresponds to the numbered markers along this route so that you may read a brief explanation regarding the points of interest.

National West Coast Recreation Area

Public campsites

The area north of Swakopmund to the Ugab River, a coastal stretch of some 210 km, is a nature reserve totally accessible to the public. The angling is superb and apart from a visit to the Cape Cross Seal Colony, this is the main reason for an excursion to the recreation area. The salt roads along the coast are excellent and in many places one can drive to the edge of the sea in an ordinary vehicle.

A good system of camp-sites has been established at Miles 4 and 14, Jakkalsputz and Miles 72 and 108. Ablution blocks are provided and petrol is available at Mile 72 and 108. Visitors must supply all their own equipment and provisions. At Henties Bay there are fully equipped bungalows for rent but visitors need to bring their own towels. The Skeleton Coast Park begins at the

Namibia

Reservations and permits required

Ugab River. Public access to the Skeleton Coast is limited to overnight visitors at Torra Bay or Terrace Bay. Reservations and permits must be secured from the DNC in Windhoek. Torra Bay is only open to campers from 1 December to 31 January. Facilities are very basic: toilets but no hot water or showers. The Terrace Bay camp consists of fully equipped bungalows and the rate includes full board. No camping is permitted. The Skeleton Coast Park north of Terrace Bay has been proclaimed a wilderness area and the only access is via a fly-in safari. For detailed information on this trip see page 64.

Sesriem and Sossusvlei

Swakopmund is a convenient departure point for an excursion south to Sesriem Canyon and Sossusvlei. Because of the distances involved, this trip needs at least one overnight stay. There is a camping area at Sesriem with ablution facilities, petrol and braai pits. Please note that you must provide all your own tents, equipment and provisions at this site. A permit is necessary to visit this area as well as Sossusvlei and you should book in advance with the DNC in Windhoek or Swakopmund.

Sesriem canyon

Quite near to the campsite is Sesriem Canyon, a narrow gorge that was carved out of metamorphic rock centuries ago by the Tsauchab River. The walls of the canyon are over 30 metres high and in one place the walls narrow to a width of only two metres. It is possible to explore the gorge on foot as the ravine is only about 1-1/2 km long. If there has been sufficient rainfall you might be lucky enough to have a swim in the pool which forms in the gorge.

From the Sesriem camp it is a 65 km journey to Sossusvlei. The gravel road is negotiable by ordinary car until you are within 3 k m of Sossusvlei. Unfortunately only four-wheel drive vehicles can proceed to the pan; if you are not so equipped, it will be necessary to walk across the sand, a trek of about an hour.

World's highest sand dunes

Sossusvlei is arguably the most beautiful spot in Namibia. Here you will find a clay pan surrounded by the world's highest sand dunes, some in excess of 300 metres. This clay pan represents the end of the Tsauchab River. Although the river may once have flowed to the Atlantic Ocean some 60 km distant, a sea of sand dunes eventually blocked its path. The Namib Desert is characterized by vast expanses of sinuously curving sand dunes. What sets the dunes here apart, aside from their height, is the presence of iron oxide which gives the sand a bright red colour. The Sossusvlei dunes, known as star dunes, have the most incredible red-orange hue with contrasting areas of taupe-coloured sand. The stark white clay of the pans *(vleis)* highlights the dramatic colour of these dunes. The best time to see Sossusvlei is at sunrise or in the late afternoon when the play of light creates shadows which heighten the visual impact. The dunescape extends as far as the eye can see and the silence here is deafening. Unbelievable as it may seem, it is common to see springbok, ostrich and oryx (gemsbok) in this area.

Scenic flights

If you are short of time or not inclined to camp, there are several other ways to visit or view this area. *See Africa Tours* in Swakopmund offers a three-hour scenic flight to Sossusvlei via Sandwich Harbour. It is an unforgetable experience and it is possibly the best way to grasp the magnitude of the Namib dunescape. Photo opportunities on this flight are unexcelled. Another option is to let one of the Swakop safari companies, such as *Charly's Desert Tours*, escort you to Sesriem. The trip requires two nights of camping but everything is provided for you. All travel is done by four-wheel drive vehicle so there is no hiking involved at Sossusvlei.

A third possibility is to drive yourself (or fly by chartered plane) to the **Namib Rest Camp**, a privately owned camp 27 km south of Solataire. Very nice, fully equipped bungalows are available for the modest price of R40.00 for two people. Meals can also be provided if you so desire. Guided Landrover excursions to Sesriem and Sossusvlei are offered so you do not have to go it alone. A special feature of the Namib Rest Camp is the unique petrified sand dunes which are found here. These huge mounds of coloured sand have hardened to stone over the millennia, a process most people only associate with wood. To book a stay at Namib Rest Camp telephone (06632), and ask for 3211, or book with the *Swakopmund Tourist Information Office*, telephone (0641) 2224.

ACTIVITIES

Fishing

Surf casting

The coastal area stretching from Walvis Bay north to Terrace Bay on the Skeleton Coast is a mecca for fishing enthusiasts. Beach access is by ordinary car and bait and tackle can be purchased at service stations and grocers. Check the *Namib Times* for up-to-date angling advice before you go, or contact one of the following companies: *Sunrise Fishing* with H.D. Herzig. Tel. (0641) 4923.

Namibia

West Coast Angling Tours. Tel. (0641) 2377; fax (0641) 2532. This company offers daily guided tours departing at 8 a.m.that include all bait, equipment, a light lunch and refreshments. Surf and rock angling as well as inshore and deep sea charters are available. The price of all tours is R150.00 per person and includes transport to and from your hotel.

The Sanpipi Fishing Lodge at Henties Bay. Tel. (011) 6096158. South Africa. Offers three-, five- or seven-day packages with luxury accommodation, full board, all tackle and bait and some sightseeing.

Golf

Namibia's finest nine-hole golf course is located just outside of Swakopmund at the Rossmund Country Club. The public is welcome. Tel. (0641)4110. There is also a mini golf course situated next to the Municipal Nursery and Gardens.

Swimming

Because the sea is rarely warm enough for prolonged swimming, an Olympic-sized, indoor heated swimming pool was constructed on the beachfront. There is a very small admission fee and changing facilities, lockers, showers and hairdryers are available.

Waterslide The pool is open daily. There is also a waterslide, children's pool and play park located on the beach at the Mole Basin. The town provides public toilets, showers and changing rooms at the beach. These are available every day of the week from 8 a.m. to 5 p.m.

Camel Rides

There is a camel farm 12 km out of Swakopmund on the road to the Rossmund Country Club. Fifteen minute rides are given daily from 3 p.m. to 5 p.m. only. Tel. (0641) 363.

Horseback Riding

Rides in the Namib dunes are offered, lasting 1½ to 2 hours. Inquire at *Blatt Shoe Store*, Kaiser Wilhelm Street.

TOURING

Charly's Desert Tours. 11 Kaiser Wilhelm St. Tel. and fax (0641) 4341. Offers daily guided Landrover trips to a variety of places in the Namib Desert. Scheduled tours include Sandwich Bay, Cape Cross Seal Colony, Gemstone Tour, Spitzkoppe and Namib Desert. The most popular trip is the full- or half-day Desert Tour during which one visits the Swakop and Khan canyons, Goanikontes oasis, the *Welwitschia mirabilis* plains and the

Organised sightseeing

Swakopmund

so-called moon landscape. The informative guide discusses the geology and plant and animal life of the Namib. Non-scheduled camping safaris to Sossusvlei, Etosha, Damaraland and Kaokoland can also be arranged on an individual basis.

Desert Adventure Safaris. Roon St. in the passage next to the Hansa Hotel. Tel. (0641) 4072. Also offers sightseeing tours of Swakopmund, the Namib, Spitzkoppe and Cape Cross, some on a daily basis, others on demand. Longer 3-12 day excursions to Caprivi, Kaokol and, Botswana and Victoria Falls are also available.

See Africa Tours. Roon St. Tel. (0641) 5243; fax (0641) 4203.

Scenic flights Offers a variety of scenic flights with a very competent pilot. The most notable are the flight to Sossusvlei of three hours' duration and the flight to Damaraland via the Skeleton Coast (four hours). If you would like to stay overnight in this region arrangements can be made for you to stay at the Palmwag Lodge.

SERVICES

TOURIST INFORMATION
Swakopund Tourist Information Office, Bismarck Street.
Open Monday-Friday, 9 a.m.-1 p.m. and 2.30 p.m.-5.30 p.m; Saturday 9 a.m.-1a.m. Tel. (0641) 2224. After hours: (0641) 4025. This office provides excellent information on Swakopmund and the surrounding region and acts as a booking agent for any tour you may wish to join. A 25-minute video of Namibia is available if you are interested. Be sure to ask for the Swakopmund Tourist Brochure.

NATIONAL PARK BOOKINGS
Directorate of Nature Conservation, Ritterburg Building, Bismarck Street. Tel. (0641) 2172.

GETTING AROUND

Car Hire
Avis: tel. (0641) 2527
Budget: tel. (0641) 2080
Imperial: tel. (0641) 61587
All three companies have offices in Kaiser Wilhelm Street.

Bus Service
Mainliner, Post Street. Tel. (0641) 4031

Airline
Namib Air, Post Street. Tel. (0641) 5123

CINEMA
Atlanta Theatre, Roon Street. Tel. (0641) 2845

TRAVEL AGENCY
Trip Travel, Post Street. Tel. (0641) 4031

THE SKELETON COAST

INTRODUCTION

The Skeleton Coast is a narrow strip of land sandwiched between the Atlantic Ocean and the vast sand dune sea of the Namib Desert. Proclaimed a national park in 1971, it stretches from the Kunene River on the Angolan border 500 km south to the Ugab River. For political, mineral and ecological reasons, the Skeleton Coast has been largely off-limits to modern man for over a century. As a result, it is today one of the only true wilderness areas remaining on the African continent. Although one doesn't tend to think of desert habitat as a delicate environment, the ecosystems here are extremely vulnerable to man's casual and often unwitting destructiveness. For instance, wagon tracks made almost a century ago still scar the landscape and the mere act of walking across fragile lichen plains can destroy an ancient life form. For this reason the Skeleton Coast from the Hoanib to the Kunene Rivers has been declared a wilderness area and access is severely restricted with the very real hope of preserving the delicate balance of life which struggles to exist here.

Fragile habitats

Namibia's Skeleton Coast is one of the most desolate and inhospitable places on earth and very few of those unfortunate souls who have been shipwrecked off its treacherous coast over the centuries have lived to tell the tale. Beaches littered with the bones of man and whale and the detritus of countless ships have given this stretch of land it's apt name. A combination of strong currents, tricky tides and reefs have sent many a ship off course to her death. Due to the influence of the Benguela current from Antarctica, dense fog blankets this region virtually on a daily basis, adding to the dangers inherent in navigating this stretch of coastline. It is this very fog however, which extends as far as 40 km inland, that brings life-sustaining moisture to the flora and fauna of the Skeleton Coast. The symbiosis that occurs between the shroud of mist and the life forms of this region is one of the amazing characteristics of the Namib Desert. Despite being the oldest and one of the driest deserts on earth, the Namib sustains an amazing array of plant and animal life. Not always visible to the unpractised eye, the creatures of the Namib are flourishing, having adapted over the millennia to their harsh, arid habitat.

Littered with shipwrecks

Life sustaining fog

GETTING THERE

Not to be missed!

My number one recommendation for any tourist to Namibia is a trip to the Skeleton Coast with Louw Schoeman's *Skeleton Coast Fly-In Safari Company*. There is no better way to experience the geology, flora, fauna and ecosystems of this desolate strip of forbidding coastline than to spend a few days in its midst with the experts. The trip is not luxurious but then this is a true wilderness area and one shouldn't expect the Hilton. However, the vehicles are first rate, the food is good and plentiful, the tents are clean and the water is hot. Best of all are the guides - naturalists who know the area intimately and who are eager to show visitors the hidden wonders and miracles of life in this remote and fascinating region. A week spent in the company of these people exploring the vast, trackless world of the Skeleton Coast is a singular experience. The beauty of the desert is astounding and the variety of terrain here makes every day's journey a new revelation. From seal colonies to lichen plains which paint the desert in a wild palette of colour, from red sand glistening with the fire of crushed garnets to boulder-strewn canyons reminiscent of the American West, from secret, subterranean rivers to thousand-foot sand dunes marching in sinuous curves to the sea, the Skeleton Coast offers a feast for the eyes and a balm for the soul. There is no place like it in Africa, or indeed the world, and the wild magnificence of its geology and vistas will be forever imprinted on your memory.

Beauty of the Namib

Skeleton Coast Fly-In Safaris offers four-, five-, six- or eleven-day excursions on a scheduled weekly basis throughout the year. If you have the time, my recommendation is Safari B which combines the Skeleton Coast with the Kunene River for six days/five nights. Louw Schoeman, the owner of the company, has the sole concession from the Government to operate tours in this wilderness area. Guests are flown in and out of the region in single-engined planes and are accommodated in igloo tents equipped with chemical toilets. The daily agenda typically features an all-day drive to visit areas of interest such as the roaring dunes, seal colonies, Agate Mountain or the nomadic Himba people. The primary purpose of these safaris is not to view game. Although game is present, notably springbok, oryx (gemsbok), ostrich, jackal, hyena and elephant, the animals are not at all accustomed to vehicles or people and as a result they tend to disappear long before you have your camera ready. The aim of a Skeleton Coast safari is to introduce

Roaring dunes

The Skeleton Coast: littered with the bones and detritus of countless shipwrecks.

you to desert geology, ecology, flora and fauna and to let you experience the freedom, unique beauty and overwhelming solitude of the region.

For detailed information, contact *Skeleton Coast Fly-In Safaris*, PO Box 2195, Windhoek 9000. Tel. (061) 22-4248 or fax (061) 22-5713. Please note that it is quite easy to combine a visit to the Etosha National Park with a Skeleton Coast safari. If you would be interested in a link-up, Skeleton Coast Fly-In Safaris can arrange this for you.

ETOSHA NATIONAL PARK

INTRODUCTION

Signature salt pans

Etosha is Namibia's largest and finest game reserve. It was originally declared a wildlife reserve in 1907 by the German colonial government and comprised some 100,000 sq km of territory. Political pressures have managed to erode a considerable portion of the park and today it is confined to 22,270 sq km. Etosha is a desert habitat and the park is characterized by and famous for the enormous salt pans which form the heart of its landscape. Twelve million years ago this region was an immense inland lake, formed by the flow from the

Kunene River. Tilting of the earth caused the river to change course and over time the lake became a pan; at 6,133 sq km it is now just a fraction of its original size.

Etosha is an Ovambo word meaning 'land of dry water', or alternatively 'great white place of dry water'. This expression is particularly appropriate given the visual impact of the terrain. The relatively monochromatic landscape is littered with limestone rubble and stunted, often barren trees. In the distance, stretching as far as the eye can see, lie the salt pans, looking for all the world as if they are full of water. From a great distance the pans assume a blue hue and it seems certain that they are shallow lakes. The mirage is ephemeral though, for as one approaches the trick of light and heat haze dissipates and the pans blaze white and bone dry under the cloudless sky. Vast plains of bleached grass and the parched earth of the salt pans are quintessentially Etosha. The occasional clump of verdant reeds which fringes a waterhole provides the only counterpoint to the arid, virtually featureless expanse of the park. There is no distraction of landscape here to vie with the wildlife for attention. The enormity of sky is so overwhelming that it seems to have pressed the desiccated earth into a narrow ribbon with its weight and the sun seems to have leached all vestiges of softness or colour from the soil. The animals stand in stark relief to the landscape and it is difficult to imagine a more dramatic spot on earth.

Heat mirages

There are large concentrations of game at Etosha and if you are in Namibia for the purposes of game-viewing, this is the spot to be. The park is criss-crossed by a system of well-maintained dirt roads and 37 waterholes are accessible to the public. Game sighting in Etosha is a bit different from what you may have experienced in other parts of Africa. Vehicles are confined to established roads and game is most easily and frequently observed at the established maintained waterholes. During the dry season when surface water is non-existent in the interior of the park, the animals are forced to migrate to this water source for survival. The variety of species and the interplay between them at the waterholes is a special feature of Etosha and photo opportunities are unmatched. When and if the rains come, the animals will head into the interior of the park. Game will still congregate at the waterholes but concentrations will be smaller. Pools of water will form everywhere and the grazing will be better in the far reaches of the park where there is less competition than in the areas surrounding

A different style of game viewing

Namibia

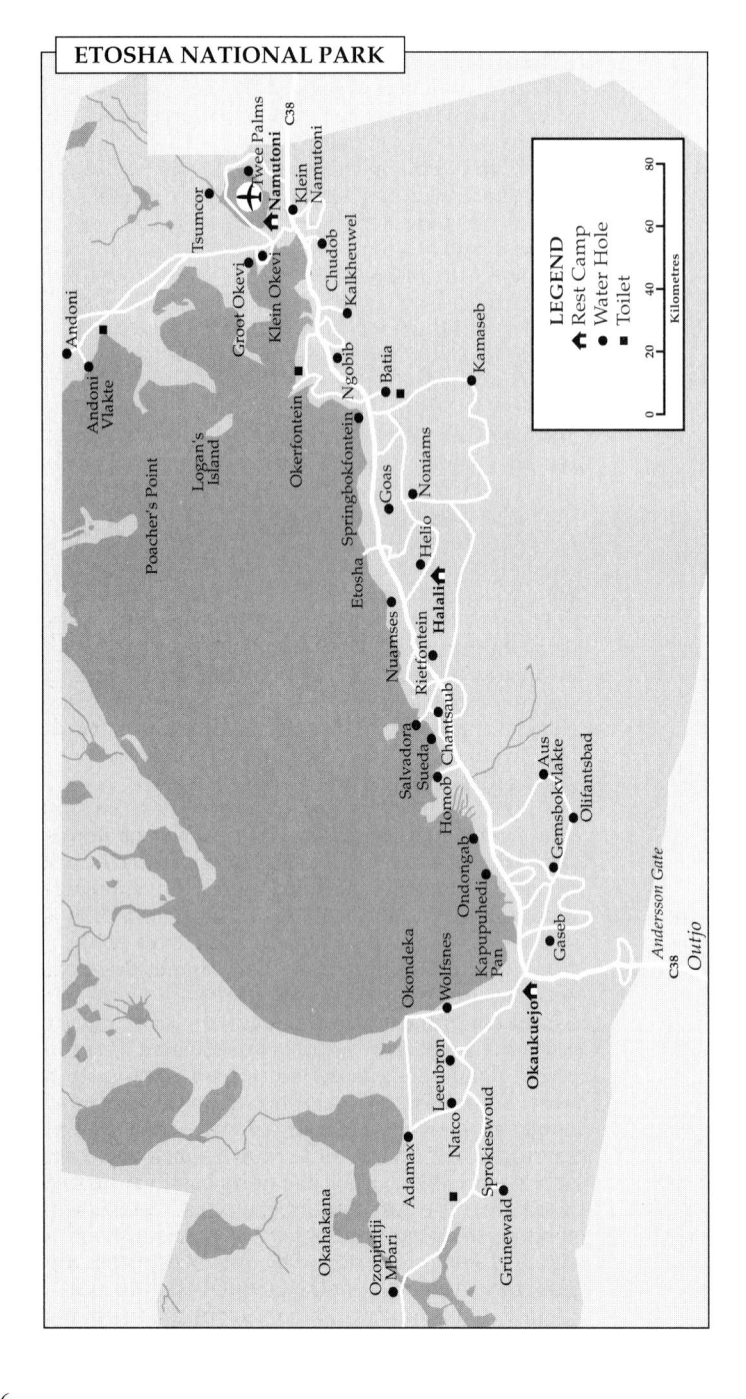

the dry-season waterholes.

Prolific birdlife Etosha also has abundant bird-life with over 325 species recorded. If the rains prevail, always a fervent wish in Africa, the pans will fill with water, attracting thousands of flamingos and waterfowl. Such an occurrence is an unimaginable sight - the transformation of this dehydrated land into a shallow sheet of shimmering water, alive with the colours of a million feathers, seems nothing short of miraculous.

GETTING THERE

Easy access It is an easy 437 km drive from Windhoek to Okaukuejo on the south-western edge of the pan. The road is paved until you reach the Andersson Gate, about 18 km south of the rest camp at Okaukuejo. It is also possible to drive from Windhoek to Namutoni, a distance of 537 km on good paved roads.

Namib Air flies to Tsumeb, the closest town to the Etosha National Park, 110 km from Namutoni. Hire cars are available at the airport from Avis. Charter flights may be arranged to the airstrips within the park through *Namib Commercial Aviation*, tel. (061) 22-3562/3. Avis now hires cars from the rest camp at Okaukuejo, which is convenient if you have been flown in. A number of tour companies also offer coach excursions to Etosha on a scheduled daily basis.

ACCOMMODATION

There are only three places to stay within the Etosha National Park and they are all managed and maintained by the Government. The services and facilities are essentially the same at each; it is their locations which differ. At the time of writing only the camps at **Namutoni** and **Okaukuejo** are open all year round; the facility at **Halali** is closed to overnight guests from 1 November to mid-March. The restrooms, pool and restaurant are open, however, to day visitors.

Okaukuejo camp is on the south-western edge of the Etosha Pan. This rest camp has one- and two-room bungalows for self-catering as well as two-bed 'bus quarters', which translates as motel rooms. Camping and caravan sites are also available. Okaukuejo has a **Floodlit waterhole** in the grounds that is floodlit for night game-viewing, a feature unique to this camp. Facilities at the camp include a petrol station, restaurant, shop, post office and swimming pool.

Halali is centrally situated between Okaukuejo and

Namibia

Namutoni, approximately 70 km from both. This is the newest of the three government rest camps but it lacks air conditioning, which is why it is closed from November to mid-March. Accommodation ranges from camping and caravan sites and dormitories with shared communal ablution blocks, to bus quarters and rondavels with en-suite bathroom facilities.

Beau Geste fort

Namutoni is the most picturesque of the three rest camps as it is centred around the old 'Beau Geste' fort built by the German colonial government. The original fort that was built on this site in 1903 was destroyed by some 500 Ovambo warriors in 1904 when the majority of German troops were away from this base fighting the Herero in the south. The fort was completely rebuilt, however, between 1905 and 1907. Its only military use after this date was to house some British prisoners of war during the early years of the First World War before the South African government assumed control of South West Africa in 1915. Today, the fort has been converted into rooms and the camp also accommodates visitors in bus quarters and three-bedroomed mobile homes. The mobile homes have seen better days and the government has plans to replace these with rondavels in the future. Camping and caravan sites are available and the same facilities exist here that one finds at the other two rest camps.

Book in advance

Bookings for any of the three rest camps within the National Park should be addressed to the DNC in Windhoek. Namutoni is especially popular and reservations should be made well in advance, especially during school holidays. There is a small **admission charge** to the park for day and overnight visitors and vehicles which is payable at the entrance gates near Okaukuejo and Namutoni. Because this is a game reserve, visitors are not allowed to enter the park or to enter or leave the rest camps between sunset and sunrise.

In 1990 a new hotel opened just 11 km outside the Von Lindquist Gate at Namutoni called the **Mokuti Lodge*****. Tel. (061) 3-3145; fax (061) 3-4512 . Operated by the Namib Sun chain, Mokuti is a three star hotel offering guests a range of accommodation including two-bed bungalows, family chalets and standard tourist rooms. All units have air conditioning, telephone and private bathrooms. The Lodge has a swimming pool, restaurant and bar and its own air-strip. The quality of accommodation and the food are better at Mokuti than at any of the government rest camps. However, it is very convenient to be situated in the park itself and all three rest camps are perfectly adequate and much less expensive.

GAME-VIEWING

As I have said, there is an excellent system of roads in the Etosha National Park linking the 37 waterholes and the three rest camps. The majority of game viewing is done at these waterholes and involves shutting off the engine and waiting patiently for the drama to unfold. This said, it is easy enough to drive oneself through the park and observe game. However, unless you are familiar with the animal and bird species of this part of Africa you might consider engaging the services of an expert for at least part of your stay. A naturalist knows which areas the game has been frequenting and the amount of information he or she can impart is staggering. To understand the ecology of Etosha properly and to maximize the game-viewing experience, I highly recommend contacting Etosha Fly-In Safaris. The owners, Klaus and Helen, are extremely personable and their game safaris are informative and professional. If you fly in to Tsumeb or one of the smaller airstrips in the park, they will fetch you. All arrangements for accommodation can also be handled through them. For additional information write to *Etosha Fly-In Safaris*, PO Namutoni via Tsumeb, Namibia, telex 3550 WK.

Guided safaris

Before the advent of the white man, game was abundant throughout Southern Africa. Nowhere was this more true than in the region now set aside as the Etosha National Park. Large-scale hunting was the white man's trademark in Africa however, and by 1880, only 30-odd years after the first European had set foot in Etosha, the entire elephant population of this region had been eradicated. When there wasn't even enough game left to feed the German troops stationed in this part of the country, the Government realized the necessity of establishing nature reserves. Today, Etosha has healthy populations of animals and game-viewing here is generally excellent. The most frequently encountered animal is the springbok, followed by zebra, oryx (gemsbok), kudu, elephant, giraffe, blue wildebeest, ostrich, eland, black-faced impala, lion and rhino. Cheetah, leopard, hyena, jackal, dik-dik, steenbok and all manner of birds are also commonly sighted.

The best time to visit Etosha is April-October. The rainy season commences in the summer which means that from November to March the animals tend to migrate to the interior of the park, away from the

Namibia

waterholes that support them throughout the dry months. The winter months are also the coolest, making game viewing a bit more pleasurable. Summer temperatures often exceed 40°C and both animals and people tend to be less active when it is hot. For those hoping to see the bird life that congregates in the pan when the rains have come, March and April are the best months. However, it should be noted that the Etosha Pan only fills with water when the rains have been especially good, something that has not occurred in over eight years.

WATERBERG PLATEAU PARK

If you are driving to or from Etosha an overnight stop at the Waterberg Plateau Park could be fitted into your itinerary without too great a detour. The entrance to the park is located 95 km south-east of Otjiwarongo; take the C22 off the B1. The Waterberg is a red sandstone mountain that rises some 200 metres above the flat plain below. This mountain plateau was designated a National Park in 1972 for the express purpose of protecting rare and endangered species. A very successful programme of relocating animals to this area has been underway since the inception of the park. Today it has healthy populations of white rhino, buffalo, roan and sable antelope and tsessebe. Other species include giraffe, blue wildebeest, leopard, eland, red hartebeest and cheetah. There is also prolific bird life including eight species of eagle. The area is very beautiful with lush deciduous vegetation and massive, wind-sculpted rock formations. There are a number of naturally occurring springs which provide a year-round source of water for the wildlife.

Almost 45 per cent of the Waterberg Plateau Park has been set aside as a wilderness area. No permanent hiking trails have been established to prevent a deleterious impact on the fragile ecology of the region. Instead, guided trail tours are given by a nature conservator who is well-equipped to talk about the geology, flora, fauna and conservation efforts of the park. Visitors are not allowed to drive through the park on their own, but tours are given in open four-wheel drive vehicles. Clever hides and viewpoints have been constructed as well to permit observation of birds and animals.

There is a new, well-designed DNC rest camp called Bernabe de la Bat where one may stay overnight. Attractive one- or two-bedroomed stone bungalows with hot plates, refrigerators and en-suite bathrooms are available as well as quite luxurious rooms ('tourisettes'), and camping and caravan sites. The camp has a licensed restaurant, petrol pumps, a kiosk and a swimming pool.

Waterberg Wilderness Trail

One of the best ways to explore the Waterberg Park is to partake in The Wilderness Trail, a four-day/three-night hike which departs on the second, third and fourth Thursday of every month from April to November. The group is limited to eight participants so it is important to book in advance with the DNC office in Windhoek. There are trail camps along the trail where you sleep in tents with bush toilets and cold water only. You must bring your own sleeping bag and food; everything else is provided.

DAMARALAND

INTRODUCTION

Black rhinos

Damaraland is a beautiful region of stark contrasts, of desert, rolling grasslands and rocky, rugged mountains. This area of Namibia is home to Africa's largest concentration of black rhino and desert elephant, two highly endangered species. For ten years, dating from the mid-1970s, rampant, unchecked poaching seriously reduced the elephant and rhino populations in this area. Great progress has been made in rectifying this situation recently and the efforts of the past five years have begun to turn the tide. Conservationists and government officials are working with the indigenous Damara people to save their precious heritage. In an attempt to involve and interest the local inhabitants, native game rangers are appointed by tribal chiefs to apprehend poachers; thus far the system has had smashing results!

Hunter gatherers

The origins of the Damara people are uncertain. Bacause they could work with metal it is thought that they might have migrated from the Sudan where copper- and iron-smelting had its birth on the African continent. Others believe that the Bushmen and Damaras are the original inhabitants of Namibia. Whatever their descent, it is known that these people were often enslaved by the Hottentots and Hereros because of their metallurgical skills. To escape this persecution the Damaras moved into the desolate mountain region on the edge of the Namib Desert where they maintained a hunter-gatherer life-style until the advent of the colonial era.

Separated from the Atlantic Ocean by the Skeleton Coast Park, Damaraland extends some 600 km from north to south and 200 km from east to west. Of the many geographical formations and Stone Age relics in this region, I have outlined those attractions that hold the most interest for the tourist. All are accessible with an ordinary car, and they can be combined in a day's outing.

TWYFELFONTEIN

Rock engravings

Twyfelfontein, located on a secondary road (the D3254) approximately 10 km off the D2612, is probably the most notable and fascinating site in Damaraland. Here you will find Namibia's largest concentration of rock engravings: over 2,000 have been etched into the huge slabs of stone which typify this region. Although the exact age of the engravings is not known they are thought to range from

Bushmen rock engravings at Twyfelfontein in Damaraland.

A desolate land

500 to 10,000 years old. The ancient Stone Age artists no doubt sought shelter from the sun and wind under the towering rock formations in this valley. With sharp bits of stone they drew and incised the animals that roamed the bush around them. The figures of lion, giraffe, rhino, oryx (gemsbok), kudu and leopard are all easily recognizable. There are also quite a few portrayals of animal tracks and a number of abstract engravings. Today the surrounding plains are all but barren of game and the land is scorched and wind-burnt. Perhaps in centuries past this area was more fertile and the waterholes were perennial, assuring the prehistoric people of good hunting. To modern man the engravings are both mystical and enigmatic. However did these people exist in such an unremittingly harsh land? Given their daily struggle for survival, the constant search for food and shelter, from what well of joy and celebration did this ancient art gallery spring?

There are several shaded picnic tables at Twyfelfontein as well as toilets ('long drops'), water taps and a curio shop. No food or beverages are available. You are expected to sign in and a local guide will escort you to

Damaraland

the engravings. Wear trainers or sturdy shoes as there is bit of climbing involved. The tour takes approximately 30 minutes and the guide will apppreciate a small tip and/or cigarettes. If you are interested in a more in-depth study of the engravings you are free to explore on your own as long as you remove nothing from the site.

BURNT MOUNTAIN

No mountain!

Ten kilometres south of Twyfelfontein is a range of lifeless hills called the Burnt Mountain. The desolate slopes in this region are devoid of vegetation although in places varying hues of red, orange, brown and purple rock contrast with the bleak panorama. The blackened mound of ash and stone which lies at the end of the access road is reminiscent of a Johannesburg slag heap. It may appear burnt but this is no mountain! Nearby there is an outcropping of basalt rock; huge vertical blocks of stone are clustered together and this geological formation has been dubbed the Organ Pipes. If you are short on time, both of these diversions could be bypassed without great loss.

PETRIFIED FOREST

Rejoin the main road and continue north until it intersects with the C39; 30 km towards Khorixas you will see a turn-off for the Petrified Forest. A brief stop here will give you an opportunity to view the 200-million-year old remains of large trees which hardened to stone over the millennia. The trees for the most part are still intact, lying where they were deposited by some huge flood eons ago. They look like wood and it is only upon touching one of the segments that you realize the wood has become stone. Along the path to the Petrified Forest you will see quite a few small *Welwitschia mirabilis* plants.

BRANDBERG MOUNTAIN

The White Lady controversy

The Brandberg is a mountain massif which juts dramatically from the flat plain of central Damaraland. It is Namibia's highest mountain with the Konigsstein peak measuring 2,580 metres. This region was undoubtedly frequented by the San people in earlier times as evidenced by the prolific rock art. A very famous and controversial rock painting called the White Lady (*Wit Vrou*) adorns a rock face in the Brandberg. The figure in question is part of a frieze and a good bit of speculation has surrounded the painting since its discovery in 1918. When the paintings were studied in 1947 by world authority Abbe Henri Breuil, they were believed to have Mediterranean origins and the central figure was deemed to be a woman. Breuil's theory was predicated on the basis of an uncanny likeness between this figure and those found on Greek vases. One must remember that at this time Europeans found it difficult, if not impossible, to credit Africa with any significant cultural, artistic or architectural heritage. Many modern scholars now believe that these paintings, which date back to 15,000 years ago, were indeed the work of indigenous people. The White Lady is thought to be a male daubed with white clay, perhaps indicating a ceremonial rite.

Senseless defacement

Sadly, over the past decade the White Lady painting has been abused and defaced by the public. The Department of Nature Conservation has attempted to prevent further desecration by constructing a cage around the rock slab. However, the damage is irreparable and the hot, one-hour walk is not worth your effort. The White Lady is totally unrecognisable.

SPITZKOPPE

Another prominent Damara landmark is the Spitzkoppe, a solid granite mountain often referred to as the Matterhorn of Namibia. The Spitzkoppe is a favourite ascent for mountaineers and there are many fascinating rock formations in this area. In the nearby Pondok Mountains there is an oasis of sorts called Bushman's Paradise where rock paintings have been discovered. Lamentably, this art has also been obliterated by vandals. I did not find a detour here very enlightening and if you are keen to explore this region I would recommend doing so with a tour guide from Swakopmund or Windhoek.

ACCOMMODATION

A good base for the area

Khorixas Rest Camp**. Tel. 0020 and ask for Khorixas 196. Khorixas is literally in the middle of nowhere, but a rest camp was established here to serve as a base for exploring the scenic attractions located nearby. If you are planning a journey to Twyfelfontein, Burnt Mountain or the Petrified Forest, you will most likely want to stay overnight at the Khorixas Rest Camp. The camp is very well maintained and has an enticing swimming pool, terrace, bar and a la carte restaurant. There are camping and caravan sites as well as 40 fully equipped bungalows with private baths, refrigerators and fans. A small shop on the premises sells cold drinks, sweets and curios. Petrol is available in the town about 2 km from the camp.

Palmwag Lodge**. Tel. (0641) 4459; fax (0641) 4664. This is another possible holiday spot located approximately 155 km from Khorixas and 110 km from Twyfelfontein. Situated adjacent to a perennial spring of the Uniab River, facilities include seven reed and grass bungalows with toilet and shower, a licensed restaurant and three swimming pools. Rates include full board but no towels; camp-sites served by ablution blocks are also available. Fly-in safaris to the Palmwag Lodge from Swakopmund are quite popular.

Hobatere Lodge***. Tel. (06532) 1602. Although this is a bit far from the Damaraland attractions, Hobatere is a well-run guest farm. The Lodge is located just outside the western boundary of Etosha National Park, some 175 km from Khorixas. Guests are accommodated in 12 bungalows all with private bath and there is a nice swimming pool on the property. As an added attraction Hobatere offers photo safaris and game drives led by professional guides; hunting safaris are also available during the season. If you are lucky you might see some of the desert rhino and elephant which inhabit this region.

Game drives

CAPRIVI

INTRODUCTION

Territorial trading

The Caprivi Strip is a narrow finger of land (482 km in length and 30-90 km at its widest) which separates Namibia from Angola, Zambia, Botswana and Zimbabwe. In 1890 Britain and Germany signed a treaty to settle their territorial interests in Africa. The British ceded the Caprivi Strip and Heligoland in the North Sea to Germany in exchange for Zanzibar Island. The Germans coveted the Caprivi as a means of access to the Zambezi River from South West Africa. The Caprivi was named after Count General Georg Leo von Caprivi who succeeded Bismarck as Chancellor of Germany. After the First World War the Caprivi was incorporated into Bechuanaland (now Botswana) but in 1939 the South African government took over its administration.

The Caprivi Strip is comprised of two distinct areas. Caprivi, which runs from Bagani to the Kwando River, is a dry, sandy region and has been proclaimed a National Park. The game, which includes elephants, kudu, wildebeest, giraffe, zebra and many antelope species, tends to inhabit the eastern end of the park near the Kwando River as there is no permanent water in the central area. East Caprivi, in contrast, is very fertile and lush as it is watered by four river systems: the Zambezi, Kwando, Chobe and Linyanti. This region receives 500-600 mm of rain annually so the farming potential is good; crops of maize, millet and sorghum are grown. Rice farming was attempted, evidently to no avail, as this has been discontinued. A new project is now underway to cultivate sugar cane which, if successful, would boost the failing economy of this region.

Katima Mulilo

Katima Mulilo is the administrative centre and only town in the Caprivi. Its location on the banks of the Zambezi River affords it a lushness of tropical vegetation and birdlife rarely encountered in Namibia. Katima Mulilo is really rather depressing however, as there is no employment for the locals and people just loiter about. One can't help but notice that there is more bottle and tin can litter here than anywhere else in Namibia, and maybe in all of Africa. The local people are conspicuously apathetic and often downright unfriendly, which is so unlike the attitude and behaviour of the inhabitants encountered throughout the rest of Namibia.

For the tourist, the Caprivi Strip is really off the beaten path. During the war for independence this region saw quite a bit of fighting which was a major deterrent to the development of a tourist industry. Today the area is totally safe for the traveller but there is little to see or do as yet. The main reason for an excursion to this area (other than as a transit corridor between Namibia and Botswana) is for the fishing and the bird-watching. The Zambezi is especially noted for its tigerfish although many other species such as bream (tilapia), catfish and largemouth are prevalent in these waters. Over 300 species of birds frequent the riverine habitat so there is plenty to keep bird-watchers occupied! One of the most unfortunate legacies of the war has been the utter depletion of all game in this section. Game-viewing along the Zambezi is non-existent so one must travel to the Chobe River to encounter hippo, elephant and antelope. If you are considering an excursion to the Caprivi, please bear in mind that February-September is the best time to visit. The summer months coincide with the rainy season, the mercury hovers around 45°C and the river is too low for boating in many sections.

A sad legacy of the war

GETTING THERE

Katima Mulilo is served three times weekly by *Namib Air*. The airport is called M'Pacha and is located 22 km from Katima Mulilo. Although it is possible to drive from

Check on road conditions Windhoek to Katima Mulilo, a distance of 1,215 km, it is a long and arduous journey. The road is tarred except for a 370 km section east of Rundu. Normally this gravel road is passable in an ordinary car but ruts and deep sand can be a problem. It is advisable to check with the AA in Windhoek about the condition of this stretch of road before setting out. Also, if there has been heavy rain, a four wheel drive vehicle will be essential.

Access to Botswana or Zimbabwe is quite easy. From Katima Mulilo to the border post at Kasane, Botswana, it is only 120 km, a two-hour trip. Once again, this trip can be done in an ordinary vehicle except after heavy rains. If you are travelling in a hired car, make sure that you have the necessary authorization and documentation to cross borders. The owner of the **Zambezi Lodge** in Katima Mulilo has the *Avis* franchise and he can arrange the paperwork and logistics involved in taking a car out of the country.

ACCOMMODATION

Zambezi Lodge. Katima Mulilo. Tel. and fax (067352) 203. The most de luxe resort in the Caprivi. Set on the bank of the river, guests are accommodated in basically furnished, air-conditioned rooms or chalets, each with private bath. All rooms are the same price but some of them are newer and larger so you might want to request one of them (Nos. 20-27). There is a swimming pool, a **Golf course** nine-hole golf course (clubs available for hire), a curio shop, a restaurant and a floating bar. A gym is currently under construction. Avis cars can be hired here and the hotel provides an airport transfer service. Camping and caravan sites are available adjacent to the property. Although the Zambezi Lodge offers fishing and sightseeing excursions on the river, this is not possible from November to January and anglers must provide their own tackle.

Hippo Lodge. Katima Mulilo. Tel. and fax (067352) 86. This Lodge is 7 km east of town, offers rustic but affordable accommodation in twelve reed and thatch bungalows, seven of which have en suite facilities. The grounds are lovely, with large expanses of grass and many shade trees. There is an open-air a la carte restaurant that serves three meals a day, a bar called the Laughing Crocodile where tribal dancing is sometimes featured, and a good-sized swimming pool. Fishing is offered but no tackle is furnished. Plans are underway to construct a floating barge for sunset cruises and evening dining on the Zambezi.

Namibia

Darts, dice and pool

A serious fishing camp

Kalizo Camp. Set on the banks of the Zambezi 37 km from Katima Mulilo, this is a camp for serious fishing, pure and simple, and if you are after big tigers, this is the place to be. Guests are lodged in reed or wood bungalows under thatch and share a large ablution block with both showers and baths. There is a cozy pub with darts, dice and pool table and Kalizo boasts no fewer than 17 motorized fishing boats. Full board, tackle, bait and airport transfers are included in the daily rate; boat hire and petrol are additional. Trophy mounting can be arranged on request. As an adjunct to the fishing camp, Kalizo offers five-day canoe safaris along the Chobe or Kwando Rivers and seven-day land safaris into West Caprivi Game Park and Mamili Reserve. Both of these adventures are geared to game viewing which is very good in these areas. Contact company headquarters in Johannesburg at (011) 886-4067; fax (011) 886-3576.

Floating casino

Zambezi Queen. This brand new 45-metre luxury cruise boat is now available for passengers who would like to spend a week on the Zambezi River in high style. Built and operated by the owners of the Zambezi Lodge, it is fully air-conditioned and offers 12 nicely furnished double rooms, each with wall to wall carpeting, toilet, sink and shower. There are two sundecks, two bars, a beautiful restaurant and a small casino. The Zambezi Queen departs every Friday between February and June on seven-day, six-night voyages. You will cruise downstream to Impalila Island, wind your way into small channels to view game, visit a native village and experience the Victoria Falls in Zimbabwe. A smaller boat is towed for fishing and sightseeing excursions. Telephone (067352) 203 or write to Alta Visagie, PO Box 98, Katima Mulilo.

Popa Falls Rest Camp. Poppa Falls. Located at the western edge of the Caprivi Strip on the Kavango River, and maintained by the DNC, this rest camp offers shady camp sites and rustic wood huts equipped with towels and bed linen. The ablution facilities are communal; there is a small kiosk but no restaurant. Book with the DNC in Windhoek.

Kavanga Motel. Rundu. Tel. (067372) 320. Although Rundu is not in the Caprivi Strip (it is 220 km west of Popa Falls), if you are driving to or from Windhoek you might wish to break your journey here. The Kavango Motel offers 11 clean but uninspired rooms, each with private bath, telephone and air conditioning. There is a fully licensed restaurant on the premises as well.

Caprivi

Kaisosi Safari Lodge. Rundu. Tel. (067372) 1230. Located 7 km east of Rundu on the Okavango River, this is a rustic camp with bungalows, tents with bedding, caravan and camp sites. There is a restaurant, bar and swimming pool and the management will arrange excursions to Popa Falls and the Mahango Game Park.

DINING
Your choices are extremely limited. The **Zambezi Lodge** and **Hippo Lodge** are your best bets.

SHOPPING

Limited shopping

In Katima Mulilo you will find a supermarket, a butchery, a bakery and an off licence. The only shopping for tourists is at the **Caprivi Art Centre**, a co-operative 'gallery' consisting of eight or nine stalls, all selling more or less the same items. Goods range from baskets and ivory and malachite jewellery to wooden carvings, predominantly of hippos. The quality of the carvings is good. Open daily from 9 a.m.-5 p.m.

SERVICES

BANKS

Bank Windhoek in Katima Mulilo is the only bank in the Caprivi and generally there are very long queues.

GETTING AROUND

Car Hire
Avis is located at the Zambezi Lodge. Tel. (067352) 203.

POST OFFICE

Unbelievably, there are two. One is in the central shopping area and the other is next to the police station.

TOURIST INFORMATION

Anything Goes is a small shop located across the street from the police station. Billing itself as 'Your Caprivi Connection' and 'The Hassle Buster', any and all arrangements can presumably be handled here. *Anything Goes* also doubles as the *Tourist Information Centre* so if you are looking for accommodation or something to do, this is an important stop. They book sunset cruises on the Zambezi (February-July), full-day or hourly fishing trips, game drives, scenic flights and canoe safaris. Tel. 067352 and ask for 86.

LUDERITZ

INTRODUCTION

Bartholemew Dias

Although the Phoenicians may well have landed in the natural harbour known today as Luderitz, the first recorded visit was in 1488. Once again it was the Portuguese navigator, Bartholemew Dias who first sailed into the harbour and erected one of his famous stone crosses. There were sporadic land and sea expeditions here over the next three centuries by the Dutch and British, but little interest evolved. Although it boasted an excellent harbour, Luderitz was bereft of fresh water and a 130 km wide belt of sand dunes separated it from the interior. It wasn't until the 1850s that the commercial potential of Luderitz was first realized. Under the auspices of a British firm, the lucrative collection of guano began on the islands just offshore; activities soon expanded to include fishing and sealing.

Colonial interests

In 1882 a German merchant named Adolf Luderitz negotiated with the Nama tribe to purchase large tracts of coastal land, including the area now known as Luderitz. Shortly thereafter, Chancellor Bismarck proclaimed Luderitz and the entire region between the Orange River and the twenty-sixth South parallel to be under German jurisdiction. Although there had been three decades of British industry in Luderitz, the British government had repeatedly expressed no interest in assuming responsibility for the territory. It was only after Germany declared its sovereignty over the area that Britain became nervous about an increasing German influence in South West Africa. In response, the British proclaimed Bechuanaland (now Botswana) a protectorate.

Discovery of diamonds

With the advent of the Hottentot War in 1904 Luderitz assumed strategic importance. A railway to the interior was built and the harbour was improved. Within one year there were four hotels, 22 shops and three bakeries in town. The war was over by 1908 and the economy of Luderitz had just begun to suffer when diamonds were fortuitously discovered. Overnight prospectors from all over the world flocked there to seek their fortunes and the population of the town mushroomed dramatically. Development continued unabated until 1914 and the outbreak of the First World War . When the British arrived at Luderitz German troops had already evacuated the town and surrendered without a shot being fired. Despite the change in government life remained much

Luderitz

The quaint seacoast town of Luderitz.

Romantic charm

the same. Diamonds were the lifeblood of the community until the Second World War, when mining operations shifted to Oranjemund. Following this the population decreased, but within a few years the town had bounced back as the centre of Namibia's crayfish industry.

Today, Luderitz is a quiet coastal town. For many, this is its principal charm. Unfortunately, years of overfishing have decimated the crayfish population and the town is experiencing difficult times economically. Although it's prosperity and populace have fluctuated over the years, ironically enough the town is once again about to be rescued by diamonds. Consolidated Diamond Mines (CDM) is in the process of opening a new mine at Elizabeth Bay. Rather than create another ghost town such as Kolmanskop when the diamond supply is exhausted, Luderitz is going to become the operational headquarters. Regardless of the rise and fall of it's fortunes, it exudes quaintness and the romantic charm of yesteryear, qualities that visitors will always find appealing.

GETTING THERE

This delightful coastal town has the distinction of being the oldest European settlement in Namibia, but it is not *en route* to anywhere. However, if you are planning an

Namibia

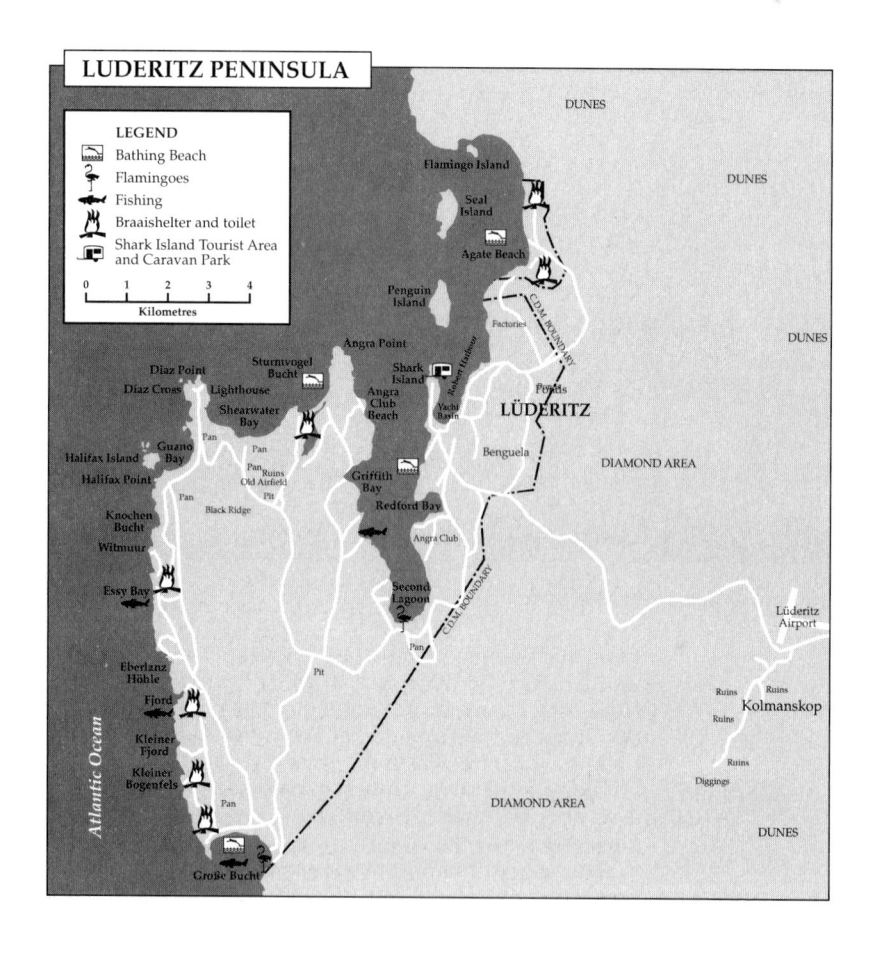

LUDERITZ PENINSULA

LEGEND
- Bathing Beach
- Flamingoes
- Fishing
- Braaishelter and toilet
- Shark Island Tourist Area and Caravan Park

extensive road trip through the country, you might consider a detour to Luderitz. The easiest access is via Keetmanshoop on the B4. The road is surfaced for all but 84 of it's 334 km. Another option would be to reach Luderitz from Swakopmund with a stop *en route* at Sesriem and possibly another at Helmeringhausen. This is a very scenic approach and an overnight stay in the Sesriem-Sossusvlei area is highly recommended (see page 58). The *Sinclair Guest Farm* (tel. (06362) 6503) on the D407 north of Helmeringhausen is a small but delightful place and is easily accessible after a morning excursion to Sossusvlei; to accomplish this, the best route is via the D826 to D407.

Castle in the sand

If time permits a short diversion to *Schloss Duwisib* would also be interesting. It is an incongruous but memorable sight to come upon this imposing stone castle perched on the very edge of the Namib Desert. A famous German architect designed it in 1908 to serve as both home and fortress for Baron von Wolff and his American wife. With the exception of the stone, which was quarried locally, all building materials, furnishings and craftsmen were imported from Europe. After arrival by sea in Luderitz, an overland journey awaited: 640 km by ox wagon through the Namib Desert! The castle is now managed by the DNC and plans are underway to convert it into a hotel. At present the Schloss Duwisib is open to visitors between 8 a.m. and 5 p.m. daily.

Namib Air offers flights to Luderitz from Windhoek and Swakopmund three times per week.

ACCOMMODATION

Bay View Hotel**. Diaz St. Tel.(06331) 2288. This hotel has 28 clean and basically furnished rooms with private bath and telephone. There is a nice swimming pool and the hotel restaurant serves breakfast, lunch and dinner.

Strand Bungalow Motel. Tel. (06331) 2398; fax (0631) 28691. Situated on the harbour 1 km from the town centre, accommodation is provided in whitewashed bungalows equipped with 2-4 beds, fridge and most with private bath. Some of the bungalows and rondavels do not have plumbing and ablution blocks must be used. The beach is very small and not very appealing but it is possible to swim here. The hotel restaurant is open daily.

Kapps Hotel*. Bay Rd. Tel. (06331) 2701. There are 25 very basic rooms, only seven of which have private bathrooms. There is a telephone in each room and the hotel has an *a la carte* restaurant for guests only.

Shark Island Camp. You couldn't ask for a more picturesque camp-site setting than this. Caravan and tent sites have electric points, ablution blocks and braai pits. Book at the DNC in Windhoek.

DINING

Delicious local crayfish

Strand Restaurant. Diaz St. Tel. (06331) 2752. Good food and a pleasant, informal setting; an outdoor terrace overlooks the harbour. The menu features grilled meats and fish as well as local oysters and crayfish. Open daily from 7.30 a.m. to 10 p.m.

Namibia

Franzel's Restaurant. Tal St. Tel. (06331) 2290. Luderitz's most popular and well-respected restaurant. The atmosphere is casual and friendly; the food is the usual selection of grilled meat augmented by local fish, oysters and lobster. It serves lunch and dinner daily.

SIGHTSEEING

Walking Tour

Walking is the best way to get a feel for Luderitz. The town is so small that you can easily stroll through its environs in less than an hour. Most of the German Art Nouveau and Imperial style architecture can be viewed by beginning at the fountain on Bismarck Street. Walk up the hill as far as Berg Street and turn right. At the Kreplin House turn left and walk up Kirch Street to the Evangelical Lutheran Church. The church is open to the public on Saturdays and Sundays at 5.45 p.m. when the bells are rung. If you wish to visit the church at another time, ask the Tourist Information Office to arrange it. The church was built with donations from Germany and the stained glass altar window was a gift from Kaiser Wilhelm II.

German colonial architecture

Kaiser Wilhelm II

Retrace your steps and at the bottom of the hill turn sharp right into Diamantberg Street. The most stunning example of colonial German architecture in Luderitz is perched on top of Diamond Hill. Known as Goerke House it is owned by CDM and serves as a guest house for CDM officials and visitors. If it is not occupied, Goerke House is open to the public on weekdays between 2 p.m. and 3 p.m. and on Saturdays between 10.30 p.m. and 11 p.m. Check with the CDM office in Diaz Street to confirm if a visit is possible.

Museum. Tel. (06331) 2526.
This small museum concentrates on the early history of Luderitz and the ecology of the Namib Desert. It is only open on Monday, Wednesday and Friday from 4.30 p.m. to 6 p.m. or by appointment.

Crayfish Factory Tour

Seaflower Lobster Corporation. Tel. (06331) 2518.
Located at the very end of Industry Street, 3 km north of town. At the gate to the factory there is a notice advertising that tours are permitted between 8.15 a.m. and 9.30 a.m. Monday-Friday. Despite this, I found it impossible to find someone able or willing to give me a tour. It would be advisable to phone in advance.

Sedina **Yacht Trip.** Tel. (06331) 2929.

Sailing cruise — Weather permitting there is a daily boat trip from Robert Harbour aboard the gaff-rigged schooner *Sedina*. The trip usually departs at 8 a.m. and lasts three hours. You will sail to Dias Point and if the seas are calm, onward to Halifax Island, noted for its large penguin colony.

Weavery, Bismarck St. Tel. (06331) 2272.
Watch pure karakul wool being hand-woven into Namibian-designed rugs at Luderitz Carpets. Worldwide shipping and custom orders are possible. Open Monday-Friday, 8 a.m.-1 p.m. and 2.30 p.m.-5 p.m. Saturdays from 8 a.m.-12 noon.

Peninsula Tour

A pleasant two hour drive will enable you to explore the Luderitz peninsula. Points of interest are Dias Point where the Portuguese navigator first landed and erected a stone cross. Today there is a wooden footbridge leading to a replica of the cross. Continuing south along the beach you will see Halifax Island, home to jackass penguins and cormorants. There are a number of small bays along the shoreline which afford good fishing and picnic opportunities. For swimming continue on to Grosse Bucht ('Big Bay'); this **Black sand beach** offers shallow but safe bathing. The road now turns inland and passes several pans *en route* back to Luderitz; springbok and oryx are often seen in this area so keep an eye out. The terrain of the peninsula is very bleak and forbidding. Much of what you see is in a restricted diamond area and it is difficult to imagine that this barren land yields such precious stones!

Back in town follow Bismarck Street down to the harbour. Turn left and then right into Insel Street and drive across the causeway to **Shark Island**. There is an old lighthouse, a hospital, a plaque commemorating Adolf Luderitz and a camp-site on this spit of land. You have excellent views of the town and bay from here. If you are in the mood for still more driving, follow Hafen Street out of town and watch for the turn-off to Agate Beach. The beach is 8 km out of town and is suitable for safe swimming and long walks.

Kolmanskop

A fascinating ghost town — The ghost town of Kolmanskop is the most interesting place in the Luderitz area. When diamonds were discovered in 1908 a town sprang up here overnight; Kolmanskop was the thriving centre of the diamond

Namibia

industry for 30 years. Despite the lack of fresh water the town flourished as evidenced by the fine buildings, bowling alley and casino. When mining operations shifted to Oranjemund, Kolmanskop slowly ceased to function. As boom town became ghost town the desert began to reclaim the site. Today CDM has restored several of the buildings while the rest have been abandoned to the ravaging influence of sun, sand and wind. An excellent one-hour tour is given at 9.30 a.m. Monday-Saturday. The museum on the premises depicts the history of mining here and after the guided tour you are free to roam through all the deserted buildings. Bring your camera and your appetite. There is a small tearoom here that serves the best pastries in Namibia during the two hours each morning that Kolmanskop is back among the living. Book for the tour at the CDM office in Luderitz on Diaz Street between 8 a.m.-12 noon and 2 p.m.-4 p.m.

SERVICES

TOURIST INFORMATION

Tourist Information Office, Bismarck Street. Open 9 a.m.-12 noon, Monday-Friday

GETTING AROUND

Car Hire
Avis is located at the airport but the counter is unmanned except when a Namib Air flight lands. In town *Avis* shares the *Namib Air* office in Hafen Street. Tel. (06331) 2054.

Taxis
Ring (06331) 2622 or 2719 any-time.

BOOK SHOPS

Luderitzbuchen Buchhandlung, Bismarck Street
Diaz Souvenirs, Bismarck Street

TOUR COMPANIES

Luderitzbucht Safaris and Tours, Bismarck Street. Tel. (06331) 2719 fax (06331) 2863. Scheduled tours are not offered *per se* but anything can be arranged on an individual basis. The owners will meet you at the airport, arrange accommodation and tailor tours to your interests. Overnight safaris to the Namib Desert and the Fish River Canyon can be planned. This company also offers a very good walking tour of Luderitz.

FISH RIVER CANYON

INTRODUCTION

The world's second largest canyon

The Fish River Canyon is Namibia's greatest natural wonder, a gigantic ravine formed over a period of 900 million years by the forces of erosion, fracturing, glacial ice and the once powerful waters of the Fish River. The canyon measures 161 km in length, is 2.7 km across at its widest point and is between 457 and 549 metres in depth. As such, it rates as the second largest canyon in the world, surpassed only by the Grand Canyon in the USA. The Fish River is Namibia's largest although it meanders through the canyon today as a mere shadow of its former self. The river only flows intermittently but there are always pools of water that glisten like jewels along the canyon floor.

The best way to experience the wildlife and flora of this gorge is to walk it. For those of us who have neither the time nor the energy for such an adventure, the lookout points will have to suffice. The Fish River Canyon is impressive, but frankly, if you have experienced the Grand Canyon, this does not compare.

GETTING THERE

To get to the Fish River Canyon plan on a two-hour drive from Keetmanshoop or 33/4 hours from Luderitz, both on very good gravel roads. An early start is advisable so that you beat the heat haze that is a daily occurrence here in the summer. Ten kilometres from the canyon lookout point there is a park gate at the Hobas Rest Camp, which is manned from 6 a.m.-10 p.m. daily. All vehicles must be registered and there is a small entry fee.

Get an early start

Hobas Camp and Hiking Trail

Hobas offers shady camping and caravan sites with ablution facilities, electric points, tiny swimming pool and braai pits; there is also a small kiosk that sells cold drinks, sweets and crisps. Hobas Camp is open all year round and bookings should be made with the DNC.

Continue past the camp to the first viewpoint. You will note that just before you reach this spot there is a turn-off leading to the Sulphur Springs viewpoint. To get to this particular site you must travel a total of 32 km over a horrendous road. Moreover, the view from here is no better than at the main lookout and the hot springs are not visible from the canyon rim. I do not recommend this deviation unless you are adept at fixing punctures!

Namibia

KEETMANSHOOP

In 1860 a Rhenish missionary station was established at what is now Keetmanshoop. This small town is the fourth largest in the country and is the centre of the karakul industry in the south. Keetmanshoop would rarely be included on a tourist's itinerary unless one is *en route* to the Fish River Canyon or the Kalahari Gemsbok Park. It is a convenient overnight spot for those who are combining these two attractions and it is easily accessible from Luderitz (334 km) or Windhoek (500 km).

If you do find yourself in Keetmanshoop you might consider a quick detour to the Quiver Tree (Kokerboom) Forest, 30 km north-east of town. The quiver tree is actually a member of the aloe family, *Aloe dichotoma*. These plants were named by the Bushmen who used their hollowed-out branches as quivers to hold arrows. The 'forest' consists of about 300 quiver trees, ranging from 3 to 8 metres in height. If you happen to be in this area during June or July by all means schedule a stop as the trees are aflame then with lovely yellow flowers.

The *Canyob Hotel* (tel. (0631) 3361) is the best hotel in town although that is not saying much. The standard rooms don't deserve their three-star rating. For an extra R20 the more de luxe rooms have clean carpets and new curtains, bedspreads and furniture. All 54 rooms have air conditioning, telephone and radio; television is available for hire for a small charge. There is a lovely swimming pool and grassy lounge area, much appreciated amenities in a hot, dusty town such as Keetmanshoop. The hotel has a decent a la carte restaurant and a cocktail bar.

Lookout point The first stopping point offers several shaded picnic tables, stone firepits and toilets. The main lookout point is 1 km further on and is the best spot for photographs. An 86 km hiking trail commences here; it takes an average of four days to trek along the canyon bottom to Ai-Ais. A permit must be secured well in advance of your planned hike. Due to the strenuous nature of the trail, a medical certificate, issued within 40 days of your hike, must be presented to the officials at the Hobas Gate. This trail is

Hiking trail only open from May to late August; contact the DNC in Windhoek for a permit application and complete details.

Ai-Ais
The Ai-Ais Hot Springs Resort is situated 80 km south of the main viewing point. To get there return to the Hobas gate and when you reach the D324 turn right. After 58 km you will cross the C10; turn right again and continue 14 km to the resort. Located in the midst of a desolate, lunar landscape, Ai-Ais is a true oasis. The Nama word Ai-Ais means firewater, an apt name for the water which wells from the earth here is an incredible 60°C. Rich in fluoride, chloride and sulphates, the water is piped to spa pools

Hot springs and jacuzzis; many people believe that the hot springs can provide relief to rheumatic sufferers.

Ai-Ais is a lovely spot to spend one or two nights. There is good bird and animal life and excellent fishing in addition to the spa attractions. The resort accommodation ranges from furnished tents, caravans and huts to fully equipped luxury flats with private baths. Day visitors are welcome between sunrise and sunset. Facilities include a restaurant, a shop, a large outdoor thermal pool and petrol pumps. Please note that Ai-Ais is only open from the second Friday in March to the end of October due to the intense heat and very real threat of flash flooding during the summer months. Reservations should be made well in advance with the DNC in Windhoek.

Day visitors welcome

THE KALAHARI

Although the *Kalahari Gemsbok Park* is located in the Republic of South Africa and Botswana, if you are travelling in southern Namibia you are only a few hours away from it. Before independence it was quite easy to get to the park from Namibia via the Mata Mata gate. However, there is no longer a border control post here so there is absolutely no crossing allowed between the two countries. From Keetmanshoop the most direct route is the C16 to Rietfontein. Once you have cleared border formalities it is another 150 km to the park. If you are driving from Ai-Ais, take the C10 to the B3 as far as Nakop; after you cross into South Africa the B3 becomes the R32. Approximately 65 km later take the turn off to the Kalahari Gemsbok Park and in just less than three hours you will be at the Twee Rivieren gate.

The Kalahari Gemsbok Park is an excellent spot for those who wish to experience the Kalahari Desert. Many consider it more scenic than Etosha but the game does not begin to compare. You will encounter far more species at Etosha and the vantage point for photographs is generally superior at the Pan. For a full discussion on the Kalahari Gemsbok Park refer to page **.

For those travellers who would like to spend a bit of time in the Kalahari Desert environment there is an alternative to an excursion to the Kalahari Gemsbok Park that does not entail leaving Namibia. The *Kalahari Safari Lodge* is a private game ranch located in the south-eastern corner of Namibia, 570 km from Windhoek and 265 km from Keetmanshoop. This region is characterized by savannah woodland and the Kalahari trademark: rolling red sand dunes. It is home to 50 mammal and 200 bird species and the ranch boasts the largest privately owned gemsbok herd in the world. Guests stay in fully equipped and serviced A-frame chalets with private bath and lapa (patio). The Lodge offers a restaurant, well-stocked shop with fresh meats, bottle store (off-licence), petrol and swimming pool. Fly-in safaris can be arranged and transport from Windhoek or Keetmanshoop is available on request. Activities at the ranch include game drives in open vehicles, walking safaris, horseback rides through the dunes and hot air ballooning. Prior booking is essential. Telephone (06 662) 3112 or write to PO Box 22, Koes 9000.

Botswana

Traditional fish traps in use along the Okavango River.

SECTION 2: BOTSWANA

BACKGROUND INFORMATION
    Travel Facts

    Country File

AROUND BOTSWANA
    Maun

    Okavango Delta

    The Panhandle

    Tsodilo Hills

    Other National Parks and Game Reserves

    Gaborone

    Francistown

BACKGROUND INFORMATION

INTRODUCTION

The essence of Botswana is untouched wilderness. To be sure, there is also magnificent wildlife but this is not unique to Botswana for other countries in Southern Africa can boast the same. The lure of the Kalahari and the wonder of the Okavango Delta are this country's primary attractions. Here one can experience an infinity of space, total isolation and freedom from distraction or restraint. Botswana still wears the face of old Africa.

Botswana is blessed with political stability and a pragmatic but conservation-minded government. Over 17 per cent of the country's territory has been set aside for parks and wildlife reserves. Although there is growing pressure to balance the demands of the people with the preservation of wilderness assets, to date the Government has managed to do so. For now the wild treasures of Botswana remain accessible to tourists, relatively untouched by modern man. How long this situation will last is anyone's guess. The Okavango is the only delta of its kind in Africa and for a number of reasons its fate is uncertain. The chance to explore it is reason enough to visit Botswana and I urge you to see it before it is very possibly condemned to death by man's greed and short-sightedness.

Although Botswana is an expensive country for the tourist, the camps are small and intimate, the level of professionalism among guides and naturalists is high and commercialization and mass tourism have not been introduced. There is much to entice the traveller to this country: peaceful, friendly people, plentiful big game and the healthiest elephant population on the continent, scenic beauty, and diverse and unique habitats. Botswana offers an unbeatable combination of wildlife, wilderness and culture: all the ingredients for a fantastic African adventure!

TRAVEL FACTS

ENTRY REQUIREMENTS

All travellers to Botswana need a passport valid for at least six months from the date of entry. Visas are not required of nationals from the Commonwealth or EC countries, the United States, Scandinavia or South Africa. Visitors are issued with an entry permit on arrival which is valid for up to 30 days. If you wish to stay longer you must have your entry permit re-issued; this can be done at a local immigration office. Generally, visits to Botswana are limited to no more than 90 days in any year, a regulation that is strictly enforced.

QUICK FACTS

TOTAL AREA: Covering an areas of 582,000 sq km, Botswana is roughly the size of Texas or France.

NEIGHBOURS: Botswana is a totally land-locked country bordered by Namibia, Zambia, Zimbabwe and South Africa.

POPULATION: 1.347 million (1990 estimate).

ETHNIC GROUPS: Although there are a number of small tribes, 95 per cent of the population is Tswana.

CAPITAL: Gaborone.

LANGUAGES: The official language is English but the national language, Setswana, is much more commonly spoken.

RELIGION: About 50 per cent of the population is Christian, mainly Anglican.

INDEPENDENCE: 1966.

TIME: GMT plus 2 hours.

CURRENCY: The unit of currency is the pula, a word meaning rain in Setswana, this of course being a very valuable commodity. There is no limit to the amount of foreign or local currency which may be imported, but you are only allowed to export P20. The rate of exchange at the time of writing is £1.00 = P3.54; $1.00 = P1.8.

CUSTOMS REGULATIONS

Visitors may bring the following into Botswana dutyfree: one litre of wine; one litre of alcoholic spirits; 250 g of tobacco; 50 cigars; 400 cigarettes. The control of firearms is strict and an import permit must be obtained in advance of entry. For such a permit, write to the Commissioner of Police, Private Bag 0012, Gaborone.

CURRENCY

The pula is the unit of currency in Botswana and it is divided into 100 thebe. There is no limit to the amount of foreign currency a visitor may bring in to Botswana but a full declaration of such currency must be made. Currency declaration forms will be presented on entry and will be checked on departure. Although I have never been asked to present my money for corroboration, it is always a possibility. Visitors are allowed to export up to P500 and whatever amount of foreign currency they declared upon arrival.

Travellers should bear in mind that there are very few banks in Botswana outside the major towns. Although you may be able to change money or travellers' cheques at some of the larger safari camps, it is best to take advantage of a bank when you find one.

GETTING THERE

Air: There is a non-stop *British Airways* flight from London to Gaborone twice a week. This is the only airline offering a direct service to Botswana from overseas. There is, however, also a direct flight from London to Harare *(Air Zimbabwe)* as well as from Sydney to Harare *(Air Zimbabwe/Quantas)*. From the United States there is a weekly service from New York to Lusaka *(Zambia Airways)*. Connections to Gaborone are relatively easy to make from either Harare or Lusaka, so this is another option you might consider.

There is reasonably good service to Botswana from several African cities. There are daily flights via Johannesburg to Gaborone, and services to Gaborone from Lusaka, Harare, Nairobi, Dar es Salaam, Lilongwe, Maseru and Mamzini, although these are not available on a daily basis.

Road: Driving from South Africa to eastern Botswana is very easy if you plan to cross at the major border posts. These access roads are rated all-weather and petrol is available. The border posts are not open 24 hours a day, however, and some close as early as 4p.m. If you are planning to enter Botswana's southern region from South Africa, a four-wheel drive vehicle will be essential for crossing the Kalahari Desert. A good deal of advance planning is necessary for a trip of this nature.

An overland trip from Namibia to Botswana can only be accomplished on sand and gravel roads. The three border crossings are at Mamuno (*en route* to Ghanzi), Mohembo (*en route* to Shakawe), or Ngoma Bridge (*en route* to Kasane or Maun). There is no official border post at Mohembo or Ngoma Bridge so travellers must report immediately to the nearest police station after entering the country. The roads from Mamuno and Mohembo cannot be driven without a four wheel drive vehicle as these routes traverse deep desert sand. The governments of both countries are at present in the process of surfacing the road from Namibia to Maun via Ghanzi but this is sure to be a five- to ten-year project. It is possible to cross into Botswana from Namibia via the Caprivi Strip (Ngoma Bridge/Kasane) in an ordinary vehicle if there have not been heavy rains.

There are two main routes (tarred) from Zimbabwe to Botswana. The border crossings are at Kazungula Road and Ramokwebena. Both posts are open from 6 a.m. to 6 p.m. daily.

Overland entry from Zambia may be accomplished at Kasane at the Kazungula Ferry border control post. This post is manned from 6 a.m. to 6 p.m. daily.

Rail: There is rail service to Botswana from Bulawayo, Zimbabwe, and from Johannesburg, South Africa.

Coach: There is regular coach service once a week from Lusaka, Zambia to Francistown, a journey of about 16 hours; twice a week there is also a bus from Harare (via Bulawayo) that runs to Francistown. UTC buses make a daily run between Kasane and Victoria Falls, Zimbabwe. These mini-buses stop at several of the safari lodges in Chobe and reservations for a seat may be made by ringing 250340 at the Chobe Game Lodge.

GETTING AROUND

Air: *Air Botswana* is the national carrier and connects all the major towns with scheduled services. For travellers who are more interested in the wilderness areas and game reserves of the country, charter flights are the most practical means of getting to these areas. For instance, although you can reach Maun on a scheduled *Air Botswana* flight, from here you will most likely charter a plane to get into the delta or to Moremi or Savuti.

Road: One look at a road map of Botswana will tell you about driving in this country: distances are vast and there are very few tarred roads. The towns along the eastern side of the country are easy to get to because this is where Botswana's main road runs. There are a few sections of tarred surface which branch off this road, notably those to Orapa (where no tourist goes). Otherwise the roads are surfaced with dirt or sand and the great majority of them must be negotiated with four-wheel drive vehicles. The Government is in the process of tarring large stretches of road to connect Maun with Kasane and Ghanzi with Gobabis in Namibia, for instance. However, these projects take an unbelievably long time to complete and so the traveller in this century must plan on coping with the existing road surfaces.

It would be remiss of me not to emphasize the difficulties that may well be encountered in an overland journey across the Kalahari Desert. Adequate advance preparation can mean the difference between life and death. Learning some basic wilderness survival techniques would be prudent. If you have never driven a four-wheel drive vehicle in deep sand before, then the Kalahari Desert should not be your first attempt. The dangers are many: water and petrol supplies are few and far between; wild animals abound and encounters can be fatal; vehicle breakdowns or getting stuck in the sand or mud necessitate long waits or mechanical know-how.

The difficulties of such a trip notwithstanding, it is the very challenge of exploring a remote wilderness that attracts many people to Botswana. There is no better way to get a feel for this country then by driving through its vast interior and camping under the stars. The thrill of encountering wildlife without the distractions of other tourists and vehicles cannot be overstated. For those intrepid travellers who wish to make such a journey, I would recommend *Visitors' Guide to Botswana*, by Mike Main and John and Sandra Fowkes. This book deals almost exclusively with overland travel and there are many useful details and suggestions for driving in the wilds of Botswana.

Rail: Railway services are available only in the eastern section of Botswana, running roughly from Francistown in the north-east to Lobatse in the south. This railway is the old BSAC line that was built in the late nineteenth century. Stops are made at numerous villages *en route* to Zimbabwe or South Africa.

Coach: Bus services in eastern Botswana follow much the same route as the railway, plying the tarred road from Lobatse in the south to Francistown in the north-east. From Francistown the bus heads north to Nata and then

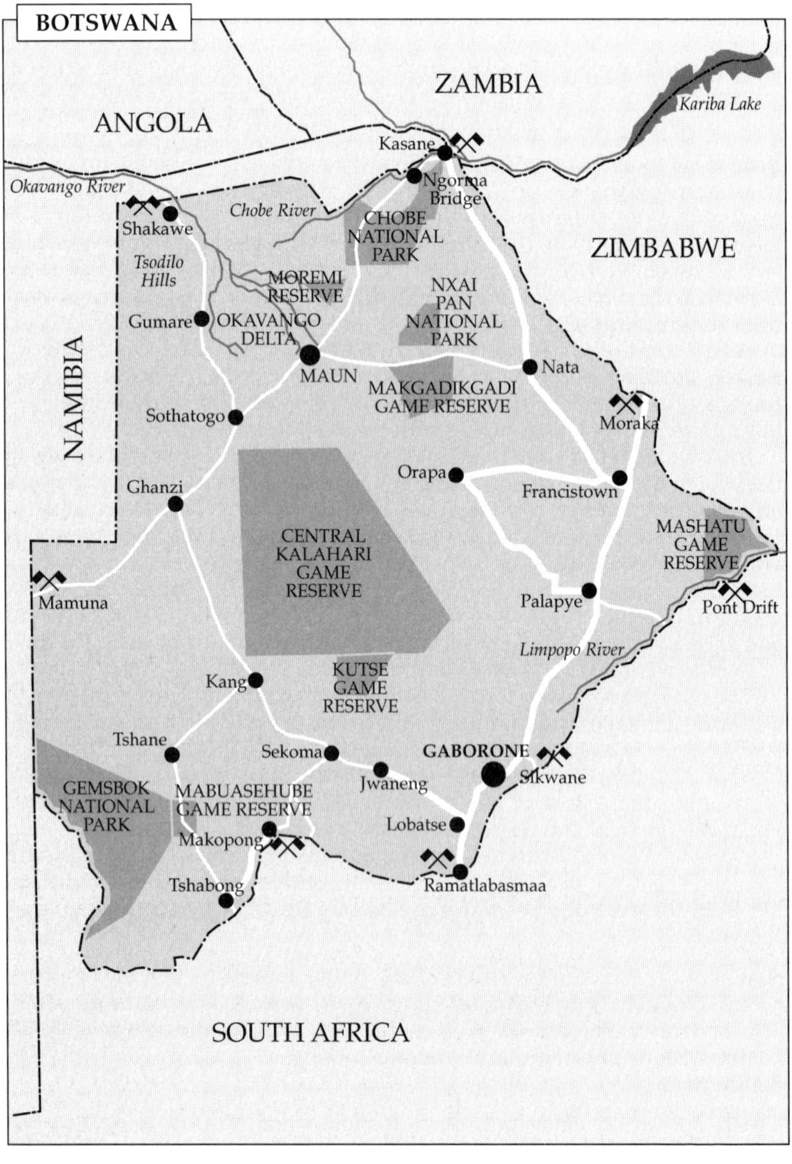
BOTSWANA
ZAMBIA
ANGOLA
Kariba Lake
Kasane
Okavango River
Ngoma Bridge
Chobe River
Shakawe
CHOBE NATIONAL PARK
ZIMBABWE
Tsodilo Hills
MOREMI RESERVE
NXAI PAN NATIONAL PARK
Gumare
OKAVANGO DELTA
NAMIBIA
MAUN
Nata
MAKGADIKGADI GAME RESERVE
Moraka
Sothatogo
Orapa
Francistown
Ghanzi
MASHATU GAME RESERVE
CENTRAL KALAHARI GAME RESERVE
Mamuna
Palapye
Pont Drift
Limpopo River
Kang
KUTSE GAME RESERVE
Tshane
Sekoma
GABORONE
Sikwane
Jwaneng
GEMSBOK NATIONAL PARK
MABUASEHUBE GAME RESERVE
Lobatse
Makopong
Ramatlabasmaa
Tshabong
SOUTH AFRICA

continues either west to Maun or straight on to Kasane. Printed timetables are rare, so it is best to ask the locals about arrival and departure times. There is no rail or coach transport to the vast western region of Botswana at present.

Car Hire: Cars are available for hire in the major towns. Of the international agencies, *Avis* is the most widely represented in Botswana. There is no extra charge for one way rentals between *Avis* locations in Botswana. Four wheel drive vehicles can be hired at Maun and Kasane. The Maun office provides guides to accompany those travellers who wish to venture into the wilderness under the tutelage of an experienced local. The price for this service is currently an extra P35 per day. If you know your travel plans will include hiring a car, I would suggest that you make a reservation before leaving home, as the rate is usually better if the booking is made out of the country. Also, it can often be difficult to secure a vehicle at some places if a prior reservations has not been made.

A local company, *Holiday Car Rentals*, hires sedan and 4x4 vehicles throughout Botswana with offices in Gaborone, Francistown, Maun, Kasane and Selebi-Phikwe. Reservations can be made through the main office, tel. 313093; fax 312205.

Bush Link Ltd. hires fully equipped Land Rovers complete with roof-top tents and all camping gear. High-frequency radios are standard in every vehicle so that travellers are in touch with a base station at all times. These vehicles can be delivered to you almost anywhere in Botswana. Telephone or fax 37-1480 for details.

CLIMATE

Botswana is a large country so there are micro-climates within the various regions. Basically it is a land of low rainfall. The north-eastern region receives the most rain, averaging 600 mm per year, and the south-west is the driest area with an average of only 200 mm. The rainy season generally falls between the end of October and late April; December, January and February are the rainiest months. Devastating droughts are not unusual, as seems to be the case across much of the continent.

The climate is subtropical ranging to temperate. Temperatures can fluctuate greatly especially in the Kalahari Desert where the mercury can dip to freezing in the winter and climb to over 40°C in the summer. The seasons are indistinct and are in reverse of those in the Northern Hemisphere. Winter (April–September) is the dry season and is characterized by clear, warm days and cold nights; summer (October–March) is rainy and it can be very hot in October and November until the rains come. In August strong winds blow from the west, dispersing Kalahari sand across the entire country.

Because of regional variations it is difficult to pinpoint exactly what time of the year is best for visiting Botswana. In the Okavango Delta, the best time for game viewing is July–October, although the fishing is at its peak from August to April, when the water is warm. Game-viewing is excellent throughout the year in the Moremi Wildlife Reserve and the Chobe

National Park. However, the dry-season months from May–November are generally a little bit better. There is less foliage at this time of year and the animals tend to congregate at permanent waterholes and rivers as the surface water in the hinterland dries up. In the Makgadikgadi Game Reserve, June–September is considered the best time to view the migratory plains game. Bird watching in Botswana is rewarding throughout the year although there are more species present during the warmer months when there is an influx of migratory birds escaping from colder climes.

HEALTH

Malaria is prevalent throughout Botswana all the year round although the threat is greatest in the wetter northern regions. Travellers should begin a prophylactic routine before their arrival in the country, under the direction of their doctor. Be sure also to pack a mosquito repellent containing DEET as an additional preventative measure.

Bilharzia (schistosomiasis) is a potential danger so it is safest to assume that all bodies of water are infected. As a rule, stagnant or slow moving water and water in populated areas is the most likely to be contaminated, so bodily contact with it should be avoided. Symptoms take a minimum of six weeks to develop and include lethargy and blood in the stool or urine. If you are concerned that you may have contracted this disease, be sure to visit your doctor on your return. Bilharzia is easily cured once it is detected.

No immunizations are required of visitors to Botswana unless you have come from a yellow fever zone. The tap water is safe to drink and overall the level of hygiene is quite high in this country. The AIDS epidemic that is raging through many parts of the continent has not hit Botswana, although it is increasing. All major towns have hospitals and most villages have medical clinics. My personal advice is to carry a supply of tablets to mitigate minor stomach upset or diarrhea.

WHAT TO PACK

Packing for Botswana is easy: leave all your dress clothes behind. Most likely you will be spending your time out in the bush so comfortable, neutral-coloured outfits are best. White clothes and garments that require pressing are impractical unless you are staying in luxury class camps where a laundry service is provided. Always take a lightweight jacket or sweater and at least one pair of long trousers, whatever the season. It can be chilly on an early morning game drive or out in a boat at sunset. The sun is strong so a hat or visor, sunglasses and sun screen are essential. A comfortable pair of walking shoes or lightweight hiking boots will come in handy if you are going off the beaten track and plan on a good deal of activity. Otherwise, trainers are fine for short walks and boating.

Those staying at the de luxe safari camps might find that a change of clothing for dinner is appropriate, although it is not required. A collared shirt for the men and a skirt or simple dress for the ladies will suffice. High heeled shoes are unrealistic as the paths from the tents to the dining room are generally sand or grass. I always include a bathing costume just in case one of the lodges has a swimming pool or there is an opportunity to take a quick dip in the Okavango Delta. You are likely to be taking a charter flight to some destination in Botswana and this will necessitate limiting your baggage to around 12 kg, excluding camera equipment. The lighter you travel, the happier you will probably be.

A camera with at least a 200 mm lens is strongly recommended. Film is difficult to come by out in the wilds so bring all that you think you might need and more. Botswana is dusty so plastic bags are useful for preventing damage to your camera. An electronic flash is helpful for early morning and dusk shots and I always carry a polarizing filter to counteract the blinding sun and sand glare. Binoculars are mandatory if you are interested in birds or game. I have found that the small, travel-sized glasses are difficult to hold steady and very tiring on the eyes. Despite the extra bulk and weight, full-sized binoculars are highly preferable. Sacrifice a pair of shoes or a book to make room for your binoculars and I guarantee you won't regret it!

NATIONAL PARKS

Seventeen per cent of Botswana's area has been set aside for wildlife parks and reserves while an additional 35 per cent of the country remains unfenced wilderness. There are a number of national parks and game reserves and all of them are open to the public. Facilities at the public campsites vary from non-existent to good, depending on the reserve. Although the Government is working to upgrade these sites, at this time they do not compare to the parks of Namibia, Zimbabwe or South Africa in terms of accommodation or ablution facilities. Botswana has many wonderful privately run lodges and camps in the national parks and game reserves, however, for those who prefer luxury to camping.

Public campsites may be found in the Chobe and Nxai Pan National Parks, Moremi Wildlife Reserve and Khutse Game Reserve. No facilities exist at this time in Makgadikgadi or Mabuasehube Reserves. The Mashatu Game Reserve is privately owned and no camping is allowed within the reserve.

There are entry fees to all the national parks and reserves with the exception of the Makgadikgadi, Mashatu and Mabuasehube reserves. The Botswana government has levied substantial daily entrance fees to its parks in an effort to keep visitor numbers at a reasonable level. To put it plainly, they wish to discourage budget travellers but attract those affluent tourists who can afford to pay. Prior to the raising of park fees there were a great many South African tourists who would drive to Botswana and spend their holidays camping. Most of these visitors were self-catering and contributed very little to the economy of Botswana. Evidently entrance fees were raised astronomically to discourage this particular type of tourist.

TOURIST INFORMATION

Tourists are pretty much on their own in Botswana as information centres are non-existent. If there is time, you might try writing to the *Division of Tourism*, Private Bag 0047, Gaborone, to ask for maps and brochures for the areas you wish to visit.

SAFARIS

Botswana is an expensive country and travel here does not come cheaply. In comparison with its neighbours – Namibia, Zimbabwe, Zambia and South Africa – a safari in Botswana can be considerably more expensive. The average cost per person, per day for accommodation with full board in a private camp runs from £125 to £250. A mobile safari can often be slightly less expensive, especially if you are with a group of four or more people. These trips generally offer very good value for money and unlike a stay in a permanent camp, you tend to see more of the country.

For the budget traveller camping is the best option. Although air charters into the Okavango are expensive, there are two privately run campsites in the delta from which mokoro expeditions can be arranged. There are also a number of public campsites in the national parks and game reserves of Botswana, but reaching these is difficult without a vehicle. Hiring a car does give you access to most of the country but this is no bargain unless you are travelling with others willing to share the cost. However, price aside, Botswana is one of the continent's last great wilderness regions and no other African country can claim such a magnificent watery paradise as the Okavango Delta. Botswana offers a wide variety of habitat, rivers, swamp, riparian woodland, flood plains, scrub, savannah, salt pan and desert. There is superb game-and bird-viewing which is, of course, most visitors' reason for going to Botswana.

A list of safari camps in each region of the country is included at the end of the relevant chapters. I have purposely neglected to specify daily rates at most of the camps, although as a general guide I have indicated price categories: expensive, slightly less expensive or reasonable. Prices tend to change frequently and while some camps charge for drinks and transfers, others don't, so price alone doesn't always make a fair basis for comparison.

If you are planning to travel with young children it is best to do some thorough checking. There is no age limit for admission to public campsites in the national parks and reserves, but few private safari camps accept children under the age of 12. In speaking with guides and camp operators on this subject, I was told that their experience has been that young children generally do not enjoy a safari. The typical safari day begins at dawn (or earlier) and involves several very long game drives where silence and patience are essential. Meal times vary and the food choices are limited. After having seen the 'exciting' big game animals most children become bored and very often they distract or bother other guests. Operators and guides believe that it is a rare child under 12 who has the interest or stamina to enjoy an African safari. There are always exceptions to every rule so if you feel strongly about bringing your children, by all means discuss this with the camps of your choice and see if something can be worked out.

Botswana is one of the last bastions of big-game hunting in Africa. Citizens have the right to hunt anywhere in the country except within national parks and game reserves. Despite the fact that licenses are inexpensive for citizens, hunting by locals alone in 1989 netted the government approximately $5 million. Five companies cater for foreign

Travel Facts

hunters. In 1989, 1,910 game animals were taken by overseas hunters in the northern Botswana region. This was equal to 400 jobs and $5 million for the economy. Although I am not personally an advocate of hunting safaris, I do recognize that it is a paradox of wildlife conservation in Africa that only by using wildlife (skins, meat, trophy fees and tourism revenues) so that it contributes to man's well-being will its survival be ensured.

A wide variety of adventures awaits the traveller to Botswana. If you are interested in the remote regions of the Kalahari Desert or Bushman rock art, special excursions led by experts are a possibility. The tiger fishing is legendary in the Okavango Panhandle and several fishing camps serve this region. There are mokoro trips for a leisurely introduction to the Okavango Delta, elephant and horseback safaris and even a journey through the Makgadikgadi Pan on all-terrain vehicles is offered. Any safari to Africa qualifies as an adventure but for those who seek the unusual, check with the following tour operators for an excellent selection of exciting and challenging holidays.

Birding Safaris
Africa Calls!, Private Bag 83, Maun. Tel. or fax 66-0351

Bush Survival Course
Africa Calls! (address above)

Bushmen Safari
Penduka Safaris, PO Box 55413, Northlands, 2116, South Africa. Tel. or fax (011) 883-4303

Canoe *(Mokoro)* Trips
Okavango Tours and Safaris, PO Box 39, Maun. Tel. 66-0220; fax (011) 788-6575 (South Africa)

Felix Unite River Adventures, PO Box 80, Rondebosch 7700, South Africa. Tel. (021) 689-8729; fax (021) 689-2706

Desert Safaris
Kalahari Kavango Wildlife Adventures, PO Box 236, Maun. Tel. or fax 66-0493

Penduka Safaris, Tel. (011) 883-4303, (South Africa)

Elephant Trails Safari
Ker Downey Selby, PO Box 40, Maun. Tel. 66-0211; fax 66-0379 (For UK and US addresses, see page**)

Okavango Horse Safaris
Travel Wild, Private Bag 23, Maun. Tel. 660493

Africa Calls! (address above)

Wilderness Camping Trips
Overland Safaris, PO Box 82, Warden 7330, South Africa. Tel. 013342 and ask for Roadside 7330

Drifters, PO Box 48434, Roosevelt Park 2129, South Africa. Tel. (011) 486-1224; fax (011) 486-1237

Walking Safaris
Educational Wildlife Expeditions/Clive Walker Trails, PO Box 645, Bedfordview 2008, South Africa. Tel. (011) 453-7645

Africa Calls! (address above).

ACCOMMODATION

The range of accommodation available in Botswana is adequate, but the Government's high-cost/low-density tourism policy has resulted in a limited number of hotels, camps and lodges and these tend to be on the expensive end of the scale. Almost without exception the private safari camps and lodges in Botswana's game reserves are de luxe and are priced accordingly. Hotels in the major towns are geared to the business traveller for the simple reason that there is little of interest for the tourist in these areas. The Government does not have a grading system for hotels or lodges, but in general the standard of accommodation in Botswana is good and rooms are usually clean. Camping is the least expensive option and public campgrounds can be found in the majority of the national parks and game reserves. A P20 camping fee is levied in most of these camp-sites.

FOOD

The cuisine of Botswana can be summed up in one word: beef. Cattle farming is one of the mainstays of this nation's economy so it is not surprising to see its end product on every restaurant menu. The beef is good, although a bit tougher than the corn-fed variety Americans or Europeans may be accustomed to eating. As for culinary trends, there don't seem to be many. Food is straightforward and generally overcooked. The big exception is the cuisine prepared in many of the luxury safari camps and lodges. Where conditions allow, vegetable gardens are tended, fresh fish are line caught and a variety of foodstuffs is flown in. Experienced chefs man the camp kitchens and much of the food is first rate and ambitious.

International cuisine is offered at most hotels throughout the country and buffets are very popular. Usually at a buffet there is a selection of salads, curries, cheeses and desserts so a vegetarian can manage to eat quite well. However, outside the major towns you are not going to find much in the way of fresh fruit and vegetables. What is available in Botswana markets is mostly imported from South Africa.

If you are camping you might try your hand at fishing when there is a river nearby. The waters of the Okavango and Chobe abound with bream (tilapia), a delicious fresh water fish. Biltong (dried, salted meat) is widely available and needs no refrigeration, making it a handy item for campers. The native people eat a cornmeal mush called *mielie-pap.* I find it tasteless but edible and it does have the virtue of being quite filling. Despite all the hunting concessions game is not served in restaurants or camps. I was told this is because there are no meat inspection facilities for game animals.

Beer is consumed in copious quantities, and it is always cold and reasonably priced. Spirits and liqueurs are widely available; all are imported from South Africa. Botswana produces no wines but a good selection of South African products is offered. Soft drinks are easy to obtain and you will see evidence of this in the form of unsightly litter all over Botswana.

TIPPING

Tipping is a matter of personal discretion as service charges are not routinely added to restaurant bills. If you are inclined to tip, 10 per cent would be more than adequate. In safari camps it is customary to tip your guide and the camp staff; although you will not meet all of the personnel, your tip will be equally divided among the staff members. It is appropriate, however, to tip your guide (or *mokoro* poler) personally.

ARTS AND CRAFTS

Generally speaking, Botswana is not a shopper's paradise. The majority of tourists spend their holiday in the bush or desert and opportunities to purchase native crafts are minimal. Furthermore, there is not a lot of art being produced, at least commercially, which also limits shopping. Baskets represent the best of Botswana's crafts but you will also find small carvings, ostrich shell beadwork and a bit of jewellery for sale. The baskets are produced in Ngamiland in the north of the country. The weavers use palm leaves and dye the fibres with tree roots to produce a variety of earth shades. The different design motifs all have their own meaning and patterns tend to be geometric or abstract. The baskets are very beautiful and quite reasonably priced. I have found that shops generally carry a good selection of small baskets as well as flat, tray-like articles which will pack reasonably well. If you are interested in basketry, Maun and Gaborone are the places to shop. Otherwise, some of the safari lodges and hotels have curio shops where crafts and baskets can be purchased.

Botswana is one of the only places where Bushman (San) crafts are available (Namibia is another). Ostrich-egg jewellery is a traditional item. The shell of an ostrich egg is broken into tiny pieces which are then painstakingly chipped into round beads, strung on sinew or leather strings and then crafted into beautiful belts and bracelets. The end product is unique. The amount of work that goes into creating these beads is mind boggling so if the price seems high, consider the labour! The other item that might intrigue some visitors is Bushman hunting sets consisting of bow, arrows and quiver. These are not antiques, but have been cleverly and realistically manufactured for the tourist. Prices are modest but most travellers will need to have an item such as this shipped home. I attempted to do this several years ago. I was told that the shipping cost would not exceed the price of the hunting kit and would take about a week by air. Months went by and nothing arrived. I decided that it was probably just as well: the bow and arrows weren't going to fit in with my decor, anyway. (These things always look so good in Africa and perfectly ridiculous at home). Two years later a customs agent in San Francisco notified me that my 'animal trophy' had arrived. Imagine my shock when I was informed that shipping and storage costs were in excess of $200.00, a full seven times the price of the item. Moreover, there was a nightmare of paperwork and government inspections involved before the Bushman hunting kit could be released! The moral of this story is to never buy uncured animal skins.

COUNTRY FILE

HISTORY

Pre-Colonial Era

In prehistoric times the area known today as Botswana was the exclusive territory of the San (Bushman) people. The Tswana people (Batswana) who now predominate in this country were Bantu-speaking pastoralists who migrated from the north between the time of Christ and 1000 AD. By the seventeenthth century it is known that they were firmly established in the Transvaal region of South Africa. Initially, the arid regions that the Bushmen roamed held little interest for Bantu tribes emigrating to the central and southern areas of the continent. By the end of the eighteenth century however, a combination of factors brought about a change in this situation. Land hunger and population increases throughout Southern Africa transformed relatively peaceful tribes into warring factions. A political split occurred among the Tswana with a resultant splintering of the tribe. Some moved north across the Molopo River into Bushman territory, or Botswana as we know it today. This migration coincided with the rise of Shaka Zulu and the *Mfecane* which was sweeping across Southern Africa. Although the Tswana were not directly terrorized by the Zulus, other tribes, displaced and fleeing from the madness, turned to marauding themselves, and intruded into the Tswana territory, adding to the northward migration. Those who remained were subjugated by the Ndebele tribe.

The Colonial Era

Shortly after the Ndebele subjugation of those Tswana who remained in what is now South Africa, the white man appeared on the scene. The Boers had set off from the Cape Colony on their Great Trek in 1835 and when they crossed the Vaal River on the frontier of modern Botswana, they found the region strangely empty, emptied of course by the *mfecane*. And so, with no one to dispute them, the Boers settled here on traditional Tswana land. With sophisticated weapons at their disposal these Voortrekkers were able to subdue the Ndebele in 1837. The Ndebele then moved north and eventually settled in Zimbabwe where they established a powerful nation. With the Ndebele driven off by the Boers, many Tswana returned to their traditional territory only to find that their land was gone, appropriated by the Boers. Without land the foundation of African tribal society was broken and a way of life was lost. The Tswana were forced to work on the white man's farms, on land they considered their own, to survive. They stayed on as squatters or labourers or tenant farmers but they were essentially serfs. When the British allowed the Boers to establish an Afrikaner republic in the Transvaal, the Tswana officially lost their independence and became subject to European law. A number of Tswana chiefs protested against Boer rule but these outspoken, uncooperative rulers were fiercely punished. On several occasions they appealed to the British government for protection but to no avail.

As history has repeatedly shown, African territories were defined and created by the European colonial powers for self-serving purposes. In 1885 the British, alarmed by German influence in South West Africa (Namibia) and by increasing Boer aggression and encroachment in the Transvaal, declared a protectorate over an area they called Bechuanaland. The rationale for this was to create a buffer zone to prevent the Germans and the Boers from joining together to block Britain's route to the north. Bechuanaland incorporated three major Tswana kingdoms and much of the territory of modern Botswana. Basically, however, the British had little interest in administering this territory; they established a military presence here and little else. After trying unsuccessfully to interest the Cape Colony in assuming control of Bechuanaland, the British divided the protectorate into two separate territories. The area south of the Molopo River became British Bechuanaland and the remaining northern sector, extended in 1891 to the Zambezi River, was called Bechuanaland Protectorate. In 1895 British Bechuanaland was annexed to the Cape Colony and subsequently became part of South Africa. A capital for Bechuanaland Protectorate was established outside the territory's borders in Mafeking, South Africa. Many construed this as evidence of just how little genuine and constructive interest the British had in Bechuanaland.

With few exceptions, the Tswana chiefs were not enthusiastic about the establishment of a protectorate. Although they welcomed British military protection against Boer incursions, they wanted to be left alone to govern their people. Despite assurances by the British government of non-interference in domestic affairs, the British South African Company (BSAC), headed by Cecil Rhodes, desperately wanted to take over the administration of Bechuanaland. Although this idea was financially attractive to Britain, the Tswana kings were in an uproar. They had seen Rhodes use his BSAC as a springboard for the colonization of Southern Rhodesia (now Zimbabwe) and they had no intention of letting a similar fate befall their nation. Three Tswana kings successfully thwarted Rhodes' scheme by travelling to London to present their objections to the Colonial Secretary, Joseph Chamberlain. Under great pressure from the British public, Chamberlain reneged on his promise to Rhodes and assured the chiefs that their people would remain under the protection of the crown, not a commercial enterprise. In exchange for this decision, the Tswana had to relinquish a strip of land along the eastern border of the country for the construction of a BSAC railway.

In 1910 the South Africa Act established the Union of South Africa, uniting the two Boer republics and the two British colonies. The South Africa Act included a provision that Bechuanaland, Swaziland and Basutoland (now Lesotho) would eventually become part of the Union. The white farmers who had settled in Bechuanaland were eager for this to occur. Additionally, South Africa wanted to extend its policy of native land reserves (separate development) to the territory. Despite all kinds of economic threats from South Africa in an effort to extract compliance, Tswana leaders were unanimously opposed to the idea of incorporation.

The British stood firm and repeatedly refused to grant this request.

The Bechuanaland Protectorate was administered by a British resident commissioner, ultimately responsible to the Colonial Office in London, and assisted by an advisory council of chiefs. Bechuanaland was never extensively colonized by the British in the manner of Kenya or Southern Rhodesia. Although some white farmers settled there and were given territory, the majority of the land remained in tribal hands. The British contributed little to the welfare of the protectorate but they did not overlook the imposing of taxes. As there was no real employment in Bechuanaland, men were forced to seek work in South Africa to pay these taxes. With virtually no industry and the great majority of workers out of the country, Bechuanaland remained a rural society. The British spent next to nothing on the development of an infrastructure of roads, schools, communications or hospitals. Although tribal chiefs received 10 per cent of the tax money they collected, few of these funds went toward improving community life either. At the time of independence most people were living subsistence life-styles and the prognosis for future prosperity did not look bright.

Independence

Unlike in so many other countries in Africa, there was no war for independence in Bechuanaland. Between 1959 and 1962 three political parties were formed but only the Bechuanaland Democratic Party (BDP) garnered broad support. Its leader was Seretse Khama, heir to the Ngwato chieftainship and husband of a white Englishwoman, Ruth Williams. Khama had met and married his wife in 1948 while he was studying law at Oxford. Bowing to pressure from South Africa, Britain refused to recognize the marriage, banned Khama from Botswana indefinitely and even attempted to offer him money to relinquish his kingship. The marriage was not much more popular within his own family. Although the majority of the men in the tribe supported Khama, despite his break with tradition, a political split resulted and some of the tribe moved away to settle among the Bakwena. In 1956, however, the family was reconciled and an agreement was reached whereby Seretse Khama and his wife could return to Bechuanaland as private citizens. In 1965 a constitution granting internal self-government was introduced to Bechuanaland; the British were continuing the policy of de-colonization which they had begun with Ghana. General elections were held and the BDP was the overwhelming victor, claiming 28 out of 31 seats. Independence was granted on 30 September 1966 and Sir Seretse Khama (knighted in the same year) became president, a position he held until his death in 1980.

Post-Independence

Bechuanaland became the Republic of Botswana, a word which translates as land of the Tswana. The capital was moved from Mafeking, South Africa to Gaborone. Legislative powers today are vested in Parliament which consists of the President and the National Assembly, a body of 32 members elected by adult suffrage. Elections for the National Assembly and president are held every five years. A House of Chiefs was established to advise the Government and no legislation may be passed that affects tribal affairs without consultation with this body. Unlike almost every other nation on the continent, Botswana did not create an army upon independence but established an effective police force instead. However, in 1977 it became necessary to form a permanent defence force to patrol it's borders and maintain order. South African forces seeking to rout ANC supporters and guerrillas were repeatedly staging incursions into Botswana's territory.

Despite the euphoria of independence, of being free at last of colonial overlords, the realities were grim. In 1966 Botswana was one of the twenty poorest nations in the world. There were just 111 km of tarred road in the entire country. The South Africans owned the railway and exercised a virtual stranglehold on the economy. However, the discovery of diamonds at Orapa in 1967 saved the country from a bleak fate. Within just a few years it had become one of the top three diamond producing nations in the world. Although the mining contract was given to De Beers, a South African cartel, the government negotiated a very favourable financial arrangement, retaining 75 per cent of the profits.

Politically, Sir Seretse Khama steered a moderate course during his 14 year tenure as president and tried to maintain friendly relationships with all of Botswana's neighbours. Despite the country's dependence on South Africa, Khama was outspoken in his criticism of that country's apartheid policies. He offered asylum to political refugees from Rhodesia, Namibia and South Africa. In 1974 Botswana joined with Angola, Mozambique and Tanzania to form the Front Line States. The aim of this organization was to provide support for the liberation movements in Rhodesia and Namibia. Although Botswana never provided military or financial support to either liberation struggle, South Africa launched several raids into it's territory on the pretext of eradicating guerrilla training camps. In 1979 the Front Line States attempted to reduce their economic dependence on South Africa by forming the Southern African Development Coordination Conference (SADCC). The participating countries - Zimbabwe, Mozambique, Malawi, Tanzania, Lesotho, Swaziland, Angola, Zambia, Namibia and Botswana - seek to attract foreign aid to the region and to develop trade networks between themselves .

Sir Seretse Khama died in 1980 after being re-elected three times. The National Assembly elected the Vice President, Dr Quett Masire, to replace him. Botswana's economy has continued to grow steadily although it is still very dependent on South Africa. South African investments, technical expertise, transport systems and markets are crucial to the financial health of the nation. Despite this situation, Botswana has not curbed its vocal protests at the racist policies of its neighbour. In apparent retaliation, throughout the 1980s South Africa continued to launch commando raids, kidnapping political refugees and bombing ANC and SWAPO houses in Gaborone in what some saw as an attempt to destabilize the country. Botswana never yielded to the pressure.

Twenty five years have elapsed since independence. Botswana has built a democracy in a region where democracy is the exception rather than the rule. To quote President Masire, 'Democracy and mutual tolerance are anchored in Botswana's tradition'. The country has an indigenous foundation of democratic tradition in the form of the *kgotla*. The *kgotla* is a public court or meeting place which is at the centre of daily life. Disputes are settled, matters of local importance are discussed and even the autocratic power of the chiefs can be checked by this forum. As the old Setswana saying goes, 'The chief is only the chief by the will of the tribe.' The *kgotla* represents a kind of village democracy and it exists today as an integral part of the nation's political structure.

Unlike so many African nations, Botswana enjoys tremendous political stability and remains a multi-party democracy with a strengthening economy. It is more fortunate than its neighbours in several ways: there is little cultural or ethnic diversity here and the country never experienced a divisive war. Overpopulation has not been a problem to date, diamond wealth provides financial stability and government corruption and mismanagement have been minimal. Wisely, the government has not squandered the country's new found wealth and profits are being used to improve the infrastructure of roads, health care, schools and irrigation systems. Everything is not perfect in Botswana, of course. There is a great disparity in the distribution of wealth in rural areas, a dramatic increase in urban living which has resulted in housing shortages and high rents, and a worrying population explosion threatens future prosperity. Despite these concerns, however, Botswana remains Africa's greatest success story since independence.

GEOLOGY, FLORA AND FAUNA

Botswana is a land-locked country with over 80 per cent of its surface area covered by the sands of the Kalahari Desert. This desert is considered to be the largest continuous sand body in the world. Botswana is essentially a sand-filled basin averaging 1,000 metres above sea level. Bush and tree savannah cover 90 per cent of the territory. With the exception of the Limpopo and Chobe Rivers on the eastern and northern borders, none of its water systems reach the sea. The most notable example of this is the Okavango River which enters Botswana as a powerful torrent only to completely expend itself in the sands of the desert.

The Kalahari is technically not a true desert. To classify as such an area must receive less than 60-100 mm of rain annually and no part of the Kalahari receives less than this amount. The southern reaches of the Kalahari are the driest, with rainfall in the vicinity of 150 mm a year. It is more accurate therefore, to refer to the Kalahari as an arid area or a thirstland. Rainfall increases as one progresses northward and it is this varying amount of rain that gives the Kalahari such diversity of habitat. Although the surface is sand, it is also covered by vegetation; indeed, it is only in the extreme southern portion, where the dune belt occurs that there is an area devoid of vegetation.

The vegetation, which takes the form of grasses, shrub-like plants and acacia thorn trees, is adapted to survive at least eight months without rain, or longer in case of droughts. In the southern parts of the Kalahari the sand is a beautiful red colour. The colour comes from iron oxide which coats the surface of the sand grains. Moving northwards, the dunes become lighter in colour and there is little evidence of this dramatic tinting; it is believed that in areas where rainfall is greater the iron oxide is washed off. However, in the south where rainfall is minimal, the sand remains a vibrant red.

In striking contrast to this sand-covered country, the Okavango Delta is an incongruous oasis, a bountiful wetland in the heart of a desert. It is not known when the Delta came into existence but evidence suggests that it is less than two million years old. In ancient times when climatic conditions were more favourable, much of Botswana was covered by a vast super-lake. Exactly which rivers were the source for this enormous body of water is unclear. The relics of these vanished lakes, however, are easily seen to day at the Makgadikgadi and Nxai Pans. The fault lines that lie beneath the Kalahari and the Okavango Delta are extensions of the East African Rift Valley system. Considerable seismic activity and continental tilting have changed the flow of rivers many times in Botswana's past, draining vast lakes, diverting river courses, forming new basins and deltas. The Savuti Channel in the southern reaches of the Chobe National Park is an excellent case in point. Several times in the past century the water has flowed here for a period of years and then suddenly there is nothing. Rainfall has nothing to do with this phenomenon. Rather, it is the result of unseen activity beneath the earth's surface which switches the flow of water on and off. The distribution of water in the Okavango Delta is also constantly changing, very likely the result of intense tectonic activity in this region. What this bodes for the future of the Delta is simply not known.

THE ECONOMY

Botswana's economic progress since independence has been nothing short of remarkable. In 1966 the UN listed the country as one of the world's least developed. Only 5 per cent of the land was arable, there were no state schools and less than 100 people held university degrees. Today, Botswana's economy is one of the fastest growing in the world, averaging 13 per cent annually. Per capita income has increased more than five-fold to $1,600 within the past decade. Botswana has one of the highest levels of foreign exchange reserves in the world relative to its size. The economy is based on two primary industries: diamonds and beef. Diamonds were discovered in the Kalahari Desert in 1967 and are currently being mined in three locations. Botswana is now one of the world's leading diamond producers and this resource is the nation's single most important export, realizing 75 per cent of its revenue. In 1989, 13 million carats were extracted at a value of $1.4 billion dollars.

Botswana also has rich deposits of copper, nickle, coal, potash, salt, manganese and soda ash. Many of these minerals are being lucratively mined at present, notably copper, nickle and soda ash. The Sua Pan soda ash project is a joint venture with a group of South African companies; the

Government is eager to reduce its almost total dependence on diamonds, a very depletable resource, and the Sua Pan deposits are expected to last 900 years.

The majority of the people raise livestock. Indeed, cattle outnumber people almost three to one! Beef is a major export with the European Community (EC) providing more than 50 per cent of the market. The EC has granted assistance to Botswana in the form of a preferred price for beef, which means that it buys at four times the world price. Cattle is Botswana's biggest earner after minerals. When the very attractive EC arrangement ends the country will need to take a hard look at the beef industry. A number of problems and pressures face it: communal versus private land ownership, destructive overgrazing and controversial veterinary cordons that were built to protect cattle from foot and mouth disease but which also block migratory routes for wildlife.

Agriculture and manufacturing are not significant contributors to the economy at present. In 1989 agriculture provided only 3.9 per cent of the Gross Domestic Product and manufacturing only 6 per cent. Subsistence crops of maize and sorghum are grown for domestic consumption only. It is doubtful whether crop farming will ever play a major role in Botswana due to the lack of water. On the other hand, the manufacturing and industrial sectors of the economy could be expanded dramatically. The Government has an overtly capitalist outlook and has professed a serious interest in attracting foreign investment.

Tourism is viewed as an important part of the economy. It contributes foreign exchange and creates jobs, especially in areas where employment is virtually non-existent. In 1989 the fees for game parks and reserves were raised 3,000 per cent in pursuit of a high cost low-volume tourism policy. The dual aim is to protect wildlife and to increase revenues to help justify retaining such huge areas of the country for nature conservation. Although regional tourism from South African and Zimbabwean residents has decreased dramatical ly as a result of the new fee structure, it has not discouraged tourists from overseas. Healthy tourist revenues are essential to ensure that Botswana's wildlife and wilderness are not squandered.

As is the case with the other countries of Southern Africa, Botswana has an unhealthy dependence on South Africa. With the exception of diamonds, the majority of imports and exports of this landlocked country are shipped by rail to or from South Africa. Botswana relies heavily on South African markets, goods, technical expertise and investments. A large sector of the population contracts for employment in South Africa because there are not enough jobs in Botswana. Although the President has recently stated that unemployment is the nation's number one social problem, it is not a situation that is easily rectified. In the mines of South Africa alone there are apporximately 20,000 Botswana workers and without the money these men earn, Botswana's economy would be hard hit. Although the Government has remained staunchly opposed to the racial policies of its neighbour, it does not want to see the dismantling of apartheid lead to an economic decline or disaster for Southern Africa as a whole.

THE PEOPLE

The original inhabitants of Botswana were the San, a hunter-gatherer, nomadic people who continue their life-style today, although in greatly reduced numbers, in the central Kalahari. The San or Bushmen as they are commonly called, are thought to number around 35,000 and the majority have been resettled by the Government in the western sector of the country near Ghanzi.

The Tswana, a Bantu people, comprise 95 per cent of the population. They are divided into 8 principal tribes, each with its own territory and hereditary chiefs. Despite the presence of these tribal groups there is considerable cultural unity among the Tswana. The absence of significant inter-tribal divisions has spared Botswana the upheaval and conflict that has marred so many other post-colonial African nations. Historically, the Tswana have been solicitous of the interests of smaller, unrelated tribes such as the Herero, refugees from Namibia during German persecution in the first decade of the nineteenth century.

Cattle, land and rain are the three most important factors in the lives of the Tswana. Traditionally, a man's wealth and stature are held in direct proportion to the heads of cattle he owns. Eighty per cent of the populace lives in rural areas to the east of the Limpopo River, subsisting on farming and income from cattle. Although this region only represents one fifth of Botswana's territory, this is where four fifths of the people try to eke out a living. However, the soil is ancient and not fertile and job opportunities are scarce.

Whites represent only a small segment of the Botswana population. The Europeans immigrated from Great Britain, Zimbabwe and South Africa for the most part. The majority live in the eastern area of the country; many own farms while others are involved in mining or business.

In terms of education Botswana has made good progress since independence. Today, more than 70 per cent of the children finish seven years of primary schooling; secondary education is still not offered to the majority of rural inhabitants. The University of Botswana was established in Gaborone in 1982 and approximately 3,200 students are enrolled. Botswana lacks a skilled work force, a legacy of the colonial era. As a result, foreigners comprise 78 per cent of the country's engineers, half of its company managers and about 30 per cent of its teachers.

Botswana is struggling with a rapidly increasing population. The growth rate is 3.4 per cent annually, among the highest in the world. In 1989, 100,000 people, representing 25 per cent of the labour force, were unemployed. In a nation incapable of feeding itself, already faced with massive unemployment, this does not augur well for the future.

RECOMMENDED READING

Augustinus, Paul, Botswana: *A Brush with The Wild*, Acorn Books, Randburg, South Africa, 1987.

Botswana

Balfour, David, *Okavango – An African Paradise*, Struik Publishers Cape Town, 1990.

Campbell, A. C., *The Guide to Botswana*, 3rd ed. Winchester Press, Gaborone, 1980.

Johnson, P. and Bannister, A., *Okavango, Sea of Land, Land of Water*, Struik Publishers, Cape Town, 1979.

Main, Michael, *Kalahari: Life's Variety in Dune and Delta*, Southern Book Publishers, Johannesburg, 1987.

Main, Michael and Fowkes, J. & S., *Visitors' Guide to Botswana*, Southern Book Publishers, Johannesburg, 1989.

Moore, R.J. and Munnion, C., *Back to Africa*, Southern Book Publishers, Johannesburg, 1989.

Murray-Hudson, Mike, *The Swamp Book: A View Of The Okavango*, Southern Book Publishers, Johannesburg, 1989.

Owens, Mark and Delia, *The Cry of the Kalahari*, Houghton Mifflin, Boston, 1984.

Patterson, Gareth, *Cry for the Lions*, Mpiti Books, Kloof, South Africa, 1990.

Potgieter, H. and Walker, C., *Okavango from the Air*, Struik Publishers, Cape 1989.

Ross, Karen, *Okavango: Jewel of the Kalahari*, Macmillan Publishing, New York, 1987.

Shostak, M., *Nisa: The Life and Words of a !Kung Woman*, Penguin, Harmondsworth, 1983.

Van der Post, Laurens, *The Lost World of the Kalahari*, Harcourt Brace Jovanovich, New York, 1958.

AROUND BOTSWANA

MAUN

INTRODUCTION

Maun is situated on the banks of the Thamalakane River and has been the traditional capital of the Batawana tribe (a branch of the Batswana) since 1915. The word Maun, which rhymes with town, is of Bayei origin and translates as the 'place of black reeds'. The village, which has a wonderful frontier air, is bisected by a 5 km stretch of tar and it sprawls without design around the original Tswana village of mud huts and earth yards. These mud houses have made few concessions to modern times although the locals do incorporate aluminum soda and beer cans into the earth wall construction, to unusual effect. A small commercial centre has sprung up around the airport and in the central area there are a dozen or so shops selling basic supplies. Just beyond the turn-off for the airport the tar gives way to a dirt road which heads north-east to Moremi and Kasane. Along this route about 12 km from Maun there are a few lodges clustered along the Thamalakane River which cater for tourists. The road is currently being tarred which will bring this 'suburb', called Matlapaneng, within easy reach of Maun.

Safari capital of Botswana

For the traveller, Maun is important because it is the safari capital of Botswana. Located at the lower end of the Okavango Delta, it is the departure point for excursions into the Moremi, Chobe, Savuti and Makgadikgadi areas as well as the delta itself.

Surrounded by sand

Maun is a scruffy little town with sand streets, mud huts and roaming goats and cattle. There are no parks or flower gardens to soften the impact of the daunting desert that completely surrounds the village. What Maun lacks in appearance is more than compensated for by its character, however. It is a hive of activity and a very interesting crowd of people call Maun home. Because this is the centre of the country's safari industry, it is also the operational base of many professional hunters, naturalists, guides and adventurers who are attracted to Maun like a magnet. There is a Wild West feeling here and the ubiquitous tanned faces, khaki uniforms and rugged men who frequent the bars and cruise the airport in their dust-coated four wheel drive vehicles rarely fail

A group of Tswana children in Maun entertain a passing crowd.

to give a thrill of excitement to the visitor, and a conviction that this, at last, is the real, untamed Africa. A kind of Hemingway mystique prevails about this raw town that attracts rovers, explorers, thrill-seekers and young people from all over. As a result there are many who settle here for a year or two in search of adventure, excitement and fun. Maun looks and feels utterly African and the local 'ex-pat' crowd fit the scene so beautifully that Hollywood could not have created a better set.

Not surprisingly, almost every safari company in Botswana maintains an office in Maun. If you arrive here without any advance travel plans, one of the safari companies or travel agencies should be able to set something up. However, the number of 'beds' in Botswana game parks and reserves is very limited, so this is not particularly advisable. If you are venturing into the desert on a mobile safari, game-viewing in the Moremi Wildlife Reserve, or fishing and boating in the Okavango Delta, you will undoubtedly depart from Maun. I think it is the most enjoyable town in Botswana so if you do have to stay here, it shouldn't be a hardship.

Maun

GETTING THERE

There are direct flights to Maun from Gaborone with *Air Botswana* every day of the week. There is service from both Francistown and Ghanzi twice a week. International connections are available to Windhoek by *Namib Air* and Victoria Falls by *Air Zimbabwe*. *Air Botswana* has recently expanded it's service to Kasane; this is a real boon to travellers wishing to combine the Okavango Delta and Chobe Game Park. As soon as the runway in Maun is extended, a jet service will be available.

There is a daily bus service from Francistown to Maun but I am told that it is erratic and that the trip can be very lengthy. If you are travelling by car, the road to Maun via Nata is notoriously difficult. At the present time it is not tarred, although surfacing work has begun. The 304 km stretch from Nata to Maun does not require a four-wheel drive vehicle but it is certainly preferable to drive one. The road can be a nightmare of ruts, owing to the calcrete composition of the soil. There is no petrol station after Nata so be sure to fill up there.

Road travel is challenging

If you are approaching Maun from Ghanzi, a four wheel drive vehicle is not necessary although it would be nice. The 280 km stretch of road is not tarred and it is riddled with pot-holes which keep driving speeds to a minimum. From Kasane a four-wheel drive is essential as the route is sand and can be deep in places. The 400 km trip generally requires ten hours of steady driving so it is sensible to break the journey in Moremi or Savuti. There is a lot of talk that the government plans to tar this stretch of road to link Maun with the Caprivi Strip in Namibia, but these projects take decades to accomplish.

ACCOMMODATION

Maun has a shortage of beds so it is wise to book a room in advance of your arrival if at all possible.

Riley's Hotel. Tel. 66-0204; fax 66005800. Located in town, this is the most convenient lodging for those without a vehicle. Part of the Crest Marakanelo chain, it is the most expensive hotel in Maun and it is considered luxury class. Despite this, it is very difficult to recommend this hotel. It is under perpetual heavy construction (now on phase 3 of seven), the service is non-existent and many of the rooms are shabby and none too clean. The restaurant is filthy and the small swimming pool is used by the general public, often making swimming difficult. On the bright side, however,

Accommodation is limited

Riley's does have a block of new rooms which are very nice and luxurious. I would recommend requesting one of these (Nos. 1–20 and 35–58) at the time of booking. Courtesy airport transfers are offered.

Crocodile Camp. Tel. 66-0265; fax 66-0493. Most people's favourite place to stay in Maun. It is a delightful bush camp on the banks of the Thamalakane River, 12 km from town. There are seven rustic reed and thatch rondavels that are charming and very clean. Only two have en suite facilities; the others share an ablution block. The grounds are lovely with many plants and huge shade trees. The bar and restaurant are the best in Maun and unless you need a telephone, pool and air conditioning to be happy, this is my recommendation. Airport transfers can be arranged although there is a substantial charge for this service. Crocodile Camp is closed for the month of February.

> **Best bet for food**

Island Safari Lodge. Tel. 66-0300; fax 66-0205. Also located on the Thamalakane River, accommodation here is provided in 23 thatch and stucco chalets each with its own private bathroom facilities. The rooms are very basic but adequate. There is also a huge riverside campsite here with communal ablution blocks, providing an inexpensive alternative to renting a room. The Island Safari Lodge caters primarily for overland and backpacking tourists. There is a restaurant as well as a pub that serves meat pies, fried chicken and pizza until late. It has a large swimming pool and offers transport to town, 12 km away.

DINING

The Duck Inn. Tel. 66-0253. Just outside the airport, this is probably the most popular watering hole in Maun. It is open daily from 8.30 a.m. to 10 p.m. and serves salads, soups, burgers and a variety of pub-style dishes throughout the day. The service is notoriously slow (this is a country where patience is truly a virtue) but the atmosphere is unbeatable. Spend a few hours drinking at the Duck Inn and you will get a full dose of Maun's local colour.

> **A Maun institution**

Crocodile Camp. Tel. 66-0265. Serves the best food in Maun and is open for dinner nightly. You must reserve a table by 4 p.m. as they only cook for a predetermined number of guests. Dinner is a set four-course meal for P30 and the food is ambitious and well executed. A typical menu might feature pear and celery soup, salad with cucumber and pecans, fillet of beef with port sauce and poached nectarines with almond custard. The service is friendly and efficient, a comment I am unable to make about any other restaurant in Maun.

Island Safari Lodge. Tel. 66-0300. Offers a pub menu in the bar for lunch and light dinners. The fried chicken is quite good but I cannot recommend the pizza. Dinner is also available in the dining room seven days a week and features a set menu. Guests who wish to dine in the restaurant are requested to book by 4 p.m.

Riley's Grill at Riley's Hotel. Tel. 66-0204. Serves breakfast, lunch and dinner daily. There is an a la carte menu that is very ambitious for Maun. The food is generally good but the service is deplorable, a situation which will hopefully change soon.

Book for dinner

SHOPPING

The best shopping in Maun is at the airport. The *Maun Gallery* and the *Bushman Curio Shop* sell high quality native crafts, basketry, sculpture, paintings and jewellery. They also offer films, postcards, videos, T-shirts and a terrific selection of books on Botswana. These two shops are open Monday–Friday, 8 a.m.–5 p.m. and at weekends 8 a.m.–3 p.m. All credit cards as well as foreign currency are accepted and shipping can be arranged.

Two kilometres from the airport there is a small shopping area optimistically called the Mall. Here you will find two banks, several clothing shops, a grocery, a beauty salon, a bottle store and a butchery. There is really nothing here for the tourist.

Arts and crafts

SERVICES

GETTING AROUND

Car Hire

All the hire companies maintain offices very near the airport. If you are hiring a vehicle and have booked in advance, ask to be met at the airport terminal building. Only four-wheel drive vehicles are available in Maun for the very good reason that most of the streets are sand. The vehicles are equipped with long-range fuel and water tanks. Avis allows you to take a car in to Namibia, South Africa or Zimbabwe although there is a drop-off fee if you do not return the car to Botswana. Hertz does not let its Maun vehicles leave the country. Holiday Car Rentals has full camping kits for hire (except sleeping bags) and will even provide a driver.
Avis: Tel. 66-0258
Hertz and Holiday Car Rentals: Merlin Services is the agent for both of these companies, Tel. 66-0351.

Airlines
Air Botswana's office is located just outside of the airport on the tarred road to town. Tel. 66-0391.

Air Charter
Aer Kavango: Tel. 66-0393; fax 66-0623
Northern Air: Tel. 66-0385; fax 66-0366
Both companies are located at the airport and offer single- or twin-engine planes.

Botswana

TRAVEL AGENCIES

Bonaventure Botswana, PO Box 201, Maun. Tel. 66-0205; fax 66-0502

London Office:, 68 St. James Street, London SW1A 1PH. Tel. (071) 499-2136; fax (071) 493-2381

Bonaventure is a travel agency that specializes in Botswana and can tailor any kind of holiday to suit a client's needs and interests. Good personal service is offered and the owner has made it a priority to get to know all the camps and operators in this country to assure that the traveller has a successful safari. Bonaventure also puts together Botswana-Zimbabwe-Namibia combinations. Call or write for their excellent catalogue of scheduled trips.

Okavango Tours and Safaris, PO Box 39, Maun. Tel. 66-0220; fax (011) 788-6475 South Africa

This very reputable company can make bookings for any camp in the Delta. It also offers a variety of scheduled safaris, some of which include other Southern African countries.

Merlin Services and Travel, Private Bag 13, Maun. Tel. 66-0351; fax 66-0571

This company is a booking agent for any camp in Botswana. Tailor-made safaris based on an individual's interests are also offered.

Travel Wild, PO Box 236, Maun. Tel./fax 66-0493

Travel Wild is conveniently located at the airport. This office is the booking agent for Shakawe Fishing Camp, Guma and Nxamaseri Camps and Okavango Horse Trails.

POST OFFICE

Located just past the Mall in town; open weekdays 8.15 a.m.-1 p.m. and 2.15 p.m.-4 p.m. Saturday 8.30 a.m.-11.30 a.m.

BANKS

Barclays and *Standard Chartered Banks* are located at the Mall. Hours of business are 8.15 a.m.–12.45 p.m. Monday–Friday and 8.15 a.m.–10.45 a.m. Saturday.

CINEMA

The *Island Safari Lodge* shows fairly up-to-date releases four nights a week in a small theatre. Usually there are two films a week; one is shown on Tuesday and Friday and the other on Wednesday and Saturday. Food and drink are available from the pub.

SAFARI COMPANIES

Photographic Safaris

Ker Downey Selby (KDS). This is a top class outfit that operates three of the very best camps in Botswana: Pom Pom, Machaba and Shinde. Not a detail is overlooked and utmost professionalism is their hallmark. For those who want the best, this is a company you should investigate.

PO Box 40, Maun. Tel. 66-0211; fax 66-0379

Also at: 14 Old Bond Street, London, W1X 3DB, UK. Tel. (01) 629-2044; fax (01) 491-9177

13201 Northwest Freeway, Suite 880 Houston, TX. 77040, USA. Tel. 800-231-6352; fax 713-895-8753

Desert and Delta Safaris. This company maintains two exquisite camps in Botswana: Camp Okavango and Camp Moremi. Luxury and first class service are paramount to the operation.

P.O. Box 2339, Randburg 2125, South Africa. Tel. (011) 886-1524; fax (011) 886-2349.

Gametrackers Botswana. A well-established and reputable company which operates eight camps in Botswana: Qhaaxwa and Xaxaba in the Okavango Delta; Khwai River Lodge and San-ta-wani in the Moremi Reserve; and Allan's Camp, Savuti South, Linyanti and Chilwero in the southern and northern sections of the Chobe National Park.

Airport Box 100, Maun. Tel. 66-0302

1000 East Broadway, Glendale, CA. 91205. Tel. 818-507-7893

Crocodile Camp Safaris. This popular outfit offers numerous top quality scheduled safaris through Botswana, Namibia, Zambia and Malawi. Tailor-made safaris are also available.
PO Box 46 , Maun, Tel. 66-0265; fax 66-0493

US representative: *Wilderness Travel*, 801 Allston Way, Berkeley, CA. 94710 US. Tel. 415-548-0420

Okavango Explorations. A local safari company which also own Xugana Camp in the Okavango Delta.
Private Bag 48, Maun . Tel./fax 66-0528

Vira Safaris, PO Box 335, Maun . Tel. 66-0383; fax 66-0593

Lloyd Wilmot Safaris, PO Box 37 , Maun. Tel. 66-0351 or (011) 53-1814 South Africa

Afro Ventures. This Johannesburg based company offers 140 scheduled adventure safaris through Southern Africa. The majority of their trips are camping safaris and guests participate by assisting with the cooking, cleaning, setting up of tents, etc.
PO Box 2339, Randburg 2125, South Africa. Tel. (011)886-1524; fax (011)886-2349

Mobile Safaris

Africa Calls! This company offers original and specialized safaris with modern vehicles and all the bush comforts from ice to hot showers. The Bushman Safari, the Cry of the Kalahari Expedition, the Livingstone Trail, the Botswana Birding Safari and the Okavango Boating Voyage are just a few of the interesting trips they feature.
Private Bag 83, Maun. Tel./fax 66-0351

Capricorn Mobile Safaris. Comfortable but basic 'under canvas' safaris with hands-on participation by the guests characterize this outfit. No cooking or camp chores are involved but you do paddle your own canoe! This company has scheduled 12-day and two-week adventures that combine hiking, boating, driving and white-water rafting at reasonable prices. Tailor-made safaris may also be arranged for a minimum of four people and a maximum group of 20.
Private Bag 21, Maun. Tel. 66-0351; fax 66-0571

Penduka Safaris. Izak Barnard has been leading mobile safaris into the Kalahari Desert for over 25 years. He is without a doubt the most knowledgable and experienced guide available: he speaks several Bushman dialects and is an authority on the flora and fauna of the Kalahari. If you are interested in the Bushman culture and life-style, Mr Barnard offers an excellent eight-day safari.
P.O. Box 55413, Northlands 2116 , South Africa. Tel./fax (011) 883-4303

Kalahari Kavango Wildlife Adventures. Four young guides operate this company and their speciality is the Makgadikgadi Pan. Clients are each assigned their own all terrain vehicle for driving through this very remote region, visiting areas where modern man has never been. Luxury tents are set up nightly by the crew and niceties such as hot showers and ice are provided. Tailor-made safaris for 2–8 guests are also offered.
PO Box 236, Maun. Tel./fax 66-0493
Overseas Booking Agent: J&C Voyageurs, Oxford, England . Fax (0235) 84-8840

Hunting Safaris

Safari South is an extremely reputable company that has been in operation for more than 25 years. Many of the most famous names in hunting are affiliated to this outfit. The company requires a minimum booking of ten days and hunting takes place in both the desert and the Okavango Delta. Tracking is done by vehicle and on foot, depending on the time available. Luxury tented camps with every bush comfort are used. For families or groups with non-hunters, photo safaris can be arranged. In addition to big game safaris, Safari South also features bird hunting trips.

This is an American-owned company but its Botswana operation is managed and run by locals from Maun.
USA Tel. 800-231-6352; fax 713-895-8753

Terry Palmer Safaris. This outfit has three private hunting concessions in the Kalahari Desert as well as over 500,000 sq km in the Okavango Delta. A maximum of two clients accompanies each professional hunter. Guests are accommodated in large tents with bush showers, laundry service and excellent meals. Terry Palmer is the son of Lionel Palmer, one of the well-known hunters associated with Safari South. Terry is extremely personable and his safaris are quite popular. Bookings can be made through Vira Travel in Maun or you can phone 66-0254 (fax 66-0593) for details.

Elephant Safaris

This is a new safari concept in Botswana that has met with smashing success since its inception. Randall J. Moore, an American biologist with 20 years' experience working with elephants, captured the world's heart and attention with his arduous struggle to return three North American circus elephants to their birthplace in Africa. His engrossing story may be followed in detail in his book, *Back to Africa.* Moore is now offering six day/five night elephant safaris in the Okavango Delta from March to September for a maximum of eight guests.

Accommodation is in a luxury tented camp with en suite facilities. Morning and afternoon 'rides' are offered as well as traditional game drives, mokoro and fishing expeditions. This is an excellent way to see game at close range. There is no engine noise and you can mingle among the other animals in the bush, your human presence totally undetectable from your lofty elephant perch. The howda accommodates two people plus a handler and is quite comfortable. Moore's elephants, which number three adults and seven youngsters at the time of writing, are not wild so they present no danger. To the best of my knowledge this is the only elephant safari in Africa and needless to say, it is an unforgetable experience! Bookings can be made in the United States through *Ker Downey Selby* or with *Bonaventure Botswana* in Maun.

OKAVANGO DELTA

INTRODUCTION

Floodwaters in the Kalahari

The Okavango Delta is one of nature's greatest wonders, a permanent sweetwater paradise incongrously surrounded by the deep sands of the Kalahari Desert. Its source is the Okavango River which rises in the mountains of Angola, gathering volume as it flows south-eastwards to Botswana. This formidable waterway courses through the Panhandle and then fans out to form one of the world's largest inland deltas, covering an area roughly the size of Wales. Each year a remarkable phenomenon occurs: the Okavango River floods and an estimated six billion gallons of water a day flow over the land. This gentle tide of water inundates the delta, renewing its resources and redefining its shape and direction. The slow, almost imperceptible flow results in a tangled network of waterways bearing clear, pure water over a blanket of yellow desert sand. It takes six months for the water to wend its way through the serpentine labyrinth of the swamp before it gives its last gasp in Maun. It has been estimated that an incredible 95 per cent of this flood water evaporates before it reaches the Thamalakane River in Maun. Here, on the edge of the Kalahari, the Okavango dies, a thousand miles short of the sea.

The people of the river

The original inhabitants of the Okavango Delta were the Banoka, the 'people of the river'. They are sometimes referred to as river Bushmen although this is not strictly correct for they were ethnically related to the Bantu. The origins of the Banoka are unknown but they were strictly hunter-gatherers, unlike the peoples who followed. Today, the Bayei people are the largest single group living in and around the delta. It is believed that the Bayei had established settlements by the eighteenth century if not well before. They were attracted to the delta by the fish and the hippos; their way of life centres on hunting and fishing although they tend some domestic livestock as well. The Bayei were followed by the HaMbukushu, who are known as the 'deep water people'. The HaMbukushu have settled predominantly in the Panhandle where they subsist as crop farmers with domestic stock.

For many, the Okavango Delta is the highlight of a visit to Botswana, the magnet that draws them to this distant land. Crystalline water meanders aimlessly across the flat desert plain creating a maze of tortuous, reed-

Taxis of the Delta

fringed channels, lily-scattered lagoons and countless secret islands. The *mokoro* (plural: *mekoro*) is the traditional mode of transport. *Mekoro* are flat-bottomed dugouts that have been crudely fashioned from the huge native trees in this region. They are propelled by polers who stand at the back of the craft and in a smooth, rhythmic tempo push the *mokoro* through narrow passageways and across floodplains covered with only 15 cm of water. The delta is a bewildering network of papyrus and water and it is mystifying how these boatmen can so unerringly find their way.

The delta abounds in wildlife; indeed, it is one of Africa's last great wildernesses. This watery wonderland is home to over 400 species of birds, elephants, lions, hippos, zebras, giraffes, buffalo, antelopes, crocodiles and Bayei boatmen, to name but a few. However, game-viewing should not be the primary reason for a visit here; although animals are plentiful they are difficult to spot in the luxuriant growth. Rather, it is the peace and solitude one can experience in this enchanted place that are its primary attractions. Come to the Okavango to watch birds, to fish, to walk, to explore a myriad of hidden channels no wider than your *mokoro*. Time slows here and man is able to rediscover the tempo and cadence of nature.

A bird's eye view

To appreciate the scope and beauty of the Okavango Delta fully, it must be seen from the air. The great majority of visitors who venture into the swamps fly from Maun to one of the many small airstrips in the delta that service the safari camps. The scenic splendour of these flights is unforgettable. As the plane lifts off from the runway at Maun, the land below appears painfully harsh, parched and dormant, the village a haphazard collection of huts afloat in a sandy sea. It is difficult to conceive that a vast cool and lush oasis extends just beyond Maun's dusty doorstep. In a matter of minutes, however, the scenery changes: we fly over the gnarled and blackened branches of a mopane grove and then gradually patches of green begin to appear. Suddenly there is soft green earth everywhere, stretching to the horizon. Sinuous ribbons of water narrowly thread through this expanse, glistening and winking in the sunlight. Below us there are thousands of animals moving singly and in great herds, in timeless rhythm with nature. Awestruck, we watch their graceful flight as they rush to escape the unseen noise of the plane overhead.

Delta transport: a mokoro *and poler.*

The role of the tsetse fly

The Okavango Delta is a study in pristine beauty, a miracle of life and water in the heart of a thirsty desert land. Its magic is subtle and evocative, sights and sounds recall an ancient Africa unsullied by modern man. But the delta is in great jeopardy today, its very existence threatened. Had it not been for the tsetse fly, it would have succumbed long ago to population and grazing pressures. The tsetse fly is the carrier of a deadly parasite, trypanosome, which causes sleeping sickness in man and nagana in cattle. Botswana has been attempting to control tsetse fly populations since the 1940s. The original methods included eradication of game, bush clearing and ring-barking. In the 1960s insecticides such as DDT were introduced and ground spraying became the predominant control technique; in the 1970s an aerial spraying programme with newer, less toxic chemicals was undertaken.

A number of scientific studies have been made to gauge the environmental impact of insecticides: aerial

Botswana

spraying has been found to maximize the effect with minimal harm to wildlife, fish and habitat. In other parts of Africa chemically impregnated odour-baited traps are being used with success to control the tsetse; these have not had positive results in Botswana because the Delta fly is a different species which relies on sight rather than smell to locate its host. Historically, man and cattle have not been able to co-exist with the tsetse, and so wildlife has flourished in the Okavango instead. However, the years of applied science and technology have at last succeeded and the tsetse fly, the delta's unwitting protector, has now been eradicated. Local people are eager to graze their cattle on the verdant pastures of the delta.

Ecology vs science

Today, only a few strands of wire called the Buffalo Fence separate this unique eden from the inexorable march of man and cattle. The cordon was erected to prevent the outbreak of foot and mouth disease; it is believed, but has not been conclusively proved, that this disease is spread by buffalo. The European Community, Botswana's primary beef market, has very strict regulations concerning the co-existence of cattle and buffalo, so it is hoped that this will allow the Okavango Delta to remain a cattle-free zone. Nonetheless, environmentalists remain gravely concerned. The Government is under pressure from many quarters to revise the protected status of this great treasure house. Sensibly, it is striving to protect the Okavango Delta while at the same time allowing people to enjoy and utilize its resources.

Land use pressures

Tourism is a viable consideration because it creates needed jobs and foreign exchange while having little deleterious effect on the environment. Although tourism is northern Botswana's largest private employer, it is difficult to reconcile the overwhelming needs of the people with the interests of foreigner visitors and conservationists. Tourism then, is just one part of the equation and the land-use conflicts facing Botswana will only be resolved by integrating conservation and development.

The lucrative diamond mining industry in this country further complicates the situation. Mining uses enormous quantities of water, a precious and scarce commodity in a parched land. Even as this is being written two dams and a reservoir are being constructed, the water for which will be diverted from the delta via a 20-mile channel from the Boro River. Ostensibly the reservoir is for the use of

Controversial water projects

the 20,000 residents of Maun but public opinion has it that the majority of the water will be funnelled to the Orapa diamond mines. To many in the Western world it seems inconceivable that this incomparable labyrinth of wildlife and water could be intentionally exploited and systematically destroyed with the consent of the Government. However, there is an undeniable hunger for the land and water that lie just beyond the fence. It is doubtful that the nation's leaders will be able to hold out in the face of mounting political pressures.

How much water can be tapped from the Okavango before the fragile ecological balance is irretrievably altered or destroyed? No one really knows for sure. All the various studies seem to prove is that numbers and percentages can be manipulated at will to substantiate whatever case someone is attempting to make. One thing is certain, however: the differences in habitat on either side of the cordon fence could not be more dramatic or telling. The profusion of lush, verdant grasslands that characterize the forbidden delta stands in stark contrast to man's domain where the earth is hard and barren, rendered lifeless by the overgrazing of domestic stock. Let us hope that Botswana's most precious heritage is not squandered, that this matchless ecosystem can be preserved for all of mankind.

Although there are over 114 species of animals in the delta, game-viewing is only a small part of the Okavango experience. If sighting game is a priority then a stay at the Moremi Wildlife Reserve on the edge of the delta is what you want. For those who wish to venture into the watery heart of the swamps, however, it should be with the intent to explore a maze of hidden waterways, view the incredible bird-life, marvel at the power of water and papyrus, fish and walk. Any game you might see here is an added bonus, not the reason for a voyage into this glorious wetland wilderness.

A different kind of safari

Moremi Wildlife Reserve

In the north-eastern sector of the Okavango Delta lies the Moremi Wildlife Reserve, Botswana's premier game park. This reserve was established in 1963 at the urging of a number of local Twsana residents, who donated tribal land to prevent the extermination of wildlife in Botswana. It was expanded in 1976 to include Chief's Island, located in the heart of the delta. Moremi encompasses a variety of diverse habitats: swamps, riverine terraces and flood plains, islands, dense mopane and acacia woodlands, sand veld and dry bush. Much of the reserve is inaccessible by vehicle or boat and remains an untouched wilderness. There is great beauty here and the game-viewing is some of the very best in Botswana.

Excellent concentrations of game

The incredible diversity of habitat supports large and various populations of animals. If you are lucky you will see almost every species found in Southern Africa at Moremi, with the exception of springbok, gemsbok and black rhino. The bird-life is also phenomenal, the answer to any ornithologist's dream. Carmine bee-eaters, fish eagles, Pel's fishing owls, storks, cranes, herons, ducks, kingfishers, shrikes, quelea and lilac-breasted rollers abound, to name but a few.

A number of luxurious private safari camps are ideally situated in the Moremi Wildlife Reserve, in addition to four public campsites. In many of the private camps guests can partake in traditional game drives on land, as well as the water activities of the delta. These lodges offer the best of both worlds in one location, making Moremi the perfect destination for those travellers who wish to combine forays into the Delta with superb game-viewing.

GETTING THERE

Charter flights

Maun is the gateway to the Delta and the great majority of travellers use charter flights to get to safari camps in this region. Generally, the camp operators make flight arrangements for their guests as many maintain their own planes and pilots; often transfers to and from Maun are included in a camp's daily rate. It is, of course, possible to make your own charter arrangements but it is doubtful that this would save you any money.

It would be foolhardy to attempt to explore the Delta on your own in a boat or canoe. Many channels are so overgrown that they are barely visible and the topography can change with the seasons, rendering maps of little help. It is extremely easy to get lost in the Okavango and people have been known to disappear without trace. If you are keen to explore the Delta on your own rather than stay at a private lodge or camp, hire a guide to accompany you and help with handling the boat. Consult the list of mobile safari operators and travel agencies on pages 118-119 or contact the Island Safari Lodge in Maun for information.

Another boating option is to travel to the delta from the north via the Panhandle. A company called *Africa Calls!* offers a 12-day trip called Delta Voyager. After a scenic flight to Shakawe guests are launched on the

DELTA ECOLOGY

There are a dozen excellent books on the market which deal expertly with the geology, wildlife and flora of the Okavango Delta. If you have the time to read even one of them before your trip it will add immensely to your enjoyment. The delta is a unique and complex ecosystem. There are, in fact, really three different ecosystems at work there; the northern reaches which are perennially flooded; the lower swamps, which are inundated seasonally and the large, dry islands, of which Chief's Island is an example. The flood waters arrive in March and April and when there is good rain the area of the delta can double. From the air it looks like just so much green grassland interspersed with small islands and curving swaths of water. What is not readily apparent from above, however, is that all of that green grassland is really marsh and much of it will not withstand the weight of man. It is only when you are down there, out on the water, that you can truly get a sense of its many elements. Towering walls of reed and papyrus prevent any chance of a panorama. These great barriers of vegetation line the waterways, blocking channels, choking off the flow of water wherever possible. Throughout the delta there is an endless, silent struggle for dominance between the jungle growth of papyrus and open water. Papyrus is one of the fastest-growing organisms on earth and despite many schemes to arrest its growth, none have proved successful.

The Okavango Delta is characterized by a number of beautiful hidden lagoons where the water is still and mirror-like, its surface disturbed only by the flowering lilies. These lagoons are home to hippos and herons. One has a sense that the moving current of the delta is at rest here, if only for a few hours, before it moves on to resume its ceaseless flow. Although the whole of this great oasis is covered with water, much of it is only a few centimetres deep. Deep water is usually confined to the main channel beds. These are lined with Kalahari sand and the current is swift enough so that vegetation does not gain much of a foothold. From these main waterways thousands of narrow and shallow channels branch off, winding through the delta at random. Most go nowhere. Hippos play an important role in the Okavango creating pathways from the lagoons where they spend the day, through the swamplands, to the islands where they graze at night. The hippo paths which result are used by man and beast to navigate the delta.

There are millions of islands scattered throughout the area. They come in all shapes and sizes: some just little hillocks barely able to keep dry amidst all the water, others quite large, capable of supporting dense vegetation and animal life, ecosystems unto themselves. Many of the smaller islands originated as termite mounds, perhaps in an era of low water levels or even at a time pre-dating the Okavango Delta itself. These termite islands, or termitaria, grew together and formed an area of higher ground, diverting the flow of the water. Subsequently, the rich soil of the termitaria attracted trees, grasses and wildlife with the result that today the delta is graced with many beautiful islands fringed with luxuriant woodland growth.

The Okavango Delta abounds with wildlife but the actual perennial delta only sustains three large animal species: crocodile, hippo and sitatunga, a rare aquatic antelope. It is in the southern reaches where the reedbeds and swamps have given way to dry land and seasonally flooded plains that more than 20 large mammal species occur, including buffalo, elephant, zebra, giraffe, waterbuck, tsessebe, sable, lechwe and impala.

Botswana

Overland route to Moremi

Okavango River; from here the group travels downstream at a relaxed pace through the delta, landing in Maun at the conclusion of the voyage.

It is possible to drive from Maun to the **Moremi Wildlife Reserve** if you have a four-wheel drive vehicle. Many of the excellent safari camps in this sanctuary are accessible by road and the reserve has four public campsites. Plan on a five hour drive and remember that there are no services such as food or petrol *en route*. The entrance gate is open from sunrise to sunset and there is an entry fee for passengers, vehicles and camping. If you have a dread of flying you may prefer this way of getting there.

ACCOMMODATION

A list of 19 private safari camps follows. I have attempted to divide the camps into price categories, but in all honesty the distinction between expensive and slightly less expensive is very fine. With the exception of the two 'budget' camps, there are no bargains in the Okavango Delta. It is important to pick a camp that will offer what you are seeking. For instance, some camps are exclusively devoted to water activities and the chances of sighting game will in all likelihood be minimal. If you have your heart set on being poled through the delta in a traditional *mokoro*, read what follows carefully for many camps are using more stable canoes and in some cases poling is not possible if the camp is located on deep water. Night game drives can only be offered at camps that have private concession land, for the Moremi Reserve is off-limits after sunset. In general, all the luxury camps are simply wonderful and a visit to any of them will represent money well and happily spent.

Choosing the right camp

Comfort and luxury

Expensive
Shinde. This is a beautiful tented camp run by *Ker Downey Selby* (KDS) just outside the northern perimeter of the **Moremi Wildlife Reserve.** Game drives, *mekoro*, motor boats and walking are offered; as an added feature there is a viewing platform nestled in a tree canopy, overlooking a waterhole. KDS has its own concession land and the game-viewing here and in neighbouring Moremi Reserve is as good as it gets. Guests are provided every possible comfort and luxury that are available in the bush. Top notch food, guides, staff and service characterize Shinde. Book through KDS (see page 118).

Camp Okavango. A favourite of mine, this luxury tented

The ever-vigilant fish eagle, quintessential symbol of the Delta.

Zoo Park in downtown Windhoek.

The much-maligned spotted hyena emerging from his den.

A baobab tree stands sentinel.

Lilac-breasted roller.

Water lilies abound in the lagoons of the Delta.

Okavango Delta

camp is located on its own small island in the heart of the Okavango Delta. Tents are spacious and beautifully appointed with private ablution facilities located some 10 metres behind each tent. The food here just might be the best in the Delta and the professional guides are super. No game drives are offered as this is strictly a water camp but walks on neigbouring islands are featured. The camp is fortunate to be situated on an island that has both shallow lagoons for poling (canoes) and deep water for motor boating and fishing. Book through *Desert and Delta Safaris*.

Pom Pom. This small, beautifully sited camp accommodates 14 guests in large, traditional canvas tents with attached en-suite bathrooms. The tents are literally on the water's edge with huge shade trees providing a canopy from the sun. Guided walks, fishing and game drives, including night drives, are featured. Additionally, *mokoro* excursions are excellent from here as the water surrounding the island is shallow. A resident group of a dozen or so hippos provides non-stop entertainment as well as orchestral counterpoints to the tranquility of the setting. As with the other KDS camps, everything at Pom Pom is top notch. Book through KDS.

Delta Camp. De luxe accommodation is offered in charming chalets, no two alike, with en-suite bathrooms. Many of the chalets incorporate the trees which shelter the camp in their structures. The rooms are very open to the elements and guests sleep under mosquito netting. This water camp is superbly situated in the central delta and activities centre on traditional *mokoro* and nature walking. There are no vehicles or motorized boats at Delta Camp as the owners are concerned for the environment. The camp can arrange a unique camping experience on nearby Chief's Island for those guests who would like to rough it for a few nights. Contact PO Box 39, Maun; tel. 66-0220 or (011) 788-5549 South Africa.

Chief's island retreat

Camp Moremi. Camp Moremi is the sister camp to Camp Okavango. It is located on the mainland in the **Moremi Wildlife Reserve** on the eastern edge of the Xakanaxa Lagoon. Five-star luxury prevails and guests are accommodated in spacious tents with private ablution facilities located just behind each tent. No water activities are offered but the game-viewing is superb and elephants freely roam the camp. Transfers between the two camps are done by motor boat and guests often combine one or two nights at each spot. Book through *Desert and Delta Safaris*.

Botswana

Machaba. This is another of the KDS camps, situated on the banks of the Khwai River just outside the perimeter of the Moremi Reserve. Machaba offers excellent day and night game-viewing, being located within 3,200 sq km of KDS concession land. Guests are accommodated in large tents with full en-suite bathrooms. Exceptional cuisine and hospitality are the hallmarks of this camp. Book through KDS.

Mombo. This luxury camp is located on the north-western side of Chief's Island and is one of the smallest camp in the Delta with only six tents available. Shaded by huge trees, each tent has en-suite facilities and is nicely appointed. Game drives in open vehicles on private concession land are featured and night drives are a possibility. Book through any tour company or travel agent.

Xaxaba. This is one of the most popular camps in the delta offering accommodation in reed and thatch chalets with private bathrooms. Sunset pontoon cruises, power boats and *mekoro* are all available and professional guides lead walking trails. There is a swimming pool which guests may use during the summer months. Xaxaba camp is frequently booked by tour groups so it is best to reserve early. Contact PO Box 147, Maun; tel. 66-0302, or 1000 East Broadway, Glendale, CA. 91205, USA; tel. 818-507-7893.

Slightly Less Expensive

Xugana. A luxury camp that can sleep 16 guests under canvas; each tent boasts *en suite* facilities. This camp is beautifully situated on Xugana Lagoon which facilitates fishing, boating, walking and *mokoro* excursions. There is a swimming pool on the premises and game drives can be organized in conjunction with Xugana's sister camp, Tsaro. Contact PO Box 48, Maun; tel. 66-0528 or (011) 708-1893 South Africa; fax (011) 708-1569 South Africa.

Tsaro Lodge. This is the sister camp to Xugana and I think it is one of the most attractive places in the delta. It is situated on the grassy banks of the Khwai River under the shade of huge trees. There is accommodation for 16 guests in luxurious thatched rondavels with en-suite facilities. The look and feeling of Tsaro are far less 'bushy' than at most camps, due in part to its manicured lawns and sparkling swimming pool. Game drives and walks are led by professional guides. (See Xuguna for booking address).

Khwai River Lodge. This is one of the largest camps in the delta, accommodating up to 24 guests in unimaginatively decorated thatch and brick bungalows. Each has a private en-suite bath and the camp is electrified. As its name suggests, this lodge is situated on the Khwai River just outside the Moremi Reserve. No water activities are offered, although there is a good-sized swimming pool. Daily game drives are featured in Moremi and they are very professionally done with extremely knowledgeable guides. Book through *Gametrackers,* (See page 118).

San-Ta-Wani. This is another *Gametrackers* operation, located at the South Gate of the **Moremi Wildlife Reserve**. 18 guests can be accommodated in cool stucco and thatch chalets each with an *en suite* bathroom. The grounds are lovely and the chalets are nestled under the shade of huge trees. Fishing and game drives in open vehicles led by professional guides are featured. Boating (*mokoro*) is said to be available subject to water levels, but if this is an important factor for you, I would check with Gametrackers because there were no water activities offered during the 1991 high-water season. Book through *Gametrackers*.

Camp Okuti. Situated on beautiful **Xakanaxa Lagoon** within the Moremi Reserve, Okuti offers basic thatched chalets with shared ablution facilities. Activities include both game drives and power boat excursions into the delta; walking and fishing are also available. Camp Okuti is one of the only camps in the Okavango to welcome children of all ages. Contact Private Bag 049, Maun; tel. 66-0205; fax 66-0502.

Children welcome

Jedibe Island Camp. This is a tented camp situated just below the Panhandle in an area of the delta where there is permanent water. Ablution facilities are communal. This water camp has a reputation for some of the best bream and tiger fishing in the Okavango (September–January). Activities revolve around power-boat and *mokoro* expeditions, overnight stays on remote islands, bird-watching and nature walks. Contact PO Box 14, Maun; tel. 66-0205; fax 66-0502.

Guma Lagoon Camp. Guma Camp is located at the very bottom of the Panhandle at the top (north-west) end of the delta. Guests stay in reed huts with private bathrooms; there are also two tents which share ablution facilities. Traditional *mekoro* are used to explore the backwaters of the Guma Lagoon; power-boat trips, bird-watching and very good fishing are offered as well as horseback riding. Six horses are stabled at Guma and day or half day hire can be arranged. This is an unusual way

Horseback safaris

to experience the delta. For the more adventurous, guided trail rides of four or more days duration are available. The game-viewing on these trips is reputed to be excellent. Tented camps with bush comforts are set up by a suppport staff at various stops *en route*. Contact Private Bag 23, Maun; tel. 660493 or (011) 659-1211 South Africa.

Xakanaxa. This tented camp can accommodate 18 guests with shared ablution facilities. It is situated on the edge of the Delta's largest lake, Xakanaxa Lagoon, within the **Moremi Wildlife Reserve**. Activities include game– and bird-viewing by both boat and vehicle. Contact PO Box 201, Maun; tel, 66-0205; fax 66-0502.

Reasonable

Camping

Oddballs. This is one of Botswana's finest campsites, located in the very heart of the Okavango Delta on the edge of Chief's Island. It is the most inexpensive way to experience the delta, a low-cost high-density alternative to Botswana's professed tourism policy. If you don't have your own camping or fishing equipment it is possible to hire it, but make these arrangements in advance of your arrival. The highlight of a trip to Oddballs is setting off

Mokoro trails with a poler-guide on a *mokoro* safari to explore the ubiquitous islands and channels of the delta. You can camp, swim, fish and walk wherever you like. Access to the **Moremi Wildlife Reserve** is easy and you are allowed to go game-viewing on foot here. Oddballs campsite offers hot showers, flush toilets, a small grocery store, a laundry, a bar and restaurant. There is a daily charter flight from Maun for P210 per person (return). Please note that it is important to pre-book a *mokoro* as the camp only has 30. Also, all campers are required to spend their first and last nights in the delta at the Oddballs Camp. At the time of writing the daily rate was P15, excluding national park fees. Book through *Okavango Tours and Safaris*, PO Box 39, Maun; tel. 66-0220; fax (011) 788-6575 South Africa.

Gunn's Camp. Sometimes called Ntswi Island Camp,

Budget option Gunn's is the only other reasonably priced place to stay in the delta. It is one of the southernmost camps, located on an island in the Boro River near the tip of Chief's Island. Access is by charter flight and guests may choose between camping in tents or basic bungalow accommodation. The bungalows are equipped with four beds, cooking equipment and gas lamps. Ablution blocks with hot water, toilets and showers are provided and there is a restaurant, a bar and a small shop selling foodstuffs. The price per person for the bungalows (minimum two people) including three meals a day is currently P240. Campers can expect to pay P120 per night and this includes all equipment, meals and use of a *mokoro* with poler. Walking, traditional *mokoro* safaris and powerboat excursions are available; four- to ten-day *mokoro* trips through the delta can also be arranged. By the way, Gunn's Camp is much smaller and quieter than Oddballs. Contact Private Bag 33, Maun; tel. 66-0351; fax 66-0571.

Camping

There are four public, government campsites in the Moremi Wildlife Reserve: **South Gate, North Gate, Third Bridge(Mboma)** and **Xakanaxa** . Driving after dark is prohibited in the reserve as is camping outside the designated areas; this is for your own safety. My favourite campsite is Third Bridge; the camp gets it name from the picturesque bridge of *mopane* logs that is close by. The camp is well-sited under good tree cover and there is wonderful swimming at the bridge in crystal clear, fast-flowing water. If you are like me, however, you won't spend too much time in the water just in case Mr Crocodile is in the vicinity. Lions are frequently seen in this area and they use the bridge as a highway. Construction of concrete block ablution facilities is currently under way at Third Bridge campsite which will upgrade it considerably. If you are not going into the Okavango Delta you might want to spend some time at the Third Bridge or Xakanaxa campsites. These camps are on the edge of the Delta and the lagoons and floodplains are very beautiful here. North Gate camp is also quite nice, located in a wooded area overlooking grassy plains. All the camps have the same very basic facilities: toilets, cold water taps and showers.

Lions at Third Bridge

CHOBE NATIONAL PARK

INTRODUCTION

The Chobe National Park was created in 1968 and encompasses 11,700 sq km of wilderness. The park abuts the Moremi Wildlife Reserve at its south-westernmost point and together these two sanctuaries form a protected range 300 km in length. Chobe is characterized by vast endless plains, ancient woodlands and riverine thickets. Wildlife roams in profusion and there is a great diversity

Stronghold of the elephant

of species. The elephant population alone is estimated to be in excess of 30,000 in the Chobe National Park and over 450 species of bird life have been recorded. The park is divided into three distinct sections: **Serondella, Ngwezumba,** and **Savuti,** and these differ quite a bit in terms of terrain, habitat and best times to visit.

There are several ways of exploring the Chobe National Park. You can fly into Kasane or Maun, hire a four-wheel drive vehicle and set off for the hinterland. This is a great way to experience the African bush if you are up to the demands of the drive and camping outdoors. There are a number of public campsites within the park although it should be noted that only Serondella Camp is accessible in an ordinary sedan car. For those with less time and more comfort in mind, there are excellent safari camps and lodges in the Serondella and Savuti regions that offer game drives, walks, bird-watching, fishing, sunset cruises or whatever is appropriate to the area. If photographing the prolific bird and wildlife of the Chobe National Park is your objective then these camps will not disappoint you. If your time is limited you should select either Serondella or Savuti for a visit, depending on the time of year and what you hope to see.

SERONDELLA

Chobe River

The Serondella is the northernmost sector of the park and activities here are for the most part focused on the Chobe River. This river actually originates in Angola where it is called the Kuando. From Angola it flows eastwards along the Caprivi Strip and where it first reaches Botswana it becomes the Linyanti River. At the town of Ngoma in Namibia, it changes names again and becomes the Chobe. From this point the Chobe River only flows a short distance before it merges with the Zambezi just above the famous Victoria Falls. The Chobe forms the northern perimeter of the national park and is one of Botswana's international boundaries as well.

The Serondella region is famous for its elephant and buffalo populations. The elephants come nightly to the river's edge to drink and bathe and there is nothing more quintessentially African than to watch the setting sun outline in silhouette a herd of these gentle giants. In contrast to many other areas of Africa, the elephant population in Botswana (like those in Zimbabwe and South Africa) is thriving. There are now too many elephants in the Chobe National Park and the

Habitat destruction Government has begun a culling program. Evidence of the intensive destruction these animals are capable of inflicting is quite apparent in the Serondella region. Huge tracts of riverine woodland and mopane forest have been devasted and the habitat degradation will be complete in a matter of years if the population is not managed. Many visitors have great difficulty with the concept of culling or wildlife management in general. However, anyone who has travelled through Southern Africa will undoubtedly reconsider the issue. The elephants destroy the habitat not only for themselves but for other wildlife. When the food source is gone the elephants will face certain starvation, for the regeneration of woodland savannah is very slow. The havoc a herd of elephants can wreak in one or two days is truly unbelievable. In

Yawning is often a sign of aggression in hippos.

consequence, despite the terrible irony of the situation, Botswana and some of her neighbours are forced to cull herds while throughout eastern and central Africa the elephant is losing ground to poachers.

The riverine terraces and flood plains of the Serondella region lend a beauty to this section of the Chobe National Park that is not matched by its counterparts. Visitors can expect to see plenty of game, including giraffe, lion, tsessebe, waterbuck, eland, roan, sable, puku, lechwe, hippo, crocodile and rhino as well as the ubiquitous elephant and buffalo. The wide flood plains along the Chobe River make game-viewing easy although there are plenty of inland areas characterized by thickets and forest. The best time to visit this region of the Chobe is during the dry season from June to October; when the surface water in the vast interior of the park begins to dry up, the animals move northwards to the river.

Best time to visit

Kasane
Before the creation of the Chobe National Park there used to be a village of Serondella; its inhabitants were relocated to the nearby town of Kasane, however, when the land was declared a reserve. In many ways Kasane is to Chobe what Maun is to the Okavango Delta. It is a nondescript town that serves as a gateway to the park.

For travellers entering Botswana from Zimbabwe or Namibia, Kasane will be the first town encountered. From Victoria Falls it is an easy drive on a fully tarred road, so many visitors to the falls combine a jaunt to the Chobe National Park with their Zimbabwean holiday (or vice versa). UTC offers a daily coach service between Victoria Falls and Kasane. Once you arrive in Kasane you can hire a car to tour the area, or if you are staying in one of the lodges nearby, game drives will be offered to interested guests. Driving from Namibia, one crosses into Botswana at Ngoma Bridge. As there is no immigration post here travellers are required to report at Kasane straight away for these formalities. For those visitors who would like to fly to Kasane from Maun or Gaborone, *Air Botswana* has a convenient service.

Victoria Falls is nearby

Kasane is located 4 km to the east of the entrance gate to the park. The town has experienced quite a bit of growth in recent years as a result of tourism; there is now a decent range of facilities here: a Post Office, a bank, a garage, a supermarket, a bottle store, and government offices. There are also several lodges and campsites in the Kasane environs that serve as convenient bases for exploring the Chobe National Park.

Accommodation

Chobe Safari Lodge. This lodge is located in the centre of Kasane and is nicely situated on a bank overlooking the Chobe River. Accommodation ranges from chalets with communal ablution facilities to modest hotel rooms with en-suite bathrooms, to campsites. There is a wonderful swimming pool on the river bank and a very popular terrace where inexpensive snacks are served. The lodge offers game drives, fishing, boat hire and a daily river cruise on the Fish Eagle Barge. The Chobe Safari Lodge is the most reasonably priced place to stay in the Serondella area, outside of camping. Contact PO Box 10, Kasane; tel. 25-0336.

Reasonably priced lodging

Chobe Game Lodge. This is the most luxurious and expensive place to stay in the Serondella sector of the park. Although this lodge will not be to everyone's taste or pocketbook, for those who like a bit of pampering or need a respite from too much time in the bush, this is the spot to pick. After all, it is a much publicised fact that Richard Burton and Elizabeth Taylor chose the Chobe Game Lodge for their second honeymoon, so you can rest assured that the amenities and cosseting will be up to Western standards. The Game Lodge is very conveniently situated within the national park alongside the Chobe River. The architectural style is Moorish: several two-storey stucco buildings are set amidst beautifully manicured grounds on the banks above the river. Guests are accommodated in 50 spacious double rooms, each with river view, air conditioning and private bathrooms. There is a wonderful swimming pool, an outdoor terrace for meals, an indoor dining room, a bar and inviting lounge areas. The lodge also has one of the best gift shops in Botswana, selling native crafts as well as the requisite postcards and T-shirts.

The ultimate in luxury

Because it is situated within the park's boundaries, wildlife is part of the decor and ambiance here. The last time I was a guest, I had slipped away to the pool for a post-prandial snooze. I had barely shut my eyes when my husband prodded me awake, frantically pointing at the ground between our lounge chairs. A family of warthogs had decided to join us at the poolside. Six homely little pigs proceeded to scrape off a layer of grass under our lounges to get at the cool dirt below. They then wriggled and squirmed until comfortably entrenched, and shaded from the sun by our bodies, decided to catch 40 winks themselves. I still regret that I didn't have my camera with me; those warthogs were so close that I could have

Warthogs abound

reached down and touched them. Needless to say, the owner of the lodge was less than enthusiastic when she passed by about 30 minutes later. She screeched and ran for our lounge chairs, disrupting my reverie as well as the warthogs, no doubt. She was quite indignant that we had 'allowed' the warthogs to make such a mess of the lawn. Of course I could see her point, but I had enjoyed the encounter so much that I just couldn't shoo them away, lawn or no lawn.

Elephants are also frequent, destructive visitors, baboons seem to consider the grounds their own private estate and even hippos and lions have been known to use the lodge as a thoroughfare. Apart from the wildlife that roams the resort, however, there is really nothing about the Chobe Game Lodge that is particularly African; for many the animals introduce a note of reality to this enclave of luxury and civilization.

Good fishing Game drives are offered several times a day in open vehicles. There is very good fishing in the Chobe River and boats and guides are available. In the late afternoon a sundowner cruise is featured. The lodge has its own aeroplane and flights to Moremi, Savuti or the Okavango Delta can be arranged. Contact PO Box 32, Kasane; tel. (011) 783-8660 (*Sun International Reservations*, South Arica). In the USA ring 800-421-8905.

Chobe Chilwero. For those travellers who would like a touch of luxury but still want the African bush feeling, Chobe Chilwero is the answer. Set on an escarpment high above the river, this intimate camp accommodates 16 guests in twin-bedded wood and thatch A-frame chalets, each with en-suite facilities. Chilwero is very well run and the professional game guides here are the best. Fishing and game-viewing by boat are also offered. Book through Gametrackers, (see page 118).

Kubu Lodge. Kubu is located 7 km east of Kasane just off the main road to Zimbabwe. Guests are accommodated in thatched chalets with private bathrooms. Kubu Lodge also offers riverside campsites and basic A-frame huts with communal ablution blocks. The grounds are lovely and there is a nice pool. Full- and half-day game drives in the park are offered and boats for fishing or river cruising can be hired. Contact PO Box 43, Kasane; tel.25-0312.

Public camping **Serondella Campsite.** Serondella is the public campsite for this section of the Chobe National Park. It is located approximately 15 km west of the park gate on the banks of the Chobe River. Facilities are limited to toilets, taps and showers (cold water only). This is a very popular campsite for the simple reason that it is the only one in the park that is accessible by ordinary car. Unfortunately it is often very crowded and marred by litter.

NGWEZUMBA

Ngwezumba occupies the middle portion of the Chobe National Park and as I have said, it is only accessible to travellers in four wheel drive vehicles. There are two public campsites in this region: **Nogatsaa** and **Tjinga**. Nogatsaa offers toilets, showers and taps with cold water; Tjinga has no facilities although there is a water tank here which may or may not be usable. The Ngwezumba River only flows in years of exceptional flood but it is dammed in the vicinity of the campsite and there is a hide overlooking the dam for game-viewing.

Best time to visit

The chances of sighting game are very good in the Ngwezumba region from November to May. The area is characterized by mopane woodlands, grassy plains and a number of pans. When the rains come and these pans hold water, the wildlife can be quite prolific with large herds of elephants and buffalo. A special feature of Ngwezumba is an antelope called the oribi; this animal occurs nowhere else in Botswana.

SAVUTI

Savuti is one of the best places for game-viewing in Botswana and November–May is the time to visit. Located in the south-western sector of the park, Savuti lies within the **Mababe Depression**. The Mababe is the bed of an ancient super-lake that once covered most of northern Botswana. Whatever rivers may have fed it eons ago have since shifted course, no doubt due to crustal movement, for this entire region is still subject to considerable tectonic activity. A sand ridge called Magwikhwe, measuring 20 metres in height, 180 metres in width and 100 km in length, runs along the western edge of the Mababe Depression and it is believed that this was the beach barrier of the ancient lake. Even with an untrained eye it is easy to see the evidence and boundaries of the former lake. Today, the Mababe Depression is a vast, incredibly flat plain covered with grass and scattered bush, edged with *mopane* scrub. This area encompasses sand veld, acacia savannah, dramatic rocky outcrops and on rare occasions, marshland. It is a mecca for wildlife especially after the rains have rejuvenated the grassland.

Prolific wildlife

Botswana

The disappearing channel

The Savuti Channel is one of the most famous and enigmatic features of the region. It is basically a tributary of the Linyanti (Chobe) River but instead of carrying water *to* the river, it carries it in the opposite direction. The water flows 100 km from its source through a breech in the Magwikhwe Sand Ridge and is then deposited in the Mababe Depression. This created what is called the **Savuti Marsh**, which varies in size with the flow in the channel. Today the Savuti Channel is dry. It stopped flowing in 1981 and no one knows if it will resume. Records show that this is not the first time it has ceased to exist. It is known that for a number of years between 1850 and 1880 there was water in varying levels in the channel. However, the flow dried up in the mid-1880s and did not resume again until 1956.

One of the distinguishing features of the Savuti is the hundreds of dead acacia trees that line the channel bed, testimony to a drier era when they were able to take root and flourish. When the waters mysteriously reappeared the trees were drowned and they stand as stark reminders of the capricious nature of the Savuti Channel. Geological studies have shown that the Mababe Depression is subject to very high levels of seismic activity. Initially, scientists thought that the flow of water in the Savuti was linked to high rainfall and the subsequent flooding of the Chobe River. However, this notion has not been borne out and it is now believed that movement within the earth's crust is the determining factor.

A channel full of water stretching 100 km through the northern Kalahari sands represented nothing short of paradise for the wildlife. When the Savuti was in flow the plains were covered with herds of impala, zebra and tsessebe numbering in the hundreds of thousands. The grasslands teemed with every species of animal and this is how it must have looked when the animals ruled the earth and the world was still young. However, even today without the presence of water in the marsh or channel, Savuti attracts large numbers of game because of the lush, nutritious vegetation and the many small pans which do hold water. When this surface water is gone some of the animals trek to the Linyanti (Chobe) River, 50 km distant, only to return when the rains come again.

An area of great beauty

Savuti is truly one of the most spectacular and beautiful regions of Africa and should not be overlooked on a visit to Botswana.

Accommodation

Lloyd's Camp. This is one of the most famous and popular safari camps in Botswana. The owner, Lloyd Wilmot, is the son of Bobby Wilmot, the legendary crocodile hunter who is reputed to have killed 45,000 of the beasts before his death during an encounter with a black mamba. Lloyd's Camp is set on the banks of the **Savuti Channel**. It is rustic rather than fancy but the food is good and the game-viewing is even better. The camp has a hide overlooking a borehole (floodlit at night), which attracts game. Guests are accommodated in eight large tents and share ablution blocks set under the stars. The camp prides itself on offering close contact with big and dangerous game. If you want to feel an intimate part of Africa, Lloyd's Camp can't be beaten. Access is by air or four-wheel drive vehicle. Book through *Lloyd Wilmot Safaris* (see page 119).

Close encounters with big game

Allan's Camp. Allan's Camp is located on the banks of the Savuti Channel overlooking the **Mababe Depression**. This 16-bedded safari camp consists of rustic wood and thatch A-frame chalets with en-suite bathrooms. There is an open-air dining room and the atmosphere here is informal and relaxed. Game drives are operated twice a day by professional resident rangers. Book through *Gametrackers,* (see page 118).

Linyanti. This camp is set on the banks of the Linyanti River just outside the Chobe National Park. The accommodation is in luxury twin-bedded tents under thatched A-frame structures; reeded ablution blocks with separate showers, sinks and toilets are provided. Activities include foot trails and fishing and game viewing trips by double-decker boat and Land Rover. Linyanti means 'the place of the buffalo' and during the dry season (May–October) vast herds of buffalo, elephant, zebra, wildebeest and other plains game migrate to the area for a permanent winter source of water. The bird life is among the best in Botswana and there are several hides at this camp that afford good photographic opportunities. Book through *Gametrackers*.

Savuti South. South Camp is a traditional safari-style tented camp located on the banks of the Savuti Channel. There are eight luxury tents unobstrusively set amongst gigantic trees, each with its own private bathroom. Twice daily game drives with professional rangers are featured. Book through *Gametrackers*.

Basic camping

Camping
There are two public campsites in the Savuti region. One is the **Linyanti Campsite**, located outside of the Chobe National Park on the Linyanti River and Swamps. The Linyanti Swamps are predominantly papyrus marsh and are permanent home to hippos, crocodile, sitatunga and lechwe. The other is the **Savuti Campsite** which runs along the Savuti Channel. Both offer rudimentary showers, toilets and cold water taps. Animals, especially elephants and baboons, roam the sites; it is very important not to feed them as they quickly become a nuisance and must be put down. Access to both of these campsites is with a four-wheel drive vehicle only.

THE PANHANDLE

INTRODUCTION

Okavango River
The Okavango River rises in the highlands of Angola and flows into a valley in north-western Botswana that was created by two parallel faults about 15 km apart. The valley is flat and the river snakes and twists across it so that the river distance is some three times that of the direct route. The river floods annually and the pastures which follow it's course are inundated; the resulting 95 km long flood plain is known as the Panhandle. The Okavango River runs strong and wide through the Panhandle and this region is primarily a Mecca for fishing enthusiasts although the bird-watching is also excellent. Eighty species of fish inhabit the Okavango River. Tiger fish are plentiful and this species is renowned as the world's best fresh-water game fish. At the base of the Panhandle the Okavango River hits the **Gomare Fault,** an extension of the East African Rift system. This geological feature causes the waterway to split and disperse into a thousand tributaries which fan out and form the Okavango Delta. At the lower end of the delta, approximately 160 km downstream, the spread of water is blocked by the uplifting of another fault called the **Kunyere.**

GETTING THERE

Shakawe
It is possible either to fly or to drive to Shakawe, a small village located in the upper reaches of the Panhandle. There are no commercial flights to this airstrip so it would be necessary to charter a small plane from Maun,

Kasane or Gaborone. The drive from Maun is a long 370 km of heavy sand and four-wheel drive is essential. All the camps in the Panhandle provide or arrange transport for their visitors, which greatly simplifies the situation.

ACCOMMODATION

Nxamaseri. This luxury camp is located halfway up the Panhandle on an island 3 km from the Okavango River. A maximum of eight guests can be accommodated in comfortable brick and thatch chalets with en-suite bathrooms. Fishing is the predominant pastime at Nxamaseri and all equipment and guides are provided. Both power boats and *mekoro* are used to travel the waterways. Bird-watching walks are offered and a flight to **Tsodilo Hills** to view the Bushman rock paintings can be arranged. Contact Private Bag 23, Maun; tel. 66-0493.

Superb fishing and birdwatching

Xaro Camp. Xaro is a luxury tented camp in the northern sector of the Panhandle overlooking the Okavango River. A total of 14 guests can be accommodated; modern ablution facilities are communal. Activities include walking, bird-watching and fishing. Contact Private Bag 14, Maun.

Qhaaxwa. One of the Gametrackers camps, Qhaaxwa is located at the western edge of the delta at the base of the Panhandle. The camp can sleep 16 guests in reed chalets, each with en-suite bathrooms. Boating in power craft or canoes is offered as well as fishing, bird-watching and walking. Book through *Gametrackers,* (see page 118).

Shakawe Fishing Camp. Guests are accommodated in newly constructed brick and thatch chalets with en-suite bathrooms. Activities centre on fishing and bird-watching and there is even a small swimming pool in the grounds. Sightings of the elusive **Pel's fishing owl** are very common at Shakawe. This camp is located in the northernmost region of the Panhandle on the westen bank of the Okavango River. The nearby village of Shakawe has an airfield so charter access is relatively easy; it is also possible to drive overland to this camp.

Bushman art

The **Tsodilo Hills** are situated a mere 40 km west of the camp and guided tours by vehicle are offered. A large, shady campsite adjoins the fishing camp. Campers may be able to use the camp's bar and restaurant as well as hire tackle and boats if these are not being used by the guests. Book through *Okavango Fishing Safaris Ltd*, PO Box 12, Shakawe; tel. 66-0493.

TSODILO HILLS

The Tsodilo Hills are Botswana's greatest archaeological legacy. A group of four rocky outcrops, cracked and burnished by the relentless sun, they loom dramatically above the flat monotony of the Kalahari Desert in the remote north-western corner of the country. The Tsodilo Hills were first brought to the world's attention in 1958 by Sir Laurens van der Post in his book, *Lost World of the Kalahari*. Of his first sighting van der Post wrote, *'They rose sheer out of the flat plain and were from the base up made entirely of stone, and this alone, in a world of deep sand, gave them a sense of mystery'*.

A place of magic and mystery

The Bushmen who inhabited this region for more than 30,000 years call the Tsodilo Hills the 'bracelet of the morning' and the 'slippery hills'. As van der Post discovered and related in his book, the Bushmen have a long and mystical connection with these hills. Testimony to the significance they attached to Tsodilo is the incredible collection of rock art that decorates the stony slab surfaces of these four hills. Over 2,750 individual paintings have been identified, evidence of the joyous creative spirit of these indigenous people who lived in such harmony with their environment. Tsodilo was a magnet to the Bushman as he roamed the Kalahari, for here among the rocky outcrops there were a number of secret, permanent springs. The Tsodilo Hills remain a place of magic, myth and mystery even today. Van der Post's vision of these hills *'as a great fortress of once living Bushman culture, a Louvre of the desert'*, may be romantic but there is an indefinable spirit here, an echo of the past that cannot be blithely dismissed.

Access is difficult

Reaching the Tsodilo Hills is no easy trick. It is possible to drive here from Shakawe, a journey of 40 km that will take at least two hours as the road is horrendous. If you fly to Shakawe you can hire a four-wheel drive vehicle from the Shakawe Fishing Camp for the trip. Alternatively, you could charter a plane from Maun to take you to the small airstrip that is within walking distance of Tsodilo. From Maun it is a twelve hour trip by vehicle; if you do elect to drive yourself, take note that there is no petrol *en route*. Camping is permitted but you must bring your own water and food because there are no facilities at the hills. Several camps in the Okavango Delta and Panhandle will also arrange guided tours (by air or vehicle) for interested guests.

The Tsodilo Hills have been accorded National Monument status and you will be asked to sign the visitors' book when you arrive at the HaMbukushu

(Bantu) village at the end of the road. Many people make the journey to Tsodilo in the hopes of encountering an authentic Bushman or two. There is a small encampment of about 25 !Kung people at the foot of Male Hill, as the largest of the four monoliths is called. However, these are not the noble hunter-gatherers of van der Post's story. Sadly, twentieth century problems and commercialism have had a negative impact on the Bushman way of life. The old nomadic ways are gone and the Bushman has not integrated into modern society with grace or success. Be prepared for Coco-Cola can litter and even curios for sale. In the village you should be able to hire a guide to show you the rock art. Don't expect a dissertation on what you are seeing however, for next to no English is spoken. It is also important to bear in mind that much of this art has mythological, religious or spiritual significance which can not be readily explained. However, even without the cultural insight necessary to interpret some of the drawings and symbols, many of the animal paintings are easily recognizable and outstanding – full of grace, movement and life.

!Kung people

Three of the four Tsodilo Hills were named by the Bushmen for their descending order of size: Male, Female, Child. The fourth and smallest of the hills remains nameless. The majority of the paintings can be found on Female, along the base of the hill on the western side. To see the rock art one climbs stony pathways that weave between the fractured cliffs and a crazy jumble of boulders. Soft sand tracks stabilized by vegetation connect the hills. One of the most famous of the painting depicts elands and giraffes on a high rock face and is known as the van der Post panel. Vandals have desecrated some of the Tsodilo paintings with graffiti, including this panel, but the majority of the art is amazingly recognizable and life-like. In common with other Bushman rock art found in Southern Africa, a great many of the paintings at Tsodilo depict easily identifiable animals although there are friezes with simple geometric designs, abstract symbols and human figures. Over 30 years ago van der Post was struck by how young and fresh the paintings appeared. Incredibly even today the vividness of the colours has not been lost, despite the fact that many of these paintings could be 10,000 or even 20,000 years old. Laurens van der Post and his group believed that spirits dwelled in the Tsodilo Hills. It would be fitting if perhaps the brooding spirits of the ancient artists linger still among these rocky hills and crevasses, keeping an eternal watch over the paintings, protecting their precious monument to the past.

Rock paintings

OTHER NATIONAL PARKS AND GAME RESERVES

Off-the-beaten track

The majority of the foreign travellers to Botswana visit only a few of the country's nine parks and reserves. The most popular destinations are the Moremi Wildlife Reserve, the Okavango Delta, and the Savuti and Serondella regions of the Chobe National Park. However, for the visitor with special interests or more time, there is much of beauty and some very good game viewing in some of Botswana's other reserves.

MAKGADIKGADI PANS GAME RESERVE

35,000 years ago Lake Makgadikgadi was a vast inland sea midway between the Indian and Atlantic Oceans; it was formed by the Chobe, Okavango and Zambezi Rivers, amongst others, and it lay at the end of the East African Rift Valley in a region of extreme tectonic instability. Repeated fracturing of the earth's crust resulted in directional changes in the flow of the river systems and over time Lake Makgadikgadi dried up. Evidence suggests that it has been 1,500 years since it held any substantial levels of water.

All that is left today of this ancient super-lake are two enormous salt pains called *Ntwetwe* and *Sua*. These pans represent the last vestiges of the lake, the deepest and **Desolate** thus the final basins to dry up when the waters **salt pans** disappeared as a result of tectonic and climatic changes. These vast pans are perfectly flat and are composed of grey clay saturated with salt. No debris of any kind mars their surface and vegetation is non-existent, unable to grow in earth with such high concentrations of salinity. Although the pans are never completely flooded today, they do hold several centimeters of water during a good rainy season. Rain transforms the pans and waterfowl from across the globe, especially flamingos, converge to breed. It is a spectacular sight. Sua Pan is particularly rich in brine shrimp and algae and this might explain why hundreds of thousands of greater and lesser flamingos migrate here. Sua is a wetland of international importance and the economic project underway to extract soda ash and the saturated brine of the pan concerns some environmentalists.

Sua is the San word for salt and for decades the pan was considered a useless wasteland. Ironically it has now been proved that a treasure lies beneath its surface. Soda ash is an essential ingredient in the production of glass, steel, detergents and paper pulp. Salt is also produced from the process which is basically one of dehydration. The project is located at the north-eastern end of the Sua Pan. Although the development area is relatively small, concern for the ecology of the region has led to the establishment of a sanctuary in the Nata River delta. The sanctuary will embrace the northern reaches of Sua Pan and the boundaries will abut those of the soda ash project. The **Nata Sanctuary** will provide protection for a crucial breeding area for water birds, and will encourage tourism in the area.

In contrast to the pans, the Makgadikgadi plains to the west are a sea of endless whispering grass dotted with clumps of palm trees and interrupted by small islands of vegetation. David Livingstone was the first to explore this region in 1851 and as he described it there were massive herds of elephants, buffalos and plains game stretching to the horizon, as far as the eye could see. Sadly, it only took a decade or so for hunters and traders to discover the riches of this area and the great herds were severely decimated. Today, the north-western edge of the Makgadikgadi, encompassing some of Ntwetwe Pan, has been proclaimed a game reserve. During the dry season thousands of wildebeest and zebras depend on the grasslands here for survival. Under the protective status of a reserve, the plains game are flourishing once again along with their attendant predators, although the elephants have never returned.

Makgadikgadi is somewhat off the beaten path for most tourists. However, some mobile safari operators do offer excursions here, or alternatively, if you are driving around Botswana on your own then this is a place you might want to include in your itinerary. The best time to explore Makgadikgadi is between June and November, before the onset of the rainy season. After that the animals tend to move north to the Nxai Pan. No public campsites or facilities of any kind exist in the Makgadikgadi Game Reserve so you must be self-sufficient. Access is via the road from Nata to Maun. The Reserve is criss-crossed by a maze of unmapped tracks and a four-wheel drive vehicle is mandatory. If you decide to explore the vast pans, the *Visitors' Guide to Botswana* by M. Main and J. and S. Fowkes will be very helpful.

Livingstone was here

Best time to visit

NXAI PAN NATIONAL PARK

Nxai Pan borders the northern edge of the Makgadikgadi basin. It is another fossilized lake bed, but unlike the Sua or the Ntwetwe Pans, it is not covered in salt. Framed by a low dune belt, it stretches for miles, a carpet of lush green grass sprinkled with many stands of trees. Great herds of wildebeest, zebras, giraffes, gemsboks, springboks and eland breed here when the pans fill with water during the rainy season; the game viewing can be spectacular.

Seasonal migrations

The ideal months to visit Nxai are December to April if the rains have come. Both Nxai and Makgadikgadi teem with game when the conditions are right; at other times, a traveller can drive for weeks without seeing anything but the odd ostrich or gemsbok.

The entrance gate to the Nxai Pan National Park is just 30 km north of the Nata–Maun road, 170 km from Nata. A four wheel drive vehicle is necessary to negotiate the Park and it is dangerous to stray from the established roads. Two public campsites are available, one at the southern end of the pan and the other at the northern end. Both have toilets and cold water but nothing else.

Colossal baobab trees

Just south of the Nxai National Pan Park boundary there is yet another pan called *Kudiakam*. Here steep banks encircle the expanse of salt and the pan's floor is dotted with many islands of vegetation covered with dense mopane and acacia. Along the northern edge of Kudiakam there is a famous clump of baobab trees which have been named Baines' Baobabs in honour of Thomas Baines, an artist who painted these trees in 1862. Baobabs are not unusual in this part of Botswana but the setting of this group is particularly impressive. These colossal monoliths rise out of the flat, featureless plain like great sentinels. Poised on the edge of the Kudiakam they seem to stand in eternal watch over the barren wasteland of salt to the south and the grass plains to the north. They appear today as they did in 1862 when Baines wrote: *'Five full-sized trees and two or three younger ones were standing, so that when in leaf their foliage must form one magnificent shade. One gigantic trunk had fallen and lay prostrate but still losing none of its vitality, sent forth branches and young leaves like the rest. The general colour of the immense stems was grey and rough; but where the old bark had peeled and curled off, the new . . . showed through over large portions giving them, according to the light or shade, a red or yellow, grey or deep purple tone'.*

CENTRAL KALAHARI GAME RESERVE

The Central Kalahari Game Reserve was established in 1961 and occupies the vast central portion of Botswana, an area encompassing 53,000 sq km of semi-arid tree and bush savannah mixed with grassland shrub. Unlike the southern Kalahari Desert the endless vistas of this reserve are interrupted only occasionally by sand dunes and dry river beds. The very size and remoteness of the reserve are its most distinguishing features. This is the second largest game reserve in the world and it was here, in **Deception Valley**, that Mark and Delia Owens undertook their famous lion and hyena research, remarkably well-told in *the Cry of the Kalahari*.

This has been the home of the San people for centuries. The reserve was originally established to provide a refuge for these nomadic people and to protect the wildlife and other resources used by the Bushman in his hunter-gatherer life-style. However, a long period of drought in the 1980s forced many to leave and it is doubtful whether more than 1,200 Bushmen or Remote Area Dwellers (RAD) as they are now officially called, live here now. The majority live at the Cade Settlement near the western boundary and basic services (schools, water and a health clinic) are provided.

Proper preparation is imperative

The reserve has always been closed to the general public in the past but recently this has changed and access is possible via the Kutse Game Reserve in the south or from the east by way of Orapa into Deception Valley. Prospective visitors should be aware that the only roads are unmarked sand tracks and there are currently no tourist facilities of any kind. It is imperative to carry sufficient water, food and petrol to cover the possibility of a breakdown. The best way to travel is with a local Setswana-speaking guide; the Department of Wildlife and National Parks staff at **Kutse** and **Matshwiri Camps** (the official entry points for the reserve) will be able to assist you in locating a guide.

Desert-adapted wildlife

The reserve is totally fenced and there is considerable wildlife within its confines. However, there are no natural water sources, and surface water occurs only for brief periods, which greatly limit wildlife populations. Those animals that do exist here must be adapted to the desert and able to obtain the moisture they need from shrubs and grasses, or in the case of carnivores, from other animals. Animals most commonly found are springbok, gemsbok, eland, kudu, giraffe, hartebeest, blue wildebeest, steenbok and duiker, with small numbers of brown hyena, lion, cheetah and leopard.

KUTSE GAME RESERVE

Kutse is a small 2,500 sq km area that protrudes from the south of the Central Kalahari Game Reserve. It is only 220 km north-west of Gaborone but the journey necessitates a four-wheel drive vehicle. Kutse is characterized by rolling scrub bush, thorn trees and a great many salt pans. Game is very seasonal and is generally not abundant unless the rains have been good. Those animals that are passing through the reserve can most likely be found congregating at the pans.

The lure of the Kalahari

The real attraction of Kutse is the Kalahari desert itself: the opportunity to experience the beauty and solitude of the land and to savour the incredible sense of space here . There are a couple of campsites, the nicest of which is at Moreswe Pan, some 65 km from the entrance gate at the end of the only road through the reserve. There is another camp at Kutse Pan, about 12 km from the entrance gate and on the border of the Central Kalahari Game Reserve. Campers should bring all of their own provisions: food, equipment, water, firewood and petrol. There is water available at the park gate (from a borehole) but it is not very tasty.

MABUASEHUBE GAME RESERVE

Mabuasehube is situated in the south-western corner of Botswana, adjacent to the Kalahari Gemsbok Park. It is the least visited of all of the reserves and parks in this country, owing largely to its remoteness and the poor quality of the access roads. It is characterized by six large pans and a number of smaller ones. The word *mabuasehube* means red soil and although all but one of the pans in the reserve are grass-covered, the northernmost is barren and is composed of the distinctive Kalahari sand showing a brick orange colour. The pans of Mahuabesube hold water during the rainy season and attract a good deal of wildlife, including gemsbok, springbok, wildebeest, eland and the predators that follow these animals wherever they go.

Distinctive red sand dunes

The best time to visit is during the rainy season from October to April. There are no facilities of any kind here and the traveller must be totally self-sufficient. The distances involved in getting to Mahuabesube are substantial and due to the nature of the drive, it should only be undertaken by the experienced and adventurous. The most common approach is from the south via Tshabong. Plans to pave the road from here to Gaborone in the future will make this trip much more feasible.

MASHATU GAME RESERVE

Tuli Block

In the north-eastern corner of Botswana at the confluence of the Limpopo and Shaswe Rivers there is a finger of land that abuts the borders of Zimbabwe and South Africa. The Mashatu Game Reserve is located here, part of a region that has been known historically as the Tuli Block or Enclave. Tuli is a narrow strip of land only 20 km at its widest which runs alongside the Limpopo River, stretching some 250 km along the border with South Africa. A large number of white farmers own land in the Tuli Block dating from the late 1800s when this land was ceded by the Tswana chiefs to the BSAC for the building of a railway. In the event, the railway bypassed Tuli because there were too many rivers requiring bridge construction.

Elephants abound

This area is usually overlooked by tourists to Botswana, which is a shame because it encompasses some of the most scenic landscape in the country and is rich in game and archaeological interest. The Mashatu Game Reserve is the largest privately owned conservation area in Southern Africa, encompassing roughly 35,000 hectares of pristine game land. Moreover, Mashatu claim to have the largest single population of elephants on privately owned land in the world. Known as the *relic herds of Shashe*, these elephants are the last living testament to the great herds that once populated the Limpopo River valley. After being hunted to extinction in this area in the late nineteenth century, the elephants have gradually struggled to re-establish themselves in the Tuli enclave and today there are over 700 in the Mashatu Game Reserve alone.

Tuli Block

The Mashatu Reserve was named after the magnificent mashatu trees that occur throughout the area. There are a number of diverse habitats incorporated in the reserve: savannah, riverine forests, marshland, open plains and eroded sandstone outcrops. In addition to elephants Mashatu has an astounding variety of bird and wildlife. Over 350 species of birds have been noted and giraffe, eland, zebra, kudu, bushbuck, impala, baboon and all of the big cats are in residence here, to name but a few.

ACCOMMODATION

Mashatu The game reserve is owned by *Rattray Reserves*, a South African concern that operates some of the most luxurious and exclusive safari camps in Africa. There are two choices of accommodation at Mashatu: the Main Camp or the Tent Camp. The Main Camp is super-de

Botswana

luxe; guests are accommodated in air conditioned chalets with his and her bathrooms and private verandahs. There is round-the-clock electricity, a swimming pool, an outdoor *boma* for evening dining and a floodlit waterhole for game viewing. The Tent Camp is the more rustic option. It is located at the remote northern end of the reserve and can sleep up to 14 guests under canvas. The spacious tents have en-suite toilets and showers and in true Rattray style, all the bush comforts are provided in camp. Game drives and meals are included in the tariff.

Night game viewing As a special feature night game drives are offered, providing an opportunity to see many nocturnal animals rarely seen during the daylight hours, such as civet, aardvark, genet, bushbaby and even leopard. Excursions can also be arranged for visitors interested in seeing some nearby ancient ruins believed to be related to the Karonga Kingdom of Great Zimbabwe.

Many visitors approach Mashatu from South Africa; it is a five hour drive from Johannesburg. If you are driving from South Africa leave your vehicle at the Pont Drift border post. The camp will send a vehicle to fetch you and clear Botswana customs. For those travellers who want to get to Mashatu from Botswana it is imperative to check on river conditions before undertaking the journey. Charter flights are also easily arranged from Gaborone, Maun or Kasane. Rattray Reserves offers daily flights to and from Johannesburg in their own luxurious Beechcraft King Air. Contact: *Mashatu Game Reserve*, PO Box 2575, Randburg 2125, South Africa; tel. (011) 789-2677; fax (011) 886-4382.

Tuli Safari Lodge This is another luxury camp distinguished by beautiful grounds and gardens and a relaxed, informal ambience. 38 guests can be accommodated in spacious chalets with en-suite facilities. Tuli Lodge is a place with few rules: you can stay out in the bush all night if you like, swim in the pool, join a guided game walk or drive through the reserve. As a matter of interest it is worth mentioning that the owner of Tuli Lodge is sponsoring Gareth Patterson's lion project. After George Adamson's untimely murder by poachers

The lions of Mashatu in Kenya in 1989, Patterson assumed responsibility for the rearing of his three lion cubs. These cubs have been brought to Botswana to the Tuli area, where they will eventually rejoin the wild. Patterson has written a moving story about the lions of Mashatu in his book, *Cry for the Lions*. Contact PO Box 335, Gaborone: tel. (011) 788-1748 South Africa.

Nokolodi Campsite Nokolodi is a beautiful site set on a forested riverine terrace along the Limpopo. A huge *mashatu* tree estimated to be at least 1,000 years old serves as the focal point of the campsite. In addition to camping however, there are a few very small, rustic huts available with self-catering facilities. A professional guide/ecologist runs Nokolodi and he leads game drives and walks for interested visitors. Contact Private Bag X1040, Waterpoort 0905, South Africa, tel. (011) 788-0740.

GABORONE

INTRODUCTION

Boomtown Gaborone was originally a traditional village but became the capital of Botswana at independence in 1966. It was chosen for this purpose because of its proximity to the railway line and the availability of water in the area. Although a development plan was formulated in the early 1960s for a city of 20,000 inhabitants, Gaborone has grown totally out of proportion to original expectations. It is the fastest-growing town in Botswana with a population that has more than doubled in ten years and currently exceeds 175,000 people. A building boom is underway and the entire town seems to be in varying stages of dusty construction, and as a result it is rather unattractive. As the capital of Botswana, Gaborone is the financial and political centre of the country. The National Assembly, government ministries and the House of Chiefs are clustered here around a small park, forming the Government Enclave.

Not much to interest travellers By Western standards Gaborone is a very small town and offers the tourist little in the way of scenic interest or recreation. If you do find yourself in Gaborone, however, there is limited shopping, one museum and a number of good hotels and restaurants.

GETTING THERE

The Sir Seretse Khama Airport is 8 km from Gaborone. *South African Airways* and *Air Botswana* offer daily services to and from Johannesburg. *British Air* has scheduled service three times a week, with direct flights to London on Tuesdays and Saturdays. *Zambia Airways* flies between Lusaka and Gaborone twice weekly. There are also services to Harare, Maseru, Mauzini, Lilongwe, Dar-es-Salaam and Nairobi at least once a week on various carriers. *Air Botswana* connects Gaborone with Francistown, Selebi-Phikwe, Kasane and Maun.

Transport to Gaborone from the airport is available via hotel courtesy buses provided by the Gaborone Sun, the Gaborone Sheraton and the President Hotel. If you want to be dropped at the town centre (the Mall) take the President Hotel bus; you do not have to be a hotel guest to use the service. There is no taxi rank at the airport so you will have to ring for one on arrival.

The railway passes through Botswana *en route* to Zimbabwe and South Africa. There is a daily service between Gaborone and Bulawayo in Zimbabwe and between Gaborone and Mafeking on the South African border. There is also a through service to Johannesburg four or five times a week. There is both a daily passenger train and a weekly express mail train (that carries people) connecting Gaborone with Lobatse in the south and Francistown in the north with numerous stops in between. The railway station is in Station Road, within walking distance of the Mall. Bookings may be made on weekdays from 7.30 a.m.to 1 p.m. and 2 p.m. to 7 p.m., and at weekends from 4 p.m. to 7.30 p.m.

Erratic bus service

There is a haphazard bus system in Botswana linking Gaborone with the main towns and villages in the eastern half of the country. Because of the nature of the roads in western Botswana, coach transport is just not feasible. Bus stops are signposted and not surprisingly, the majority are on tarred roads or near towns rather than in rural areas. There never seems to be anyone at the bus station in Gaborone to answer questions so it is next to impossible to determine when the buses will arrive or depart. A printed schedule does not exist so the best course of action is to find a bus stop and ask the waiting passengers for information.

ACCOMMODATION

Hotel rooms are in demand

Gaborone is a growing town and there is quite a lot of new hotel construction going on. As it is often difficult to find a room, with the large numbers of business people and government officials who frequent Gaborone, this is just as well. The standard of accommodation is quite high with prices to match.

Gaborone Sun Hotel, Nyerere Drive. Tel. 35-1111. This is one of the city's most luxurious hotels, and is located about two km from the Mall. It has a beautiful swimming pool, a golf course, tennis courts, two restaurants and a casino. If you have a long wait in transit at the airport I

Gaborone

Casino would suggest you catch the hotel transport bus and while away the hours here. There is a small entrance fee to the casino and only the slot machines are open during the day.

Gaborone Sheraton Hotel and Towers. Molopolole Road. Tel. 31-2999; fax 31-2989. Situated on the western side of the town this brand-new international Sheraton is really two hotels in one. The Towers is a fifth floor 'hotel within a hotel', consisting of 36 rooms and suites with VIP amenities. The hotel itself has 200 rooms, three restaurants, satellite TV and video, 24-hour room service, a swimming pool, tennis courts and a gym with a sauna.

President Hotel, The Mall. Tel. 35-36310. This is Gaborone's most centrally situated hotel, right in the centre of the Mall. It is operated by the Cresta Hotel chain and although the price of a room is comparable to the Gaborone Sun, there are far fewer facilities and amenities.

Oasis Hotel. Tlokweng Road. Tel. 35-6396; fax 31-29680. Some 5 km from the city centre, the Oasis offers 50 suites, all with air conditioning, telephone, TV and video, at slightly more reasonable rates than the central hotels. There is a large swimming pool, a seafood restaurant, a mini golf course and a fitness centre. The Cameo Club offers good live entertainment and is a very popular night spot.

Morning Star Motel. Tlokweng Village. Tel. 35-230. This is a budget class hotel with basic but clean rooms. Located 6 km out of town, it is somewhat difficult to get to without a car. Try flagging down one of the many combis (mini-buses) that ply this route; the locals use these as their primary mode of transport and although they are always full, you can generally squeeze in.

YWCA. Notwane Road. This is the least expensive place to stay in Gaborone but it accommodates women only in dormitories. The Y is within walking distance of the Mall.

DINING

La Pergola. Tel. 35-3631. At the President Hotel, La Pergola has a pleasant second floor open-air terrace where snacks and cocktails are served during the day except on Sundays.

The Cattle Post. Tel. 35-3631 Also at the President Hotel, this restaurant is open daily for lunch and dinner and the menu features burgers, steaks, ribs and salads.

The Savuti Grill. Tel. 35-1111. This is the main dining room of the Gabarone Sun and it serves buffet-style breakfast, lunch and dinner daily.

The Taj Restaurant. Tel. 31-3569. Situated in the African Mall (behind the President Hotel) specializes in Indian cuisine with Chinese and Mauritian dishes also represented on the menu. Open for lunch and dinner.

The Bull And Bush. Off the Francistown Road. Tel. 37-5070. This is the only pub in Gaborone. It has a good atmosphere, good steaks and live entertainment.

SHOPPING

The Mall

Gaborone may be the capital of Botswana but the shopping, in tourist terms at least, is unexciting. In this rapidly growing town which seems to be developing at random, the Mall is an anomaly; it was formally designed and laid out to serve as the central pedestrian shopping centre. One end of this very pleasant tree-lined walkway is framed by government buildings and at the other end sits the Town Hall, the Library and the National Museum and Art Gallery. There are a number of shops on the Mall selling food, hardware, clothing, books, furniture, curios and photo and stationery supplies. The post office and two banks – *Barclays* and *Standard Charter* – are also here. If you need help with your itinerary there are several travel agencies in the Mall in addition to the *Air Botswana*, *British Airways* and *Zambia Airways* offices.

Quality crafts

The only shop in the Mall that sells hand-made native products is *Botswanacraft*. High quality baskets, jewellery, weavings, pottery and carvings are featured and they will arrange shipping. Be sure to take a stroll down the Mall even if you do not intend to do any shopping. This is where the action is and it is fun to browse and watch the people.

There are two other quality curio shops in Gaborone but neither is on the Mall. *Sun Bird Curios* is in the Gaborone Sun Hotel and it offers beautiful leather products in addition to jewellery and carvings. The other is the *Bushman Gift Shop* in Tlhwane Road in Broadhurst, a suburb of Gaborone. The selection here is much the same.

Behind the President Hotel there is a haphazard collection of stalls known as the *African Mall*. This is where many of the locals shop and there are several interesting restaurants in this sprawl. Although there is little here that a tourist would buy, it is interesting to mingle with the shoppers and see just what is for sale.

SIGHTSEEING

Basically there is no sightseeing in Gaborone. Apart from the Mall, the only real attraction is the **National Museum** and **Art Gallery**. I wouldn't recommend a stop in Gaborone just to see these collections, but if you are in town, by all means visit them.

The wildlife collection is of interest as are the cultural artefacts and the displays relating to the hunter-gatherer way of life in the Kalahari Desert. The Art Gallery is very small but it has some appealing paintings and sculptures. Many of the pieces are from other African countries but are of interest nonetheless. The museum is open from Tuesday-Friday, 9 a.m. to 6 p.m. and on weekends and holidays from 9 a.m. to 5 p.m. Admission is free.

SERVICES

TRANSPORTATION
Car Hire

Avis and *Hertz* are both represented at the airport. There is no extra fee if you hire a car in Gaborone and then leave it at another Avis or Hertz location in Botswana. Four-wheel drive vehicles are also available for hire. If at all possible, book a vehicle from overseas to ensure you get the most reasonable rate.

Holiday Car Rentals also maintains an office at the airport and both cars and 4x4's are offered. Telephone 35-3970; fax 31-2280.

If you are planning a road trip through the country, *Bush Link Ltd* hires fully equipped Land Rovers complete with rooftop tents and all camping gear. High-frequency radios are standard equipment in every vehicle so that you are in touch with their base station at all times. Telephone or fax 37-1480 for details and prices.

Airlines
Air Botswana: Tel. 35-2812
South African Airways: Tel. 37-2397

Air Charter
Kalahari Air Services: Tel. 35-1804

POST OFFICE

In the centre of the Mall; open weekdays from 8.15 a.m. to 1 p.m. and 2 p.m. to 4 p.m.; Saturdays from 8.30 a.m. to 11.30 a.m. Public telephones are located just outside the entrance. There is also a post office in the main terminal at the airport.

BANKS

Banking hours in Botswana are 8.15 a.m. to 12.45 p.m. Monday–Friday and 8.15 a.m to 10.45 a.m. on Saturday. There is a banking window in the Seretse Khama Airport but it is often not manned.

BOOK SHOPS

The best bookshop in the country is the *Botswana Book Centre* on the Mall.

CINEMA

Capitol Cinema, the Mall

LEFT LUGGAGE

None is available at the airport but there is a left luggage office at the railway station; it is only open on weekdays, however.

FRANCISTOWN

INTRODUCTION

Francistown is Botswana's second largest town and its oldest commercial centre. It originated as a gold-rush boom town in the 1860s but today its economy is based on agriculture and industry as most of the mines are no longer in operation. Francistown is experiencing rapid commercial growth, notably in light manufacturing and chemical industries.

At the crossroads of Botswana

In comparison with Gaborone, Francistown is compactly laid out and quite attractive although it, too, holds no interest for the tourist except as a possible overnight stop. All roads lead to Francistown in this country; as a result there are several good hotels and a decent array of shops if you need to stock up before heading out into the wilds.

GETTING THERE

Francistown is on the main north–south road, roughly at the halfway point, at the junction of the roads leading to Bulawayo, Kasane, Maun and Gaborone. The railway line runs parallel to the tarred road, so there are numerous small hamlets near the railway stations where it is often possible to obtain food, drinks and petrol.

The town is served once a day by the passenger train that runs from Bulawayo to Mafeking and once a week by an express train. The railway station is in Haskins Street right in the centre of town and it is open on weekdays only from 8 a.m.–1 p.m. and 2–4 p.m.

The bus terminus is at the southern end of Haskins Street, within easy walking distance of the railway station. There is a service to Lusaka, Zambia, once a week and to Harare, Zimbabwe, twice a week.

The small airport is served by *Air Botswana*. There is no bus transport to town so you must ring for a taxi or hire a car. There are also no banking facilities at the airport.

ACCOMMODATION

Thapama Lodge. Tel. 21-3872. This is your best choice if you want to stay in the town centre. It is run by the Crest Marakanelo chain and is popular with businessmen. This hotel offers 48 air-conditioned bedrooms with TV, radio, in-house video, telephones and en-suite bathrooms. There is a swimming pool as well as two restaurants and

Francistown

The African or Cape Buffalo.

. two bars and a small shopping arcade.

The Marang Motel. Tel. 21-3991. This is the nicest hotel in Francistown but it is 4 km south of town on the Old Gaborone Road. Set on the banks of the Tati river it has beautiful shaded grounds and is a cool and relaxing spot to unwind after a hard day of travelling. Accommodation ranges from luxury wood and thatch chalets to de luxe air-conditioned rooms and rondavels. Facilities include a swimming pool, a one-hole golf course, a bar and an a la carte restaurant. There is also a superb campsite at the Marang with clean ablution blocks . This is a popular hotel, so advance bookings are advisable.

SERVICES

TRANSPORTATION
Car Hire
Avis's office is at the airport; tel. 21-3901
Holiday Car Rentals: tel. 21-4524

Taxis
Telephone 21-2260.

Airline
The *Air Botswana* office is in the Thapama Lodge; tel. 21-2393.

BANKS
Barclays and the *Standard Chartered Bank* are both in Haskins Street.

CINEMA
Cine 2000, Blue Jacket Street

LEFT LUGGAGE
There is a left luggage office at the railway station, which is manned from Monday to Saturday.

SWIMMING POOL
There is a public pool in Baines Street that is open daily.

SECTION 3: SOUTH AFRICA

BACKGROUND INFORMATION
Travel Facts

Country File

AROUND SOUTH AFRICA
Johannesburg

Sun City

Eastern Transvaal: The Panorama Route

Kruger National Park

The Drakensberg

Durban

The Game Reserves of Zululand

Capetown

The Winelands

The Garden Route

South Africa

SOUTH AFRICA

NAMIBIA

Windhoek

Lüderitz

Keetmanshoop

Province of The Orange Free State

Province of The Cape of Good Hope

Kalahari Gemsbok National Park

Twee Rivieren

Kuruman

Upington

Britstown

Carnarvon

Calvinia

Victoria

Vanrhynsdorp

Atlantic Ocean

CAPE PROVINCE

Beaufort West

Saldanha

Worcester

Oudtshoorn

Cape Town

Paarl

Stellenbosch

George

Simonstown

Strand

Somerset West

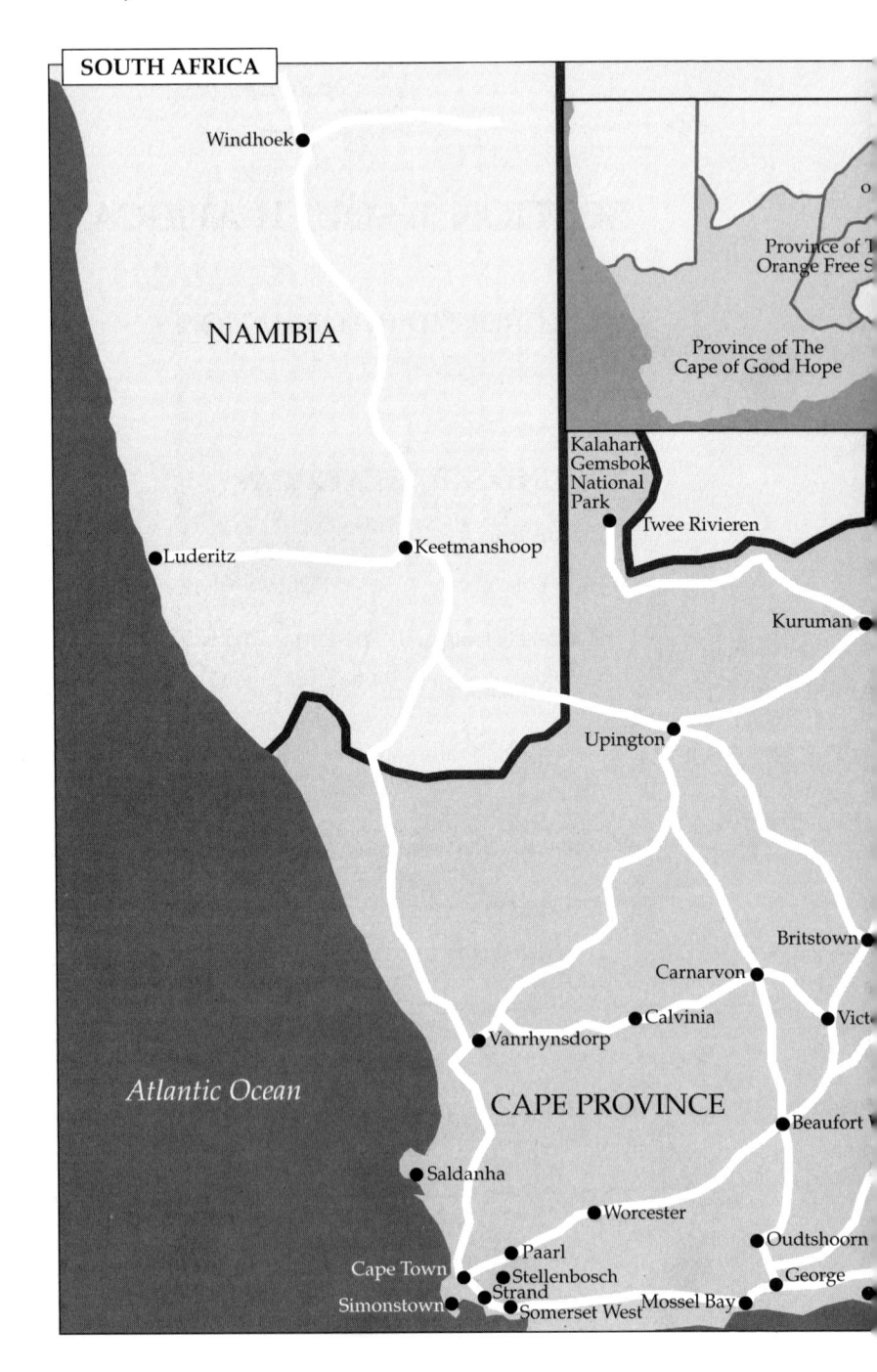

Mossel Bay

Map

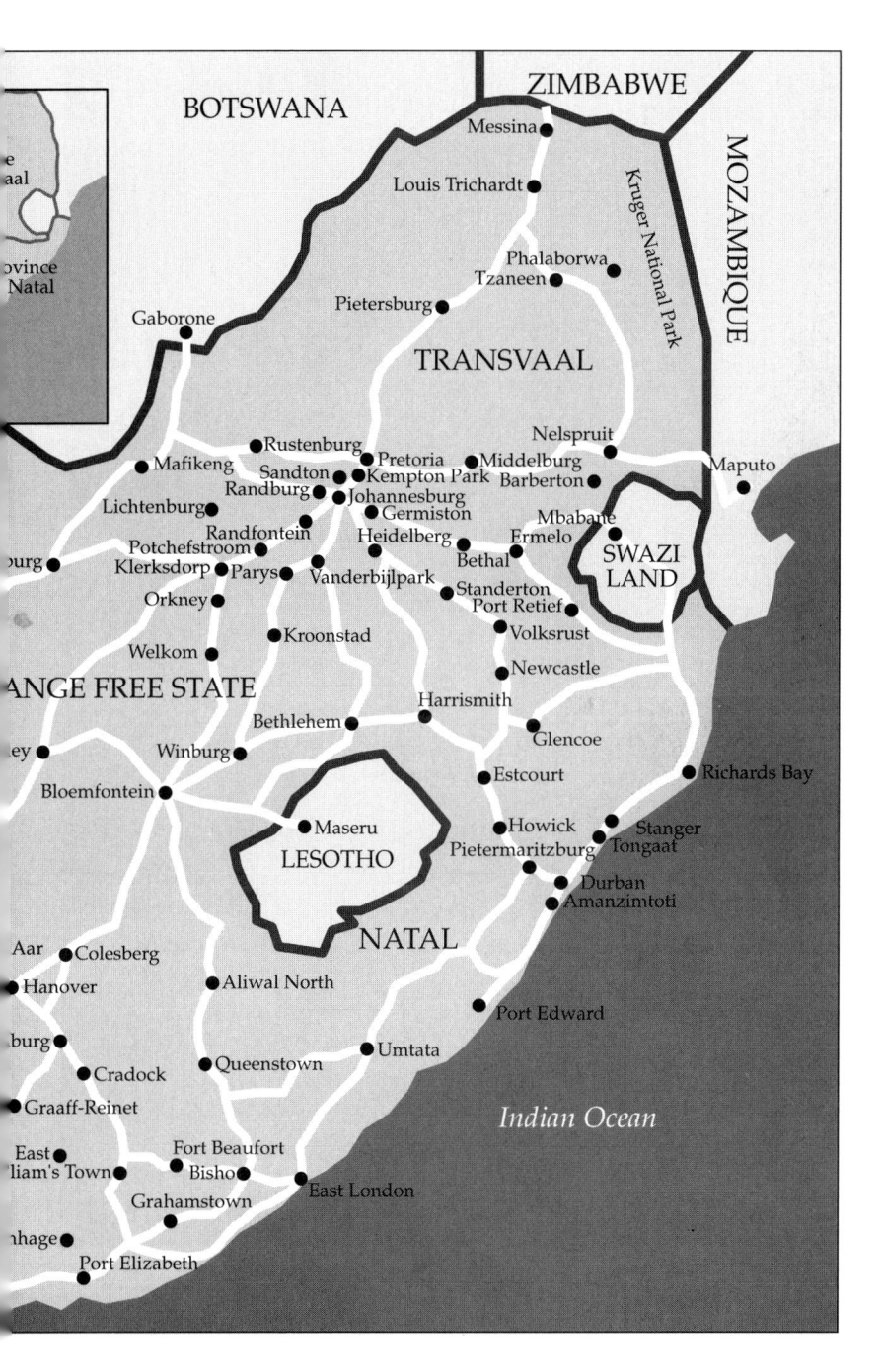

South Africa

The leopard is one of the most elusive predators.

BACKGROUND INFORMATION

INTRODUCTION

South Africa is a land of legendary beauty, of stunning landscapes and breathtaking diversity. The South African tourist industry boasts that visitors can experience 'the world in one country' and indeed it seems an accurate claim. Most travellers who have spent time in the other 49 countries of Africa are pleasantly surprised by the first-world facilitites and infrastructure in South Africa. Things work here and unless you are off the beaten track or in the bush, it is possible to forget that you are in Africa!

Despite the scenic splendour and fascinating destinations however, it is impossible for travellers to disregard the political and social realities of this country. South Africa, for all its look and feeling of normality, is in the throes of an inevitable transition. It is clear to most of its citizens, as well as to the rest of the world, that apartheid has been an abysmal failure and that the future of this country depends on communication and cooperation between black and white. Things are changing in South Africa; too rapidly for some, too slowly for others. The future belongs to the black majority and they know it; only the logistics and time-scale need to be resolved.

This is a guidebook, not a political or ideological primer, but it would be naïve to not address the current situation. Very few Westerners are unaware of the fear and violence that are interwoven into the life of people of all races. The media thrive on the sensational and there is plenty of grist for their mill in the townships. Barely a day passes without a new headline of yet another senseless massacre of ANC members by Inkatha or vice versa. Potential visitors are understandably left with an impression that South Africa is unsafe to visit. Is it or isn't it?

My personal view is that it is quite safe at present. I have every confidence in leading tours and planning itineraries to this country. As a white who has travelled extensively throughout the land, without benefit of a guide or a group, I can say quite categorically that I have never once been afraid for my safety. Moreover, as a white person, I have never experienced any racial animosity or hatred during my six years of extended visits to South Africa. It is actually my impression that there is more racial tension between blacks and whites in the United States than in this tormented country; why this is so, I cannot even begin to guess. South Africa has long fascinated and repelled the Western world; I wholeheartedly recommend that individuals intrigued by its potential and its dilemmas visit the country and see for themselves.

It would take at least six months to see all of South Africa, so I have just concentrated on its many highlights. In combination, even these selected destinations would necessitate a full month's holiday, so it is essential to plan your itinerary carefully, taking into account the time of year, your personal interests, your mode of travel, etcetera. A trip to South Africa should be as diverse as the country's terrain. A combination of outdoor activities, relaxed destinations, city lights and the indefinable wonder of the African bush will allow you to experience and savour the essence of the country. There is something here for everybody and any month is a good time to visit. In addition, the people are warm and friendly, the climate wonderfully agreeable, and travel is easy to all corners of the country. South Africa is a beguiling and powerful land: I have yet to meet an individual who has been there and not been bewitched by its beauty and its overwhelming potential. I hope you will find it equally thrilling and memorable.

TRAVEL FACTS

ENTRY REQUIREMENTS

All visitors to South Africa require valid passports. In addition, visas must be obtained except for those citizens of the United Kingdom, Ireland, Switzerland, Lichtenstein and Germany who are travelling to South Africa on holiday. To apply for a visa, contact the nearest South African consulate or embassy for an application form. There is no processing fee but allow

---

QUICK FACTS

TOTAL AREA: 1,220,430 sq km, five times the size of Britain or half the size of Europe, but still only 4 per cent of the area of Africa.

NEIGHBOURS: The Republic of South Africa is bordered by Namibia, Botswana and Zimbabwe to the north, Mozambique and Swaziland to the north-east, the Atlantic Ocean to the west and the Indian Ocean south and east.

POPULATION: In 1991 there were an estimated 38 million inhabitants, comprising a mere 5 per cent of the total population of Africa.

ETHNIC GROUPS: There are approximately 29 million blacks in South Africa, an overwhelming numerical majority. Whites number 5 million, coloureds (mixed race) 3 million and Asians 1 million. Within the black population there are ten distinct ethnic groups, each with its own cultural identity and language.

CAPITALS: South Africa has three capitals: Cape Town for legislative matters, Pretoria for administrative and Bloemfontein for judicial.

LANGUAGES: Afrikaans and English are the official languages of the country, and there are also a number of African languages.

RELIGION: 80 per cent of the population is Christian; Hindus, Muslims and Jews comprise the other major religious groups, in that order.

ELECTRICITY: 220/230 volts AC at 50 cycles per second

TIME: GMT plus 2 hours

CURRENCY: The unit of currency is the rand, which is divided into 100 cents. At the time of writing the rate of exchange was £1 = R4.80 and $1.00 = R2.80.

several weeks unless you are obtaining the visa in person. If you are travelling into neighbouring countries and then returning to South Africa, make sure you request a multiple entry visa.

Upon entering the country you will receive a temporary residence permit specifiying the length of time you may stay. Although I have never seen this happen, you may be asked to furnish proof of funds to support yourself, as well as an onward airline ticket. If you do not have a return ticket you may be asked to pay a cash deposit of R2,000 which is refundable upon departure.

CUSTOMS REGULATIONS

All valuables must be declared on entry; personal effects are duty free. Duty-free allowances are allowed as follows: one litre of spirits, two litres of wine, 50 ml of perfumery, 250 ml toilet water, 400 cigarettes, 50 cigars and 250 g of tobacco.

CURRENCY

The unit of currency is the rand which is divided into 100 cents. Visitors are allowed to bring as much foreign currency as they like into South Africa. On departure, only R200 in South African Reserve Bank notes may be exported. Any amount of foreign currency may be exported, provided it can be established that the foreign bank notes were brought into South Africa.

TAXES

South Africa has just switched from a general sales tax system to value added tax (VAT). At present, the rate is 10 per cent and applies to most purchases and services, with the exception of food.

GETTING THERE

Air: British Airways, Lufthansa, South African Airways (SAA), Olympic, Sabena, SAS, Swissair, TAP, UTA, Iberia, LuxAir, Alitalia and KLM all link Europe with South Africa. British Airways has daily flights from London to Johannesburg and flies to Cape Town (via Johannesburg) twice a week. Lufthansa has a scheduled service from Frankfurt to Johannesburg five times a week. SAA flies from London to Johannesburg daily, and from London to Cape Town twice a week. SAA also has services from Paris, Brussels, Amsterdam, Lisbon, Milan, Vienna and Zurich twice a week.

Although the fare structures on SAA and British Airways are similar, it bears mentioning that the London–Johannesburg route is one of the most expensive in the world. Virgin Airlines has recently applied for the route from London and has announced that it will reduce the ticket price dramatically if and when it begins service.

On 3 November 1991, SAA resumed its service from New York to Johannesburg, eliminating one day's travel time and a European stopover for US passengers. At present, the service is limited to four days a week in each direction; there is also once weekly service from Miami to Capetown.

South Africa

Direct flights from the US on a Super Apex fare cost roughly half what it costs to travel via Europe.

Direct flights from Australia to South Africa have also recently resumed; SAA and Quantas fly this route. SAA also connects Johannesburg with Hong Kong, Taipei, Singapore, Bangkok, Mauritius, Reunion, the Comoros, Nairobi, Abidjan, Lusaka, Harare, Gabarone, Windhoek, Maputo, Lilongwe, Manzini, Maseru and Kinshasa. Cathay Pacific has re-instituted a service from Hong Kong on a weekly basis and undoubtedly a number of other carriers will be flying again to South Africa in the very near future.

Sea: Few travellers arrive in South Africa by sea these days. However, there is one line which carries 128 passengers between Avonmouth and Cape Town. The voyage takes 30 days of which eight are spent on St Helena. There are departures from Britain six times a year; for complete details and fare structure, contact *Curnow Shipping*, c/o The Shipyard, Portleven, Helston, Cornwall; tel. (03265) 63434; fax (032665) 64347.

Since the lifting of sanctions, *Salen Lindblad Cruising* is offering a de luxe 24 day voyage that begins in Dakar and ends in Cape Town with a number of interesting stops along the way. For more information ring 202-967-2900 in the USA.

Road: It is quite easy to drive to South Africa from any of the neighbouring countries. From Botswana, Namibia and Zimbabwe the major roads to Johannesburg are tarred. A number of border posts are maintained between the countries; hours of attendance are generally 6 a.m.–8 p.m. but these can vary so it is best to check in advance. Ring (011) 314-8911 or contact the AA of South Africa for exact details (Tel. (011) 403-5700).

GETTING AROUND

Air: SAA is the national carrier and connects Johannesburg with Cape Town, Durban, George, Port Elizabeth, East London, Kimberley, Bloemfontein and Nelspruit. Smaller regional airlines serve these and other principal towns in South Africa. The various routes are too numerous to list here so it is best to consult your travel agent or SAR Travel. The names and telephone numbers of many carriers are listed under **Service** in the relevant chapters of the text.

Visitors who travel to South Africa on SAA should be aware of a special offer called the 'See South Africa Fare'. Overseas travellers are permitted to purchase five flight segments on SAA for travel within the country for R799. There are certain restrictions on these tickets but if you plan to visit different regions of South Africa, this is a good buy.

Road: The road network in South Africa rivals that of any Western country. Motorists drive on the left-hand side of the road, a legacy of the British administration. Standard international signs are used, and most are bilingual. The use of seat belts is mandatory and although it is relatively rare to see highway police on the roads, radar cameras are used to monitor speed. South Africa has one of the highest motor accident rates in the world, so extra caution is needed.

Travel Facts

> **THE BLUE TRAIN**
>
> This train, which plies the route between Pretoria and Cape Town, is one of the most fabled in the world. The salons, lounge and bar compartment and dining car are elegantly and tastefully decorated. The cuisine is gourmet and passengers dress for dinner. Accommodation is divided into four categories, ranging from one exclusive three-roomed suite, complete with bath, to twin and single compartments with private bathrooms, to a number of compartments with shared ablution facilities. Service is flawless and there are few more romantic and relaxed ways to travel. All coaches are fully airconditioned, windows are tinted with a layer of gold to make sightseeing more pleasurable and the train is virtually noiseless. As an added incentive, the scenery is magnificent, especially the passage through the winelands of the Cape Province. The Blue Train is extremely popular and reservations are difficult. The journey takes approximately 24 hours and departs on Mondays, Wednesdays and Fridays in both directions all year round. To book, phone (011) 774-3929 or consult SAR Travel offices world-wide, or your travel agent.
>
> *The Trans-Karoo.* If you are unable to make reservations on the Blue Train or if the fare is too steep, consider the Trans-Karoo. It also covers the distance from Johannesburg to Cape Town, and although the train is not nearly as luxurious, it is perfectly adequate. For reservations and information, ring (011) 773-2944.

Rail: There is an extensive railway system in South Africa and most cities have a direct link with Johannesburg. There are additional services to Zimbabwe, Namibia and Mozambique. The trains are clean and punctual and the food is good. This country is one of the last bastions of the steam engine so if you are an aficionado, you will be ecstatic. There are several excursions by steam train discussed in this book, notably Rovos Rail, the Outeniqua Choo Tjou and the Banana Express.

Coach: Coaches in South Africa are of the first world rather than the third world variety. The concept is still rather new in this country but the system is being expanded and offers the budget traveller an alternative to costly hire cars and flights. Service currently connect Pretoria, Johannesburg, Nelspruit, Durban, Cape Town, Port Elizabeth and George, with stops *en route*. For more detailed information contact one of the SAR Travel offices (see page 168) or Greyhound Inter-City on (011) 7 62-2544.

Car Hire: There are hundreds of companies hiring vehicles in South Africa in addition to the international firms such as Avis and Budget. If you are planning to tour the country by car, some advance research is advisable. Unless you are doing a circular tour it may be more advantageous to arrange for a car which can be dropped at a different town from where it was originally hired. The large agencies are usually able to offer this service as they maintain offices in all major towns and airports. Kilometre charges can also add up fast; ask if there is a rate that includes unlimited mileage. In most cases, too, the rate is lower and there is no excess kilometre charge if you make a reservation before you leave home. It is always worth shopping

South Africa

around for the best deal as it is surprising how varied the tariffs can be.

To hire a car in South Africa you must be at least 23 years old and have a valid driver's licence. If your licence does not bear your photograph, obtain an international driver's licence before you leave home. Some of the major South African car hire firms are:

African Self-Drive Safaris (fully equipped Land Rovers), PO Box 39859, Bramley 2018. Tel. (011) 802-2282

Imperial Car Rental (formerly Hertz), PO Box 260177, Excom 2023. Tel. (011) 337-6100

Europcar, P.O. Box 16736, Doornfontein 2028. Tel. (011)402-6328

The Automobile Association (AA) of South Africa is happy to assist international members of this organization with all aspects of road travel in the country. Their address is:
AA House, 6 de Korte St, Braemfontein, Johannesburg 2000. Tel. (011) 403-5700; fax (011) 339-2058

Caravans: South Africa has over 650 caravan parks and the great majority of these are located in areas of scenic beauty and interest. With fine weather all year round and an excellent road system, a caravan holiday is a super way to tour the country. A number of reputable companies offer fully equipped caravans for hire; a partial list is given below. For more information on parks and facilities, contact the *South African Tourist Board*, the AA (see above), or the *Caravan Club of South Africa* (P.O. Box 50580, Randburg 2125) .

Capricorn Tours & Campers, 39 Elsenham Ave., Somerset West 7130. Tel. (024) 55-2331; fax (024) 55-4062

Priclo Caravans, 299 Koeberg Rd, Brooklyn 7405. Tel. (021) 511-4208

Campers Corner, 357 Jan Smuts Ave., Craighall Park. Tel. (011) 787-9105; fax (011) 0787-6900

Natal Sprite, 6 Kirk Rd, Pinetown 3610. Tel. (031)72-7291; fax (031) 72-7209

CLIMATE

The climate of South Africa is usually temperate and sunny, with mild winters and warm summers. It is a large country, however, and there are many regional and seasonal variations that make it difficult to generalize. More than 40 per cent of South Africa's total area lies above 1,220 metres, a factor that contributes directly to climatic conditions.

There are two main climatic regions in the country. One is the coastal belt which extends from Cape Town to Port Elizabeth (the Garden Route) and north from Cape Town to the Namibian border. In this region the climate is considered Mediterranean. In Cape Town and inland, the rain falls in the winter and summer is dry and sunny; to the east, along the Garden Route, the rains are evenly distributed throughout the year. The second climatic region is by far the largest, occurring along the Natal coast and throughout the vast interior of the country. Influenced by the currents of the Indian Ocean, Natal is blessed with a subtropical climate and is warm and humid all the year-round. The vast interior of South Africa consists of an enormous plateau which varies in altitude from 1,800 metres in the Transvaal area to 900 metres in the north-western Karoo. Here the weather is typically dry with rainfall in the summer. Summer temperatures are high, around 25°C; winters are sunny with cold nights and snow occasionally falls in the highest areas.

South Africa is blessed with more hours of sunshine than most places in the world, a fact which undoubtedly adds to travellers' enjoyment. It lies well to the south of the equator, and its seasons are therefore the reverse of those in the northern hemisphere.

AVERAGE TEMPERATURE CHART (Celsius)

	Summer	Winter	Hrs. of Sun	Ocean
Cape Town	21.4	13.0	8.4	21.0
Durban	24.0	16.5	6.6	18.5 -26.5
Johannesburg	21.0	10.5	8.7	—
Port Elizabeth	21.0	13.5	7.9	17.0 -23.5

HEALTH

South Africa has the highest health standards on the continent and modern medical treatment is readily available. However, as with Africa in general, there are hazards which necessitate precautionary measures. Malaria is the most serious of these, although only in the Transvaal *lowfeld*, which includes the Kruger National Park, and in Zululand in northern Natal is malaria endemic. Check with your doctor before you leave home and get anti-malarial medication. If this is inconvenient, they are available over the counter in South Africa and they give them out at the Kruger National Park.

Schistosomiasis or bilharzia as it is commonly called, exists in some rivers in Natal and the Transvaal. You can't tell by looking, so the best prevention is to stay out of the water, especially in populated areas where the current is slow. Bilharzia is a parasite which infects the liver. It is easily curable but the danger lies in the difficulty of diagnosis in Europe or North America, where this parasite is uncommon and thus likely to be overlooked.

There is no yellow fever or cholera in South Africa and inoculations are not required unless you are entering the country via an infected area. Many doctors recommend updating your tetanus, hepatitis and polio vaccinations as a general precaution for overseas travel.

Because the level of hygiene is high and there are modern sanitation facilities, travel in South Africa is much simpler and safer, from a health point of view, than most places in the world. A number of AIDS cases have been reported but the problem is very small at the moment in comparison to the rest of Africa or the Western world. There is no national health service here, so visitors should be aware that they are responsible for their own medical expenses. It is wise to obtain medical insurance before leaving home.

WHAT TO PACK

If you are spending time in the cities of South Africa, dress standards are much the same as in any cosmopolitan city in the West. Businessmen wear suits and ties at the office, in exclusive hotels, and at night when dining out. If your holiday is centred around game parks and beach resorts then your selection of clothing should be much more casual. Neutral-coloured clothes that don't need a lot of pressing will be most useful on safari. Sturdy shoes, a lightweight jacket and long trousers are mandatory for any time of the year in the game parks. At the beach, dressy clothing for evenings might be suitable in the luxury hotels and elegant restaurants, but would not be obligatory. The trend is toward 'smart casual', which on the one hand means no shorts, dungarees or sandals but on the other hand means forget ties and jackets.

SHOPPING

There is plenty to spend your money on in South Africa. It produces a full range of consumer goods as well as luxury items. Unlike most of its neighbours, South Africa experiences no shortages and imported goods are readily available. Because the value of the Rand is so low at present against most foreign currencies, there are very good bargains to be had. Clothing, shoes, leather goods, art, wine and handicrafts all seem inexpensive. However, gold, diamonds and precious gems are comparable in price to jewellery in the USA and Europe, so don't look for big savings in this department. Foreigners are often given discounts upon presentation of their passports and return air tickets, so if you see something special, be sure to ask.

There are many shops throughout the country specializing in African art, artefacts, antiques and curios. The quality of the work tends to be very high and shipping can easily be arranged. Ostrich, crocodile and other exotic leather items are sold at some of the lowest prices I have ever encountered anywhere in the world; ostrich and crocodile farms are big businesses in this country, so it is not surprising that prices are reasonable. Workmanship is excellent; in some cases the skins are sent to Italy for crafting. Prices are lowest at the farms themselves, but selection and sizes are often limited in these small shops. If you purchase crocodile goods and are returning to the United States, be sure to ask for the CITES paperwork, which certifies that the skins were legitimately farm-raised.

Shopping hours are generally 8 a.m.–5 p.m. Monday–Friday and 1 p.m. on Saturday. Very few shops are open at night, on Sundays or holidays. Credit cards are widely accepted throughout the country.

NATIONAL PARKS

South Africa was the first country on the continent to establish game reserves. It was recognized as early as the mid-seventeenth century that certain animals needed protection from unregulated hunting. By the late

Travel Facts

nineteenth century, there were moves to establish sanctuaries to avoid the wholesale extinction of entire species of flora and fauna by hunters, zoologists and scientists. Today there is a widespread system of national parks in South Africa, as well as over 100 municipal parks and sanctuaries and dozens of game reserves. They are extremely well organized and maintained, with excellent facilities and easy access. In addition, some of the parks have a number of wilderness hiking trails with strategically located overnight huts.

Of the 18 national parks, the Kruger is the most renowned ; because of its incredible wildlife, it is also the most popular. However, each has something unique to offer the visitor and a common aspect of them all is spectacular scenery. Accommodation facilities are available in all of the parks and may be reserved up to one year in advance. To describe each one adequately would need a book in itself; instead, those most likely to be of interest to the traveller are covered in the relevant regional sections. For detailed information and reservations contact one of the following National Parks Board (NPB) offices:

PO Box 787, Pretoria 0001. Tel. (012) 44-1191; fax (012) 44-1171 Ext. 2112

PO Box 7400, Roggebaai 8012. Tel. (021) 419-5365

PO Box 774, George 6530. Tel. (0441) 746-9241

Natal Parks Board, PO Box 662, Pietermaritzburg 3200. Tel. (0331) 47-1981; fax (0331) 94-7374

TOURIST INFORMATION

The *South African Tourist Board* (SATOUR) maintains offices in most European countries and in the United States. These offices have numerous first-rate publications and maps that are available free of charge.

London Office, 5-6 Alt Grove, Wimbledon, London SW19 4BZ. Tel. 081-944-6646

U.S. Offices, 747 Third Ave., New York, NY 10017. Tel. 212-838-8841
9465 Wilshire Blvd., Suite 721, Beverly Hills, CA. Tel. 213-275-4111

There are also offices in Toronto, Sydney, Paris, Frankfurt, Amsterdam, Milan, Zurich, Hong Kong, Tokyo and Tel Aviv. Within South Africa there are regional SATOUR offices in all of the major cities and at Jan Smuts Airport in the international arrivals hall. Many small towns have excellent information bureaux and will assist with hotel and restaurant suggestions, sightseeing and maps.

If you need help booking accommodation or flights when you are planning your itinerary, a number of *SAR Travel* offices abroad are ready to assist you. SAR Travel is a division of *Transnet,* South Africa's largest transport company which owns SAA and the railways. Essentially these are government travel agencies and they are able to arrange most anything, including excursions to neighbouring countries. There is no fee for their service and you can contact them direct or get your travel agent to work through them.

London Office, 266 Regent Street, 5th Floor, London W1R 5DA. Tel. 071-287-1133; fax 071-287-1134

US Office, 1100 East Broadway, Glendale, CA. 91205. Tel. 818-549-1921 or 800-727-7207; fax 818-507-5802

ACTIVITIES

I've tried, but I just can't think of a single sport or activity that is not available in South Africa. From the relative simplicity of hiking to the excitement of caving or paragliding, an incredible diversity of sporting and leisure activities await the visitor.

The various sections of the book deal with the activities available in particular places. Tennis, squash and golf are easy to find just about anywhere in the country so I have concentrated on compiling a list of some of the organizations and companies that specialize in more unusual activities.

Gliding
The Witswatersrand Gliding Trust, PO Box 6875, Johannesburg 2000. Tel. (011) 615-2461

Hang Gliding
Drifters, PO Box 48434, Roosevelt Park 2129. Tel. (011) 673-7012

Hot Air Ballooning
Lifestyle Travel, PO.Box 67, Randburg 2125. Tel. (011) 705-3201; fax (011) 705-3203

Game Fishing
Garden Route Tours, PO Box 4179, George East 6539. Tel. (0441) 70-7993

African Fishing Safaris, PO Box 124, Bergvliet 7945. Tel. (021) 72-1272; fax (021) 75-3283

Mountaineering
Trailblazers, PO Box 18692, Hillbrow 2038. Tel. (011) 724-5198

Hunting
SATOUR offices can provide information and fee schedules or contact:

The Professional Hunters' Association of South Africa, PO Box 770, Cramerview 2060. Tel. (011) 706-7724

M. Flanagan Associates, Hunting, 18 Fouche St, Pierre van Rynevald Park, Verwoerdburg 0140. Tel. (011) 331-9671

Skiing
Rhodes Ski Resort (North-eastern Cape; open June–August). Tel. (02211) 64-2092

White Water Rafting/Canoe Trips
River Runners, PO Box 583, Constantia 7848. Tel. (021) 705-8878

Aqua Trails, 2 Tudor Mansions, Leeuwenvoet Rd, Tamboerskloof 8001. Tel. (021) 24-7686

Mine Visits

With the exception of the *Crown Mine* at Gold Reef City and the *Premier Diamond Mine* in Cullinan, the general public has little access to the mines of South Africa. Professionals in the field and individuals who are seriously interested in a closer look at the mining industry, can request tours by writing well in advance to the *Public Affairs Advisor, Chamber of Mines*, PO Box 61809, Marshalltown 2107; tel. (011)838-8211.

Travel Facts

ADVENTURE SAFARIS

If you want to do more than sightsee, there are hundreds of adventure trips available specializing in novel and exciting ways to see South Africa. For detailed information, prices and itineraries, please contact these companies directly or consult your travel agent.

Canoe Safaris
Fish River Canoe Adventures, PO Box 207, Grahamstown 6140. Tel. (0461) 2-7855

River Runners, P.O. Box 31117, Braamfontein 2017. Tel. (011) 403-2512

Venture Trails, P.O. Box 231, Howard Place 7450. Tel. (021) 25-2886; fax (021) 21-7209

Cycling/Hiking
Drifters, PO Box 48434, Roosevelt Park 2129. Tel. (011) 486-1224; fax (011) 486-1237

Horseback Trails
Drifters (see above)

Sunwa Ventures , PO Box 1595, Parklands 2121. Tel. (011) 788-5120

Overland Safaris
Afro Ventures Ltd., PO Box 2339, Randburg 2125. Tel. (011) 789-1078; fax (011) 886-2349

Overland Safaris (specializes in Lesotho), PO Box 82, Warden 9890. Tel. (013342) ask for Roadside 7330

River Rafting
River Rats, PO Box 1157, Kelvin 2054. Tel. (011) 786-5482 or (021) 72-5094; fax (011) 786-5497

Sunwa Ventures Pro Rafting Tours, PO Box 1595, Parklands 2121. Tel. (011) 788-5120

River Rafters, P.O. Box 1157, Kelvin 2054. Tel. (011) 786-5482; fax (011) 786-5497

Sailing
Lifestyle Travel, PO Box 67, Randburg 2125. Tel. (011) 705-3201; fax (011705-3203

Scuba Diving
Ocean Divers International, PO Box 5624, Walmer 6065. Tel. (041) 51-5121; fax (041) 56-3791
(Diving in Shark Cages Adventure is offered)

ACCOMMODATION

The South African Tourist Board controls the standard of hotels and awards gradings from one to five stars. One star denotes a good hotel and five stars signifies an establishment comparable to the best anywhere in the world. There are also non-graded establishments which include guest houses, game lodges, rest camps, holiday flats, bungalows and cottages, youth hostels and guest farms. The fact that these are not assigned a rating does not mean that they are inferior. On the contrary, some of the ungraded game lodges, such as MalaMala, are among the most luxurious and expensive in the world.

South Africa has several major hotel chains. *Southern Sun/Holiday Inns* owns a number of hotels in the 3–5 star range. The company also has a division called Sun International with four and five star hotels throughout the nominally independent homelands as well as in Namibia, Botswana, the Comoros, Mauritius, Swaziland and Lesotho. Another large hotel chain in South Africa is called *Protea Hotels and Inns* and it has a preponderance of

South Africa

1–3 star hotels, formerly family-owned, in most small cities. At the budget end of the spectrum, *City Lodge* is a good bet. Regardless of where you choose to stay, the standard of accommodation, cleanliness and service is very high throughout the country.

A number of publications are available free of charge from SAR Travel offices which detail accommodation possiblities. Of particular interest is the *Portfolio of Country Places*. This booklet advertises a number of lovely country retreats and game lodges, all of which are characterized by attention to detail, service and remarkable location or setting. A similar publication is *The Independent Small Hotels of South Africa*. The dozen or so hotels pictured in this brochure are all luxurious and represent some of the finest establishments in the country. To make advance reservations at any of South Africa's hotels, consult your travel agent or SAR Travel.

The YMCA and YWCA maintain accommodation in the major cities of South Africa. There are also youth hostels, although not many. Camp and caravan parks abound, providing a less expensive and more flexible alternative to hotels. The campsites are located in some of the country's most beautiful regions and facilities are always top-notch. The following addresses may be helpful in researching accommodation.

South African Youth Hostels Association, PO Box 4402, Cape Town 8000. Tel. (021) 419-1853

YMCA National Office, 104 Rissik St, Johannesburg 2001. Tel. (011) 724-4541

YWCA National Office, 408 Dunwell House, 35 Jorissen St, Braamfontein 2001. Tel. (011) 339-8212

Bed and Breakfast Ltd, PO Box 31124, Braamfontein 2017. Tel. (011) 726-6915

FOOD

There is no shortage of restaurants in South Africa and in the metropolitan areas just about any kind of cuisine can be found. Not all restaurants are licensed to sell spirits or wine and beer. Some establishments carry a full licence, others can serve only wine and malt beverages, and a number sell nothing alcoholic at all. It is always best to check in advance, because if a restaurant is unlicensed you may bring in your own alcohol.

South Africa has the best food in Africa, no great surprise when one considers that this country grows most of the food on the continent. With its fortuitous position, sandwiched between two great oceans, seafood is fresh and plentiful. Oysters, rock lobsters (called crayfish), mussels, abalone (called perlemoen) and dozens of species of salt water fish are harvested from the sea. Of the fish, kingklip, snoek, kabeljou (cob) and steenbras are among the most popular. In addition, agriculture is a thriving industry in South Africa. All kinds of fresh fruits, vegetables and dairy products are available and are reasonably priced.

South Africa is a nation of meat lovers: excellent beef, Karoo lamb, pork, *boerewors* (sausages) and a wide assortment of game meats are abundant. The national passtime is the barbecue, called a *braai* (pronounced 'bry' and short for *braaivleis*). *Braai*-mania has swept the country and no park, campsite or back yard is without its *braai*. Sauces are *de rigueur* (the unfortunately named monkey-gland sauce is a favourite) and special varieties of wood and cuts of meat are considered essential for the proper *braai*. Often the grilled meat is accompanied by *mielie pap* (cornmeal mush), which gets a hefty dose of special sauce, presumably to lend it some flavour.

A number of cultural influences have left their mark on the cuisine of this country. British, French, German, Indian, Chinese, Malaysian and Indonesian influences are all evident and the piquant spices of the Portuguese are also frequently detectable. South Africa's most interesting and unique cuisine is referred to as traditional Cape or Malay fare. This cuisine is the legacy of the indigenous population of the Cape Province and was greatly influenced by the food and spices of the Dutch East Indies. The slave cooks, brought to South Africa from Indonesia and Malaysia, introduced their spicy recipes and a wonderful amalgamation of local and exotic ingredients was the result. No visitor to this country should miss trying one of the hallmark dishes, such as *bobotie* (minced meat with apricots, almonds, curry and chutney), *bredie* (vegetable or lamb ragouts), or *smoorsnoek* (smoked fish).

South Africa has a highly regarded wine industry centred near Cape Town. The wine is excellent and is extremely reasonably priced by European or American standards. Unlike the locally produced wine in many African countries, which is barely potable, South Africa's wineries date back to the seventeenth century and the arrival of the French Huguenots. Varietal grapes from European stock are grown so much of the wine will be very familiar to overseas visitors. South Africa also has two native varieties: Pinotage, a cross between Pinot Noir and Cinsaut, and Steen, believed to be a mutation of Sauvignon Blanc. Most restaurants that are licensed to sell alcoholic beverages will offer a good to excellent selection of South African wines. Many older vintages are available in the finer establishments; foreign wines, however, are difficult to find and quite expensive.

A number of brands of lager beer are brewed in South Africa and they are all very good; Castle and Lion are two of the most popular. A full range of international spirits and liqueurs is available; in comparison with most countries, prices are very fair. South Africa also produces two interesting liqueurs: Van der Hum, made from tangerines and Amarula, distilled from the marula berry.

TIPPING

Service is not added to licensed restaurant or hotel bills in South Africa, by law. If an establishment is not licensed to sell alcohol or wine and malt beverages, they may add a service charge, so long as it is prominently stated on the menu. Tipping tends to be less generous in South Africa than in America or Europe. Gratuities should reflect the quality of service received, so it is difficult to generalize. Ten per cent seems to be the norm for restaurant staff, taxi drivers and tour guides. I usually tip porters two rands per bag and leave 3–5 per day for chambermaids.

COUNTRY FILE

HISTORY

Prehistory

The history of man in Southern Africa is believed to have begun some 2–3 million years ago. As in East Africa, there is fossil and artefactual evidence that evolutionary processes occurred over the millennia in the subcontinent culminating in the transmogrification of hominids into beings classified as humans. These earliest peoples were strictly hunters and gatherers well into the Late Stone Age. The San and Khoikhoi people who populated the region that is now called South Africa are believed to have developed from an ancient African stock that evolved in the subcontinent. The Late Stone Age life of the indigenous San and Khoikhoi is known to some extent through the magnificent cave and rock paintings found in several regions of South Africa. From this art it can be determined that the Khoikhoi people (popularly called Hottentots), had established a pastoral culture based on cattle and sheep by the time of European contact, some 2,000 years ago. The San people (commonly known as Bushmen), on the other hand, never became pastoralists, leading a hunter-gatherer life-style well into the twentieth century. Today, very few San retain this indigenous culture, having been forced to adapt as best they can to modern influences and pressures.

The Pre-Colonial Era

Historians suggest that as early as the third to fifth centuries AD and through to the fifteenth century, Bantu-speaking groups from Central and East Africa began migrating and settling in parts of South Africa, bringing with them Iron Age skills and culture. An accumulation of wealth occurred in a number of societies, spurred by the long-distance trade in copper and gold which flourished in South Africa from the eleventh century on. The Iron Age mines and remains of impressive stone settlements such as that at Mapungubwe in the northern Transvaal, indicate the great power and wealth that were amassed. With the advent of such prosperity, social organizations and hierarchies, settled village life, agriculture, pottery and iron-working technologies evolved and it is believed that many of the indigenous Stone Age peoples were absorbed, leaving remnant groups in the more arid and southern fringes of the continent. In any event, archaeological and linguistic evidence points to a close association between the indigenous San and Khoikhoi and the Bantu communities. Without a doubt, these early Bantu-speaking peoples are the ancestors of the majority of the black population in South Africa today.

Not all of the Bantu settlements revolved around mining and trading of course, for farming was a predominant way of life for the majority. The agriculturalists were not really affected by the trade and accumulation of power and wealth by the elite societies. They lived in small communities based on kinship, and were ruled by a chief presumably chosen by virtue of royal genealogy. By the beginning of the sixteenth century, these Iron Age farming tribes were for the most part established in their present locations along the Highveld escarpment and south-eastern coast of South Africa. Cultural and ethnic identities distinguished the societies, although population pressures, finite resources and the militarization of certain tribes ensured that the situation would not remain static for long.

Colonialism in the Cape Colony

The first recorded European to arrive in South Africa was the Portuguese navigator, Batholemew Dias, who sailed around the southern edge of the continent in 1488, landing in Mossel Bay. His mission was to find a sea route to India although this was only achieved by his successor, Vasco da Gama, a decade later.

Although the Portuguese went on to conquer and rule a number of countries in Africa along both coasts, they never turned their attention to the southern perimeter of the continent. Colonization of South Africa was left to the Dutch and subsequently the British. In 1652 a Dutchman by the name of Jan van Riebeeck was sent by the Dutch East India Company with an entourage of 125 men to establish a permanent revictualing station at the Cape of Good Hope. By the late sixteenth century the Cape had become a crucial stop for European ships *en route* to the Indies; fresh water was needed and in addition, the indigenous Khoikhoi were willing to barter cattle in exchange for tobacco, brandy and metal beads and implements. The very powerful Dutch East India Company had the foresight to see that a refreshment stop for their trading vessels was a necessary investment . It was never their intention, however, to colonize the region, merely to establish an outpost which would procure and grow such provisions as were needed for the outbound crews.

Inevitably, however, the small original colony grew in population and area and before long the Dutch East India Company was having difficulty controlling the farmers, who became known as Boers (which is Dutch for 'farmers'). The climate of the Cape region was suited to European settlement and agriculture, and although the indigenous Khoikhoi were resistant to white expansionism, they were unable to stop the rapid advance of the new cattle farmers, or *trekboers* as they came to be known. The *trekboers* settled just far enough away from the Cape Colony for government control to be unfeasible. They became accustomed to making their own rules and solving their own problems. With very few white women around, interbreeding between *trekboers*, San and Khoikhoi was commonplace and a separate ethnic group known as 'Cape coloured' resulted. By the mid-eighteenth century a rigid racial hierarchy had evolved, the precursor of a legalized system of discrimination called apartheid.

At the heart of the Khoisan resistance to the Dutch was the issue of labour. From the outset the Dutch had prohibited the enslavement of the San and Khoikhoi and had instead imported slaves from the East Indies beginning in 1658. Both the farmers and merchants of the Cape and the semi-nomadic *trekboers* were utterly dependent on slave labour and as the settler population grew, there was a corresponding increase in the number of slaves in the Colony. As the indigenous population lost their land and

South Africa

livestock, they too were forced to enter into service with the whites in increasing numbers. However, the existence of a large slave labour population endangered their opportunities and status. Although the Khoikhoi had been afforded the legal status of 'freemen', in fact their condition closely resembled that of slaves, and they became virtual serfs on white farms.

As the Cape's role in the world market expanded, it was matched by an intensive exploitation of labour, culminating in a virtual guerrilla war between the Boers and the Khoikhoi. Decimated by European diseases, outnumbered and outgunned, the Khoikhoi managed nonetheless to mount a resistance largely based on continual cattle raids which interrupted colonial expansion northwards for a period of thirty years. Despite the vigour of their response, ultimately the natives were unable to stop colonial expansion, and were eventually subordinated to the white system or absorbed by Bantu tribes. The San people on the other hand, were without cattle, land or agricultural skills but they also fared badly as the settlers encroached into their traditional territory. Many were driven into arid and mountainous regions and thousands were killed in retaliation for cattle raiding.

Encountering resistance and challenges on the northern frontier of the Cape, a number of *trekboers* looked eastwards as demands for fresh meat escalated and reserves of Khoisan cattle were exhausted. These *trekboers* however, found their path blocked here by the established Xhosa settlements in the area of the Great Fish River. Peaceful contact and trade with the Xhosa had begun in the early years of the eighteenth century, but within 50 years the whites and blacks were on a collision course, competing for grazing land and water in this region. By the end of the century the frequent cattle raids and skirmishes had escalated into a full-scale frontier war that was to erupt periodically for almost 100 years.

In 1795 the British took possession of the Cape for a period of eight years during the Napoleonic Wars. In 1803 rule reverted to the Dutch, but only until 1806 when the British once again gained control. By this time the settlement had grown to number 22,000 whites dominating approximately 25,000 slaves and countless Khoisan serfs.

To say that British rule was unpopular with the established Afrikaner (Dutch) community would be a gross understatement. For over 150 years the burghers and farmers had been more or less left to their own devices, isolated from the changes occurring in the rest of the world. When Britain assumed sovereignty, the Industrial Revolution was in full flow in Europe, with its attendant complex social, economical and ideological concerns. The British colonial government had 'modern' notions of land reform, taxation, legislation, commodity production and labour relations that outraged and threatened the Afrikaners and their very way of life. Some 5,000 British settlers arrived in 1820 and a solid middle class was formed. The crown granted representative government to the colony and in 1853 a colour-blind franchise was introduced that included the substantial coloured population. The British hoped that this would swing the coloured vote in their favour and counteract the influence of the Afrikaners.

If the Boers were aghast at this step, a more crucial and inflammatory issue was the abolition of slavery; this the British engineered by banning the slave trade in 1807, followed by the emancipation of existing slaves in 1834. It was readily apparent to the British that a mere decree was not going to effect change in South Africa, and so the Government attempted to regulate the relationship between masters and servants to ensure equality before the law and a transition from serfdom to contracted wage labour. The British notion of free labour was anathema to the Afrikaner and this issue, combined with increasing government interference in their lives, prompted several thousand of them to gather their possessions (and slaves) and leave the colony on what has become known as the Great Trek. Little in Afrikaner history is more romanticised or revered than this self-imposed exile and the subsequent trials of this pioneer group. The mythology is potent today and the National Party which has governed South Africa since 1949 still relies on the imagery and history of the Great Trek to instil in its white constituency a sense of destiny and righteousness in the face of world-wide condemnation. The trekkers migrated northwards and crossed the Orange and Vaal Rivers, establishing the Boer republics of Orange Free State and the Transvaal; both were granted autonomy from British rule in the 1850s.

The nineteenth century was not an easy time for either British or Boer in South Africa. Colonial expansion was the order of the day and as we have seen, since the early days of the Cape Colony there was concerted resistance to this on the part of the Khoisan and Xhosa people. The Cape's eastern frontier was the scene of the fiercest and most prolonged fighting. By 1811 British soldiers were permanently stationed along this front and the Xhosa had retreated east of the Great Fish River. Despite the apparent superiority of the settlers, there were constant skirmishes and no less than ten wars were waged between 1795 and 1879. Land was the issue on which most of them were fought. The Xhosa, used a pastoral life-style and the freedom to move on to new pastures when the need arose, did not understand the formal notion of ownership which the British introduced. They were formidable opponents, well armed and well versed in guerrilla tactics. Their downfall was really caused by internal strife, not superior British forces. For too long they had been crowded into progressively smaller areas, causing friction among the chiefdoms. By 1880, exhausted by a century of struggle, impoverished and displaced, the Xhosa were finally defeated. From this point on, the remaining African strongholds and territories between the Cape and Natal were annexed peacefully to the British Colony

The Independent Boer Republics

The two Boer republics established in the Transvaal and the Orange Free State in the 1850s were also the scene of constant friction between whites and blacks; notably, the trekkers suffered grievously at the hands of the treacherous Zulu king, Dingane. The issues were the same here as in the ever-advancing Cape Colony: land and livestock.

The trekkers' arrival in this central interior region had coincided with the rise to power of the legendary Zulu king, Shaka. Historians agree that Shaka possessed a great military genius, hitherto unparalleled in Southern Africa, that was given full expression in the first quarter of the nineteenth century. His reign of terror became known as the *Mfecane*, which means 'the crushing'. Drought, population pressures and competition for land were the catalysts for a mounting disorder among the chiefdoms; Shaka was opportunistic enough to take advantage of the inexorably deteriorating situation. He organized and trained his Zulu warriors into an efficient fighting machine, which in turn subdued and subjugated neighbouring tribes. In a matter of just a few years Shaka had created a ruthless military kingdom which stretched from Delagoa Bay, in what is today Mozambique, to Pondoland, south Natal.

Many treatises on South African history would have you believe that when the Boer settlers reached the Transvaal and Orange Free State, they found it empty; that they had not appropriated any black territory for it was unoccupied and thus theirs for the taking. There is no doubt that the Zulu hordes, led first by Shaka and then by the renegade, Mzilikazi, had disrupted African life and that many tribes had fled in response to the Zulu reign of terror. Evidence of their established pastoral communities would have remained, however, so it is naïve to believe that the white trekkers were unaware of African settlements in this area that predated their arrival. When the *Mfecane* had run its course and the Africans gradually returned to their traditional lands, it was only to discover that both their cattle and land were gone. A way of life had been irretrievably shattered and there was no recourse but to seek employment on white farms, on the very land that had previously been their own. A ready source of labour was now at hand.

Meanwhile, two portentous discoveries altered the course of South African history; first, diamonds were discovered in 1868, followed by the discovery of gold on the Witwatersrand in 1886. The diamond fields were annexed to the Cape Colony, but the gold mines were under the political control of the Boers. All at once the economy of the area was booming, immigration soared, foreign investments flooded in, and suddenly, this unimportant backwater became one of the most vital and lucrative pieces of territory in the world. Across the land economic development increased rapidly in every sector from transport to manufacturing to agriculture. Social changes were a necessary corollary to the expansion and growth as a predominantly agrarian society became an industrial giant virtually overnight. An overiding theme of this development was the insatiable need for labour; unskilled workers in the mines were a paramount necessity and the unprecedented growth in all spheres of the economy required a mass labour pool as well. Following on the heels of the devastation and disruption wreaked by the *Mfecane*, the timing couldn't have been better from the colonists' point of view.

The South African (Boer) War
By the end of the nineteenth century it had become apparent that despite continued British attempts to coerce the independent Boer republics into a South African confederation, the Boers had no desire whatsoever to join in partnership with their perceived enemy, the British. In view of the prize at

CECIL RHODES

No history of South Africa would be complete without a brief glance at a man who was one of the most important in shaping the country's destiny. No individual better personifies the nationalistic interests and goals of the British than Cecil John Rhodes (1853-1902). The story of Cecil Rhodes' arrival in South Africa as a sickly young man and his subsequent rise to fame and fortune by the age of 30 is legendary. Rhodes made his millions on the diamond fields of Kimberley; his farsighted vision enabled him to consolidate the disparate rights of individual miners and to parlay his holdings into the De Beers consortium, monopolizing the industry.

Not content merely to count his money, Cecil Rhodes turned to politics and entered the Cape Parliament in 1880 in order to protect his extensive interests. Within ten years he had become Prime Minister of the Cape Colony and was deemed to be the most powerful and influential man in South Africa. He had grandiose plans for his country and was enraptured by the vision of a British empire that extended from Cape Town to Cairo.

Constantly on the lookout for new mining concessions, Rhodes formed the British South Africa Company (BSAC) and was granted a royal charter by the crown to exploit and extend administrative control over most of southern and central Africa. The British government was interested in pre-empting its European rivals' territorial claims in the region. It also wanted to populate central Africa with white settlers to solidify British occupation and interests and to develop its resources at minimum cost. Moreover, great mineral riches were suspected in the region north of the Zambezi River in what is now Zimbabwe and Zambia. Under Rhodes' guidance, the BSAC wasted no time in securing land concessions from the local chiefs, who agreed to accept British jurisdiction over external affairs and over the non-Africans in their domains.

Never one to lose sight of an opportunity to realize his dream of an empire, Rhodes' downfall came about when he plotted with his lieutenant, Leander Starr Jameson, to overthrow the independent Boer republic in the Transvaal that encompassed the lucrative gold fields of the Witwatersrand. The uprising was a complete fiasco and Rhodes was forced to resign his post as Prime Minister of the Cape Colony. The Afrikaners in the Cape viewed his subterfuge as treachery and the trust and rapport that he had fostered between the English and the Afrikaners was destroyed. The Afrikaners in the Cape united in support of their brethren in the independent Boer republics and denounced British imperialism.

South Africa

PAUL KRUGER

If Cecil Rhodes embodied the vision and energy of the English-speaking citizenry, Paul Kruger (1825–1904), or Oom (Uncle) Paul as he was affectionately called, symbolized the hopes and spirit of the Afrikaner nation. Born to farming parents of Dutch descent, Kruger was only a young boy when his parents joined the Great Trek and yet he was profoundly influenced by the hardships the emigrants endured in their struggle to form a government of their own. While still a teenager, Kruger began taking an active role in public life, combining military and civic duties. By 1855 he was a member of the commission that was entrusted with writing a constitution for the new South African or Transvaal Republic.

When the British annexed the Transvaal in 1877, he became the champion of the struggle to regain independence. His cause took him on several occasions to London where he pleaded with the British government to reverse the annexation. When diplomacy and passive resistance failed to alter the situation, Kruger led his people into military opposition to the British, culminating in victory in 1881. Limited independence was restored to the Transvaal and in 1883 he was elected President of the Republic.

Kruger's problems were really just beginning however, for when gold was discovered in the Witwatersrand in 1886, the population of the Transvaal suddenly mushroomed overnight. Within a very short time a cosmopolitan British community became entrenched in the midst of the rural Boer society. Kruger viewed this as a threat to the ethnic identity of the Afrikaners, who he believed were 'God's people'. As the mining industry grew, Kruger was increasingly unable to satisfy the demands of the industrial magnates and *uitlanders* (outsiders). Cecil Rhodes had extensive gold interests as well as enormous political clout, and predictably, he sided with the *uitlanders* against Kruger's regime. Rhodes, in his passion to create an empire, was determined to bring the Transvaal Republic into a South African confederation; his efforts met with no success, however, and as we have seen, he then resorted to the abortive Jameson Raid.

Kruger recognized the inevitable and began to rearm his people. Despite Rhodes' fall from grace and power, British imperialist interests could not be ignored and issues reached a crisis point in October 1899 when Kruger demanded the withdrawl of British troops from the Transvaal border. War erupted within two days and Kruger was forced to retreat, escaping to Holland where he lived until the end of the war in 1902; he died just two years later in Switzerland and was interred in Pretoria. Paul Kruger is credited with being the father of South Africa and his memory and image are kept alive across the nation, for almost every town has a statue or a street named in his honour.

Country File

Boer farmers on the eve of the Boer War.

stake – supremacy over the richest gold mines in the world – it was probably inevitable that war would determine the issue. The South African or Boer War began in 1899 and lasted until 1902.

It has the sorry distinction of being one of the most brutal and costly colonial wars ever waged and its consequences are still being felt today, so badly did it scar the Afrikaner consciousness. The British mustered half a million men against a Boer force of 65,000. Despite British superiority in numbers and weaponry, the Boers were not easily defeated and casualties were heavy on both sides. An estimated 22,000 British soldiers died in battle or from disease; for the Boers, casualties were proportionately much greater: 14,000 men were lost in action and another 26,000, mostly women and children, died in concentration camps. The tally of black lives lost was never officially recorded, but conservative estimates place the toll at 13,000.

The Boers were justifiably bitter at their treatment by the British. Especially unforgivable was the round-up of women, children, the elderly and the infirm and their subsequent incarceration in concentration camps. Disease was rampant in the camps, conditions were unbearable, and the loss of life was unconscionably high. After the war, many British citizens and liberal politicians renounced their country's barbarism and to this day, the South African War remains a blight on Britain's conscience and record. For the Afrikaners it appeared to be the end of a dream and of an era, for when the peace accord was signed in May 1902, the Boer republics were annexed to Britain as new colonies.

Twentieth Century South Africa
South Africa on the threshold of the twentieth century was a world divided. The Boers had been vanquished in battle and subjugated once again. A combination of rural poverty, droughts and unstable markets had forced many to a bandon the land they had toiled and fought for. The black Africans, too, had been forcibly displaced from their lands, the very fabric of their culture and life-style irreparably torn. For the first time they were drawn into the world economy as workers and peasants, faced with progressive urbanization. Boers and blacks alike found it was necessary to migrate to the mines and cities for survival.

Here they encountered a world totally foreign to their respective heritages and the roots of several of South Africa's most deeply seated problems may be traced to this fracturing of Boer and African societies. Never before in South African history had a situation arisen where whites and blacks were in competition for the same unskilled jobs. Afrikaners had long suffered feelings of inferiority to the British, but now they felt like second class citizens in their 'own' country; without the structure of the master/servant relationship, they were greatly threatened by the mass black labour pool and by the evolution of African class-consciousness. To counteract this problem a racist ideology was intentionally developed, an ideology which would form the foundation for the future doctrine of apartheid. The Afrikaners insisted that all blacks remain inferior to the poorest white labourer and so devised a hierarchal system with differentiation in terms of job opportunity, wage scale and social conditions.

So firmly rooted did this paranoia of self-protectionism become that it was elevated to the status of law, with discrimination still persisting today, if not always in practice, then certainly in the minds of the people. The winds of change were blowing and for the black African, they carried little in the way of hope or promise for the future. Even before the turn of the century, the progressive electoral stance initiated by the British when they assumed control of the Cape Colony had been substantially weakened. Universal franchise was no longer deemed feasible with the annexation of African territories and the creation of a mass black working class. In 1887 and again in 1892 the franchise qualifications were altered to restrict the numbers of black voters. When the four South African territories – now all British colonies – were joined in the Union of South Africa in 1910, the coloureds and blacks in the Cape retained voting rights only if they could meet the educational and economic criteria imposed. A full 93 per cent of the electorate was white, however, and non-whites were prevented from serving in Parliament. Furthermore, the new constitution prevented the extension of even this limited non-white franchise beyond the Cape Province to the rest of South Africa.

With union, 1¼ million whites had assumed control over almost 5 million blacks, coloureds and Asians. The new government had plans to incorporate the British High Commission Territories of Swaziland, Basutoland (now Lesotho) and Bechuanaland (now Botswana) into the Union, but this proposal met with British resistance, a humanitarian outcry, as well as concerted opposition from the native inhabitants. Although it seemed likely that eventually these territories would join the Union, ultimately, this did not happen. To this day the kingdoms of Swaziland and Lesotho remain independent enclaves within the territory of South Africa, and Bechuanaland, as we have seen, made the transition from a British protectorate to the independent Republic of Botswana.

In the early years of the twentieth century mining interests dominated the economy and politics of South Africa. The need for a steady labour force remained the recurrent theme in this country and it prompted the enactment of the Native Lands Act of 1913, revised and expanded in 1936 as the Native Land and Trust Act. What it boiled down to was this: the mining interests wanted tribal reserves for the African populace so that they could use these as home bases for migrant labour. The farmers on the other hand, wanted the reserve land for their own use; at the same time they could then eliminate African agricultural competition. The objectives of both groups were fulfilled with the Native Land Act, which baldly relegated more than four million blacks to 13 per cent of the land, giving roughly 87 per cent of the country to the whites, who at that time numbered just over one million. The existing tribal reserves were recognized and Africans were only allowed to remain on 'white' land if they were employed as labourers; this legislation formed the basis for South Africa's misguided and notorious homelands policy of the 1950's.

With the advent of the First World War South Africa sided with Britain, hardly surprisingly considering the countries' close political and economic ties. This alliance was repugnant to many of the Afrikaners however, and gave further impetus to the rising tide of nationalist sentiments which had been brewing in the aftermath of the Boer War. The very powerful Dutch Reformed Church was instrumental in fostering Afrikaner nationalism and by 1914 an Afrikaner National Party had been formed by General J.B.M. Hertzog. Within a decade, Hertzog's Nationalists had formed a 'Pact' government with the predominantly English-speaking Labour Party and Afrikaans replaced Dutch as the second official language of South Africa.

The overwhelming priority of the National Party and its coalition governments over the next 20 years was the problem of white unemployment. By 1930 one in every five was classified as a 'poor white'. Lacking the skills of their English-speaking counterparts, competing for jobs with a huge black working class that in many cases was more proficient in industrial labour, the Afrikaners were in a bad way. The Government turned its full attention to improving their lot, generally at the expense of blacks. A 'civilized labour' policy was instituted which ensured the employment of whites in certain sectors and replaced blacks in government service with Afrikaners; a colour bar reserved certain jobs for whites only; and revenues from industry and mining were channelled into improving the social welfare of whites. Meanwhile, the plight of the blacks worsened: working conditions were appalling and hazardous, social and health services were virtually non-existent and wages remained low.

The years between the First and Second World Wars were a time of tumultuous social upheaval, rapid political transformation and wild economic fluctuations. Strikes among both black and white mine workers were common and the progression from an agrarian, rural society to an industrial, urbanized one proved neither quick nor painless. Despite the political alliances forged during this era between the two white groups, the outbreak of the Second World War destroyed the fragile peace between Afrikaner and English-speaker. Once again South Africa joined the Allies in the face of widespread Afrikaner opposition. Hertzog resigned from Parliament and a group of Afrikaners often likened to neo-Nazis or Fascists in their ideology broke away from the coalition United Party and formed the Purified Nationalist Party. The Purified Nationalists pledged to advance the interests of the isolationist Afrikaner community and the party steadily gained momentum, fuelled by the heady notion of ethnic power.

After the war the National Party swept into power and for the first time in its history, South Africa was in the control of a solely Afrikaner government. Vowing to never lose their grip on the nation, the Arikaners entrenched themselves in all levels of government and then went on to legislate their continued supremacy over the ever-increasing population of Africans. South African politics had always been dominated by the maintenance of white supremacy and if the past three centuries were characterized by repression and racism, this was nothing in comparison to the draconian measures to follow. In the early years after the Second World War, the National Party built its platform on the doctrine of apartheid, a word meaning 'separateness' in Afrikaans. It was a systematic and comprehensive programme of racial segregation that not only served to separate white from non-white, but that fixed blacks and whites at opposite ends of the economic, social and political sprectrum. Although racism and segregation were hardly new to the world, nor peculiar to South Africa, this country can claim the dubious credit for elevating and refining the practice to a fine art.

It would need a book in itself to review the legislation of apartheid during its 40-odd year span; there are excellent treatises on this subject for those who seek the grim details. For the purposes of this historical review, suffice it to say that the madness inherent in apartheid and its basically untenable nature, finally caught up with South Africa and that its protracted application not only earned the country world-wide condemnation, but has cast grave doubt on the long-term welfare of the nation. The bitter legacy of apartheid is one of hate and fear; the blacks have spent their lives in fear of whites, and ironically, the reverse is also true. South Africa is a country of great beauty and potential but it is, nonetheless, a country haunted by fear, a hostage to the hideous, crippling repercussions of apartheid.

The accession to power of the National Party ushered in an era of growing violence as unrest among non-whites increased in the face of repressive apartheid policies. The black response to apartheid has been continual and vigorous, although for a great many years it assumed the form of non-violent resistance and was largely ineffectual.

In 1912 educated blacks formed the South African Native National Congress which was renamed the African National Congress (ANC) in 1917. Its stated aim was to address and represent African grievances, gain individual land tenure, improve educational oppportunities and overcome tribal divisions. The ANC has the longest continuous history of any African political movement on the continent. Until its banning in 1960, it relied on constitutional methods to effect change despite suggestions that a more militant approach might yield better results.

A number of trade union organizations had been formed in the years after the First World War, but these groups were largely impotent when they sought a political role . In 1959 a number of young and more militant members of the ANC broke away from the organization and established the Pan Africanist Congress (PAC). The more aggressive approach of the PAC occasioned a protest demonstration in the town of Sharpeville in March 1960.

The march was peaceful but the police opened fired and 69 Africans, many of them children, were shot dead and another 178 wounded. World attention turned to South Africa and Sharpeville became the single most important catalyst to activate a mass African consciousness. A turning point had been reached and at long last passive resistance (*satyagraha*) as advocated by Mahatma Gandhi in Natal during the 1920s, was abandoned as a viable course of action.

The South African government promptly banned both the ANC and the PAC, forcing the movements to go underground. All known leaders of the opposition were imprisoned or exiled, among them Nelson Mandela, Raymond Mhlaba, Oliver Tambo and Govan Mbeki. Although sporadic terrorist attacks marked the next three decades, black protest was largely characterized by marches, riots, flagrant abuse of pass laws and the like.

One must not forget that the Africans had suffered subjugation and discrimination in their own land for over three centuries and so it was unlikely that political awareness would develop quickly. Moreover, education had been scanty and the vast majority of blacks had to attend to the needs of basic survival, such as food, shelter and employment, rather than dwell on or contribute to the rhetoric and protest of the politically conscious. In addition, it is important not to underestimate the strong grip the government, police and military forces in South Africa exercised during this period. South Africa was increasingly becoming a police state and although it was nominally still a democracy, freedom of speech and assembly had been curtailed and banning or indefinite detention without charge was a very real possibility for citizens of all colours.

But perhaps the most important reason why the Africans with their vast numerical majority didn't just collectively rise up and overthrow their white tormentors is the fact that the homogeneity of the African populace had been fractured; the blacks had been systematically separated along tribal lines and then banished to distant homelands, some of which were even granted the nominal status of independent nationhood. This was no mere accident; it was rather a deliberate policy to divide the Africans into tribal nations so that the development of a national black consciousness would not occur. The success of this policy is visible today in the factional fighting taking place in the townships; although it has political overtones (ANC versus Inkatha), the parties are to some extent split along tribal lines; many of the ANC leaders are Xhosa, while Inkatha is a Zulu-based party (although it must be said that many urban Zulus support the ANC). The government has demonstratably taken sides with Inkatha, and many believe that it has instigated much of the township violence in an effort to discredit the ANC and derail the transition to universal franchise and black rule.

The 1970s were marked by continued resistance and escalating violence, culminating in mid-1976 with the worst race riots in South African history in the township of Soweto; it took the police an incredible three weeks to suppress the violence. By the end of the decade it was obvious to most people that apartheid was both an anachronism and a failure and that civil war would be inevitable, sooner or later, unless South Africa discarded its white supremist policies. Constant criticism from the United Nations and widespread economic sanctions against South Africa certainly paved the way for change. Under the triple pressures of sanctions, world ostracism and a costly and unpopular war in Namibia, the economy sank to its knees. In 1989 South Africa admitted defeat in Namibia and withdrew its troops.

President F.W. de Klerk took the next crucial step and in February 1990, releasing the world's best known political prisoner, Nelson Mandela, after 27 years of incarceration. All political parties were unbanned and the state of emergency that had been in effect since 1986 was lifted. Freedom of speech and assembly were restored, political exiles were welcome to return to South Africa and at long last the way was paved for a meaningful dialogue about the future of the country. As I sit writing this, new chapters in South African history are being written and the conclusion is unclear. Great progress has been made in a very short time; in the space of less than two years non-whites in South Africa have gained more freedoms and concessions than at any time in history. The apparatus of apartheid has been largely dismantled and discarded so that, in theory at least, segregation and discrimination on the basis of colour no longer exist. Unfortunately it is not that simple. As has been the case in other countries, centuries of racist thought and practice are not so easy to erase and discrimination can still persist even if legislation dictates otherwise. The issues facing South Africa are dauntingly complex and there are no easy solutions at hand. It seems unlikely that the road to non-racial democracy will be smooth or direct; South Africa has more than its share of extremists who will be impossible to please. For some, whatever is accomplished will be too little, too late; for others, it will be too much, too soon. There is a great deal at stake here not only for the citizens of South Africa but for the rest of the continent as well; one can only hope that the right choices are made.

Whatever the outcome, matters appear to be moving in the right direction. Multi-party talks are in progress to devise a new constitution and to discuss the make-up of an interim government. Although peace and progress are threatened by the chronic flaring of violence in the townships, the momentum has begun and there is no turning back now. It is the world's fervent wish that all South Africans will join hands and rise above the obvious obstacles to weld a new harmony and order within their beautiful land.

GEOLOGY, FLORA AND FAUNA

The landscape of South Africa is strikingly diverse and few travellers to this country are not impressed by its great physical beauty. In geological terms, there are three main regions: the vast interior plateau called the highveld; the escarpment of mountain ranges that rim this plateau to the east, south and west; and a coastal belt lying between the escarpment and the sea. The central plateau is actually the southern end of the Great African Plateau that rises out of the Sahara Desert roughly 5,000 km to the north. The plateau is an enormous inverted saucer ranging from 600 to 3,400 metres above sea level, encircled by a collar of mountains. The highveld is basically a vast plain characterized by rolling grasslands, and includes the Witswatersrand and the Limpopo River basin to the northeast, as well as the southern fringes of the Kalahari and the semi-arid middleveld to the west.

The Great Escarpment, as the chain of mountains which rim the plateau are called, is the most continuous topographical feature in the country. It runs for a distance of 1,050 km and is most pronounced in the east and south where it incorporates the Drakensberg range with peaks exceeding 3,300 metres. Some of the oldest rocks in the world are found in South

Africa and several of the escarpment mountain ranges are older than the Himalayas or Alps.

The marginal region which lies between the sea and the escarpment varies in width between 60 and 240 km and is bordered by two oceans: the Atlantic and the Indian. The coastal belt is widest to the east of the Transvaal Escarpment; this area is called the *lowfeld* and is home to the majority of South Africa's game parks. South of the central plateau lie the semi-desert Great and Little Karoo tablelands; to the west in the northern Cape and Namaqualand where the strip is narrowest, the southern extension of the Namib Desert is encountered.

Before the arrival of the whites, South Africa supported a large and diverse animal population. Uncontrolled hunting, however, decimated the game and resulted in the extinction of a number of species. Elephants, for instance, once roamed throughout the country but today, apart from the Kruger National Park, only small remnant herds remain in the Knysna Forest and Addo Elephant National Park. The same holds true for the white rhino, which is now confined to reserves in Natal.

Fortunately South Africa was the country that initiated wildlife and flora conservation in Africa, so it is not surprising that today this land is still rich in both. A system of 17 national parks has been established across the country and in the Kruger Park alone there are more species of game than in any other sanctuary on the continent. These reserves protect all the many habitats to which animal and plant life have adapted over the millennia: desert, alpine, bushveld, savannah, riverine and marine. There are also over 900 species of birds in South Africa, representing 22 of the world's 27 living orders.

South Africa is basically a dry country receiving less than 450 mm of rain a year. As a result, the vegetation is primarily xerophytic, meaning it is adapted for growth in dry or drought conditions. But the land is vast and varied, defying simple botanical classification. In general terms, the indigenous vegetation is divided into five groups: desert and semi-desert, Mediterranean-type, bushveld or savannah, forests and temperate grasslands.

The Cape region is extremely complex botanically speaking, and supports a very large number of plant species. Among these are the *Protea* and *Erica* species which have made the wild flowers of the Cape famous around the world. In the northern Cape true desert vegetation occurs in a narrow strip along the coast; when spring rains fall, the desert bursts into spectacular colour and bloom. The vegetation of the northern and eastern regions of the country is characterized by bushveld: dense thornbush, sparse grass, and numerous scrub and tree species. The vast central highlands are covered with temperate grassland while indigenous forest is found only in isolated patches along the southern and eastern coastal belt where rainfall is considerably higher. In South Africa as a whole there are over 22,000 species of indigenous flowering plants. *Visitors should note that all native flora is protected and it is against the law to pick or destroy any wild flowers.*

ECONOMY

The South African economy is the most vital and viable on the continent . Although the country comprises only 4 per cent of Africa's area, it accounts for 25 per cent of the continent's Gross National Product (GNP) and 80 per cent of the GNP of Southern Africa. South Africa has a free-market system based on private enterprise and ownership. The main pillars of the economy are mining, manufacturing and commerce, in that order. South Africa has the world's largest known reserves of gold, platinum, chromium, vanadium, manganese, fluorspar and andalusite; about 85 per cent of all mineral production is exported. In monetary terms, gold is the country's most important export; South Africa produces 35 per cent of the entire world's gold.

Industry is a well-developed sector of the economy and represents 25 per cent of the Gross Domestic Product (GDP). A large labour pool, abundant natural resources, a high level of technological expertise and the need to become self-reliant because of sanctions and divestment, have all contributed to the growth of manufacturing.

Although only 12 per cent of the country is arable, South Africa is one of just six net food-exporting nations in the world. The land is dry, rainfall is unreliable and severe droughts are a perennial problem. By world standards, South Africa has relatively little land with high agricultural potential. Nonetheless, agriculture is an important contributor to the economy although it ranks only fifth in overall monetary contribution. South Africa's temperate climate is such that just about every known crop can be grown there, with the aid of irrigation, of course. The most important food export is maize and it is a lifeline for most of the countries in Southern Africa. Other major crops are wheat, grain sorghum, ground nuts, sugar cane, fruit and vegetables. South Africa is also an important producer of meat (beef, poultry, lamb and pork), wool, milk, hides and skins.

With a 3,000 km coastline it is not surprising that fishing is a mainstay of the economy. 90per cent of the fish are taken from the cold waters of the Atlantic Ocean on the west coast; anchovies, herring and pilchards are the principal species of shoal fish caught. Deep sea trawlers take Cape hake, kingklip, snoek, monkfish and several varieties of mackerel. Approximately 90 per cent of the total catch is exported.

Foreign trade accounts for about 50 per cent of the GDP. Many of the country's commodities are vulnerable to world inflation and demand, however, so there is a good deal of economic uncertainty from year to year. There is no doubt that sanctions and divestment have taken their toll, and in combination with high inflation rates, a world-wide recession and a drastically devalued rand, they have weakened the South African economy. The Government was traditionally the largest employer, but it has recently initiated a privatization programme. Agresssive schemes in industry, transport, communications and utilities are now underway in an attempt to stimulate the sagging economy.

The South African economy is a curious mixture of first-world technology and sophistication and third-world poverty and underdevelopment. Like other African countries, it is faced with a burgeoning population and is unable to create enough new jobs and housing to keep pace with black needs. The manufacturing sector is under close scrutiny at the moment; it is capable of considerable expansion and will provide substantial job opportunities. Furthermore, foreign investment, which formerly played a major role in this country's economy, is expected to regenerate if the political situation continues to improve. This will unleash a much needed influx of capital and create additional employment.

As this guide goes to press the economic future of South Africa is uncertain. The ANC has repeatedly and publicly advocated the nationalization of mines, banks and major industries; in contrast to the current trend, it envisages a greater degree of state intervention. Redistribution of wealth to narrow the disparity between rich and poor will undoubtedly be a vital priority of any new black or coalition government. Just how this will be accomplished is difficult to surmise. The technological infrastructure and the immense natural resources of this country will not disappear with the end of white rule; how they are managed and utilized in the future remains to be determined.

THE PEOPLE

Probably nowhere in the world has so much attention and emphasis centred on race as in South Africa. It is an issue fraught with great political, social and emotional tension and after decades of enforced separation, it is no wonder that the peoples of South Africa are fragmented into distinct and rigid ethnic groups. Subjected for decades to the divisive policies of apartheid, South Africa now has a completely heterogeneous society. It is likely that a new government and constitution will sweep away the few remaining vestiges of apartheid; how quickly three centuries of bias and ethnicity can be eliminated is less clear.

The South African government recognizes four racial groups: white, coloured, Asian and black. The whites are the descendants of early Dutch, French, English and German settlers, leavened by later immigrants from other parts of western Europe. The Dutch were the first arrivals, settling at the Cape in 1652. They were followed by a small group of French Huguenots who fled to South Africa to escape the religious persecution in Europe which followed the revocation of the Edict of Nantes. Immigration by the British began in 1820 after the Cape had come under the British flag. Today, just over half the white population speaks Afrikaans; English is the other official language.

The term 'coloured' is an official label used by the government to denote persons of mixed ancestry. These people are descended fro m indigenous Khoikhoi (Hottentots) and San (Bushmen) and the imported slaves from the Dutch East Indies, who mixed with Europeans in the early days of settlement. The coloured population is very westernized. Almost 90 per cent are Christian, Afrikaans is their language, and in culture and lifestyle they are closely aligned to Europeans. Until the 1950s, the coloured community had the vote and lived in close association with the whites in the Cape

Province. Unfortunately, the enforced segregation measures of apartheid resulted in their relocation from traditional areas in Cape Town to townships on the periphery of the city; understandably, a good deal of enmity was engendered by this action. The coloured population is found predominantly in the western part of the Cape Province, where they form a majority of the population.

Of the Asians in South Africa, 99 per cent are Indian, the descendants of indentured labourers who were brought to Natal from 1860 onwards to work on sugar plantations. When their term of contract had expired these workers could choose repatriation or remain as settlers on land given to them by the British government. The majority chose the latter option and 85 per cent have remained in Natal. Today the Indians are prosperous, with a successful merchant class, and they have maintained their cultural identity. The remaining 10,000 Asians are of Chinese descent.

Black Africans outnumber whites in South Africa by roughly six to one. Apartheid strategies have long focused on building on the ethnic divisions within this majority, constantly emphasizing the nine separate tribal groups. This formed the basis for the homeland policy where blacks were relocated to areas 'historically' inhabited by their tribes. The nine tribes fall into four main ethnolinguistic groups: Nguni, which includes the Zulu, Xhosa, Swazi and Ndebele peoples; Venda; Tsonga; and Sotho, which can be divided into Southern Sotho, Northern Sotho and Tswana.

Centuries ago the ancestors of modern black South Africans migrated south from central Africa in successive waves. The tribes settled in different areas, living more or less harmoniously until the population pressures of the nineteenth century led to internecine struggles, culminating in the *Mfecane*. Decades of upheaval among the black tribes coincided with an all-out battle for land with the white man; by 1910 the whites had won and territorial bases for the major ethnic groups had been defined. Today, many rural Africans maintain tribal affiliations but the majority of the population does not. Over one third of the black population in South Africa is already urbanized and tribal structure has been largely eroded in the townships. The customs and traditions of old Africa still persist to varying degrees in the countryside but it is only a matter of time before the values and priorities of the modern world supercede. Exposure to Western society, increasing urbanization, and the mutual need for black labour are inexorably drawing the rural African into the twentieth century.

RECOMMENDED READING LIST

Abrahams, Peter, *Tell Freedom*, Faber & Faber, London, 1981.

Brink, Andre, *Rumours of Rain*, W.H. Allen, London, 1978.
    A Dry White Season, W.H. Allen, London, 1979.

Courtenay, Bruce, *The Power of One*, Random House, New York, 1989.

Gordimer, Nadine, *The Burger's Daughter*, Viking, New York, 1979.
    A Sport of Nature, Knopf, New York, 1987.

South Africa

Haggard, Rider, *King Solomon's Mines*, MacDonald, London, 1956.

Hildebrand's Travel Guide: South Africa, Hippocrene Books, New York, 1987

Hochschild, Adam, *The Mirror at Midnight*, Viking, New York, 1990.

Lelyveld, Joseph, *Move Your Shadow*, Penguin Books, New York, 1985.

Malan, Rian, *My Traitor's Heart*, Atlantic Monthly Press, New York, 1990.

Manning, Richard, *They Cannot Kill Us All*, Houghton Mifflin Co., Boston, 1987.

Matthee, Dalene, *Circles in a Forest*, Penguin, London, 1985.

Michener, James, *The Covenant*, Random House, New York, 1980.

Morris, Donald, *Washing of the Spears*, Jonathan Cape Ltd., London, 1965.

Paton, Alan, *Cry, the Beloved Country*, Chas. Scribners & Sons, New York, 1948.

Sinclair, Ian, *Field Guide to the Birds of Southern Africa*, Stephen Greene Press, Inc., Lexington, MA., 1987.

Smith, Wilbur, *The Burning Shore*, Doubleday, New York, 1985.
        Power Of The Sword, Heinemann, London, 1986.
        Rage, Heinemann, London, 1987.

Sparks, Allister, *The Mind of South Africa*, Heinemann, London, 1990.

Thompson, Leonard, *A History of South Africa*, Yale University Press, New Haven, 1990.

A pride of lazy lions in Kruger National Park.

AROUND SOUTH AFRICA

JOHANNESBURG

INTRODUCTION

City of Gold Johannesburg, the City of Gold, is just over 100 years old, but it is the most modern and prosperous city in Africa. It is 1,760 metres above sea level and straddles a chain of gold-rich hills called the Witwatersrand. The Witwatersrand, which means 'ridge of white water', is the richest gold reef in the world. In 1886 a penniless prospector named George Harrison fortuitously stumbled upon the only surface outcropping of this reef ever discovered. Harrison staked the first claim on the Witwatersrand and then later sold it for a mere £10. He subsequently disappeared without a trace, but not before unleashing the greatest gold rush the world has ever witnessed. Prospectors, fortune-seekers and opportunists flocked here from all corners of the globe. For the past century the bulk of the world's gold and uranium has been extracted from the deep, sloping reefs of the Witwatersrand.

Despite its humble beginnings as a dusty shanty town, Johannesburg is now the largest city in South Africa, and is the centre of the country's industrial, financial, commercial and mining operations. Johannesburg alone generates over 25 per cent of South Africa's gross domestic product.

There is little that is beautiful or memorable about this city. It lacks the magnificent setting of Cape Town or the tropical, colonial flavour of Durban. The Johannesburg skyline is punctuated by glass skyscrapers, yellow slag heaps and mine headgear, all byproducts of feverish mining activity. The central area is slightly drab and has an old-fashioned air about it, despite the building spree which threatens to eradicate all remnants of the past. Although gold production is no longer centred in Johannesburg today, the Chamber of Mines of South Africa has its headquarters here. The Johannesburg Stock Exchange is the largest gold share market in the world.

Transit hub For the tourist, Johannesburg is the transit hub of the country and for this reason, one-night stays are common. This type of visit generally does not lend itself to much sightseeing. If you do have the time and interest,

South Africa

JOHANNESBURG

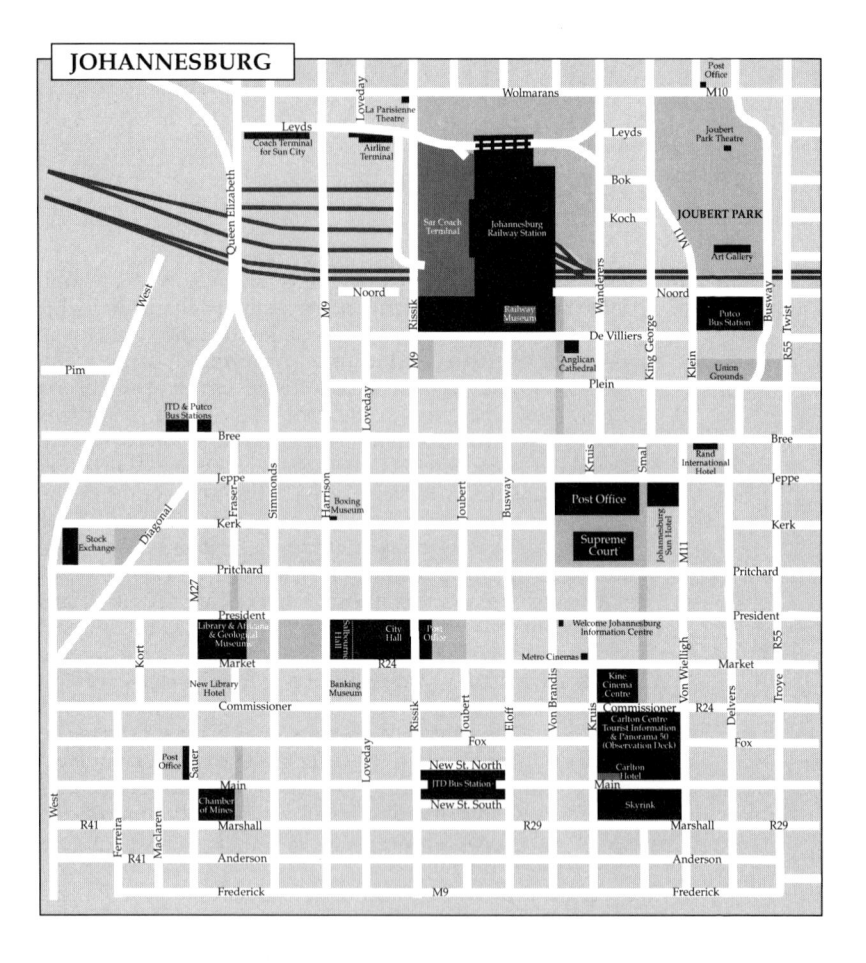

City crime

however, Johannesburg offers several tourist attractions as well as excellent shopping and dining. One note of caution: the city centre is totally deserted after 6 p.m. and it is not safe to wander the streets after dark. As is the case with most major metropolitan areas in the world, crime is a problem in Johannesburg. Exercise caution on the streets and do not carry large sums of money, cameras or expensive jewellery when you leave your hotel.

GETTING THERE

Johannesburg is the hub of South Africa and all international and domestic airlines serve the city. *SAA*

Johannesburg

has daily flights to Cape Town, Durban, George, Kimberley, Bloemfontein, Port Elizabeth and Upington. A number of private companies such as *Link, FliteStar* and *Comair* serve the smaller cities and towns.

Jan Smuts Airport is 24 km east of Johannesburg in the suburb of Kempton Park. The taxi fare, which is metered, averages R50.00. Scheduled bus services to the city centre and to Pretoria are also available for substantially less.

Excellent rail system

There is good rail service between Johannesburg and the major cities in South Africa. The **Trans Karoo** and the **Blue Train** run to Cape Town, the *Trans Natal* to Durban, the **Amatola** to East London and the **Algoa** to Port Elizabeth via Pietermaritzburg. For detailed information contact *SAR Travel* in London on (071) 287-1133 or in the United States on 213-507-5894 or toll-free on 800-4 21-8907. The railway system is called *Spoornet* and for information in South Africa ring (011) 774-4957.

There are long-distance luxury coach services between Johannesburg and Cape Town, Durban, Pretoria, Nelspruit, Port Elizabeth and George with stops *en route* at the larger towns. The *SAR Travel* offices abroad can help with schedules and reservations; in South Africa contact *Greyhound Inter-City* on (011) 762-2544 or the *Connex* central reservation office on (011) 744-4504.

It is quite possible to drive from any of the neighbouring countries to Johannesburg. Roads are tarred and are in good condition. If you are planning to drive between the countries of Southern Africa, be sure that your car hire company allows this and that you have the necessary documents and visas.

ACCOMMODATION

City Centre
Carlton Hotel and Court***. Main St. Tel. (011) 331-8911; fax (011) 331-3555. The Carlton is the city's premier hotel offering five-star luxury and service. The very tastefully furnished rooms have large marble bathrooms equipped with magnifying mirrors and hair dryers. CNN news and in-house videos are offered in addition to normal TV programmes. If you want even more luxury and extra-attentive service, the Carlton Court wing will please you. Rooms are larger, there are mini-bars and fax machines and each bathroom has a jacuzzi tub. Prices are slightly higher in the Court.
Johannesburg Sun and Towers Hotel***. 84 Smal St. Tel. (011) 29-7011; fax (011) 29-0515. The standard rooms in the Sun are disappointing and characterless and don't

deserve a five star rating. The more expensive rooms in the Towers do have all the amenities one would expect with this rating, but with the same price structure, the Carlton Hotel is the far better choice in my opinion.
Braamfontein Protea Hotel**.** De Korte St, Braamfontein. Tel. (011) 403-5740. A nice hotel in the university section of Johannesburg, a short distance from the central area. This hotel has a heated indoor swimming pool and all rooms are suites.
Hillbrow Protea Hotel*.** Abel Rd, Hillbrow. Tel (011) 643-4911. This hotel has reasonably priced rooms with standard facilities. Hillbrow is a five minute drive from the city centre. It is one of the liveliest areas of Johannesburg, with lots of street activity at night. It also has the highest crime rate in the world, or so I've been told.
Rand International*.** 290 Bree St, City Centre. Tel. (011) 29-2724; fax (011) 29-6815 A well-situated hotel within walking distance of shops and cinemas. The rooms are nice and the hotel offers the usual services and amenities, but no pool however.
New Library Hotel*. 67 Commissioner St, City Centre. Tel. (011) 832-1551. For the budget-conscious traveller this hotel is an excellent choice. It is centrally located, and although there is nothing luxurious about the rooms, they are clean and have private bathrooms. The dining room serves decent food at reasonable prices.
Youth Hostel. 4 College St, Fairview. Tel. (011) 614-8743. This new hostel is in a large, old-fashioned house, just 3 km from the city centre. It is conveniently on a direct bus route to the city (bus No. 32 or 33). The hostel is open all day; the latest you can check in is 7 p.m.

Sandton
Sandton Sun Hotel***.** Corner of Alice and Fifth St, Sandton. Tel. (011) 783-8301; fax (011) 783-0421. If you prefer to stay in one of the fashionable suburbs outside Johannesburg, this hotel is your best choice. It is luxurious and is situated at one end of the very upmarket Sandton City centre. This gives you access to the eight cinemas and more than 500 specialty shops in the shopping complex. You need never venture into the centre of Johannesburg if you stay in Sandton. It is north of Johannesburg, about 30 minutes by taxi from the airport. Hire cars are available from the hotel.
Sandton City Lodge.** Sandton. Tel.(011) 884-5300. The City Lodge chain offers standard rooms without frills for budget travellers . This hotel is relatively new, is

A fashionable suburb

Johannesburg, the city that gold built.

attractively designed and represents excellent value for money. There is no restaurant on thepremises but there are several nearby.

Airport
Jan Smuts Holiday Inn ***. Kempton Park. Tel. (011) 975-1121; fax (011) 975-5846. Of the three hotels in the immediate vicinity of t he airport, the Holiday Inn is closest to the terminals, a three minute drive by courtesy coach. It is a large, busy hotel with clean, uninspired rooms, convenient for an overnight stay if you have an early flight to catch the next morning. Day rooms are generally available.
Airport Sun Hotel***. 6 Hulley St, Kempton Park. Tel. (011) 974-6911; fax (011) 974-8097. The rooms here are on a par with the Holiday Inn in terms of size, decor and amenities. This hotel is 1 km from the airport and there is an around-the-clock minibus shuttle service.

DINING

Expensive
Linger Longer. 94 Juta Street, Braamfontein. Tel. (011)339-7814. This is consistently rated as one of the top

restaurants in Johannesburg every year. Not surprisingly, the service and food are superb and the ambience is elegant. The menu is somewhat French but not classically so, and there is an emphasis on fresh fish. Lunch is served Monday–Friday, dinner, Monday–Saturday.

Dentons. 125 Fox Street. Tel. (011) 331-3827. An elegant French restaurant that serves very creative and delicious food. Open for lunch only Monday–Friday.

Les Marquis. 12 Fredman Drive, Sandton. Tel. (011) 783-8947. This was recently voted the best French restaurant by *Hello Johannesburg*, the monthly guide to city dining and entertainment. The dining room is very elegant but I found the service inattentive and the food mediocre. If you are staying in Sandton you might consider giving it a try, but I wouldn't drive from central Johannesburg to eat here. Closed Saturday lunch-time and all day Sunday.

Leipoldts. 94 Juta St, Braamfontein. Tel. (011) 339-2765. If you want to try traditional South African food, this is the spot. The restaurant is elegantly decorated and serves an incredible 50-dish buffet. This is an excellent way to sample the various regional specialities; moreover, the food and service are superb. Open for lunch weekdays and dinner Monday–Saturday.

De Fistermann. 131 Commissioner Street. Tel. (011) 23-8006. A busy city-centre restaurant specializing in fresh fish and seafood. The menu also features traditional South African dishes which the kitchen prepares very well. Lunch is served Monday–Friday; dinner Monday–Saturday.

Moderate

Gramadoelas Restaurant. 31 Bok Street, Joubert Park. Tel. (011) 724-3716. This elegant and attractive restaurant, housed in a Cape Dutch manor-style residence, serves some of the best traditional South African and Cape Dutch Malay cuisine in Johannesburg. Closed Monday and Saturday lunch-time.

Rugantino. 6 Twist Street. Tel. (011) 29-9788. A large Italian restaurant with the standard selection of dishes. A dozen or more daily specials rescue this menu from boredom, however. The portions are generous and the prices are reasonable. Open every day for lunch and dinner.

The Perfumed Garden. 43 King George Street, Joubert Park. Tel. (011) 724-6316. This is one of the oldest restaurants in Johannesburg and if you are in the mood for something different, consider trying it. The menu features dishes from the Arabian nights and guests a re served in a mud-walled casbah. Lunch is offered Monday–Friday, dinner Monday–Saturday.

Inexpensive
Marialva. 108 Kerk Street. Tel. (011) 23-4415. A licensed, authentic Portuguese restaurant that serves simple but deliciously spicy food. There is fresh fish daily as well as calamari and bacalhau. Open for lunch and dinner daily except Sunday.
Hard Rock Cafe. 204 Oxford Rd, Illovo. Tel. (011) 447-2583. A perennial favourite the world around for quality burgers, salads and sandwiches. Open seven days a week until late.
Toty. Carlton Centre. Tel.(011) 331-6006 This restaurant is conveniently located in the Carlton Centre (bottom level). The menu is Italian and features pasta dishes and delicious pizzas cooked over wood fires. The ambience is casual and there is often entertainment after 9 p.m. on weekends. Open 11 a.m. to midnight, Monday–Saturday.

SHOPPING

As you might expect in this cosmopolitan city, the shopping is excellent and varied. Huge, de luxe shopping centres are numerous and once inside, it is easy to forget you are in Africa! The Carlton Centre is the largest complex in the business district, with almost 200 shops, several restaurants and 3 cinemas. Also in the city centre is the **Smal Street Mall**, a four block arcade connecting the Johannesburg Sun Hotel and the Carlton Centre. Here you will find dozens of clothing boutiques and several high quality art galleries.

The largest and most exotic market in Johannesburg is the **Oriental Plaza**, between Main Road and Bree Street, west of the city centre in Fordsburg. Here you will find a sprawl of almost 300 shops selling Indian and Western goods. Bargaining is *de rigueur* and part of the fun.

If your timing is right, visit the **open-air artists' market** for arts and crafts. It is held on the first weekend of every month at the Zoo Lake in Jan Smuts Avenue. Every Saturday morning there is also a **flea market** in the square in front of the Market Theatre, on the corner of Bree and Wolhuter Streets. A variety of goods is sold, some interesting, some junk. On Saturday mornings there is also an **antique market** on the lower level of the Parkview Shopping Centre from 9 a.m.–1 p.m.

Shopping opportunities are even greater outside Johannesburg at Sandton City, Sandton, the Rosebank

Shopping Complex, Rosebank, and the Eastgate Shopping Centre, East Rand. For a country fair atmosphere, visit the **organic village market** on the corner of Culross and Main Roads, Bryanstown, on Thursdays and Saturdays from 9 a.m.–1 p.m. There are 120 stalls selling quality arts and crafts and organic produce.

The following lists give a selection of the speciality shops to be found.

Diamonds
Binyan Diamonds. Republic Bldg, corner of Noord and Quartz St
Diamond Discount **Co.** 94 Pritchard St
Messias Diamond Cutting Works. 99 Eloof St

Duty Free Jewellers
The Midas Touch. Carlton Centre
Tanur. Carlton Centre, Sandton City, Smal Street Mall and Eastgate
Hong Kong Jewellers. Sandton City and Smal Street Mall

Art & Antiques
Totem Gallery. Carlton Centre, Sandton City and Rosebank
Primitive Arts & Crafts. 169 Oxford Rd, Rosebank
Gallery 21. 34 Harrison St
Antique Brokers International. 120 Plein St
Zalah Wildlife Gallery. 21 Barnacle Rd, Forest Hill

Indigenous Art & Crafts
The Bushman Gallery. Carlton Centre
Indaba Curios. Sandton City
Kraal Gallery. Carlton Centre and Sandton City
Rowland Ward Ltd. Carlton Centre

ENTERTAINMENT

Johannesburg boasts a full roster of cultural events. For an up-to-date listing of concerts, ballet, theatre and art exhibitions, consult a newspaper or the monthly publication, *Hello Johannesburg*. This magazine is distributed free of charge and may be found in the major hotels.

Theatre
Of the city's numerous theatres, the *Market Theatre* complex is the largest, with multiple stages, halls and a restaurant. The Market Theatre presents several productions simultaneously, including experimental

theatre. Jazz concerts are often held on Sundays. Bookings through *Computicket*, tel. (011) 28-3040.

Nightclubs
Caesar's Palace. Corner of Jorissen and Simmonds St, Braamfontein
Thunderdome. Corner of Claim and Noord St
Kippies Musician Bar. At the Market Theatre complex

SIGHTSEEING

Geological Museum
Located on the first floor of the Public Library in Market Street. There is a treasure house of information here for those interested in rocks, minerals and gems. The museum is open Monday–Friday 9 a.m.–5.30 p.m.; Saturday 9 a.m.–5 p.m., Sunday and holidays 2 p.m.–5 p.m. Admission is free.

Johannesburg Stock Exchange

Guided tours This is in Diagonal Street and offers guided tours 11 a.m. and 2.30 p.m., Monday–Friday, so that you can see the trading frenzy. Tel. (011) 833-6580.

Johannesburg Art Gallery
Situated in Klein Street, Joubert Park. South African and international art are on permanent display here. Guided tours are conducted upon request. The gallery is open Tuesday–Sunday, 10 a.m.–5 p.m. Tel. (011) 725-3180.

Johannesburg Zoo
This is one of the best zoos in Africa but it is a far cry from seeing the animals in their natural habitat. If you are going to any game reserves, you can skip the zoo without any qualms. If the zoo is as close as you are likely to get to any African wildlife, it will at least introduce you to the majority of species. The zoo is open daily, 8.30 a.m.–5.30 p.m.; there is a small entrance fee. Also on the same site is the **Museum of South African Rock Art** with a collection of 90 prehistoric rock engravings, displayed in an indigenous garden. The zoo is in Jan Smuts Avenue, Parktown. Tel. (011) 646-2000.

Botanical Gardens
Hedges, herb and rose gardens and hundreds of exotic trees can be seen in this 125 hectare garden in Thomas Bowler Avenue, Emmarenta. The Gardens are open daily from 10 a.m.–4 p.m. Guided tours are given at 9 a.m. on the first Tuesday of every month. Tel. (011) 782-0517.

Carlton Panorama

A bird's eye view

If the skies are clear, visit the Observation Deck on the fiftieth floor of the Carlton Centre for a splendid panorama of Johannesburg. There is a small admission fee and remember to bring 20 cent coins for the telescopes. There is a slide show entitled *A Day in Johannesburg* that runs every 10 minutes. Unfortunately the film has deteriorated terribly so the viewing is poor. The Panorama is open daily from 9 a.m.–11 p.m.

Africana Museum

Located in the Johannesburg Public Library in Market Street, this museum comprises two interesting galleries which house a collection of items relating to the history of South Africa. The development of Cape Town and Johannesburg are emphasized and there are interesting coin and silver displays as well. The museum is open Monday–Saturday 9 a.m.–5.30 p.m. and Sunday 2 p.m.–5.30 p.m. Tel. (011) 834-3766.

Soweto Tours

The good, the bad and the ugly

Many visitors are interested in a tour to Soweto (an acronym for South Western Townships), home to over four million black inhabitants. Tours are offered by a private company called *Jimmy's Face to Face Tours* and depart daily from the Carlton Hotel at 9 a.m. and 2 p.m. (Sunday at 9 a.m. only). Tel. (011) 331-6109. If you are not staying in the city centre you can arrange for them to collect you at your hotel. The charismatic owner, Jimmy, promises to show all facets of Soweto: the good, the bad and the ugly. The tours last three hours and at the time of writing costs R45.00 per person. The drivers give an excellent and humorous commentary and for visitors looking for an insight into some of South Africa's dilemmas, this tour is a must. It is not recommended that you explore Soweto on your own. However, as an organized group led by black guides, the tour seemed perfectly safe to me.

What immediately struck me in Soweto was the ubiquitous litter, the staggering number of small children and the pervasive acrid smell of coal smoke and dust. I was surprised to find that much of the township is middle class. In contrast, the squatters' camps were sad and shocking; it was heartbreaking to note the pride the occupants displayed in even this most lowly form of housing. Possessions are treasured and the interiors of the tin shacks are kept scrupulously clean. I found the workers' hostels the most appalling aspect of Soweto:

they are curiously reminiscent of concentration camps. The tour certainly serves as an introduction to the myriad of problems facing this black city, but the sense of hope and the indomitable spirit of the people were palpable and encouraging.

Gold Reef City

If you only have limited time for the sights in Johannesburg, this is one of my top recommendations. It is the perfect outing for a Sunday when everything else is closed and Johannesburg becomes a ghost town. Although this is a tourist theme park, pure and simple, it does offer the opportunity to visit a gold mine. Gold Reef City is 8 km south-west of the city centre. It is a historic recreation of Johannesburg at the turn of the century. There are faithful replicas of the architecture, furniture and costumes of South Africa 100 years ago, when the gold rush brought about the birth of Johannesburg. In addition, there are exhibitions, shops, restaurants, tribal dancers, steam train rides and a Victorian fun fair. Best of all is the underground tour of Crown Mine 17, a 3,000 metre deep gold mine that once yielded tons of gold. Although the mine was closed in 1977 due to unprofitability, miners give a very informative lecture and demonstrate the drilling and tunneling processes. Up above, visitors are welcome to watch a fifteen minute demonstration of a gold pour. Gold Reef City is open Tuesday–Sunday, 9.30 a.m.–5 p.m. The admission fee covers all activities except the underground tour, for which there is an additional small charge.

Gold mine tour

ACTIVITIES

Balloon Safaris

For those who are looking for something really different, consider a hot air balloon ride over some beautiful country north of Johannesburg. The *Balloon Safari Company* offers a daily 1 1/2 hour flight that includes brunch and transport. Tel. (011) 705-320 1.

Gold Reef City Helicopters

Scenic flights over Johannesburg and Soweto are offered on Saturday, Sunday and public holidays. The flights last five or six minutes, and are very reasonably priced. Book at the kiosk across the street from the Gold Reef City entrance gate. Tel. (011) 496-1600.

City Tours

Half day and night tours of Johannesburg are offered by

South Africa

a number of companies, which also offer a full schedule of day tours to Zulu kraals, the Heia Safari Ranch, Pretoria and Soweto.
Springbok Atlas. Tel. (011) 493-3780
Welcome Tours & Safaris. Tel. (011) 403-2562
Tour-Rite. Tel. (011) 802-7592

SERVICES
TOURIST INFORMATION
SA Tourist Board, International Arrivals Hall, Jan Smuts Airport. Tel. (011) 970-1669
Open daily from 8 a.m.–5.30 p.m.

Johannesburg Publicity Association, Markwell House, Corner of Market and Von Wielligh Streets. Tel. (011) 337-2727

Johannesburg Tourist Information Centre, 46th Floor, Carlton Centre. Tel. (011) 331-5241

GETTING AROUND
Airport Bus
There is coach service to and from Jan Smuts Airport every half hour from 8 a.m. to 10 p.m. The terminus is at the Rotunda (railway station). Tel. (011) 773-9374

Airline Offices:
SAA, Main Street at the Carlton Hotel. Tel. (011) 333-6504
Air Botswana. Tel. (011) 975-3614
Air Zimbabwe. Tel. (011) 331-1541
Bop Air. Tel. (011) 339-2314
British Airways. Tel. (011) 331-0011
Lufthansa. Tel. (011) 484-4711
Namib Air. Tel. (011) 331-6658
Comair. Tel. (011) 31-5001
Link. Tel. (011) 973-3841
Cathay Pacific. Tel. (011) 883-9226
FliteStar (Lux Air). Tel. (011) 331-3034

Camper Hire
Campers Corner, Jan Smuts Ave., Craighall Park. Tel. (011) 787-9105

Car Hire
Avis. Tel. (011) 974-2571
Budget. Tel. (011) 484-1685
Imperial. Tel. (011) 337-2300
U-Drive. Tel. (011) 331-3735

Rail
Information. Tel. (011) 774-4957
Reservations. Tel. (011) 774-4128
The Blue Train. Tel. (011) 774-3929

PRETORIA

Pretoria, the administrative capital of South Africa, is 50 km north of Johannesburg. It is a spacious, open city, home to 800,000 residents and numerous government offices and buildings.

Travellers rarely base themselves in Pretoria unless they have business in the city; truthfully, there is not a lot to see or do here.

Pretoria is called the *Jacaranda City* and if you are visiting South Africa in October or November, I do recommend an excursion to see the blossoming trees. An incredible 300 miles of streets have been planted with 55,000 jacarandas, and when in bloom, the lilac-coloured flowers are spectacularly beautiful. If you do want to see Pretoria, I would suggest taking a city tour with one of the coach companies based in Johannesburg, such as *Springbok Atlas* or *Welcome Tours & Safaris*.

Johannesburg

CULLINAN PREMIER DIAMOND MINE

Cullinan, a small town which owes its existence to diamonds, is approximately 45 km east of Pretoria; the drive from Johannesburg can be managed easily in 1½ hours. Guided surface tours of the Premier Diamond Mine are given to small groups at 9 a.m. and 10.30 a.m., Tuesday–Friday. It is essential to book in advance by ringing (012) 133-0050. Your tour starts with a short video presentation illustrating the mining process.

As this is a working mine with extremely strict security, visitors do not go underground or anywhere near diamonds for that matter. However, the mine is still of interest for it is centred around the oldest volcanic diamond pipe in the world (1.2 billion years old).

The Premier Mine yields three million carats annually, 20 per cent of which are gem quality. The Cullinan diamond, discovered in 1905, is the largest stone found anywhere to date – a record 3,106 carats in the rough. It yielded the two biggest cut stones in the world: the Star of Africa at 530 carats and the Lesser Star of Africa at 317 carats. The Premier Mine is also the only diamond mine in the world where blue diamonds are found and where stones in excess of ten carats are recovered daily. Despite Kimberley's claim to having the largest diamond pit, the mine at Cullinan is six times bigger. If you are really keen on seeing the subsurface operation, you may request a special tour by writing to the general manager at least three weeks in advance.

Taxis
Taxis are not hailed in Johannesburg but they do queue at the luxury hotels in the city centre. Tel. (011) 725-3333 or (011) 23-4555.

LEFT LUGGAGE
There are good-sized lockers available for hire at Jan Smuts Airport. They are located on the parking garage level of the international terminal. For 50 cents you can reserve a locker for 14 days. The storage room is attended so if you don't have the correct change, the attendant will assist you. Sometimes I have needed to store my luggage for longer than two weeks and have made arrangements to do so with the attendant. I simply left a 50 cent coin on the shelf inside the locker; after 14 days the attendant opened the locker and deposited the coin to extend the hire period.

If you need to get to the lockers at a very early or late hour, and the room is locked, speak to any security guard and he will find someone to open the room for you. These lockers are a godsend if you are going to Zimbabwe or Botswana for a short safari, where luggage needs to be kept to a minimum. It is worthwhile to note that only in Johannesburg will you find left luggage facilities.

SUN CITY

The Las Vegas of South Africa

Sun City is in the nominally independent homeland of Bophuthatswana, 170 km from Johannesburg. If you want to try your hand at a bit of gambling, Sun City is conveniently accessible to Johannesburg by train, coach, car or plane. Gambling is illegal in South Africa, but legal in the homelands, and as a result Sun City has developed into the African equivalent of Las Vegas. Despite its arid, semi-desert setting, clever landscaping and vast quantities of water have created an oasis of lawns, flowers and exotic trees. There is a world-class 18-hole Gary Player-designed golf course, an enormous man-made lake with a full range of water sports, a crocodile farm, a casino, cinemas, discos, and cabaret and concert halls where international stars used to appear (and may again in post-apartheid South Africa).

GETTING THERE

It is an easy three hour drive from Johannesburg to Sun City. Take the R24 via Krugersdorp to Rustenburg. From Rustenburg go west on the R27 until you get to the R565 turnoff; follow the R565 and the signs to Sun City.

Buses depart from the Leyds Street Terminus (Rotunda) daily at 9 a.m. On Thursday, Friday and Saturday there are additional services. They return at 10 p.m.

The Sun City Express

There is a also a special train, the Sun City Express, which leaves Johannesburg at 8.30 a.m. every Saturday and most holidays, arriving at Sun City station at 12.15. You have the day to spend at the resorts and then the train whisks you back to the city at 10.30 p.m., arriving at 2.30 a.m. Book for both buses and train at *Computicket*, tel. (011) 331-9991.

Bop Air has daily scheduled flights from Jan Smuts International Airport. Tel. (011) 975-3904.

ACCOMMODATION

All three hotels in Sun City are owned and managed by Sun International. To book, ring (014651) 2-1000 or (011) 783-8660.

The Cascades is the most expensive and luxurious of the three. As its name suggests, water is the theme of the hotel and its liberal use has resulted in lush, tropical grounds. The enormous swimming pool is very inviting and there is even a rain forest with streams, waterfalls, paths and bridges through which guests may wander.

The rooms are large and nicely furnished.

The Sun City Hotel has comfortable, spacious rooms but lacks the glitter of the Cascades. The casinos, cabaret theatres, discos and cinemas are located here.

The Cabanas offers the most reasonable prices and accommodation is geared to family units that are basic but more than adequate. All three resorts are linked to the casino, crocodile farm and each other by an aerial monorail. Each hotel has its own swimming pool and all have access to the golf course and lake.

EASTERN TRANSVAAL: THE PANORAMA ROUTE

INTRODUCTION

Man-made forests

In the Eastern Transvaal where the savannah of the *lowfeld* meets the massive flank of the Drakensberg Mountains, lies some of the most dramatic and awesome scenery in South Africa. The Drakensberg escarpment stretches for roughly 300 km and its length is punctuated by gorges, eroded rock formations, rivers, waterfalls and breathtaking passes. Formerly a thriving centre of gold mining activity, this region now focuses on forestry and tourism. There was little indigenous forest when the gold rush of the late nineteenth century occurred. The mines were in dire need of timber, however, and this prompted the development of a forestry industry. Today, large-scale farming of pine, eucalyptus and wattle is carried out and the groves of trees seem to stretch endlessly in all directions, carpeting the undulating hillsides in geometric patterns. The Eastern Transvaal region now encompasses the largest man-made forest in South Africa, supplying half the country's timber needs.

Scenic vistas

One of the best introductions to the Eastern Transvaal is to travel the Panorama Route. This is an informal term for a scenic journey through the historic towns and spectacular landscapes of the region. The scenery and vistas are unrivaled and in addition, out door activites abound. Late spring and summer are the ideal months to visit this area. Then the hillsides and canyons are intensely green and the rivers are running high. However, the vistas are always breathtaking regardless of the season, and avid trekkers might actually prefer to visit during the cooler months. The Eastern Transvaal has a wide range of resorts offering every amenity and

South Africa

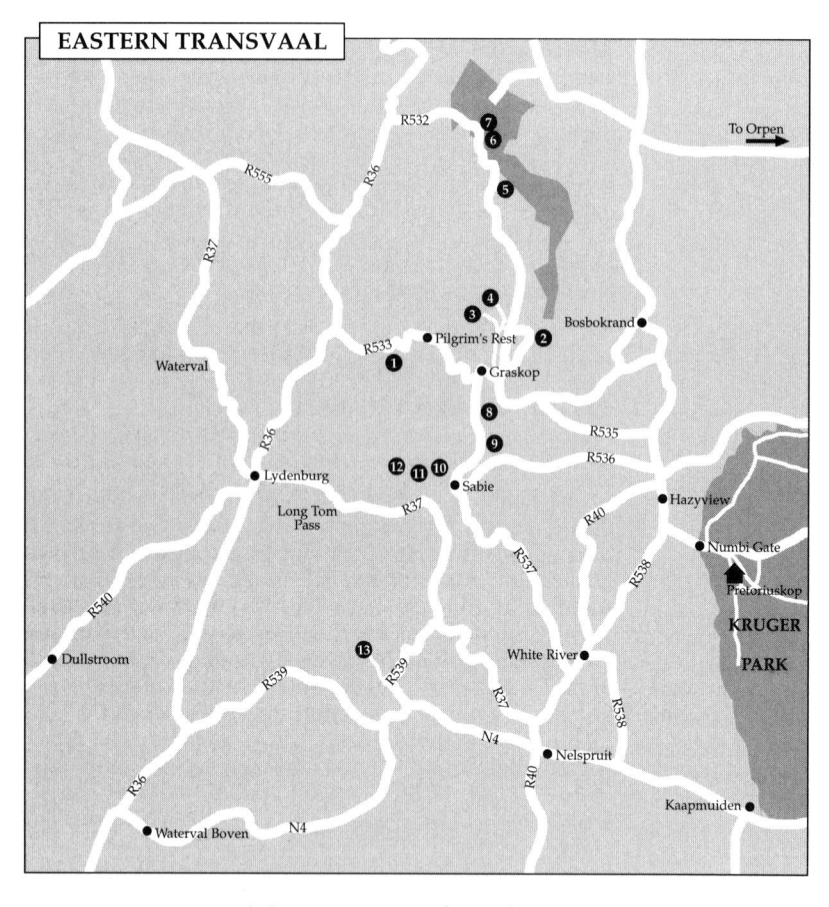

activity; caravan parks and camp-sites are numerous. Allow a minimum of two full days to explore this region and if you have more time, a foray into the neighbouring Kruger National Park is highly recommended.

GETTING THERE

From Pretoria or Johannesburg it takes about 3 1/2 hours to Pilgrim's Rest. The N4 is an excellent road and is your most direct route.

Alternatively, *Link Air* flies from Johannesburg to Nelspruit at least six times a day; the flight time is approximately 35 minutes. You will need to hire a car in Nelspruit to tour the area, and *Avis* has a desk at the airport.

ACCOMMODATION

Pilgrim's Rest
The Mount Sheba Hotel***. Tel. 0131532 and ask for Pilgrim's Rest 17. This is a wonderfully charming and scenically situated lodge just outside Pilgrim's Rest. Perched on the edge of the escarpment, it offers many kilometres of hiking trails, a small trout pond, a tennis court, a swimming pool and an excellent restaurant. Rooms or cottages are available and all have fireplaces.

Overvaal Pilgrim's Rest. Tel. 0131532 and ask for 4. **The Royal Hotel,** built in 1888 and centrally located in the heart of the historic village, is owned by the *Overvaal Resorts Group.* Rooms are small but have been lovingly restored and decorated with period pieces. Guests may also be housed in some of the restored miners' cottages adjacent to the Royal. There is a caravan park along the banks of the Blyde River and a number of restaurants.

— Miner's cottages

Sabie
Glass's Bungalows. Tel. 0131512 and ask for 110. This unpretentious resort is located along the banks of the Sabie River. Accommodation may be taken in bungalows or chalets, all of which are fully equipped. There is a good restaurant here called the **Loggerhead,** which specializes in trout dishes.

Ohrigstad
F.H. Odendaal Camp. Tel. (013231) 881. This resort is situated on the rim of the Blyde River Canyon and offers a variety of possibilities: fully equipped chalet s and cottages or camping and caravan sites. It is a very popular resort as it is often used as a stopping off point by visitors *en route* to the Kruger National Park. For a full description of the activities available here see page**.

White River
Cybele Forest Lodge. Tel. (01311) 5-0511; fax (01311) 32-839. This intimate hunting lodge is a member of the highly respected **Relais et Chateaux**, the only hotel in South Africa to attain this status. It is set in 300 acres of magnificent terrain and all the rooms and suites are exquisitely decorated. The restaurant is one of the finest in the country. Riding, trout fishing, walking, swimming and scenic helicopter trips are featured. The lodge also offers a unique five night/four day combination package with Londolozi.

— Superb accommodation

Hazyview
Casa Do Sol***. Tel. 0131242 and ask for 22. This is a lovely hotel complex in a private nature reserve amidst lush gardens and towering groves of bamboo and palm. The feeling here is reminiscent of a Mediterranean village. The buildings are whitewashed stucco with red tiled roofs, arched windows and doors. Walled, narrow brick walkways meander up the hillside and a profusion of bougainvillea spills everywhere. There are seven walking trails on the property and daily game drives to the neighbouring Kruger Park are offered. Riding, fishing, swimming and tennis are also available.

Close to the Kruger

PILGRIM'S REST

Pilgrim's Rest is a delightful and charming town situated at the heart of the Panorama Route. When Alec 'Wheelbarrow' Patterson discovered gold here in 1873, a town literally sprang up overnight. A prospector who joined Patterson named the site Pilgrim's Rest because he believed his search for fortune had ended at last. In six weeks, 1,600 prospectors from all over the world had arrived in the hope of striking it rich. Their journey was an exceedingly difficult one for there were no roads or transport to this region.

The perils of prospecting

The diggers landed at Delagoa Bay in neighbouring Mozambique; from there they faced an arduous and perilous 300 km trek across the *lowveld*. Hostile black tribes, malaria, sleeping sickness and dangerous animals claimed many lives.

For those who succeeded in reaching Pilgrim's Rest, life was very difficult and only a few found their fortune. Most of the gold discovered by the diggers was all uvial and the small stream that ran through town was jammed with panning prospectors. Several large nuggets were found and during 1875 alone, gold to the value of £200,000 was recovered from the stream. However, the alluvial gold was quickly exhausted and most of the diggers moved on to seek their fortunes elsewhere. The real wealth of gold, as it turned out, lay just under the surface of the stony outcrops on top of the hills of this valley. The Pilgrim's Rest – Graskop – Sabie triangle forms the largest and richest gold field in South Africa. A full-scale mining operation was mounted, which lasted until 1971. At that time the price of gold was $35.00 an ounce and the mines in this area were deemed to be unprofitable and were subsequently closed. With the price of gold standing at ten times that figure today, the

Richest gold field in South Africa

Pilgrim's Rest, once a thriving gold mining town, is now a national monument in the Eastern Transvaal.

Information bureau

Rand Mining Company, which owns all mineral rights in this region, is now opening two new mines near Pilgrim's Rest. The company is also reprocessing the old slag heaps to extract whatever gold was overlooked, an estimated twenty per cent!

Pilgrim's Rest is now a national monument and has been preserved as a living museum of the gold rush era. It is a small, sleepy village with an authentic frontier feeling, not spoiled by out-of-place shops and attractions. There is an information bureau opposite the Royal Hotel. Guided tours of the town leave here twice daily and once on Saturdays. The small museum in Main Street is quite interesting and pictorially portrays the gold mining process. There are also a number of antique, craft and curio shops and several tea-rooms.

If you have the time, buy a ticket at the museum for a tour of the diggings. The price is minimal and tours are given at 10a.m., 11a.m., 12noon, 2p.m. and 3p.m. The site is 1.2 km beyond the museum. To set the scene, the

Tour the diggings — knowledgeable guide first gives a brief synopsis of the colourful personalities that settled this mining town. You then descend to the stream, passing through actual claims or diggings as evidenced by the heaps of dirt and rubble. At the stream there is a sluice box and a demonstration of gold panning is given. Very often gold tailings are found and occasionally a nugget turns up. From the sluice you proceed to the rock crusher, which is run by a waterwheel. The tour finishes with a look at a mine shaft entrance and then you are free to wander through several replicas of the miners' houses. All in all, this is a very informative and interesting tour.

PANORAMA ROUTE: NORTH

On leaving Pilgrim's Rest you pass through the small village of Graskop. There are two restaurants as well as a bakery here. You might consider buying provisions for a picnic lunch to enjoy later in the day. For a quick bite, try **Harriet's Pancake Bar**; the menu features sweet and savoury crêpes at very reasonable prices. From Graskop turn north along the R532 for the real scenic wonders of the Eastern Transvaal. Follow the signs to **God's Window** and stop for a panoramic view of the *lowveld*. Beyond the car park there is a network of paths which leads to several look-out points. On a clear day you can apparently see Maputo and the Indian Ocean. In the late 1880s the only source of timber was in the *lowveld*. The miners used cables thrown down from **God's Window** to drag the wood 1,000 metres up the sheer escarpment.

God's Window

In addition to the views there is a short trail leading to a 'rain forest'. There are also picnic tables and *braai* pits here so you might want to plan ahead and bring lunch.

Continuing along the R532 you will see signposts for two waterfalls. To reach the **Lisbon Falls** drive 2 km back toward Graskop and then turn at the sign and follow the access road for an additional 2 km. A series of pools are the source of a rushing cascade of water which falls over sheer rock walls. The **Berlin Falls** are 2 km north of the point where the loop road to God's Window rejoins the R532. Here the water plunges 48 metres down a rocky cliff and falls to a deep circular pool at the bottom of the chasm. The volume of water is not particularly impressive but the setting is lovely. There is a footpath which leads above the falls and along to the opposite side of the gorge.

Rejoin the main road and continue heading north to **Bourke's Luck Potholes.** Tom Bourke was a prospector

Sun City

A geological oddity

lured to the region during the gold rush of the 1880s. Although he predicted the presence of gold in this part of the river, he never personally discovered any. Others were more fortunate and a small mine was established in the vicinity. The confluence of two rivers, the Blyde and the Treur, results in turbulent, swirling waters which have formed numerous deep and cylindrical 'potholes' over the ages. An excellent system of pathways and bridges crosses the river.

However, before you set out on a walk to the Potholes, it would be a good idea to spend 15 minutes at the information centre. Here there is a brief but very comprehensive schematic guide which succinctly portrays the geological forces that created this region. The flora and fauna of the area are also shown and there is a well-executed diorama of the vegetation and wildlife that inhabit the gorge. To the left of the entrance you will find a printed sheet of paper with an interpretation of the walk you are about to undertake; it is quite helpful.

The Potholes are unusual and fascinating and it is easy to see the vestiges of dozens of other holes that were carved into the rock when water levels were much higher. There is a nominal entrance fee to get to this area but it is well worth the price. Picnic tables, *braai* pits, restrooms and a snack bar are conveniently located near the entrance gate.

Stone buttresses

Beyond Bourke's Luck on the R532 is the **Blyde River Canyon** a 26 km ravine which runs parallel with the escarpment. The road meanders along the rim of the canyon for 14 km, providing breathtaking vistas. The far canyon wall has huge weathered stone buttresses in all shapes and sizes. The stratified layers of rock are multi-coloured and the lower slopes, which run to the river, are covered in dense vegetation. For the most scenic vantage point of the canyon, turn off at the sign for the **Three Rondavels**. From the car park it is only a two minute walk to the lip of the ravine. A reservoir is clearly visible from here as is the flat expanse of the lowveld that can be seen beyond the rim of the escarpment. Three enormous stone towers with vegetated 'roofs', resembling rondavels, are directly across the canyon from this spectacular lookout point.

Returning to the main road it is only another 3 km to the end of the Panorama Route. The **F.H. Odendaal Camp** is situated here and it offers both day or overnight visitors many activities. There is an admission fee per person and vehicle; a petrol station, bottle store and food

South Africa

Hiking trails

store are conveniently located at the gate. As a guest you can enjoy nine holes of golf, miniature golf, horseback riding, playgrounds, swimming pools and tennis. There is a good airfield here and scenic flights through the canyon are offered daily. There are also four hiking trails which originate near **World's End**, a scenic viewpoint at the far perimeter of the camp. The views do not rival those from the Three Rondavels, but the trails are perfect for a short walk, ranging from 2 to 5 km in length.

This is the northernmost point of the Panorama Route. From here you have three options: you can backtrack on the R532 to Graskop; you can continue on past the F.H. Odendaal Camp to where the R532 intersects with the R36, follow the R36 south to Ohrigstad and back to the R533 and Pilgrim's Rest; or you can drive back as far as Bourke's Luck and take the gravel road back to Pilgrim's Rest. The quickest option is to retrace the original route, but your choice will depend on the time of day and where you are staying. Exploring Pilgrim's Rest and following the Panorama Route North takes a full day.

PANORAMA ROUTE: SOUTH

Twelve kilometres south of Graskop on the R532 there is a turnoff for the **Mac Mac Falls**. In the heyday of the gold rush there were so many Scottish prospectors in this area that it became known as MacMac. At this spot the river comes crashing down a narrow course above the falls, then rushes out over the cliff's edge in a torrent of water. The river splits into two falls at the very lip of the gorge and then plunges down a 65 metre drop. The twin cascades resulted when the rocks at the top of the cliff were blasted apart more than a century ago, after prospectors had discovered gold embedded in the stone. The only observation point for the falls is at the end of a long series of stone steps. The viewing angle, although a bit oblique for photographs, is adequate. The views of the dramatic gorge alone make this stop worthwhile.

Twin cascades

Two kilometres past the falls there is an attraction known as the **Mac Mac Pools**. Here a gently meandering stream has cut a path down a beautiful, grassy hillside. Rocks have slowed the flow, resulting in a series of pools. The water is crystal clear and swimming is a delight. There is a small entrance fee at the gate but it is well worth the charge. There are very clean restroom facilities where you can change into a bathing costume. I can't think of a nicer spot for a picnic and a swim after a day of touring this region.

A terrific swimming spot!

Continuing south on the R532 a further 10 km you will reach the town of **Sabie,** another of the gold rush towns in this region. Today it is the centre of the country's forestry industry. There are a number of restaurants, hotels and shops, as well as the **Cultural Historical Forestry Museum**, in Ford Street. This may be the only museum of its kind in the world, and the exhibits are interesting to many visitors. It is open 9a.m. – 1p.m. and 2p.m. – 4p.m. Monday – Friday and 9a.m. – 11.30a.m. Saturday.

A short distance beyond Sabie there are three scenic waterfalls. To find the access road, turn at the sign to **Lone Creek Falls**. The first waterfall along this route is called **Bridal Veil**. You must turn off the tarred road on to a dirt logging track and drive for 3 km to reach it. At the parking area you will find public restrooms and a trail leading to the cascade. It is a fairly strenuous 15-minute hike to the Bridal Veil falls. As the name suggests, the flow of water is not great and the lower half is misty. Of the three waterfalls, this is the least impressive and the most difficult to get to.

Once back on the tarred road, look for the turn off on the left to **Horseshoe Falls**. At the car park there is an enterprising individual selling cold drinks and some souvenir carvings. It is a three minute walk to the viewpoint. These falls are in a pretty setting although they are not very high.

Rejoin the tarred road and continue to the very end where you will find **Lone Creek Falls**. If you only have the time or energy for one waterfall, this should be it. The cascade falls from a great height (68 metres), dramatically pouring off a sheer rock cliff lush with green moss and ferns. The pool of water at the base is rimmed with large boulders and although it is not deep, it looks inviting for a quick dip.

Most impressive of the three waterfalls

This completes the Panorama Route South. From Sabie you might consider heading east to Hazyview or south to White River for another night. This area abounds with beautiful resorts and is just a stone's throw from the Kruger National Park. If, however, you are driving back to Johannesburg, there is a fascinating cave at **Sudwala** that you might like to visit. To reach it, follow the R532 south until it intersects with the R539; look for the signs to **Sudwala Grotto**. At the bottom of the access road to the cavern there is a hotel and restaurant; take-away food is available. From here a narrow, winding road leads to the cave entrance where guided tours are given daily

The Sudwala Grotto

from 9a.m. to 4p.m. There is a moderate entrance fee for adults; it lasts about 45 minutes and is not strenuous.

Situated in the dolomite **Mankelekele Mountains**, this cavern has had a long and colourful history of human occupation. Rock art and artefacts found in the cave indicate that Stone Age people inhabited it eons ago. In more modern times it was used for a period of more than 20 years, between 1815 and 1836, as a refuge for the Swazi people who were fleeing from the militant Zulus. Later, in 1855 the heir apparent to the Swazi throne and 3,000 of his followers (and their cattle) were trapped in the Sudwala Caves for several months, this time as a result of a family feud between two brothers . During the Boer War, ammunition was secreted in the caves and a rumour persists to this day that the legendary Kruger millions are buried within the cave's passageways.

The Sudwala Caves are the oldest on earth and the largest in South Africa. Much of the grotto has yet to be explored; the complex of caverns is believed to extend for at least 30 km. Lights, especially coloured ones, are kept to a minimum, and there is no music in an effort to maintain a natural, realistic setting. The stalagmites and stalactites are impressive and the main chamber is large enough to stage musical events for an audience of 3,000. For avid cavers, a special five hour adventure is offered on the first Saturday of each month. For R45.00 per person, you will be able to crawl and squirm through 1.6 km of wet passages to the **Crystal Chamber**. Unfortunately, my visit didn't coincide with a special Saturday so I am unable to report first-hand on this experience. However, the literature advises that this is not for the claustrophobic or for anyone 'very large'! For details, write to *The Crystal Tour*, PO Box 48, Schagen 1207 or ring 0131232 and ask for 3911.

Spelunking for the adventurous

ACTIVITIES

Mountain Magic
This is a very special experience which highlights the spectacular beauty of the Eastern Transvaal. A jet-powered helicopter flies you over wooded valleys and cascading waterfalls, past Pilgrim's Rest and through the Blyde River Canyon. You are then set down on top of a remote mountain that overlooks the expanse of the *lowfeld*. Here you enjoy a champagne breakfast or lunch. Book through *DragonFly Helicopter Adventures*, PO Box 1042, White River 1240; tel. (01311) 5-0565; Fax (01311) 3-2839.

Winged Safari
A helicopter whisks you from your hotel to a private game reserve on hte edge of the Kruger Park. Here you are met by an experienced guide and tracker and taken for a three hour game drive in an open Land Rover. Breakfast or lunch is served in the bush. Book through *DragonFly Helicopter Adventures* (see above).

A very special journey

Pride of Africa Steam Train Safari. This is a unique excursion through some of the most spectacular scenery in South Africa. As the brochure so enticingly says, *'The golden age of steam trains and luxury travel has been revived in the heart of the African bush'*. The Pride of Africa consists of seven faithfully restored vintage passenger carriages drawn by steam locomotives. Facilities on the train are elegant and luxurious, the cuisine is divine and the service impeccable. A maximum of 28 guests may participate in this four day/three night adventure which starts in Pretoria and travels to Graskop with stops at Pilgrim's Rest, Bourke's Luck Potholes and the Blyde River Canyon. Passengers spend two nights on the train and one at a private game reserve outside the Kruger National Park. Sightseeing in the Transvaal is by luxury coach. There are departures every Saturday. For brochure and prices, contact *Rovos Rail*, PO Box 2837, Pretoria 0001; tel. (012) 323-6052; fax (012) 323-0843.

KRUGER NATIONAL PARK

INTRODUCTION

Kruger statistics

In 1895 President Paul Kruger proclaimed a sanctuary in the Eastern Transvaal called the Sabi Game Reserve for the preservation of wildlife, whose extinction he feared and foresaw at the hands of hunters. This marked the very first time, on a continent where man and animal seemed to be at perpetual odds, that steps were taken to protect the unique heritage of Africa. In 1926 this sanctuary was enlarged with the appropriation of 70 farms and the Kruger National Park was established. Today, the Kruger is one of the largest game parks in Africa and it continues to grow from private land donations and acquisitions. It extends for a length of 350 km along the Mozambique border, from the Crocodile River in the south all the way to the Limpopo River on the border with Zimbabwe in the north. It averages 60 km in width and there are a number of private game reserves

221

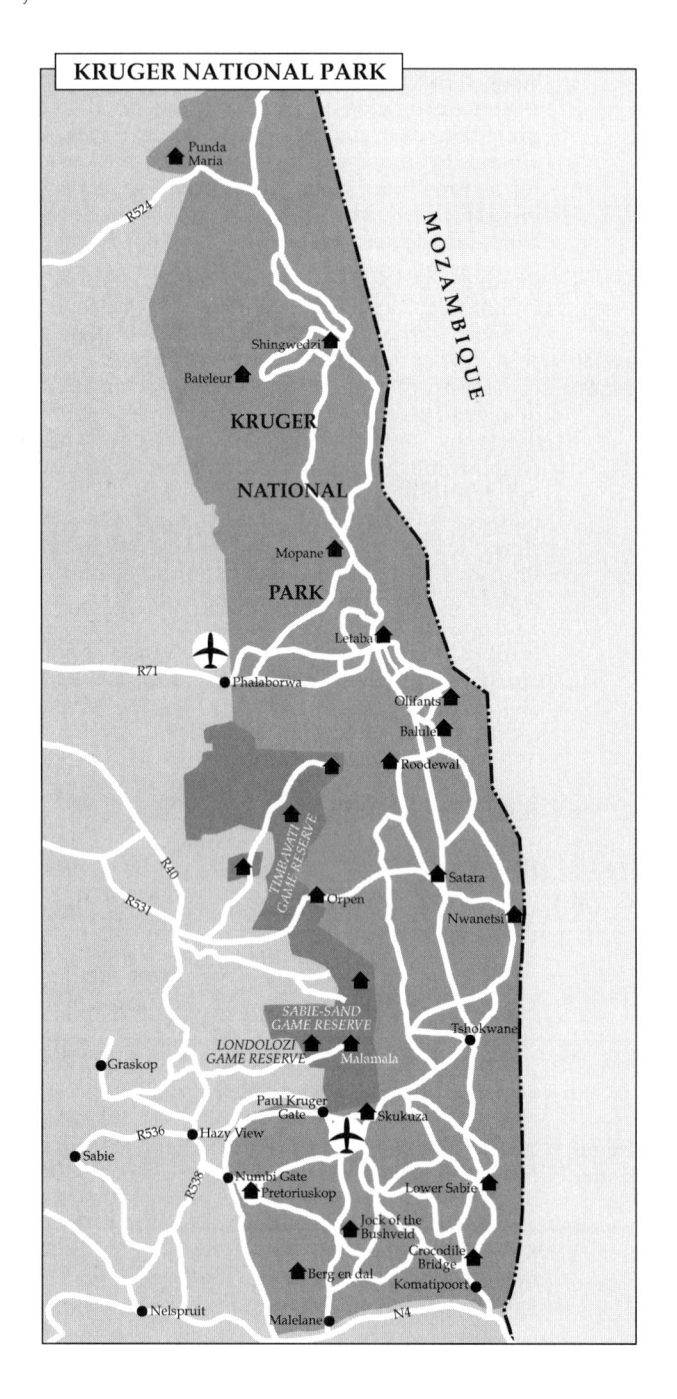

South Africa

222

along its western edge. The terrain is characterized by mopane and acacia scrubland. The climate is temperate with hot summers and cold winter nights. The park protects a staggering 137 species of mammals, 112 of reptiles and almost 500 of birds, a greater number than any other reserve on the continent.

Planning your safari

No trip to South Africa would be complete without a foray into the Kruger or a visit to one of the private game reserves adjacent to it. Here is a corner of the country still in tune with the ancient rhythms of Africa. There are several ways to experience the park, depending on the time available, your budget and your expectations. If you want to rough it there is an excellent system of campsites and basic huts, part of a network of 24 rest camps with varying amenities scattered throughout the park. For budget-conscious travellers and family groups there is no other game reserve in Africa that offers such varied, well-organized and reasonably priced accommodation. If your luxury quotient needs replenishing, the private game camps bordering on the park are unmatched in service, setting or facilities anywhere in Africa. However you choose to visit the Kruger, it is guaranteed to be one of the highlights of your holiday.

GETTING THERE

Excellent access from Johannesburg

The drive from Johannesburg takes approximately five hours on excellent roads. There are eight entrances to the Kruger National Park so your route will depend on which area of the reserve you want to visit. The southern reaches are the easiest to get to and the majority of camps, services and visitors are concentrated in that area. Four-wheel drive vehicles are not necessary in the park; the gravel and tarred roads are more than adequate.

A large number of tour operators offer scheduled coach trips to the Kruger National Park from Johannesburg, Nelspruit and Durban.

There is a scheduled service daily from Johannesburg and Durban to Skukuza (Paul Kruger Gate) on *Comair*, telephone (011) 973-2911 . At Skukuza you can hire a car from *Avis*; tel. (0131252) 141. *Comair* also flies from Johannesburg to Phalaborwa, 170 km north of Skukuza. *Avis* cars may be hired at the airport; tel. (01524) 5169.

The park gates are open from sunrise to sunset and all visitors must sign in, pay an entrance fee and accept a leaflet outlining the rules of the park. The gates are closed between 1 and 1.30p.m. and the reception offices between

South Africa

Park entrances 1 and 2 p.m., so plan your visit accordingly. Visitors are advised to take a malarial prophylaxsis (available at the gates) upon entering the Park. The eight entrances, listed from south to north, are: Crocodile Bridge, Malelane, Numbi, Paul Kruger (Skukuza), Orpen, Phalaborwa, Punda Maria, Pafuri.

ACCOMMODATION

There is an excellent selection of private and public rest camps in the Kruger Park; indeed I cannot think of any other game reserve in Africa that is so well organized. However, tourist demand is high and it is advisable to reserve accommodation through the *National Parks Board offices;* tel. (012) 343-1991. Bookings can be made one year **Book in advance** in advance and if you are planning to go during the school holiday period in July and August it is essential to do so.

To explore the entire expanse of the park you would need at least a week as the distances are vast. Many visitors choose to move between two or three camps so that they can experience the variety of habitats within the park. There is a range of accommodation at most of the camps. The five private camps are only available on a block-booking basis, meaning that you must reserve the entire camp. They can sleep 12 – 19 people and they only make sense if you are travelling with a group; for that reason I have included them in the list below, but I have not detailed the facilities at each camp.

Rest camps The rest camps described are all exceptionally nice and comfortable. The types of accommodation include luxurious, fully equipped guest cottages, two-bedroomed family cottages with en-suite bathrooms, with or without kitchenette, thatched rondavels with showers and toilets; and basic 2 – 5 bed huts close to communal ablution blocks and field kitchens. Many of the camps have restaurants and food shops; if not, you must bring all your own supplies. The following list is arranged from south to north.

Crocodile Bridge Camp. Nicely situated overlooking a river, this small camp offers two- and three-bed thatched chalets with bath and refrigerator but no kitchen, as well as 12 camping sites. There is a small shop and petrol station.

Malelane Private Camp

Berg en Dal. This is a large, well-organized camp with attractive accommodation built from native materials. Visitors may choose to stay in family cottages with

Cape Peninsula flora.

Cable car ascending Table Mountain with the distinctive "sugarloaf" peak of Lion's Head in the background.

Cape Town's newest tourist attraction – the rejuvenated Victoria & Alfred Docks.

Amazing red sand dunes of the Kalahari Desert.

Tsitsikamma's rugged coastline.

The Huguenot Monument in Franschhoek.

Sociable weavers' nests in the Kalahari Desert.

kitchenettes, three-bed thatched rondavels with bathrooms and kitchens, fully equipped guest cottages or at one of 70 tent and caravan sites. Facilities include a shop, licensed restaurant, swimmming pool, laundry, petrol station and visitor centre.

Jock of the Bushveld Private Camp

Lower Sabie. Guest cottages, thatched chalets with bathroom and refrigerators, five-bed family cottages with kitchens and 27 camping sites are offered at this pleasant camp. There is a restaurant, a shop and a petrol station.

Pretoriuskop. The game viewing is generally very good here as there is a network of roads in this area. This camp holds 300 people and there is a full range of accommodation including 50 camping and caravan sites. There is a restaurant, a shop, a petrol station and a swimming pool.

Park headquarters **Skukuza.** This is the largest camp in the park and serves as the central headquarters. Five hundred guests can stay here in all the types of rondavels and cottages mentioned. Skukuza also has a large campsite, an airport, a post office, a petrol station, car hire, a bank, medical services, a shop and two restaurants. The information centre at Skukuza is the most extensive in the park, with films, exhibitions and a library.

Narina. As I am writing this, a new luxury-class rest camp is under construction on the Sabie River just 6 km from Skukuza. Two bedroomed, two bathroomed, air-conditioned chalets with private balconies will be offered along with all the amenities and comforts of a five-star hotel.

Nwandezi Private Camp

Satara. Satara is the second largest of the rest camps with a range of guest cottages, family cottages with kitchenettes and self-contained thatched rondavels. The camp also has 30 camping and caravan sites, a restaurant, an information centre, a shop, a laundry, a petrol station and a garage. Bird-watching is particularly rewarding here and lions are frequently sighted.

Marula Caravan and Camping Park. A well-situated camp on the banks of the Timbatavi River for campers only; common ablution blocks, no electricity.

Orphen. A very small rest camp with several thatched rondavels that share ablution and kitchen blocks; there is no electricity in this camp. There is a petrol station and a shop, but no perishable foods are sold.

Roodewal Private Camp

Balule. A very basic bush camp with a small number of

White rhino in Kruger National Park.

three-bed thatched rondavels, ten camping and caravan sites, shared ablution facilities, and no electricity or kitchen. Firewood and a communal freezer are available.

Olifants. Olifants Camp is beautifully situated high on a bluff overlooking the river of the same name. All types of accommodation are available here and there is a shop, a licensed restaurant, a petrol station, an information centre and an amphitheatre where films are shown. A special feature of this camp is the lookout platform built for game viewing from a height.

Olifants means elephants in Afrikaans

Letaba. Lovely grassy and tree-shaded grounds make this one of the park's most attractive camps. Visitors may stay in family cottages with bathrooms and kitchens or in self-contained thatched huts with bathrooms and fridges. There are also 20 camping and caravan sites, a restaurant, a shop, a petrol station, a laundry, a post office and a garage.

Boulders Private Camp

Bateleur Bushveld Camp. By definition, a bushveld camp is smaller, more basic or rustic, with few if any facilities. Bateleur offers family cottages alongside the Tsange River.

Shingwedzi. Guests are accommodated in two-, three- or

Kruger National Park

four-bedroomed chalets with en-suite bathrooms and kitchens; a large camping and caravan ground is available. Camp facilities include a licensed restaurant, a shop, a swimming pool, a petrol station and an information centre.

The northernmost rest camp

Punda Maria. This is the northernmost of the camps and it is located in one of the most interesting areas of the park. Family cottages with kitchenettes, rondavels with baths and fridges, and camping and caravan sites are available. There is a restaurant, a shop and a petrol station.

GAME VIEWING

Superb game-viewing

The Kruger National Park offers some of the finest game-viewing in the world. The facilities are excellent and the impressive 2,000 km network of roads is well maintained. The park encompasses a wide range of habitats, which allows for a great diversity of species. In my opinion there is no game park in the world that can compare. You will undoubtedly encounter many members of the antelope family: kudu, eland, impala, reed-buck, duiker, sable, waterbuck, steenbok and dik-dik. There are also large numbers of zebra, wildebeest, buffalo, giraffe, white and black rhino and elephant. The chances are good that you will spot all or several of the predators: lion, hyena, leopard, cheetah and wild dogs.

The Kruger is so immense that it is difficult to know exactly where to start your game-viewing. Although it is impossible to say which areas will be most rewarding on any given day, a bit of general information may be helpful in selecting your route. Hippos and crocodiles are most easily spotted between the Lower Sabie and Crocodile Bridge Camps. Lions seem to be most numerous in the vicinity of the Jock of the Bushveld Camp, in an area called Pretoriuskop. This is the region where white rhinos were reintroduced to the park, so the chances of seeing one are good. Elephants and leopards are frequently spotted in the northern section of the park near Shingwedzi. At Nwanedzi Camp, there are large concentrations of zebra, giraffe and wildebeest; elephants are also numerous along the Sweni River adjacent to this camp. The park's largest area of grassy plains is near Satara Camp; these plains attract large herds of buffalo, zebra and wildebeest, as well as their attendant predators.

There is good game viewing all year round in the Kruger. It is easiest to spot the animals in the winter

When to visit months when the trees and shrubs have lost their leaves and animals tend to congregate at waterholes. The summer months are better for bird-watching, however. If you are visiting the park in the summer, be prepared for temperatures that hover around 40°C. Most of the camps have airconditioning and you might consider hiring an airconditioned car as well. Game viewing with a professional guide in a four-wheel drive vehicle can be arranged. It is best to book in advance for this service with the *National Parks Board* offices or at the information centre at Skukuza.

WILDERNESS TRAILS

Walking safaris Four wilderness trails have been established in the Kruger National Park. Four day/three night walking safaris are offered twice weekly all year round under the guidance of qualified game rangers. They leave on Mondays and Fridays; groups are limited to eight people between the ages of 12 and 60. It is not necessary to carry your own gear as tents and food are supplied. Advance booking is essential through one of the *National Parks Board* offices.

PARK REGULATIONS

There are only a few rules and they are for the protection of animals and visitors alike. Vehicles *must* keep to the public roads at all times. Although closed tracks may be alluring, visitors stand no better chance of spotting game on them than on the official roads.

The speed limit of 50 kph on tarred roads and 40 kph on gravel is strictly enforced. There is little sense in hurrying through the park if you are game viewing. Bear in mind that on an organized safari the driver rarely exceeds 20 kph.

If you are staying overnight at one of the rest camps, you must be in camp by sundown and you are not allowed to leave before daybreak.

Don't feed the animals Never feed any of the animals. Monkeys and baboons, in particular, quickly become a nuisance and have to be put down. As it is, the baboons in the Kruger Park are very bold and it is common to see them climbing all over cars that have stopped along the road for game-viewing. If this happens to you, just be sure to keep your windows shut.

The most important rule of the park is to never get out of your vehicle except in the designated camp or picnic

South Africa's private game lodges outside of Kruger Park are the most luxurious in Africa.

A close call

areas. It is the animals that are free to roam here, not the human visitors! On my last visit we had stopped along a river bank to watch some hippos. The driver of the car parked next to us got out to get something from the boot, and his children opened the other doors, probably to get some air. The setting looked harmless enough but the man hadn't been out of his car for a minute when a lion strolled by, not even 5 metres from where he stood. It only takes seconds for the unthinkable to happen. Don't be stupid and break rules that have been made for your own protection!

PRIVATE GAME RESERVES OF THE EASTERN TRANSVAAL

One of the unique features of the Kruger National Park is the large bloc of privately owned land along its western edge. A number of private game reserves have been established in this area, dedicated to promoting wildlife and habitat conservation. Guests may stay at a dozen or so luxury lodges where service, food and amenities are

Fewer rules and regulations

top-notch. Because the game lodges are on private rather than government land, game viewing is much less restricted here than in the Kruger National Park. Safaris are conducted in open vehicles, walking is encouraged, breakfast may be eaten in the bush and night drives are featured. The guides are not confined to designated roads and are thus able to follow the game over hill and dale. As a result, you get very close indeed to the animals in these reserves. Night drives are especially exciting and rewarding because this is when the animals, especially predators, are most active. None of the private camps is inexpensive, but they are worth every penny if you can afford the tariff. If you want to see as many animals as possible in a limited amount of time, these lodges will rarely disappoint you.

Rattray Reserves:
Rattray Reserves is the largest tract of privately owned game land in South Africa (18,000 hectares). There are three camps in the reserve and although the style of accommodation differs, the service and professionalism of the staff is the same in all three.

MalaMala. This is the flagship of the company. It has been voted the top safari lodge in the world and the list of visitors is star-studded. A maximum of 50 guests is accommodated in spacious thatched rondavels, complete with telephones and his and her bathrooms. The grounds are lovely and the camp is set on a knoll overlooking the perennial Sand River. Personalized service is assured by a staff to guest ratio of three to one. The hand-picked game guides are some of the best in the world and they are assisted by trackers who are masters at spotting and tracking game. Sightings of the big five (elephant, rhino, buffalo, lion and leopard) are extremely common here. I have been on hundreds of safaris but I have never got closer to the game than at MalaMala. Although there is not much African bush feeling here and the standard of accommodation approaches that of a hotel, this is a very special experience.

Top safari lodge in the world

Kirkman's Kamp. Situated in the southern region of the reserve. A historic homestead dating from 1902 is the centrepiece of this camp, and now serves as the dining room and lounge area. Twenty guests are accommodated in cottages overlooking the Sand River.

Each room has its own bathroom and veranda and is decorated with authentic period furnishings, in keeping with the historic nature of the place. Air conditioning is one of the only concessions to modern conveniences you will encounter at Kirkman's.

Harry's. This is the smallest and most intimate of the Rattray camps. Low-slung buildings are decorated in the Ndebele style. A maximum of 16 guests can be accommodated in seven en suite double rooms. Meals are taken outside at the river's edge and the atmosphere is casual and rustic.

Trekker Trails. The newest addition to the Rattray collection. For those who want a bush experience unadulterated by electricity and permanent structures, this intimate tented camp provides an alternative. A mere six guests can be accommodated in three well-appointed double tents with private ablution facilities. The day is spent walking with an armed ranger and an experienced tracker. In the evening, guests are taken on a night drive.

To get to the Rattray Reserves, enter the Kruger National Park at the Paul Kruger (Skukuza) gate and follow the MalaMala signs. There is a private airstrip at MalaMala and Rattray offers daily direct flights from Johannesburg in chartered, pressurized King Air aircraft. If you fly to Skukuza with *Comair*, Rattray staff will meet you at the airport. To book directly ring (011) 789-2677 or fax (011) 886-4382. Reservations may also be made through any of the *SAR Travel* offices.

Londolozi Game Reserve

The owners of Londolozi have been at the forefront of conservation planning in South Africa. They are committed to a programme of habitat management, a concept at odds with that of the Kruger National Park, where nature takes its own course without the help of man. Their mission, as they put it, is to create a model in wise land management and to demonstrate that man and wildlife can interact on a sustainable basis. The three Londolozi camps all overlook the Sand River. Each is independently run to ensure exclusivity.

Main Camp. This camp accommodates a maximum of 24 guests in either luxury chalets with bathrooms or in rustic thatched rondavels with showers. Daytime meals are taken on a balcony suspended high above the river; dinner is served under the stars in a reed-enclosed *boma*.

Bush Camp. Offers four luxurious rock cabins with private bathrooms. Everything here has been created from indigenous materials and integrates harmoniously with the habitat.

Tree Camp. The *pièce de résistance* of Londolozi. It was originally built for the owners' personal use but has now been converted to sleep eight guests. There are four luxury bedrooms with bathrooms en suite and an open living area perched high up in the canopy of a massive ebony tree. The Tree Camp has its own personal ranger and vehicle. Wonderful sights and sounds abound in this very special camp.

All three of the camps feature daily and nightly game drives as well as walking safaris. Londolozi has a reputation for leopards due in part to the film *The Silent Hunter*, which was filmed here by the owner, John Varty. The camp has its own airstrip and air charters can be arranged; otherwise, guests will be met at the Skukuza airport. To book, ring (011) 803-8421; fax (0 11) 803-1810. Or contact *SAR Travel*.

Sabi Sabi Game Reserve
There are two lodges at Sabi Sabi: the **Bush Lodge** and the **River Lodge**. Both offer air-conditioned accommodation in luxury thatched chalets complete with en-suite bathrooms. Bush Lodge is slightly bigger, with 25 twin-bedded chalets; River Lodge has 20. Day and night game drives are offered in open vehicles with professional rangers and trackers. Walking safaris are also offered. A nice feature of Sabi Sabi is the game-viewing hide which overlooks a waterhole. There is a private airfield or guests can be collected at Skukuza. For reservations ring (011) 880-4840 or contact *SAR Travel*.

Inyati. Situated on the Sand River in the Sabi Sand Game Reserve, this camp sleeps 16 guests in thatched chalets with en-suite tiled bathrooms. Daily and nightly game drives, walking safaris and a treetop viewing platform are offered. Inyati has its own landing strip or will meet guests at Skukuza airport. Tel. (011) 883-5484 or book through *SAR Travel*.

Timbatavi Game Reserve
Timbatavi is in the northern sector of the private reserve land and it covers an area of about 750 sq km adjacent to the Kruger Park. This reserve has long been famous for its rare white lions. Until recently only one remained and it was feared that the recessive gene would be lost forever when she died. The good news is that one of her offspring, a normal tawny lion, gave birth to cubs not long ago and one of them was pure white!

There are several private game lodges in this reserve, my favourites of which are **Motswari Game Lodge** and its sister camp, **M'Bali**. Motswari can sleep 22 guests in

The white lions of Timbatavi

11 air-conditioned chalets. M'Bali is a bit different and if you are seeking a 'bush' experience, this may be the camp for you. It is 9 km from Motswari Lodge and consists of seven 'habitents' strung out along the Shlaralumi River, high above the ground on wooden platforms with extended balconies that afford wonderful views of the river and bushveld. The canvas is protected by a huge canopy of thatch and timber and each habitent has its own fully appointed bathroom on ground level. Night and day drives, walking safaris, bush breakfasts, bush barbecues and hides at waterholes are featured at both camps. M'Bali is the most affordable of the private camps outside the Kruger Park but service, game-viewing and cuisine are still good. Access is easiest from Phalaborwa Airport which is served by scheduled daily flights on *Comair*. To book, ring (011) 463-1990; fax (011) 463-1992. Or contact *SAR Travel*.

Ngala Game Lodge is located in the southern Timbatavi, right on the western boundary of the Kruger National Park. A maximum of 28 guests can be accommodated in air conditioned rondavels with private bathrooms. Game drives and walking are offered. This camp has its own charter aircraft and will fly you to its own airfield. For reservations, ring (011) 803-4132.

[margin: Habitents]

THE DRAKENSBERG

INTRODUCTION

The Drakensberg is the highest mountain range in Southern Africa and its majestic scenery is unrivalled in the land. The mountains stretch for a distance of 450 km and separate the low-lying coastal belt from the higher plateau of the interior. Drakensberg means 'dragon mountains', a name given to this impressive basalt range by the Voortrekkers; influenced by black folklore, they believed the rugged chain of peaks resembled a dragon's spine. Perhaps there was something prescient in the name, for dragons, in the guise of dinosaurs, did once roam this region, as their fossilized bones and three-toed footprints show.

The weather in the Drakensberg is suitable for tourism all year round and each season has its own appeal and beauty. Occasionally snow falls on the highest peaks in winter but the air is crystal clear and the sky a cloudless blue; with the proper clothing, this can be an ideal time

[margin: Dragons and dinosaurs]

for walking. Summer cloaks the Drakensberg in a blanket of brilliant green and afternoon thunderstorms keep the vegetation lush and verdant.

Concerted conservation efforts have ensured the preservation of flora and fauna in the Drakensberg. Although the lions and elephants that once flourished in this area were shot out before the end of the last century, 12 species of antelope, over 1,000 varieties of plants and three of the world's seven species of cranes may be seen here. There are two main parks in the Drakensberg: The **Royal Natal National Park** and **Giant's Castle Game Reserve**. In between lie a number of idyllic resorts and reserves, all of which offer a multitude of sporting and leisure activities in addition to scenic splendours. The **Trout fishing** trout fishing is excellent and may be done in streams, lakes or dams. The hiking here is unmatched in Southern Africa and there is a superb system of trails throughout the escarpment. Most hotels and resorts offer daily guided hikes and it is also quite easy to walk on your own. Riding is very popular in the Drakensberg and there is decent game-viewing on foot, provided that you spend enough time walking around.

These mountains were the exclusive domain of the San people (Bushmen) for thousands of years until the advent of the whites, and as a result, the entire region is a **San rock art** treasure house of rock art. As was the case in so many places in Southern Africa, the Bushmen were displaced from the Drakensberg but a wonderful record of their lives remains for posterity in the rock shelters of these mountains. Many of the caves and paintings are easily accessible on foot from the parks and resorts.

GETTING THERE

The Drakensberg can be reached from Johannesburg or Durban via the N3. A number of rural routes branch off the main road, most of which end at the mountains. It is important to take a good look at a map before setting out to this region. Because of the nature of the terrain, it is not possible to drive directly from one resort to another; there is no road that winds along the foot of the escarpment. To travel between resorts by car you must constantly backtrack to the N3 and then choose another exit, following the signposts to your next destination.

INFORMATION

Drakensberg Publicity Association, PO Box 1608, Estcourt 3310. Tel. (0363) 2-4186.

The Drakensberg

Natal Parks Board, Reservations Office, PO Box 662, Pietermaritzburg 3200. Tel. (0331) 47-1981; fax (0331) 47-1980.

THE ROYAL NATAL NATIONAL PARK

Imposing scenery

The Royal Natal National Park (RNNP), in conjunction with the neighbouring Rugged Glen Nature Reserve, encompasses 8,000 hectares of some of the most splendid scenery in Southern Africa. The focal point of the RNNP is an 8 km arc of rugged cliffs and mountain peaks called the **Amphitheatre.** Scenic vistas abound in the Drakensberg, but the Amphitheatre is without doubt the most notable and dramatic. Anchoring one end of this imposing crescent-shaped wall is **Mont aux Sources**, at 3,282 metres one of the highest mountains in South Africa. Its slopes are the source of the Tugela River which cascades 853 metres off the edge of the Amphitheatre forming the **Tugela Falls**. In addition to the dazzling scenery, miles of hiking and riding trails await the energetic visitor.

Activities

Hiking trails

Hiking. Upon entering the Park your first stop should be at the Visitor's Centre. Detailed trail maps are available as well as hiking guidelines, weather advice and information on various ranger-led treks. The RNNP has no less than 25 hiking and walking trails to choose from, at all levels of difficulty. One of the easiest and shortest is to the Cascades and McKinlay's Pool. The Mont aux Sources Trail is the most thrilling, although it is also very demanding. It takes two hours and the ascent to the summit involves climbing two chain ladders up a sheer rock face. The incredible panorama from the top is breathtaking and most people spend one or two nights camping on the summit in a convenient cave (check with the Visitor's Centre to reserve space in the cave). If you prefer the company and leadership of others, daily guided walks are also offered by the hotels.

Fishing. The RNNP has the biggest trout hatchery in Natal and as a result of stocking, the fishing is excellent. Fly fishing is permitted in the rivers and the Dam but you must obtain a licence at the Visitor's Centre first. No equipment is available for hire.

Horseback rides

Riding. The Park maintains a stable and guided rides are offered three times a day at 9 a.m., 10 a.m. and 2 p.m. They last two or three hours depending on the departure time you choose. If you enjoy riding, this is a good way to experience the countryside.

235

Accommodation

Karos Mont aux Sources*** Tel. or fax (0364) 38-1035. A beautifully situated 86-room hotel with superb views of the Amphitheatre, located just outside the gate of the RNNP. The large rooms have been totally refurbished and there are gorgeous grounds. Tennis, volleyball, bowls, trout fishing, two swimming pools, mini golf and riding are all on offer.

Royal Natal National Park Hotel** Tel. (0364) 38-1051. Conveniently located within the park, this establishment offers accommodation in thatched cottages or traditional rondavels. A visit in 1947 by the royal family resulted in the title 'royal' being granted to the hotel and the national park. The hotel is old-fashioned but cozy, with beautiful lawns and gardens and a huge swimming pool. The rates are reasonable and include full board. Smart casual dress is required at dinner.

Centrally located

Tendele Lodge and Hutted Camp. Located within the park, at the base of the Amphitheatre. The setting is unbelievably scenic and the facilities are of the usual high standard encountered throughout this country. Cottages and bungalows are available and cooks are on hand to prepare meals (bring your own provisions). To reserve here book with the *Natal Parks Board*; tel. (0331) 47 -1981.

Mahai Camp Site. Also at the base of the Amphitheatre, this camp can accommodate 360 visitors and has two kitchens and five clean ablution blocks. Contact the camp superintendent at (0364) 38-1303 for reservations.

Cavern Berg Resort. Off the R74 at Bergville. Tel. (0364) 38-1118. Situated on a 600-hectare wilderness area adjoining the RNNP, this friendly resort offers magnificent views and country-style hospitality and charm. Guests are accommodated in thatched cottages set amidst terraced gardens. The daily rate includes all three meals and afternoon tea; no alcohol is served. A full range of activities is offered and in addition, the resort organizes Land Rover trips along mountain trails to view the region's spectacular scenery.

CENTRAL DRAKENSBERG RESORTS

Cathedral Peak

This region is dominated by the towering 3,004 metre Cathedral Peak which gives its name to a spur of mountains branching off the main range. The walking is very good in this region and there are foothills as well as peaks to climb. There is also a hiking trail to the **Sebeyeni Caves** where a number of Bushman rock paintings are to be found.

Rock paintings

The Drakensberg

The three-star **Cathedral Peak Hotel** (tel. (0364) 38-1381) offers splendid panoramas of the Drakensberg range. This family-run hotel has 92 very nice rooms with a restaurant, a swimming pool, squash and tennis courts, a gym, a sauna and a TV lounge. Fishing, riding, hiking and bowls are all available.

Cathkin Peak and Champagne Castle

Alpine peaks

Cathkin Peak looms above the Sterkspruit Valley at 3,148 metres and has long presented an irresistible challenge to mountain climbers. Champagne Castle is even higher (3,377 metres) and both of these areas are spectacularly beautiful with great walking, fishing, riding and climbing possibilities. Nearby is the **Monk's Cowl Forestry Reserve** and there are a number of wonderful walks, waterfalls and resorts in the region. Just before the road (the R600) ends, you will pass the **Drakensberg Boys' Choir School**, modelled after the Vienna Boys' Choir. If

Boy's choir practice

you should happen to pass on a Wednesday afternoon, the public is welcome to listen to a rehearsal session.

Dragon Peaks Park (tel. (0364) 38-1031) is a first-class resort at the foot of Cathkin Peak, and offers fully equipped, self-catering cottages as well as 140 caravan and tenting sites. There are petrol pumps, a laundry, a shop, a recreation centre, a swimming pool and a tennis court, and it also offers riding, guided walks and Bushman rock art.

The two-star **Champagne Castle Hotel** (tel. (0364) 38-1063) offers 49 comfortable and attractive thatched cottages as well as all the standard sporting facilities and activities popular in this region. It is a favourite with climbers.

The **Drakensberg Sun Hotel** (tel. (0364) 38-1018) is the only four-star hotel in the Drakensberg, and in the true Sun tradition, everything is of the highest quality. The grounds are extensive and every amenity and facility from a golf course to stables to a private lake are available.

GIANT'S CASTLE GAME RESERVE

Nestled in a beautiful valley dominated by a 3,000 metre wall of solid stone is an unspoilt wilderness area called Giant's Castle Game Reserve, comprising grassy meadows, forested hills, numerous streams and deep

Wildlife

ravines. Two animal species are especially associated with it: the eland and the rare lammergeyer (bearded vulture) with its remarkable 2 metre wing span; a number of other antelopes are also commonly found. In addition to animal life, there are 50 km of hiking trails, and over 5,000 Bushman rock paintings, representing almost 40 per cent of all known South African rock art.

Accommodation

Visitors can stay at one of three camps in the reserve; because of demand, advance reservations are highly recommended. To book, contact the *Natal Parks Board* at (0331) 47-1981.

The **Main Visitors' Camp** consists of fully equipped thatched cottages and huts. There is no restaurant or shop so you must bring your own food; cooks are on hand to prepare meals in the communal kitchens, however. Activities here centre on trout fishing and walking. A 20 km trail begins at the camp and climbs to the ridge below the summit of Giant's Castle (3,314 m). This trek takes 4–6 hours and the panoramas are unbeatable. From the camp hikers can also walk to Battle Cave and Main Caves to see the Bushman rock art. At the Main Caves alone there are over 500 paintings in one vast shelter. An interesting museum has been established near by that depicts the traditional San life style through tableaus and artefacts.

Thirty kilometres from the Main Camp there is a camping area with ablution blocks called **Hillside Camp**. Daily horse rides are a feature here and ther are also twice-weekly guided mountain trail rides of 2–4 days. Bookings for these trail rides should be made in advance with the *Natal Parks Board* office in Pietermaritzburg (see above).

Injasuti Hutted Camp is the third rest camp in the Giant's Castle Game Reserve. It is located at the base of South Africa's highest peak, Injasuti (3,459 metres). The accommodation here includes tent sites and fully equipped two-bedroomed cabins; bring your own food, as there is no shop or restaurant.

THE SOUTHERN DRAKENSBERG:

The resorts along the southern spine of the escarpment are a bit far afield for visitors who are stealing away for a day or two in the Drakensberg en route to Durban or Johannesburg. However, if time and interest allow, there is a very intriguing detour off the main road (the N3) which is worth mentioning. Take the R617 off the N3 to the pretty village of Himeville which is just a few kilometres from Underberg. Check into the **Himeville Arms**, an old country inn that is a favourite of trout

The Drakensberg

fishermen. Here guests are accommodated in cozy, attractively furnished cottages, each with en-suite facilities. Meals are served in the Trout House dining room and there is an English pub for evening socializing.

Via the Sani Pass to Lesotho

From the hotel, Land Rover excursions to **Lesotho** via the **Sani Pass** are organized (passport essential). The Sani Pass is an incredible, unforgettable, hair-raising route over the Drakensberg. Only four-wheel drive vehicles can negotiate the hairpin bends and rough surface. This is the only eastern road from Natal into Lesotho and it was originally a bridlepath for pack animals carrying supplies into the mountain kingdom. Many would say it still seems more suitable for mules than vehicles! Needless to say, the panoramas from the top of the pass (2,700 metres) are terrific and visitors may stay overnight at the **Chalet**, a small mountain-top hostelry in the independent kingdom of Lesotho. Walking and bird-watching are excellent from this spot and excursions to other parts of Lesotho are possible. The Himeville Arms can make bookings for the Chalet; tel. 033722 and ask for #5.

DURBAN

INTRODUCTION

Durban is in the province of Natal and is South Africa's third largest city. There are four provinces in South Africa and Natal is the smallest, occupying a mere 8 per cent of the nation's territory. Despite its small size, its climate and terrain are extremely varied; the landscape ranges from the alpine peaks and forested meadows of the Drakensberg to lush rolling sugarfields inland from the coast, to a subtropical dune beach barrier.

Vasco da Gama

History records that the Portuguese navigator, Vasco da Gama, sighted land along the east coast of Southern Africa, and on Christmas Day 1497 anchored before the lagoon that was later to become Durban harbour. He named the coastal area Terra de Natal. More than three centuries passed before the British established a trading post here in 1824 in order to barter with the powerful Zulu nation. The settlement was originally called Port Natal but was renamed Durban in 1835 in honour of the Governor of the Cape Colony.

Today Durban is a vital, modern city which boasts the largest and busiest harbour in Africa, ranked ninth in the world. Fertile land and a temperate climate have combined to make Durban the centre of a thriving

South Africa & Lesotho

> ### LESOTHO
>
> The independent kingdom of Lesotho is often referred to as the Switzerland of Africa. Much of the land in this tiny country lies above 3,000 metres and forms part of the Drakensberg mountains. Although the country is totally surrounded by the Republic of South Africa, it is an independent enclave.
>
> Lesotho offers little to entice most visitors, with the possible exception of an excursion through the Sani Pass (see page **) or pony-trekking. Four day treks on sturdy Basotho ponies are offered from the **Molimo Nthuse Pass**, 60 km outside the capital Maseru; for details contact the *Basotho Pony Project*, PO Box 1027, Maseru, Lesotho.
>
> Access to Lesotho is possible from Johannesburg via road (Bloemfontein to Maseru via Ladysmith is the easiest route), rail or air. Once inside Lesotho, you will find that the road system is primitive, and much of the country is only accessible with a four-wheel drive vehicle; backpacking and pony-trekking are the best ways to get around. There is a *Sun International* hotel at **Maseru**, complete with casino, which is an attraction for South Africans. The country is really rather remote for most overseas travellers but if you want detailed information, contact the *Lesotho Tourist Board*, 132 Jan Smuts Ave, Parkwood, Johannesburg; tel. (011) 788-0742.

Golden sand beaches

agricultural and sugar industry. Despite its major industrial, commercial and transport interests, however, the city is first and foremost a holiday resort, catering for over three million visitors a year. Durban is synonymous with the beach and is never out of season: an endless summer if you will. Lapped by the warm waters of the Indian Ocean, its Golden Mile of sandy shore is a magnet for South Africans and visitors alike. In the last decade an ambitious urban renewal project has been undertaken and the beachfront has received an impressive facelift.

Action is centred on **Marine Parade** along the famous **Golden Mile** where hundreds of modern, high-rise hotels and holiday apartments face the sea. All manner of arcades, fun fairs, wading pools, entertainment and amusement centres and even an aerial cable car line the beachfront. This strip is lively and colourful, especially at night, and although in all honesty it is somewhat brash, activities and attractions abound.

Durban doesn't have a monopoly on wonderful beaches however, for it is in the middle of over 300 km of sandy coastline, effectively dividing the North and South Natal Coasts. In either direction the shore is strung with popular resorts, offering every imaginable activity and facility to the holiday-maker. Although I wouldn't say that Durban is a 'must' for the first-time visitor, I do like its friendly character, easy-going spirit and sunny skies.

Durban

Subtropical climate

For international travellers, the main attractions are its year-round subtropical climate and the warm waters of the Indian Ocean. However, it is also rich in history and culture and there is a broad ethnic mix here which is less prominent in other regions of the country. Indians, for example, were originally brought to this region to work on the sugar plantations and they now comprise the majority of Durban's population; indeed, more Indians live in Durban than in any other city outside India. The amalgamation of many ethnic and racial groups, each with their own cultures, traditions, religions, and personalities has helped make Durban a far more cosmopolitan and open city than most in South Africa.

Large Indian population

GETTING THERE

Durban is served by *SAA's* international and domestic services; there are weekly flights from London, Mauritius, Manzini and Harare. Several other international airlines also serve Durban, notably *British Airways* to London, *Air Mauritius* to Mauritius, *Air Zimbabwe* to Harare and *UTA* to Reunion.

SAA has a number of daily flights connecting Durban with all the major South African cities. Smaller domestic airlines such as *City Air, FliteStar* and *Link Air* fly from Durban to Ladysmith, Nelspruit, Skukuza, Richards Bay and Manzini, as well as to other destinations.

Durban is served by Louis Botha Airport, 14 km south of the city. Charter flights and private aircraft use Virginia Airport just north of the city. Green or red **airport buses** depart from the domestic terminal and ferry passengers to the SAA building on the corner of Smith and Aliwal Streets. These buses meet every SAA flight that arrives in Durban. **Taxis** queue in a rank in front of the international terminal and Southern Sun Hotels also offers courtesy transport to its Durban hotels; check with their desk in the domestic hall.

Airport transfers

The major **car hire** firms maintain kiosks in the domestic terminal and there is a **bank** here that opens when overseas flights are scheduled. Please note that there is no luggage storage facility at this airport.

Airport services

There is excellent **coach service** between Durban and the other major cities in South Africa. The four companies offering inter-city travel are *Greyhound, Citiliner, Golden Wheels Intercity* and *Translux.* Contact *SAR Travel* for information. There is also a good **regional service** within Natal operated by *SAR Travel* and the *Durban Transport Management Board;* for information ring the DTMB at

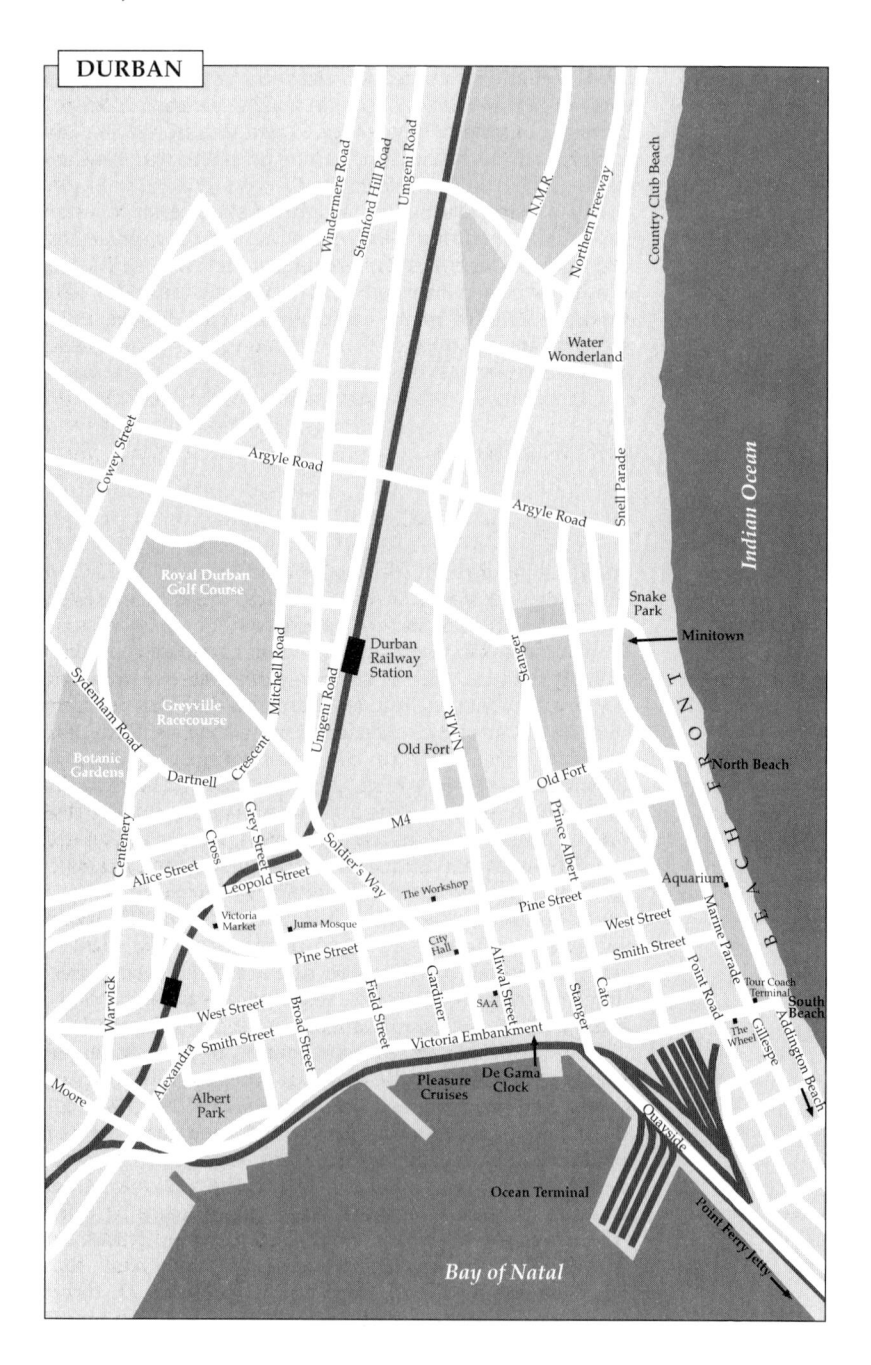

South Africa

DURBAN

Durban

(031) 368-2484. **City bus services** in Durban are excellent and inexpensive; especially convenient are the **Mynah** buses, which ferry passengers between the city and the beaches. Contact the *Durban Publicity Association* offices or the DTMB for complete details.

The **railway station** is in Umgeni Road. There is regularly scheduled service to Johannesburg, including the express overnight **Trans-Natal,** which takes 15 hours. Once a week the **Trans-Orange Express** runs to Cape Town, a journey of about 40 hours. Locally, there is a regional service that extends down the South Coast as far as Port Shepstone.

Durban is also easily reached by road from just about any area of the country. Roads are tarred and well-maintained and there are any number of scenic routes that could include a stay in Durban.

ACCOMMODATION

Maharani Hotel***. 81 Snell Parade. Tel. (031) 32-7361; fax ext.112. Managed by the *Sun Hotel* chain, this is one of the most luxurious hotels in Durban. It is just across the road from North Beach, an area less hectic and crowded than the Golden Mile. As its name suggests, the hotel has an Indian theme and ambience. The 243 rooms are large and very tastefully furnished with all the facilities and amenities consistent with a five-star rating.

Royal Hotel***. 267 Smith St. Tel. (031) 304-0331; fax (031) 307-6884. The Royal is the *grande dame* of Durban hotels, dating back 140 years to its origins as a frontier inn. Today, colonial elegance and modern conveniences have been superbly blended, and if you are looking for a central location, this is an excellent choice. The 272 rooms are spacious and beautifully furnished. There are no less than seven restaurants, as well as a health centre, a roof top swimming pool, squash courts and a sauna.

> Colonial elegance

Elangeni**. 63 Snell Parade. Tel. (031) 37-1321; fax (031) 32-5527. Dazzling white and 21 storeys high, the Elangeni towers over the beachfront; it is next to the Maharani opposite North Beach. It is considered the city's top business hotel and has 450 recently renovated de luxe rooms as well as conference facilities for 1,800. The hotel is only ten minutes from the city centre and offers three restaurants, two swimming pools, a sauna and a jacuzzi.

Marine Parade Holiday Inn*. 176 Marine Parade. Tel. (031) 37-3341. This stunning hotel is centrally situated on the Golden Mile just 3 km from the city centre. Every room has a sea view as well as a king-size bed, air conditioning, TV, telephone and radio. The 30-storey building is sleek and modern and there is a nice roof-top swimming pool in a garden setting offering wonderful views of the city and beach.

City Lodge Durban**. Corner of Old Fort and Brickhill Rd. Tel. (031) 32-1447; fax (031) 32-1483. The City Lodge chain is known for its reasonable prices and this new, very attractive hotel is no exception. It is situated four blocks from the beach and about eight from the city centre. If the situation doesn't bother you, this is quite a nice place to stay. Rooms are good-sized and have TV, radio, air conditioning, telephone, desks and relaxation areas with sofas and coffee tables. There is a large swimming pool and a restaurant adjacent to the hotel is convenient for meals.

— Reasonable prices

Parade Hotel*. 191 Marine Parade. Tel. (031) 37-4565. Centrally located across the street from the beach and in the middle of all the action, this unpretentious, clean hotel offers good value for money. Rooms do not have air conditioning, telephones or television but the hotel has a good family-style restaurant.

The Palace. 211 Marine Parade. Tel. (031) 32-8351; fax (031) 32-8307. Offers fully equipped holiday apartments accommodating 2–6 people. It is a striking Art Deco structure overlooking the sea. Each apartment has a dining area, a kitchen with microwave oven, a bedroom and a bathroom. Facilities include two swimming pools, a gymnasium, a restaurant and a bar.

DINING

Expensive

Les Saisons. Maharani Hotel, 81 Snell Parade. Tel. (031) 32-7361. Beautifully presented French cuisine accompanied by exquisite service are the hallmarks of this highly regarded restaurant. The menu is very ambitious and there is an emphasis on fresh fish and lobster. Dinner is served from Monday to Saturday.

— Mauritian cuisine

Le St. Geran. 31 Aliwal St. Tel. (031) 304-7509. Mauritian cuisine is the speciality of this casual yet elegant restaurant. French and creole ingredients are combined to delicious effect and the wine list is outstanding. Dinner is served daily.

Ristorante Scalini. 237 Marine Parade. Tel. (031) 32-2804. For very good, authentic Italian food with an emphasis on home-made pasta, this is your best bet in Durban. Open every day except Monday for lunch and dinner; licensed to serve wine and beer only.

Moderate
Aldo's. 15 Gillespie St. Tel. (031) 37-0900. This is a bistro-style eating house with a fun atmosphere and excellent food. The restaurant is unlicensed so you must bring your own drinks. Lunch and dinner are served daily except Sunday.

Langoustine by the Sea. Waterkant Rd. Tel. (031)84-9768. An excellent place for those seeking fresh fish or lobster; the selection is large and the prices are fair. Lunch and dinner daily except Saturday lunch.

Ville D'Este. 29 Gillespie St. Tel. (031) 37-0264. Homemade pasta, Italian specialities and good pizza in a casual atmosphere. The restaurant is unlicensed so you must bring your own drinks. Open daily except Monday for lunch and dinner.

The British Middle East Indian Sporting & Dining Club. 16 Stamford Hill Rd. Tel. (031) 309-4017. The colonial structure housing this establishment has been declared a national monument and there is no lack of historical ambience here. The dining room decor appears to have been untouched since Kitchener's day and I think the original staff are still at work! The cuisine is excellent: a blend of Middle Eastern and Indian dishes with curries as a special attraction. The dining room is open for lunch and dinner daily; if the weather is nice, ask to sit on the veranda.

A Durban landmark

Ulundi. Royal Hotel, 267 Smith Street. Tel. (031) 304-0331. This is one of Durban's most famous Indian restaurants. It features an extensive menu and the food is as authentic as it can be outside India. The ambience is casual and the service is excellent. Open for dinner Monday–Saturday.

Inexpensive
Durban has a full range of reasonably priced restaurants ranging from Kentucky Fried Chicken and Pizza Hut to Mike's Kitchen. Many of them can be found in Marine Parade. Also of note is the Royal Coffee House in Smith Steet at the Royal Hotel, which offers tea and scones, light sandwiches, espresso coffee and a tempting array of cakes in a beautiful English tearoom to the accompaniment of a wonderful pianist.

SHOPPING

Shopping in Durban does not compare to Johannesburg or Cape Town in terms of scope, variety or price, but there are a number of interesting shopping centres selling a diverse range of Eastern, African and Western goods.

Business hours are extended in Durban, a refreshing change from the rest of the country: most shopping centres and a number of shops on the seafront are open seven days a week and in the evening.

The Victoria Street Market. Corner of Queen and Victoria St. Durban's colourful Indian market has been re-established on its original site in a newly built complex, complete with 11 domes, each styled after a famous building in India. This bustling bazaar houses a vast array of goods from silver jewellery and silks to Indian art and curios. The pungent smell of exotic spices greets you and there are over 180 shops and stalls for entertaining browsing. Remember that you are expected to bargain here! The Market is open daily and parking is available.

Shopping Centres
The Wheel. Gillespie St. Three levels of shopping and 12 cinemas are available at Durban's largest shopping centre. All the major department stores are represented here as well as numerous boutiques and speciality shops. You can't miss this building: it has a huge green ferris wheel attached to the facade. The Wheel is open every day of the week.
The Workshop. Old Durban Railway Station. Durban's newest addition to the shopping scene, this two-storey complex of shops and restaurants is housed in the old railway station workshop. It offers 120 speciality boutiques, several cinemas and what is billed as the largest food emporium in South Africa (Pick n Pay). It is also open seven days a week and has ample parking.

Arts, Crafts and Curios
African Art Centre. Guildhall Arcade, off Gardiner St. This is a combination art gallery and shop specializing in authentic Zulu arts and crafts.
African Beadwork Market. Marine Parade. Zulu crafts with an emphasis on beaded items are sold in this open-air stall which is a permanent fixture in Marine Parade.
Graham Gallery. 16 Fenton Rd.
Elizabeth Gordon Gallery. 18 Windermere Rd.
Zells Curios. 78–80 West St.

Flea Markets
On the second and last Sunday of every month there is a flea market at the Amphitheatre Gardens in Snell Parade, North Beach.

ENTERTAINMENT

As a major holiday destination, it is not surprising that Durban has a full range of entertainment. Almost every hotel on the beachfront has live bands and dancing. The following is a small selection of what else is available.

Jazz
Coltrane's, 23 Hill St Arcade, Pinetown
The Octagon Jazz Club, Corner of Queen and Field St

Disco/Dancing
Nellos, 185 Smith St
Monte Carlo, 24 Stanger St

Classical Music
The City Hall hosts a variety of concerts and recitals, including lunchtime and Sunday afternoon performances. The *Publicity Association* has complete programme details.

Theatre
The Natal Playhouse in Smith Street is an authentically restored historic landmark that now accommodates five performing theatres under its roof. Ballet, opera, drama and concerts are presented here throughout the year. There are several restaurants and cafés in the Playhouse, some of which are open until late. Tours of this interesting building are conducted at 10 a.m. on Tuesdays, Thursdays and Saturdays. Book tour or theatre tickets through *Computicket*, tel. (031) 304-2753.

Performance centre

SIGHTSEEING

The Golden Mile
Durban's famous Golden Mile consists of four contiguous beaches: Addington, South, North and Battery. South Beach is the most central and the most crowded: many of the shops, amusement centres, water slides and pools are here, as is Seaworld (see below). A series of piers reach out into the sea along the shore and certain areas of the beaches are reserved for fishing, surfing and swimming. Facilities along the Golden Mile include life guard stations, changing rooms and toilets; all beaches have shark nets for safety.

City Walkabout Tours
The *Durban Publicity Association* has organized five very interesting walking tours of the city led by knowledgeable guides. Each 2½-hour tour features a

Theme tours different aspect of the city: historical, architectural, cultural, Oriental. The cost is R15.00 per person and bookings can be made at any of the Publicity Association offices, or tel. (031) 304-4934 or 32-2595

City Hall
Erected in 1910, this very impressive building would look at home in any European city; indeed, it was modelled on Belfast City Hall in Northern Ireland. Situated in Smith Street, this edifice houses government offices as well as the **Natural Science Museum** and **Durban Art Gallery**. The Science Museum can be found on the second floor and has exhibits of mammals and birds, including the world's most complete skeleton of the extinct dodo. The museum is open daily and entrance is free.

The Art Gallery is on the third floor and has permanent collections of South African artists as well as European works. It is also open every day of the week, although weekend hours are slightly shorter.

Botanic Gardens
Begun originally as an agricultural station in 1847, the gardens are a lovely spot to spend a few hours. Highlights include a spectacular orchid house with over 3,000 plants, tea and herb gardens, a cycad collection and a special fragrant garden for the blind. The gardens are in Sydenham Road, Berea, and are open daily from 7.30 a.m. to 5.30 p.m. Tel. (031) 21-1303.

Orchids galore

Fitzsimons Snake Park
More than 80 species of indigenous and exotic snakes, lizards and tortoises are on display and there are several handler demonstrations during the day. This attraction is in Marine Parade and is open daily from 9 a.m. to 5 p.m. Tel. (031) 37-6456.

Seaworld, Marine Parade
Seaworld consists of an aquarium and a dolphinarium in Marine Parade. Shows are given throughout the day, featuring performing dolphins, penguins and seals. In the main tank divers feed fish and sharks at scheduled times. Tel. (031) 37-4079.

Ricksha Rides
Highly colourful rickshas (two-wheeled 'carriages') with ornately bedecked ricksha drivers are available for hire along the seafront. The rates are set according to the length of the journey and you must pay for the privilege of taking photographs.

Durban

Minitown
Opposite the Maharani Hotel in Snell Parade, a faithful replica of Durban has been made in miniature, at a scale of 1:24. Children enjoy this unusual and charming attraction which is open every day except Monday.

Umgeni River Bird Park
A superb collection of over 2,000 exotic and indigenous birds, rated the third best in the world. There are three large aviaries, complete with waterfalls, cliffs and tropical plants that you may stroll through to observe the birds in their natural habitats. It can be found in Riverside Road, Durban North (tel. (031) 83-1733 and is open daily from 9 a.m. to 5 p.m.

Sugar Tours
The *South African Sugar Association Reception Centre* in Maydon Road offers a 20 minute audiovisual presentation dealing with all aspects of the sugar industry. There is a guided tour of the twin-siloed Terminal, a bulk storage site, after the show. The public is welcome on Mondays and Wednesdays at 9 a.m., 11 a.m. and 2 p.m. Tours of an operational mill can also be arranged on Tuesdays, Wednesdays and Thursdays by booking with the Public Relations Department at (031) 305-6161 or 301-0331. The mills are in operation between 1 May and early December only.

All you ever wanted to know about sugar

Juma Mohammedan Mosque
The largest mosque in the southern hemisphere is on the corner of Queen and Grey Streets, and visitors are welcome. Guided tours may be arranged by phoning (031) 306-0026.

EXCURSIONS

Natal Sharks Board, Umhlanga Rocks
Just 15 km north of Durban in the popular resort of Umhlanga Rocks, there is a fascinating shark control organization – the only one of its kind in the world. It supervises the servicing of 306 shark nets in the waters of 42 beaches along the Natal coastline, from Richards Bay in the north to Port Edward in the south. Sharks are common denizens of the warm Indian Ocean waters and all Durban's beaches are netted and patrolled as protection against attacks. For those who are still not totally reassured, it is comforting to know that beaches are closed if there is any danger of sharks; the most problematical months are June, July and August when

Beaches are netted

huge schools of sardines swim near to shore and attract the sharks. Over 1,000 sharks are caught in these nets each year and they are subsequently destroyed by the ASMB.

The public is welcome to visit the Board's headquarters and will be shown an audiovisual presentation on shark control, followed by a discussion and dissection of a shark caught in one of the many protective nets. Shows are given on Tuesdays, Wednesdays and Thursdays; ring (031) 561-1001 for times and directions.

The Banana Express

Old-fashioned steam train

The Banana Express is an old-fashioned steam-powered train that carries passengers along the coast from Port Shepstone, south of Durban, and then winds inland through the rolling hills of Natal. The scenery is lush and tropical and there is ample opportunity to view the sugar cane and pineapple fields that blanket the countryside as the train slowly chugs along. The round trip from Port Shepstone to Izotsha takes $2^1/2$ hours and includes a stop for tea and scones. For most of the year the train operates on Thursdays and Sundays, departing at 10 a.m. and 12.15 p.m. respectively. During school holidays there are additional services. For reservations, ring (03931) 7-6443.

Valley of a Thousand Hills

If you're tired of the beach and want to take a short drive (40 km) into the countryside, consider a scenic excursion along the old main road (the R103) between Durban and Pietermaritzburg. The route winds through the towns of Hillcrest and Botha's Hill and there are a number of craft shops, farm stalls and tea gardens along the way. This region is called the Valley of a Thousand Hills, an aptly descriptive name suggested by the endless rolling hills that stretch to the horizon. This is Zulu country and the hillsides are dotted with their traditional beehive-shaped huts.

Zululand

A major attraction of the valley is the **PheZulu Kraals**, a living museum centred around a collection of beehive huts where various aspects of traditional tribal life are illustrated; most popular is the very spirited demonstration of Zulu dancing. In my opinion the dancing is the only reason to make this excursion; shows are given at 10 a.m., 11.30 a.m., 1.30 p.m. and 3.30 p.m. The price of admission (R 10) includes entry to the **Assagay Safari Park**, 1 km further down the road; crocodiles and snakes are featured here.

Zulu dancing

PheZulu is a favourite stop on the coach tour circuit and the complex has capitalized on tourism by providing a tearoom, a curio shop and a nature trail. Open daily from 9 a.m. to 4 p.m.; tel. (031) 777-1208.

The Wild Coast

Transkei

The rugged and remote stretch of coastline that runs for 250 km from Port Edward to East London is called the Wild Coast, and is part of the nominally independent Xhosa homeland of Transkei. As its name suggests, it is a wild, untamed region, with unspoilt beaches, lagoons and forests, rocky promontories and superb fishing. Unfortunately, access is difficult because there is no coastal road, owing to the fact that 20-odd rivers cut through to the sea. Instead, one must drive along the N2 and choose one of the roads that branches eastward to the coast.

I do not recommend Transkei as a tourist destination at the moment; the few holiday resorts and hotels still in operation since the advent of 'independence' are run down and offer very little for the overseas visitor. I spent a few days at one of the best resorts the region has to offer and despite the brochure advertisements promising a swimming pool, tennis, fishing and boating, none of these was available. Furthermore, the road access to the Transkei coast is frightening and dangerous, the water undrinkable and the surf too wild for bathing.

Gambling is an attraction

Having said all this, there is one resort on the Wild Coast that I can recommend: the **Wild Coast Sun**, located just inside the northern border of Transkei, 225 km south of Durban. Operated by the very reputable Sun International hotel group, this resort is very popular as a day or overnight excursion from Durban. Gambling is legal in Transkei so this is the big drawing card for many visitors. In addition, the beaches are splendid (and netted), and there is a wealth of activities awaiting the energetic: golf, tennis, squash, bowling, and all manner of watersports. You may drive yourself or take one of the many coach tours operating from Durban. For information contact one of the companies listed on page 253 or phone *Computicket* at (031)304-2753.

ACTIVITIES

Diving
Durban Undersea Club. Tel. (031) 32-5850
Ocean Divers International. Tel. 32-8309

South Africa

Zulu dancers at PheZulu Kraal, Natal.

Fishing
Isle of Capri. Tel. (031) 37-7751

Golf
Windsor Park Golf Course. Tel. (031) 23-2245
Papwa Sewgolum Golf Course. Tel. (031) 262-6355

Harbour Cruises
Sarie Marais Harbour Cruises. Gardiner St. Jetty. Tel. (031) 305-4022 **DTMB Tours.** Tel. (031) 368-2848
Royal Cruiser Pleasure Cruises. Maydon Wharf 1. Tel. (031) 304-4810

Helicopter Rides
Court Helicopters. Virginia Airport. Tel. (031) 83-9513

Horse Racing
Durban Turf Club. Tel. (031) 31-5882

Paraflying
Flights leave from Addington Beach on the hour daily. Tel. (031) 52-3863

Durban

Sailing
Magic Sailing School. 46 Fenton Rd. Tel. (031) 304-1500
Dinghy Sailing Adventures. Tel. (031) 21-4766

White Water Rafting
African Ventures offers a one-day expedition down the Umkomaas River in inflatable rafts, including a gourmet lunch, champagne, cocktails and transport. Trips depart from the **Umhlanga Sands Hotel.** Ring (031) 561-2323 or (031) 561-2166 to book.

SERVICES

TOURIST INFORMATION

The *Durban Publicity Association* maintains two offices to assist tourists with tour information, maps, brochures and details of events and attractions. There is a seafront office across from the Balmoral Hotel, tel. (031) 32-2595; the other is in Church Square opposite the City Hall, tel. (031) 304-4981. The offices are open 8.30 a.m. to 4.30 p.m. Monday–Friday, 8.30 a.m.–12.30 p.m. Saturday. Another visitor's aid is the *Teletourist Service,* a 24-hour hotline dispensing taped information on interesting events in the Durban area; tel. (031) 305-3877. Additional tourist information is available at the *South African Tourist Board's Information Bureau* at 320 West St.; tel. (031) 304-7144.

GETTING AROUND

Car Hire
Budget. Tel. (031) 304-9023 (city centre), (031) 42-3809 (airport)
Avis. Tel. (031) 42-6333
Windermere Car Hire. 81 Windermere Rd. Tel. (031) 23-9477
Forest Drive Rent-a-Car. Tel. (031) 52-5866

Bicycle Hire
Ride A While, Corner of Tyzack and Gillespie St. Tel.(031)32-5294

Taxis
Eagle Taxis. Tel. (031) 37-8333;
Aussies. Tel. (031) 304-2345.
Taxis do not cruise the streets looking for fares so you must phone or find a taxi rank. A charming alternative to conventional taxis are *tuk-tuks,* the three-wheel motorized rickshas that are universally associated with Thailand. They are less expensive than taxis (prices are negotiable), may be hired at the beachfront, and will ferry passengers anywhere within a three km radius of City Hall.

BUS SERVICES
City
Durban Transport Management Board. Tel. (031) 368-2484

Inter-City
Greyhound. Tel. (031) 37-6478
Translux. Tel. (031) 302-2921
Golden Wheels. Tel. (031) 29-2894
Citiliner. Tel. (031) 304-2753 *(Computicket)*

Airlines
City Air. Tel. (031) 42-2136
Link Air. Tel. (011) 973-3841
SAA. Tel. (011) 733-6618
For general airline information, telephone (031) 42-6111

Air Charter
Tel. (031) 844-7200

Rail
Information. Tel. (031) 310-2792
Reservations. Tel. (031) 310-2931

Tour Companies:
DTMB Coach Tours. Tel. (031) 368-2848
Welcome Tours & Safaris. Tel. (031) 32-2756
Venture Tours & Safaris. Tel. (031) 42-4541
1000 Hills Tours. Tel. (031) 83-2302

South Africa

Zulu chief in full regalia.

THE GAME RESERVES OF ZULULAND

INTRODUCTION

Natal has traditionally had a rich wildlife heritage. In its eastern reaches, highveld grasslands, bush savannah, adequate rainfall and a sultry climate combine to form an ideal habitat for ungulates, big game and predators alike. Tsetse flies made human habitation impractical for centuries and it wasn't until the 1890s that hunters began to seriously decimate the huge herds that migrated through this region. In 1895, three game reserves were created: **Hluhluwe, Umfolozi** and **St Lucia**. **Mkuzi** and **Ndumu** followed in 1925 and today all are open to the public, providing accommodation, organized game trails, viewing hides and picnic sites.

If you are driving from Durban to Swaziland, or vice versa, a stop at Lake St Lucia or one of the other Game Reserves discussed in this chapter might interest you. To do justice to this area, several days are needed. My recommendation is to choose a central base for your stay so that you can visit at least two of the parks. The fully tarred N2 highway runs from Durban to the Swaziland border and four of the reserves are within easy reach of this road. Travellers should note that they are all malaria risk areas.

Choose a central base

ST LUCIA GAME RESERVE

St Lucia is the largest estuary in Southern Africa and its shallow waters are an important flamingo and pelican breeding ground. The St Lucia Game Reserve encompasses Lake St Lucia and a 1 km strip of land around its perimeter. It was established to protect hippos and today they are quite prolific here, as are crocodiles. The reserve has many varied habitats, most of which are linked to wetland systems; from mangrove swamps to dune forests, the terrain supports numerous mammals and 367 bird species.

Hippos and crocodiles abound

The St Lucia lake system is home to some of the finest fishing grounds in South Africa. The village of St Lucia, at the southern end of the reserve, exists to serve anglers and it seems as if every shop sells bait and ice and hires boats or tackle. The main species caught here are grunt, kabeljou and river bream, in that order. There are several demarcated bathing beaches but none of them has shark nets, which makes swimming an anxious proposition. Apart from these beaches, there is no swimming allowed

Swimming is risky!

anywhere in the estuary or lake: the large hippo, shark and crocodile populations in these waters make it a little risky!

Getting There
The St Lucia Game Reserve is 245 km north of Durban. It is a three hour drive and the best route is via the N2 to the R620 exit at Mtubatuba.

Accommodation
The Boma Hotel. St Lucia. Tel. 03592 and ask for 9. The only hotel in St Lucia village. Formerly the Estuary Hotel, it has just undergone a much needed renovation, and has 60 luxury rooms with modern amenities and facilities.
Sugarloaf Camp. A Natal Parks Board campsite on the beach at the estuary mouth. It is very nicely maintained and the grounds are shaded by tall trees.
Cape Vidal. Cape Vidal is 32 km north of the village of St Lucia and can be reached in an ordinary car. Here there is a safe but unprotected swimming area, a reef for snorkelling and excellent fishing. The Natal Parks Board maintains campsites and 20 fully equipped log cabins. Visitors must bring all of their own food and drink; only petrol and firewood are available for purchase. The camp is in a dense coastal forest and the walking is excellent. Book through the *Natal Parks Board Reservation Office*, PO Box 662, Pietermaritzburg 3200; tel. (0331) 41-7981; fax (0331) 47-1980.
Charters Creek and Fanies Island. North of St Lucia village there are two comfortable rest camps: Charters Creek and Fanies Island. Fishing is the main attraction of these camps although both offer swimming pools, self-guided walking trails, and at Charters Creek launch tours on the lake are available. Bookings for both should be made through the *Natal Parks Board* (see above).
False Bay. There is a caravan park 16 km from the village of Hluhluwe at the north-western end of the lake at False Bay. The bird watching is particularly good in this area and a viewing platfrom has been erected here for this purpose. In addition to the campsite, the False Bay park offers four fully equipped rustic huts.

Activities
The Natal Parks Board Reception Centre is just inside the park gate in St Lucia. Fishing licences and information on the lake region can be obtained here. Film shows focusing on the wildlife and ecology of the park are shown periodically.
Lifeboat trips are offered at 10.30, 12.30 and 2.30 every

Cruises in the estuary day except Tuesday. They last two hours and the boat leaves from the Natal Parks Board jetty. A game ranger gives a commentary on the wildlife and ecosystem of this region during the leisurely cruise into the 'Narrows', a 9 km journey up into the estuary. Book at the *Natal Parks Board Reception Centre*, tel. (03592) 20 or 47.

Inkwazi Wildlife Tours offers three hour guided excursions in 4x4 vehicles into the restricted **Eastern Shores Nature Reserve**. They leave at 8 a.m. and 2 p.m. daily and cost R30.00 per person. Fishing and beach tours to **Cape Vidal** are also available, depending on the weather and tides.

Deep-sea fishing charters are arranged by a number of local companies. A list of telephone contacts at any petrol station or bait shop. It is easy to hire small boats with motors by the hour or day from a dozen or so operators in town if you prefer to fish on your own.

The **Crocodile Centre** is a research centre maintained by the *Natal Parks Board* and is open to the public daily. The crocodiles are fed on Saturdays at 3 p.m.

Self-guided walks Self-guided walks on nine established trails are a special feature of the reserve. They range from 1½ to 18 km in length and the bird life and hippo viewing is excellent. On some of the trails there are hides for this purpose. Check with the reception centre for maps and advice.

UMFOLOZI GAME RESERVE

Umfolozi is justifiably the most famous of the Natal Game Reserves for it was here that the white rhino was saved from extinction. In 1895 when the reserve was designated, there were only an estimated 50 white rhinos left in Southern Africa. The campaign to save them has been an unqualified success, and to date, more than 3,500 of the animals have been relocated in other game reserves in Africa or given to zoos around the world. Umfolozi was formerly the personal hunting ground of the famous Zulu king, Shaka, but today it is home to large populations of wildlife, including the big five, and over 300 species of bird life have been recorded. Game-viewing hides at several waterholes as well as 84 km of good roads ensure some good game-viewing. Part of the reserve is out of bounds to vehicles and guided three-day hikes on wilderness trails are offered instead. This is a wonderful way to experience the magic of the African bush.

White rhino sanctuary

Umfolozi is 270 km from Durban and is reached by

Rest camps leaving the N2 at the R618. There are two very nice rest camps where one can stay. **Mpila Camp** has thatched chalets and huts with pretty river views; chalets have their own kitchens and bathrooms, while the huts share ablution and kitchen facilities. **Masinda** is a small hutted camp near the entrance gate on the banks of the Black Umfolozi River, with similar facilities to Mpila Camp. There are no restaurants or shops in the reserve, so you must supply your own provisions. If you are staying in a hut, however, the food you bring will be prepared for you by experienced cooks. For accommodation on the wilderness trails, book through the *Natal Parks Board* (see page 235).

HLUHLUWE GAME RESERVE

Hluhluwe is one of the smallest of the Natal reserves but it is noted for excellent concentrations of game. Rainfall is higher here than elsewhere owing to its higher position, **Lush landscapes** and as a result, the landscape is very beautiful. Watered by two rivers, the terrain alternates between undulating forested hills, grass-covered ridges, open savannah and woodland and dense bush in the valleys. This incredible variety provides habitat to all the different species of animals and birds.

Hluhluwe is situated west of the N2; there are two entrance gates, so your exit point from the main road will depend on which part of the park you want to get to. Hluhluwe is only 40 km from Umfolozi and a good gravel road links the two.

The Natal Parks Board maintains a rest camp beautifully situated atop a high ridge, with 20 two-bed, fully equipped rest huts. It has communal ablution blocks and cooks are available, but once again you must provide your own food. In addition to this rest camp, you can stay outside the reserve at the luxurious three-star **Zululand** **Private** **Safari Lodge**, located on a private game ranch. The **lodging** unfenced grounds are gorgeous and game wanders freely. Humorous notices in the rooms request that guests should not fraternize with the locals (zebras, kudus, ostriches and giraffes) nor entertain them in their rondavels. Accommodation is provided in spacious thatched rondavels with air conditioning; facilities include a restaurant, a bar, a TV room, a curio shop and an enormous swimming pool. The Lodge offers breakfast **Organised** in the bush and morning and evening game drives in **game drives** open vehicles with professional guides on a daily basis (additional charge for the drives). From this resort you can easily explore the Hluhluwe and Umfolozi Game Reserves on your own. The Zululand Safari Lodge is operated by the *Southern Sun* hotel chain. To book, telephone (03562) 63 or fax (03562) 193.

MKUZI GAME RESERVE

Mkuzi is in northern Zululand, approximately 335 km from Durban. Access is via a 21 km gravel road off the N2. Unlike the other game reserves in Natal, Mkuzi is extremely arid and vegetation is limited to dry savannah and acacia woodland. The only permanent surface water here is found at the Nsuma Pan in the south-eastern corner of the reserve. As in other arid parks throughout Southern Africa, at Mkuzi water is pumped into artificial *Waterholes* waterholes to support the animal populations. The waterholes naturally attract game and hides have been erected at four of these spots, making game viewing a delight. The reserve boasts a good road network through the bushveld habitat; white and black rhino, eland, nyala, giraffe, kudu and hippo are commonly sighted, while leopard, cheetah and hyena are rare.

A special feature of Mkuzi is walking: self-guided *Day walks* trails are available as well as short day walks (three hours or less) led by a game ranger. Mkuzi has camping and caravan sites in addition to the **Mantuma Hutted Camp** where basic accommodation and trained cooks are provided; visitors must supply their own provisions.

CAPE TOWN

INTRODUCTION

The Mother City Cape Town is indisputably the loveliest city in Africa. Indeed, there are few places on earth where land meets sea in such a splendid and unforgettable fashion. For beauty and drama of setting its rivals are few: Rio de Janeiro or San Francisco, or perhaps Sydney. It nestles at the base of Table Mountain, its most famous landmark. Established as a revictualing station by the Dutch East India Company in 1652, it became the Tavern of the Seas for ships making the long journey from Europe to Asia. Its dramatic backdrop, visible 200 km from the shore, has served as a welcome beacon to seafarers for over three centuries.

Today, Cape Town is a thriving city of almost two million inhabitants. It is blessed with a Mediterranean climate, botanical riches and some of the most magnificent, unspoilt coastline on earth. A multitude of sights and activities await the visitor. A week is needed even to scratch the surface, for in addition to the attractions of historic Cape Town, the Winelands and the Peninsula are less than an hour's drive away. Here beautiful beaches and bays, craggy mountains, fertile valleys carpeted with a patchwork of vineyards and orchards, and charming Cape Dutch homesteads grace the landscape. In a country renowned for its diverse and scenic beauty, Cape Town is the crown jewel.

GETTING THERE

Cape Town is linked by air to all the major cities of South Africa. *SAA* has pretty much had a monopoly on the country's lucrative domestic routes for the past several decades, but new airlines have recently been allowed to compete. *SAA* and *British Airways* also have direct flights from London to Cape Town twice a week each. The BA flights stop in Johannesburg for just under an hour and then continue on to Cape Town; SAA offers the only non-stop flights. Otherwise, international carriers use Johannesburg as their destination and connections to Cape Town are made on SAA. Once a week there is also a service from Cape Town to Rio de Janeiro on an SAA flight originating in Johannesburg.

Airport transfers
The D.F. Malan Airport is 22 km from the city centre. A shuttle bus service operated by *InterCape* (tel. (021) 934-4400) plies the route between the airport and the city. In addition there is a taxi rank in front of the domestic terminal. There are no left luggage facilities at the airport at the time of writing.

There is an excellent **luxury bus service** connecting Cape Town with all regions of the country. *Greyhound* has a scheduled overnight service from Johannesburg to Cape Town daily except Wednesdays. *InterCape* covers the coastal route to Port Elizabeth (via the Garden Route) as well as a west coast route through Namaqualand to Upington. *Translux* connects Cape Town with Worcester and Stellenbosch and serves Port Elizabeth via the Garden Route as well.

From Johannesburg, rail travellers can travel to Cape Town on the world famous and prestigious **Blue Train** or on the **Trans-Karoo**. The **Trans-Oranje** operates between Cape Town and Durban. Three classes of accommodation are offered on all main-line trains. Third class accommodation is very economical and no advance reservations are necessary. Pre-booking for first and second class is required.

Cape Town is easily reached by car from anywhere in the country. Major trunk roads between cities are tarred and well-maintained.

ACCOMMODATION

Book ahead

Cape Town is a major business and holiday centre and the standard of accommodation is high. Because of its popularity, however, especially in the summer, it is a very good idea to book ahead. If you arrive without reservations an emergency Hotel and Accommodation Booking Centre is available to personal callers only from 1 October to 30 April. This office is at the *Captour Visitor Information Bureau*, Strand Concourse, Cape Town; tel. (021) 419-1961.

Cape Sun Hotel***.** Strand St. Tel. (021) 23-8844; fax (021) 23-8895. A modern, luxury hotel centrally situated with 302 spacious rooms, and all amenities including indoor pool and health studio.

Mount Nelson Hotel***.** 76 Orange Street, Gardens. Tel. (021) 23-1000; fax (021) 24-7472. A bastion of elegance and the indisputed *grande dame* of hotels in Cape Town, the Mount Nelson has 151 beautifully appointed rooms furnished with antiques. The hotel is set amidst lovely grounds beneath Table Mountain, ten minutes' walk from the city centre. It has tennis and squash courts, a swimming pool, a putting green and three restaurants.

The Bay Hotel***.** Victoria Rd, Camps Bay. Tel. (021) 438-4444; fax (021) 4455. This is my favourite hotel in the whole of South Africa. If it is not imperative that you be based in the city centre, you might consider a stay here. It is brand new, super luxurious and best of all, situated across the street from one of the most beautiful beaches in the world. The rooms are large and airy and have mountain or sea views. Attention to detail, privacy and comfort are the hallmarks of this establishment. There is a swimming pool, tennis courts, two restaurants, a bar and beachside service.

On the beach

Cape Town Holiday Inn***. Corner of Coronation and Melbourne Rd, Woodstock. Tel. (021) 47-4060; fax (021) 47-8338. This hotel is 3 km from the city centre and is situated just above Eastern Boulevard, with a good view of the harbour. There are 279 modern rooms and excellent facilities. This is rated as one of the best Holiday Inns in South Africa.

Victoria and Alfred Hotel. Pierhead. Tel. (021) 419-6677;

fax (021) 419-8955. Just recently completed, this hotel is the centrepiece of the Victoria and Alfred Waterfront. Located in a historic 1904 warehouse, the V & A boasts 68 ultra-large bedrooms with all modern amenities and facilities. There are terrific views of the harbour and Cape Town and there is a shopping arcade, dozens of restaurants and quite a bit of live entertainment just outside the door of the hotel. A regular shuttle bus runs to and from the city centre, a few minutes away.

Harbour location

Ambassador by the Sea***. 34 Victoria Rd, Bantry Bay. Tel. (021) 439-6170; fax (021) 439-6336. If you want to be on the beach, this is one of your best bets in Cape Town. Bantry Bay is a tiny cliffside village just ten minutes outside the city. The Ambassador literally hangs over the sea and is a stone's throw from the famous beaches of Clifton. This is one of the only areas along the peninsula where the shore is protected from the ubiquitous wind, and as a result this stretch of coastline boasts some of the most expensive property in the country. The hotel has 71 nicely furnished rooms, each with en-suite facilities, TV and radio. In addition, there is a good seafood restaurant, a cocktail bar, a swimming pool and a garden area.

Clifton beaches

The Town House***. 60 Corporation St. Tel. (021) 45-7050; fax (021) 45-3891. A very elegant central hotel with 104 nicely decorated rooms furnished with antiques and full of country charm. There is a very good gymnasium, an indoor pool, a sauna, a jacuzzi and squash courts, as well as two restaurants and a charming Victorian pub.

Alphen Hotel***. Alphen Drive, Constantia. Tel. (021) 794-5011; fax (021) 794-5710. The Alphen is in the wine producing Constantia Valley, 20 minutes from Cape Town. The hotel is an historic Cape homestead and there are 30 charming rooms as well as lovely gardens, a swimming pool, squash and tennis courts and an aerobics centre.

Carlton Heights Hotel**. 88 Queen Victoria Street. Tel. (021) 23-1260; fax (021) 23-2088. A well-situated hotel just across from the **Botanical Gardens**, offering 57 comfortable but uninspired rooms with private baths, kitchenettes, telephones and room service.

Villa Lutzi Guest House. 6 Rosmead Ave., Oranjezicht. Tel. (021) 23-4614; fax (021) 26-1472. Located in a quiet residential area at the foot of Table Mountain, this guest house offers nicely furnished, clean rooms with en-suite facilities, fridges and telephones.

Stans Halt Youth Hostel. The Glen, Camps Bay. Tel. (021) 438-9037. Basic dormitory accommodation in a beautiful setting, high above the sea in a forested preserve. A car or bicycle would be most helpful here.

Self-Catering Apartments
Portofino Apartments. Beach Rd, Sea Point. Tel. (021) 434-9321; fax (021) 439-9437. Fully equipped luxury apartments with sea views only 6 km from the city centre, including daily maid service, laundry and porter service.
Houtkapperspoort Cottages. Constantia Nek Farm, Hout Bay Rd, Hout Bay. Tel. (021) 794-5216; fax (021) 794-2907. A luxurious village of fully equipped cottages built of stone and timber, located 15 minutes south of Cape Town. There is a daily service, a heated pool, TV, telephone and laundry facilities. One-, two- or three-bedroomed cottages are available.

DINING

Cape Town has superb seafood, fabulous wines and a heritage of traditional dishes that combine to make this city a dining delight. Lobster, callled crayfish locally, is especially prized and oysters, mussels, perlemoen (abalone) and line fish are perennial favourites. Dishes drawn from a rich heritage of Dutch, French Huguenot and British ancestors compete with what is called Cape Malay fare. These traditional dishes are hearty, subtly sweet and spicy and well worth a try. What follows is of necessity a selection of the restaurants available, but those that I mention are noteworthy.

Cape Malay cuisine

Expensive
Floris Smit Huis. 55 Church St. Tel. (021)23-3414. A small intimate restaurant in a historic house with rustic and charming decor. The food is first-rate, ambitious and beautifully presented. Open for lunch and dinner, Monday–Friday and Monday–Saturday respectively. This restaurant is not licensed, so bring your own drink.
Ons Huisie. Jansen Rd, Bloubergstrand. Tel. (021) 56-1553. This restaurant has long been renowned for its excellent Cape traditional fare. Open for lunch and dinner every day except Tuesday.
Buitenverwachting. Klein Constantia Rd, Constantia. Tel. (021) 794-3522. This is indisputably the finest restaurant in Cape Town. Not only is it spectacularly situated in the midst of vineyards and mountains, but the cuisine will rival that of the finest kitchens in the world. The menu changes daily but there is an emphasis on game and meat, with only a few fish selections. The chef is a master

Finest restaurant in town

at sauces and when I last dined here, seven different vegetables accompanied the main course. Service and ambience are elegant; the lunch and dinner menus are identical. Reservations are essential and very difficult to get. Lunch: Tuesday–Friday; dinner: Tuesday–Saturday.

The Round House. The Glen, Camps Bay. Tel. (021) 438-2320. Originally a hunting lodge, this establishment is now a popular restaurant. It is set in the forest high above Camps Bay and the dining room is small and cozy, as befits its past. The menu features ostrich fillet, rabbit, duck, Karoo lamb and fresh fish, all with French sauces. The food is excellent, as is the service and wine list. Lunch is served on weekdays and dinner Monday–Saturday.

Peers. Victoria and Alfred Waterfront. Tel. (021) 21-7113. This is one of Cape Town's newest restaurants, dramatically situated at the Pierhead, overlooking the harbour. The menu is incredibly ambitious, featuring avant-garde *nouvelle cuisine*. There is an equal balance between meat and seafood items, and all dishes have marvellous sauces and accompaniments. Lunch is offered on weekdays and dinner is served every day except Sunday; reservations are recommended.

Moderate

Jonkershuis. Groot Constantia Estate, Constantia. Tel. (021) 794-6255. The Jonkershuis is an unpretentious restaurant housed in the old slave quarters on the Groot Constantia estate. The food is home-made and excellent and the menu features several traditional Cape dishes; chicken pie and bredie are especially good. Breakfast, lunch and tea are served daily; dinner is served Tuesday–Saturday.

Blues. The Promenade, Camps Bay. Tel. (021) 438-2040. This is one of Cape Town's most popular and successful restaurants. It overlooks the beach at Camps Bay and the food and design of the place are pure Californian. The kitchen is a focal point of the dining room and it is interesting to watch a well-orchestrated crew at work. The menu features pizzas, pasta, huge salads, fresh fish and a full range of meats. Dessert should not be missed, especially the Malvavert Tart. Open daily from noon to 11 p.m.; reservations are essential.

A locals' favourite

Quaffers Wine Bar and Restaurant. Victoria and Alfred Waterfront. Tel. (021) 419-0520. There are many restaurants to choose from at the new V & A, but this is one of my favourites. The ambience is terrific and there is a good selection of South African wines, by the bottle or the glass. The menu is extensive and there is something for everyone, from soups and salads to fresh seafood and steaks.

Oriental Restaurant. Sir Lowry Rd. Tel. (021) 461-5858. A casual restaurant specializing in very good Indian curries of all degrees of spiciness. Lunch and dinner are served Monday–Saturday.

The Green Dolphin. Pierhead, Victoria and Alfred Waterfront. Tel. (021) 21-7471. If you are wandering round the V & A project, this is an excellent spot for lunch or dinner. The menu is enormous and ambitious, with six veal dishes alone. There is good live jazz entertainment at night.

Inexpensive
Hard Rock Café. 288 Beach Rd, Sea Point. Tel. (021) 434-1573. A noisy 'cult' restaurant right on the sea with great views. A full range of dishes is served but hamburgers are a speciality. Lunch and dinner daily.

Squares. Stuttaford Town Square. Tel. (021) 24-0224. This bright and modern restaurant overlooks the St George's Street Mall and is open for breakfast and lunch every day except Sunday, with an extensive menu of omelettes, sandwiches, salads, pasta and pizzas.

City centre dining

SHOPPING

The city centre has numerous department stores, boutiques, jewellery and curio shops. For the best selection of shops head for **St George's Street**, a pedestrian mall near Adderley Street. Halfway down the mall you will find **Stuttafords Town Square**, a two-level arcade of speciality shops. At the end of St George's Street are the major department stores. There is additional shopping at the **Sun Gallery** below the Cape Sun Hotel on the corner of Strand and St George's Streets; here you will find more than 50 fine boutiques and galleries. The **Golden Acre** in Adderley Street is a more mundane centre with about 100 shops. It conveniently connects with the Sun Gallery via an underground passageway. There is a car park attached to the Golden Acre complex and this is a good spot to park if you drive into the city.

Outside the city, most of the residential suburbs have shopping centres. Of these, the best is **Cavendish Square** in Claremont, an elegant and upmarket complex with 80 shops. Factory outlet shopping, all the rage in the United States, has surfaced in Cape Town at a centre called

Suburban shopping

South Africa

Access Park. It is off the M5 in Kenilworth and offers 50 factory shops selling merchandise at bargain prices.

A **flea market** is held daily except Sundays in **Greenmarket Square**; the bulk of the merchandise is T-shirts, clothing and jewellery. On Fridays between 9 a.m. and 3 p.m., the **Church Street market** in the pedestrian precinct between Long and Burg Streets gets underway, selling antiques and knick-knacks. A delightful **flower market** is held every day except Sunday at the railway station in Adderley Street; the *proteas* are an incredible bargain here. Just around the corner at **Grand Parade**, opposite the City Hall, there is a collection of stalls offering flowers and bric-a-brac; a **flea market** takes place here every Wednesday and Saturday morning. And on the first Sunday of every month an excellent **antique fair** is held at the Dock Road Venue on the Victoria and Alfred Waterfront.

Proteas at bargain prices

Shopping hours in Cape Town are extended, at least in comparison to much of the rest of the country. Generally, shops are open from 9 a.m. to 5 p.m. Monday–Saturday. In addition, outside the city centre in the suburbs and coastal towns, shopping is possible until 1 p.m. on Sundays. Speciality shops include:

Art & Antiques
Cape Gallery. 60 Church St
Atlantic Art Gallery. 71 Burg St
Sun Art Gallery. Shop 5, Cape Sun Hotel
Peter Visser Antiques. 117 Long St
African Art Centre. Riverside Shopping Centre, Main Rd, Rondebosch
Capetiques. Corner of Cavendish and Vineyard Rd, Claremont
African Market. Pearl House, Heerengracht St
Skylights Art Gallery. Union Castle House, Victoria and Alfred Waterfront

Books
Clarke's Bookshop. 211 Long St (antiquarian and Africana books)
Exclusive Books. Stuttaford's Town Square

Crafts
The Kraal Gallery. 22 Long St
Master Weavers. 6 Strand Concourse
Cape Gallery African Crafts. 108 Long St
Waterfront Trading Co. Victoria and Alfred Waterfront (open Sundays)

Curios
Indaba Curios. Victoria and Alfred Waterfront
Kwazulu Curios Ltd. 7 Castle St
Zimbabwe Curios Ltd. St George's Street Mall
Pezulu. 70 St George's Street Mall

Jewellery
Prins & Prins. 2 Long St
Penny Murdock. 50 Victoria Rd, Camps Bay
The Jewellery Mall. Victoria and Alfred Waterfront
Bruins of Amsterdam. 48A Strand St
Myra's Antique Jewellery. 78 Church St
Cape Diamond Exchange. 10th Floor, Tulbagh Centre
Franz Huppertz. Stuttaford Town Square

Leather
Frasers. Stuttafords Town Square
Lorenzi. Victoria and Alfred Waterfront
Du Artes. Constantia Village Shopping Centre, Constantia

ENTERTAINMENT

Music & Dancing
The Pumphouse. Victoria and Alfred Waterfront (live rock and jazz bands)
Dock Road Café. Victoria and Alfred Waterfront (dixie and jazz)
The Green Dolphin. Victoria and Alfred Waterfront (jazz)
Rosies & All That Jazz. Victoria and Alfred Waterfront (jazz)
The Base. 88 Shortmarket St (live bands, dancing)
Charlie Parkers. Main Rd, Sea Point (disco)
The Cat Club. 83a Loop St. (late-night dancing)
Nico Malan Theatre Centre. D.F. Malan St (opera)
Blakes at the Nico. D. F. Malan St (cabaret)
Hohenort Hotel. Hohenort Ave., Constantia (classical music and jazz)
City Hall. Darling Street (Cape Town Symphony Orchestra performs Thursdays and Sundays)

Theatre
There are 12 theatres in the Cape Town area offering a full spectrum of performance entertainment, including ballet and opera. The daily papers give complete details and bookings can be made through *Computicket,* tel. (021) 21-4715.

SIGHTSEEING

Visitors and South Africans alike consider Cape Town to

South Africa

The fairest city in the land be the most beautiful city in the country. Blessed with a rugged natural beauty, a mild and temperate climate, perfect white sandy beaches and a staggering diversity of flora, Cape Town is a marvellous spot for a holiday. No short-term visitor could hope to explore all of its attractions, so I have concentrated on the best and easiest to get to.

City Sights

Walking tours Cape Town is a superb city to walk in and for an introduction, consider joining the two hour 'city on foot' tour which takes place at 3 p.m. on Saturday from September to April. For specific details of this tour as well as brochures describing self-guided walks around the city centre and waterfront, contact *Captour* at (021) 25-3320.

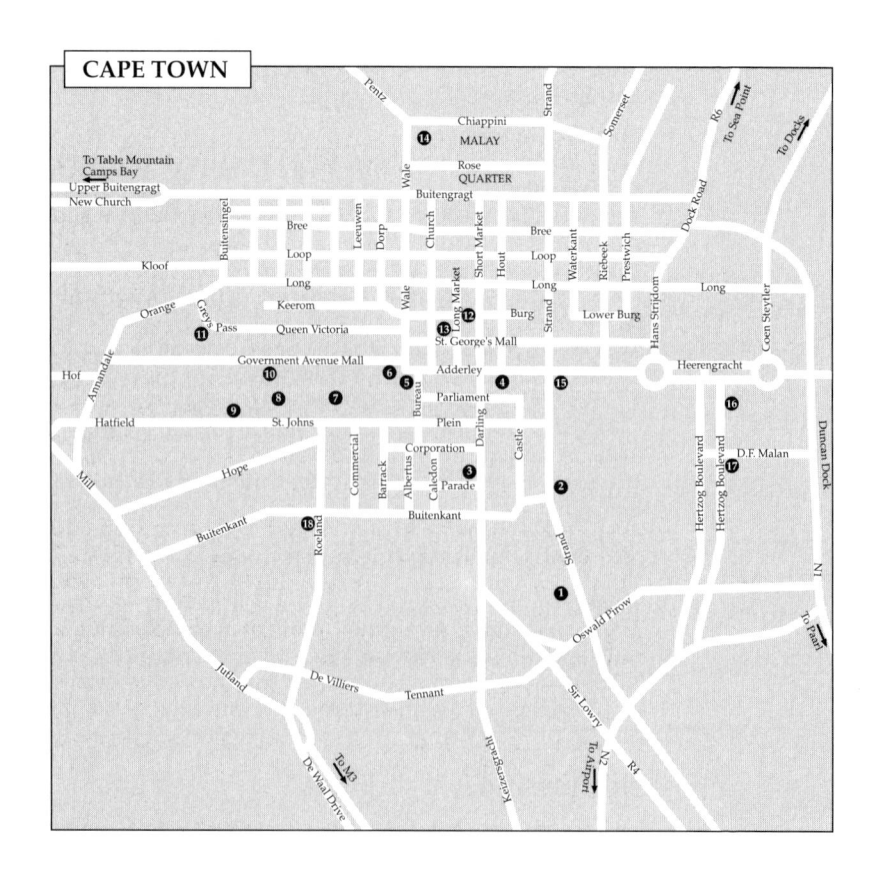

Cape Town is really quite a compact and manageable city. To orient yourself, find Adderley Street on the map. It is the heart of the shopping and commercial area; the bus and railway stations are here as well. Most of the sites described in this section that follows are accessible by foot from Adderley Street; the numbers correspond with the numbers on the map opposite.

Castle of Good Hope (1). Buitenkant St. Tel. (021) 408-7911. Located in the very heart of the city centre, this is the oldest building in South Africa, dating from 1666. The early governors of the Cape lived in this pentagonal fortress; its unusual star-shaped design presumably made it impregnable. Today, the castle houses an important collection of paintings and antiquities as well as historical memorabilia. A changing of the guard takes place every day at noon; a full ceremonial change, complete with band, is held on Fridays at noon. Very good guided tours, *en plein air*, are given daily at 10 a.m., 11 a.m., 12 noon, 2 p.m. and 3 p.m. The grounds are lovely and there is also a military and maritime museum.

Pentagonal fort

Company's Garden (10). Upper Adderley St. This lovely park is situated on the site of Jan van Riebeeck's original vegetable garden, established in 1652 to grow produce for the settlers and ships *en route* to the East. The garden today is only a third of its original size and is now devoted to botanical displays, a small aviary, a restaurant and government buildings. Lovely old oak trees line a gravel walk known as Government Avenue that runs for about half a mile through the garden; a stroll along these shady paths will give you a good view of the historic buildings that form the perimeter of the garden. Be sure to note the ubiquitous grey squirrels which Cecil Rhodes introduced from America. They love to be fed and are so tame that they will hang from your finger.

City park

Houses of Parliament (6). Government Ave. Tel. (021) 403-2911. The Houses of Parliament were completed in 1885 and the edifice is architecturally stunning. Parliamentary sessions convene in Cape Town from January to June only. Tickets are available in Room 12 for any visitor who would like to watch a session from the gallery; you may also book in advance by ringing the number listed above. Foreigners are requested to present a passport and a jacket and tie are required for admission. During the recess period guided tours are given Monday–Friday at 11 a.m. and 2 p.m.

Stunning architecture

South Africa

Planetarium

Tuynhuys (7). Off Government Ave., adjacent to Houses of Parliament. This stunning building was built in 1751 as a pleasure lodge and today it serves as the Cape Town residence and office of the State President. It is not open to the public.

The South African Museum (11). Queen Victoria St. Tel. (021) 24-3330. Devoted to natural history and archaeology, the museum has a number of excellent dioramas that portray the prehistoric and traditional lives of some of the black tribes of Southern Africa. Of especial interest is the exhibit of Bushman rock paintings. A planetarium has recently been added and shows change every three months. The museum is open daily from 10 a.m. to 5 p.m. The planetarium has shows on Tuesdays and Thursdays at 1 p.m., on Tuesday evenings at 8 p.m. and on Saturdays and Sundays at 2 p.m. and 3.30 p.m.

South African National Gallery (8). Off Government Ave., Gardens. Tel. (021) 45-1628. A permanent exhibition of South African and international artists is housed in the Main Gallery. Film shows and lectures are given throughout the year; consult the newspaper or *What's On* for details. The gallery is open to the public daily from 10 a.m. to 5 p.m., except Mondays when it opens at 1 p.m.

Cultural History Museum (5). Upper Adderley St. Tel. (021) 461-8280. This museum is housed in a structure originally built by the Dutch East India Company in 1679 as a slave lodge. The building underwent alterations in 1810 when it was remodelled to serve as the Cape Supreme Court. The collection is eclectic and represents the many countries from which South Africa's population is derived. The museum is open Monday–Saturday, 10 a.m.–5 p.m., and there is a small admission fee.

Jewish Museum (9). 84 Hatfield St, Gardens. Tel. (021) 45-1546. The Jewish Museum is housed in the oldest synagogue in South Africa, dating from 1862. The collection is comprised of items of Jewish historical and ceremonial significance. Open on Tuesdays and Thursdays from 2–5 p.m. and on Sundays from 10 a.m. to 12.30 p.m.

Rust-en-Vreugd (18). 78 Buitenkant St. Tel. (021) 45-3628. The William Fehr Collection of early South African art and valuable Africana is presented in this restored two-storey townhouse, *circa* 1777. The public is welcome on weekdays from 9.30 a.m. to 4 p.m. and guided tours can be arranged.

Greenmarket Square (12). This centrally situated cobbled square was the site of Cape Town's first market, where fruit and vegetables were sold. The tradition continues today in the form of a flea market held Monday–Saturday from 7.30 a.m.–3.30 p.m. Bordering Greenmarket Square is the **Old Town House (13)**, a mid-eighteenth century baroque extravaganza that served as the city hall of Cape Town from 1761 to 1905. The building currently houses the Michaelis Collection of Dutch and Flemish art, representative of the era when the Cape was being settled. It is open daily from 10 a.m. to 5.30 p.m., Saturdays 10 a.m.–1 p.m.

Flea market

The Malay Quarter (14). Bordered by Wale, Waterkant, Rose and Chiappini St. The descendants of the Malay slaves brought to South Africa by the Dutch still live in this area, on the slopes of Signal Hill, within walking distance of the city centre. Narrow streets are lined with traditional flat-topped, pastel-coloured houses dating from the eighteenth century. The Malays are Muslim and there are a number of interesting minarets and mosques in this district. If you have time, visit the **Bokaap Museum** at 71 Wale Street, tel. (021) 24-3846. This house was built in the eighteenth century and is furnished with period pieces, portraying the lifestyle of a typical Malay family in the nineteenth century. It is open every day except Monday and Wednesday from 10 a.m. to 4.30 p.m.

Traditional Malay houses

Table Mountain

It is certainly fair to say that Table Mountain is Cape Town's most notable landmark. Over a million visitors per year ascend to its heights to enjoy the panoramic views. In the summer season when the south-eastern wind known as the Cape Doctor sweeps across the peninsula, Table Mountain sports a 'tablecloth'. A layer of white clouds will hover above the summit and settle just slightly so that it appears as if a cloth has been draped across the flat table-like top of the mountain.

The signature tablecloth

Towering 1,086 metres above Cape Town, this imposing monolith, comprised of layers of granite, shale and sandstone, is covered with wild flowers and silver trees and is criss-crossed with over 350 hiking trails. On a clear day you can see the **Cape of Good Hope** and there are few better spots to watch the sun slip into the Atlantic or the light show of Cape Town after dark. There is a restaurant and souvenir shop at the summit and visitors can wander along a well-worn path to look for wild flowers and savour the view. Don't miss the collection of

Excellent network of hiking trails

hyraxes (rock rabbits) which lives on the stone precipice just beyond the walled terrace area. They love to be fed and are extremely photogenic.

Tramway

The **Cableway** (tel. (021) 24-5148) operates every day of the year, weather permitting, from 8 a.m. to 6 p.m.; in the summer season (December–April) it stays open to 10 p.m. The journey to the summit takes seven minutes and if the car is not too crowded, the photo opportunities are excellent. There is a R9.00 fee for the round trip; the queue can be very tedious in the peak season, so consider purchasing a voucher in advance from *Captour*, tel. (021) 25-3320. To reach the Cableway from Cape Town catch the Kloof Nek bus from Adderley Street (in front of the OK Bazaars) to the Kloof Nek terminus; from here change to the small Cableway Company bus.

For the more adventurous and athletic, there are a number of trails up the mountain but some are dangerous and poorly marked. If you want to climb to the summit rather than take the cableway, a company called *Camp and Climb* (tel.(021) 23-2175) can provide a guide. Otherwise, a relatively easy and signposted trail starts at **Platteklip Gorge**, 3 km from the Kloof Nek turn-off to the cableway station. Allow three hours for the walk to the top.

The Victoria and Alfred Waterfront

Harbour re-birth

The Victoria and Alfred Basins, located on the western side of the waterfront, are currently undergoing some exciting renovation. As with most major port cities, the dock area is not particularly picturesque: it is a working harbour not a tourist attraction. However, away from the cranes, dry docks and container terminals, the waterfront is being reborn; the oldest piers are being restored as part of a four-phase, five-year project. A number of shops, over a dozen restaurants and a new luxury hotel have recently opened and many more are underway. The **South African Maritime Museum**, which consists of a tugboat and a boom defence vessel, is located at the West Quay of Victoria Basin and is open daily. Across from the pierhead is the lovely **Victorian Clock Tower** which was built in 1883 as a signal tower; today it houses a small shipping museum and is open on Saturdays from 2.30 to 5 p.m.

More than a penny today

A quaint way to reach the Clock Tower is via the **Penny Ferry** (tel. (021) 218-2812) which runs from Quay Four from Monday to Friday, at a cost of somewhat more than a penny today (70c to be exact). Harbour cruises are a major attraction and helicopter flips over the city and

Cape Town

harbour are organized from the parking lot. Most of Cape Town's nightlife is centred here with a number of spots offering jazz, dixie and rock bands. In 1994, an ambitious **Sea World** is scheduled to open and should prove to be a real magnet, especially with shopping, dining, museums and accommodation also available.

A working harbour

As befits one of the great waterfronts of the world, the pulse of the city is still very much centred here. Despite the upmarket renovation of the docks in the Victoria and Alfred Basins, hundreds of working tugs and fishing boats are based in this section of the harbour. If you arrive just after noon, you should be able to watch them unload their catch. A stroll along the brick and cobbled docks, past the gaily coloured Victorian buildings, will quickly give you a sense of the vitality of this harbour. Tugs and tankers come and go, men scurry about ships in dry dock, seals frolic in the basins and gulls wheel and scream overhead. The V & A Waterfront may become Cape Town's premier tourist attraction, but there is nothing artificial or contrived about its setting. Moreover, the view from the piers across the water to Cape Town and Table Mountain alone justify an excursion here.

Sightseeing Outside the City Centre
Kirstenbosch Botanic Gardens. Rhodes Drive, Constantia. If you are at all interested in the flora of South Africa, don't miss an excursion to the world-renowned Kirstenbosch Gardens. This 560 hectare tract clings to the eastern slopes of Table Mountain and was a gift to the nation from Cecil Rhodes; in 1913, a decade after his death, South Africa's first botanical garden was established. Today over 6,000 of the country's 20,000 species flourish here. The best months to visit are August, September and October, but any month will be rewarding. The gardens are open daily from 8 a.m. to 6 p.m.; guided walks are given in the summer on Tuesdays and Saturdays at 11 a.m.

A gift to the nation from Cecil Rhodes

Rhodes Memorial. Off Rhodes Drive, Rondebosch. Built as a memorial to Cecil John Rhodes, this imposing granite monument, reminiscent of a small Greek temple, is a fitting tribute to a man who envisaged himself as something of an emperor. The drive to the beautifully situated memorial is very pretty and one can often catch glimpses of fallow deer. Behind the memorial there is a path that winds up the slopes of Devil's Peak; this is a popular walk with local residents. In addition there is a quaint and charming tearoom here that is open daily except Monday from 9.30 a.m. to 5 p.m.

The imposing Rhodes Memorial on the slopes of Devil's Peak.

EXCURSIONS

Constantia Wine Route

The beautiful countryside

South of Cape Town lies the Constantia Valley, a beautiful bit of countryside with a wine-making heritage dating back to the eighteenth century when its red wines were in demand by world leaders such as Bismarck, King Louis Phillipe and Napoleon. Today this bucolic valley is a mere 15-minute drive from the city centre and there are three estates on the M42 that can be visited: **Groot Constantia, Buitenverwachting** and **Klein Constantia**. All are part of the original farm, Constantia, that was granted in 1685 by the Dutch East India Company to Simon van der Stel, the first Dutch governor of the Cape. Constantia is the oldest viticultural area in the country and **Groot Constantia** has the distinction of being South Africa's very first wine estate.

Classic Cape Dutch architecture

Today the estate is still producing superlative wines and because the demand is great and the supply small, some vintages are only available from the vineyard direct. The manor house, designed by van der Stel himself, is a classic example of Cape Dutch architecture and is the oldest and grandest homestead in the country. A tour through this exquisitely proportioned and lavishly furnished house is worth the trip to Groot Constantia on its own, even if you don't like wine! There are cellar tours and wine tastings and you can buy the wine if you like it. There is an excellent restaurant called **Jonkershuis** that serves lunch and tea.

Buitenverwachting is a very old wine estate with historic farm buildings, sweeping vineyards and spectacular views of the countryside. The manor house and outlying buildings have been beautifully restored and the vineyards were re-established just ten years ago. The wines have already won awards and an enviable reputation. Cellar tours are given at 11 a.m. and 3 p.m. on weekdays and at 11 a.m. on Saturdays. The restaurant is considered to be Cape Town's finest.

Klein Constantia is the third winery on this route and it has also been lovingly restored and replanted with new cultivars to produce only quality wines. The estate is open for wine sales on weekdays from 9 a.m. to 5 p.m. and on Saturdays from 9 a.m. to 1 p.m.; cellar tours, however, require advance booking (tel. (021) 794-5188).

Superlative wines

Bloubergstrand
A few miles north of Cape Town along Marine Drive (the R27) there is a small seaside village called Bloubergstrand. There is nothing particularly appealing about this resort, but the view back to the city is superb. If you want the quintessential angle for a photograph of Cape Town and Table Mountain, this is the spot.

Best angle for photos of Table Mountain

Cape Peninsula Tour
Despite the attractions of the city, no visitor to Cape Town should miss a drive around the Cape Peninsula to the Cape of Good Hope. If you aren't hiring a car then join one of the many half- or full-day tours. If you are driving yourself, I suggest making it a full day excursion so that you have ample time to explore the beaches, villages and nature reserves of the peninsula. From Cape Town take the N2 (toward the airport and Somerset West) until it joins the M3. Follow the M3 to the colourful seaside town of Muizenberg, which is famous for its safe bathing beach along the shores of False Bay.

The exact origin of the name of this bay is unclear. One explanation is that long ago navigators sailing from the Indian Ocean thought they had reached the Cape of Good Hope and the open waters of the Atlantic Ocean when they saw Cape Hangklip at the eastern end of False Bay. Once inside the sheltering arms of the bay they realized their mistake, only to discover that the wind had

False Bay

died. Lengthy delays often resulted until the sails could fill with enough wind to carry the ships beyond the strong currents at the opening of the bay. Another story I have read claims that early settlers assumed that there would be a deep water anchorage in False Bay and were disappointed to discover that it was quite shallow.

Whatever the true origin, this beautiful inlet of water, ringed by miles of sand dunes and white sand beaches, is a favourite of swimmers, anglers and surfers alike. The waters of False Bay are influenced by the warm Mozambique-Agulhas current and so swimming is much pleasanter here than on the Atlantic coastline.

Beach towns

Muizenberg is one of South Africa's most popular resorts, and was, incidentally, a favourite spot of Rudyard Kipling's, who wrote, *'White as the sands of Muizenberg, spun before the gale'*. The town became fashionable about a hundred years ago when Cecil Rhodes bought a cottage nearby. It still retains some of its turn-of-the-century charm although the seafront facilities have been modernized and updated.

Along the main road just outside Muizenberg, on the way to Kalk Bay, you will pass **Rhodes Cottage**, where Cecil Rhodes spent his last few years. His home is now a museum open to the public every day except Monday from 10 a.m. to 1 p.m. and 1 p.m. to 5 p.m.

Heading south towards the Cape of Good Hope you will pass through **St James**, a charming beach town with Victorian bathing boxes, and then **Kalk Bay**, the home of the False Bay fishing fleet. Fish auctions are held here when the boats return to port and if you need a meal or refreshment, try the **Brass Bell**, a waterfront pub and restaurant that serves good seafood (tel. (021) 88-5456).

Continue along the curve of False Bay to **Simonstown** which has a long history as a naval base. Developed by the British in 1814 as a base for the South Atlantic fleet, it is now the headquarters of the South African Navy. To me it looks like any other military town although there are a number of historic buildings here dating from the seventeenth century.

From Simonstown it is approximately 10 km to the **Cape of Good Hope Nature Reserve**. The entire southern end of the Cape Peninsula was placed under protection in 1936 to preserve the indigenous flora and fauna. There are 40 km of coastline in the reserve and the coves and beaches are indescribably beautiful. Few trees can survive in this rugged landscape but proteas and heather thrive, despite the constant buffeting by wind, fog and salt. A number of animals live in the reserve and if you have time to explore the side roads you may encounter ostrich, springbok or eland. One animal that you will most undoubtedly see is the baboon for they are multitudinous. There are signposts everywhere warning visitors not to feed the apes, as they have become quite a nuisance and are very bold. These Chacma baboons are very unusual for they exist on a marine diet, apparently the only such group in the world to do so. When you park at the car park before climbing to Cape Point, be sure to lock your car and close all the windows or you might be extremely sorry when you return: baboons make quite a mess!

Pesky baboons

The famous journal entry of Sir Francis Drake, *'The Cape is the most stately thing, and the Fairest Cape we saw in the whole circumference of the earth'*, was a reference to the peninsula that is now occupied by the Cape of Good Hope Nature Reserve. For the sake of clarification, the peninsula actually divides into three at the tip: Cape Point on the eastern face, Cape Maclear in the middle and Cape of Good Hope to the west, also the most southerly of the three. The peninsula was originally dubbed Cape of Storms by the intrepid Bartholomew Dias in 1488 when he first rounded this point under adverse conditions. However, on his return voyage it was revealed in all its splendour and he changed his map notation to read the Cape of Good Hope.

For the most panoramic view, Cape Point is the place to go. A small bus called the *Flying Dutchman* shuttles visitors from the car park to the highest point on the headland accessible by vehicle; from here you must climb the stairs to the summit. The original 1860 lighthouse is the centrepiece of the observation point, although it is no longer in use, having lost out to modern technology. The new beacon is not visible from Cape Point but it does have the distinction of being the most powerful in the southern hemisphere.

Lighthouse

From the towering granite cliffs of **Cape Point** you can see the entire expanse of False Bay to the east and the Cape of Good Hope to the west. Although it is commonly thought that the treacherous meeting of the Atlantic and the Indian Oceans occurs at this stormy cape, in fact that distinction belongs to **Cape Agulhas**, the southernmost point of the continent 200 km to the east. Nonetheless, Cape Point is far more scenic and it is thrilling to stand on top of the 260-metre cliffs and watch the cormorants, gulls and petrels ride the updrafts and the Atlantic rollers

Meeting place of the Atlantic and Indian Oceans

crash and foam against the sheer precipice beneath you.

The Cape of Good Hope Reserve is open daily from 7 a.m. to 8 p.m. although the hours are slightly shorter in winter (May–July). There is an entrance fee per person and per vehicle. There are a number of walking trails, picnic sites, changing rooms, a tidal pool and a launching ramp available for use; also a restaurant and kiosk. A small charge is levied for the Flying Dutchman shuttle service but you can to walk up the road if you prefer.

For the return journey to Cape Town, retrace your route along the main road through the reserve and then turn left on to the M65 towards Scarborough. You will pass a number of small holiday villages and after the town of Kommetjie, the inviting white sandy shore of Chapman's Bay comes into view. At this point the road climbs and becomes the famous **Chapman's Peak Drive**. Over 70 years ago a narrow ribbon of road was carved out of this rocky mountain spine high above the Atlantic Coast. The 10 km road is reminiscent of the Grande Corniche with its cliff hugging, hairpin bends. The vistas are spectacular and this marine drive has to be one of the most scenic and memorable in the world. The sheer rock escarpment is composed of layers of red, yellow and orange sandstone which have been laid down on deposits of granite. In the spring and summer the hillsides are ablaze with the colour of millions of proteas and wild flowers. There are several lookout points and picnic sites.

Africa's Grande Corniche

Hout Bay is the next stop on your route. It is the home of the crayfish fleet and of many fishing boats. The picturesque harbour is set against the backdrop of a verdant mountain called the **Sentinel** and the town sprawls along the lower slopes of this buttress. Fishing is big business in Hout Bay and there are a number of processing plants here. At the far end of the harbour several casual take away shops sell lobster, smoked products and line fish. The **Laughing Lobster** has good fish and chips as well as grilled crayfish and calamari; customers can eat outside on picnic tables. In the centre of the marina there is a complex called **Mariner's Wharf** which features nautical gifts, souvenir shops, an art gallery, fish and lobster markets and seafood restaurants.

Scenic cruises

If you have time, consider taking a cruise around the bay to **Duiker Island**, a cluster of sea-worn rocks opposite the Sentinel that has been established as a bird and seal sanctuary. The excursion lasts one hour and there are usually hundreds of Cape fur seals cavorting and snoozing on the rocks.

Cape Town

Sunset cruises are offered from Hout Bay to Cape Town in the summer months by *Circe Launches*, tel. (021) 790-1040, and for those who like to sail, Bay Yacht Cruises arranges one hour trips on an 18-metre, twin masted, classic sailing boat called the *Laura Rose* (tel. (021) 438-9208).

From Hout Bay take the road north to **Llandudno**, a tiny little hamlet that cascades down the mountain slope to the shores of a lovely sandy beach. If you continue past the Llandudno turn off the main road to Cape Town, you can look back to get a good view of the town. In 1977 a tanker ran aground on some rocks in the bay and its rusted remains are still clearly visible today. The beach is very nice but the water is too cold for any but the hardy to swim, a statement that applies to all the Atlantic coast beaches of South Africa. Accessible only on foot, 2 km south from the beach car park at Llandudno is **Sandy Bay**, a secluded stretch of sand popular with naturists (a euphemism for nudists).

Coastal panoramas

Continuing north the road hugs the coastline, flanked by the long finger of mountain peaks called the **Twelve Apostles**. This fascinating range is actually a continuation of the back of Table Mountain and it forms a dramatic and stunning backdrop for some of the most exclusive residential property in South Africa. On the drive from Camps Bay to Clifton it is possible to imagine that you are on the French Riviera. The road skirts the base of **Lion's Head**, with its distinctive 'sugar-loaf' peak. Whitewashed houses with tiled roofs and high walls hang precariously from the sheer rock cliffs. Everywhere there is a riot of exuberant colour from a profusion of creeping bougainvillea. Only when you look to the sea, at the rocky bays and secret coves and almost pure white beaches, do you realize that these beautiful vistas far surpass the Mediterranean!

The beach at **Camps Bay** is long and wide with a neatly mowed grass verge adorned with a picture-postcard-perfect row of palm trees. **Clifton** has four sandy beaches that can only be reached by steep steps leading down from the road. These beaches are sheltered from the annoying south-easterly wind that blows in the summer months and so are quite popular.

Lion's Head

Lion's Head and **Signal Hill** are two Cape Town landmarks that join Table Mountain to encircle the city and separate it from its southern suburbs. Lion's Head is actually connected to Table Mountain by a saddle of land known as Kloof Nek and by turning inland at Camp's

South Africa

Camps Bay, only 5km from Cape Town, is a popular spot for beach volleyball and surfing.

Bay, one can drive over the hump and quickly drop into Cape Town, bypassing Clifton and Sea Point. The origin of the name Lion's Head is unknown; some suggest that the mountain resembles the head of a lion, with Signal Hill the rump and the connecting ridge forming the body. A profusion of silver trees and wild flowers covers the upper slopes of Lion's Head and there is a path to the peak for the energetic and athletic.

Every day except Sunday at exactly twelve noon, a signal gun is fired from the summit of Signal Hill. In days of old a post was maintained here to signal ships in the harbour. A road winds to the summit and the vistas are dramatic. This is a popular hang gliding spot and a good point for watching the lights of Cape Town at night.

Scenic lookout

After rounding the flank of Lion's Head you will reach **Sea Point**, a large bustling suburb of Cape Town. Drive along the coast on Beach Road; you will pass a 3 km long seafront promenade that boasts the largest salt water swimming pool in the southern hemisphere. Sea Point is tower block country and many South Africans rent flats here during the summer holiday season.

At the traffic lights at Three Anchor Bay, turn left and follow the road out to **Green Point Lighthouse**. Still in use today, it was built in 1824 and is South Africa's oldest lighthouse. Continue along Beach Road to its end and you will find yourself back in the city, at the western end of the harbour just by the entrance to the Victoria and Alfred Waterfront.

ACTIVITIES

Bird Watching
Rondevlei Bird Sanctuary, Perth Rd, Grassy Park. Tel. (021) 72-5711.
Open daily from 8 a.m. to 5 p.m.; small entrance fee. Waterside hides also offer very good hippo viewing.

Boat Charter and Pleasure Cruises
A number of scenic and informative cruises around the peninsula are offered on a scheduled basis by several reputable companies.
Ocean Star Yacht Charter (hourly harbour cruises & daily yacht charters). Tel. (021) 25-4292
Sealink. Tel. (021) 25-4480
Condor Charters. Tel. (021) 417-5612
Lowland Lancer (evening casino cruise). Tel. (021) 461-6798
Le Tigre (8 cruises daily on luxury catamaran). Tel. (021) 419-7746

Caving
Speleological Association (WP Mountain Club). Tel. (021) 790-3318

Deep Sea Fishing
Big Game Fishing Safaris. Tel. (021) 64-2203
Bluefin Charters. Tel. (021) 83-1756
African Fishing Safaris. Tel. (021) 72-1272

Diving
P.J.'s Dive Charters. Tel. (021) 685-1316
Ocean Divers International. Tel. (021) 23-5898

Hang Gliding
Cape Albatross Hang-gliding Club. Tel. (021) 438-9093

Hiking
Contact the National Hiking Way Board at (021) 402-3093 for maps and information on the many trails in Cape Town and vicinity. Also:

Roaming Tours. Tel. (021) 761-7489
Wanderlust Walks. Tel. (021) 438-1948
WP Mountain Club. Tel. (021) 790-3318
Hoeri Kwaggo. Tel. (021) 762-1578

Parasailing
Dynaflight. Tel. (021) 61-6361
Daedelas' Paragliding Adventures. Tel. (021) 790-4121
Parapente. Tel. (021) 761-6187

Riding
Horse Trail Safaris. Tel. (021) 73-4386 or 73-1807

Tours
Safair (tel. (021) 934-0344) offers a one-day tour to Oudtshoorn, and there are helicopter trips available from *Court Helicopters* (tel. (021) 25-2965) and *Civair* (tel. (021) 948-8511).
Dozens of companies also offer private and scheduled tours of Cape Town and its environs, including:
Hylton Ross. Tel. (021) 438-1500
Sealink. Tel. (021) 25-4480
Safari Escapes. Tel. (021) 794-4832
Specialized Tours. Tel. (021)2 5-3259
Walking tours include city tours with *Judy Oliver* (tel. (021) 591-4763) and the Malay Quarter and Harbour with *Mr. Annoni* (tel. (021) 762-3262).

Whale Watching
Captour has a brochure entitled **The Whale Route** which is very helpful if you are interested in whale-watching. The best time of the year is from June to November. For further details contact the *Dolphin Action and Protection Group* at (021) 82-5845.

Surfing on the Cape peninsula.

SERVICES

TOURIST INFORMATION
There are two excellent information offices with hundreds of brochures and booklets available for the taking.
Captour Visitor Information Bureau, Strand Concourse. Tel (021) 25-3320.
SATOUR, Sanlam Centre. Tel. (021) 21-6274.

GETTING AROUND
Airlines
S.A.A. Tel. (021) 25-4610
FliteStar. Tel. (021) 25-4085
British Airways. Tel. (021) 25-2970
Namaqualand Airways. Tel. (021) 931-4183
Air Cape. Tel. (021) 934-0572
National Airlines. Tel. (021) 934-0350
Safair. Tel. (021) 934-0344

Motoring Organisation
The *AA of South Africa* maintains two offices in Cape Town: Adderley Street (lower ground floor of Garlicks), tel. (021) 21-5329; and 7 Martinhammer Schlag Way, tel. (021) 21-1550.

Bus Services
There is an excellent bus service within Cape Town and to just about anywhere in the country. The bus station is at the Central City Terminus behind the Golden Acre Shopping Centre. For timetables and details of city bus services ring (021) 45-5450. The following companies offer an inter-city service:
Translux. Tel. (021) 218-3871
Intercity Greyhound. Tel. (021) 25-9514
Connex (SAR Travel). Tel. (021) 218-2191
InterCape. Tel. (021) 934-4400

Car Hire
Avis, Imperial and *Budget* all have desks at the airport and offices in the city centre. There are a number of local companies that also hire vehicles at lower prices.
Avis. Tel. (021) 24-1177
Imperial. Tel. (021) 434-9921
Budget. Tel. (021) 419-3290
Pride Car Hire. Tel. (021) 439-1144
Marine Car Hire. Tel. (021) 434-0434

Caravan Hire
Capricorn Tours & Campers. Tel. (024) 55-2331; fax (024) 55-4062
Priclo Caravans. Tel. (021) 511-4208
Camperent. Tel. (021) 25-1056
Royal Clipper Tourist Services. Tel. (021) 946-2777

Rail
There is an excellent regional rail network linking Cape Town with the Western Cape and the southern peninsula. The **Cape Town–Simonstown excursion** is an especially scenic journey. The railway station is in the city centre and for enquiries ring (021) 218-2991; ring (021) 218-3871 for reservations. If you need information regarding the **Blue Train**, the number is (021) 218-2672.

Taxis
To hire a taxi you need to phone; you cannot hail them.
Marine Taxi Hire. Tel. (021) 434-0434
Peninsula Taxis Service. Tel. (021) 434-4444
Star Taxis. Tel. (021) 419-7777

Groot Constantia Manor - quintessential Cape Dutch architecture.

THE WINELANDS

INTRODUCTION

Early viticulture

Within a 150 km radius of Cape Town there is a region called the Winelands where distinguished wines have been made for over three centuries. Vines were planted in South Africa early as 1652, when Jan van Riebeeck and the original Dutch settlers transplanted the root stock they had brought with them from Europe. After these first experimental plantings in the Company Gardens, vines were introduced to the outlying valleys by pioneer farmers. Van Riebeeck and his compatriots had no skill or knowledge of viticulture, but the vines survived, although there is little evidence that the resulting wine was especially well regarded. What was needed was a bit of expertise, and this was fortuitously provided with the arrival of the Huguenots in 1688. The majority of these 200 French refugees settled in Franschhoek and winemaking began in earnest. At approximately the same time Governor Simon van der Stel established Groot Constantia as a model Cape wine estate and the rest, as they say, is history.

The Winelands are located just a short drive from Cape Town in a corner of the country rich in natural beauty and history. Despite a relatively small area of cultivation, the diversity of soils and micro-climates

The Winelands

Explore the countryside on the wine routes

within the valleys yields a full range of grape varieties and styles of wine. Wine making is a serious business here and the wine routes are well organized, the winemakers are friendly and the restaurants and accommodation in the various villages are first rate. Hopefully, most visitors to the Cape will have an opportunity to explore one or more of the routes. Because of their proximity to the city, it is quite easy to travel several of the routes in the better part of a day.

However, this region encompasses some of the most magnificent scenery on earth and one short day of touring cannot do it justice. Although the vineyards may be the calling cards of the Winelands, they are only one facet of the many diversions and pleasures which await the leisurely traveller. Taste the wine, but also meander the winding country lanes and breathtaking passes as they skirt ancient stands of forest, tumultuous rivers, crystalline lakes and whitewashed Cape Dutch homesteads. Life moves at a slower, more gracious pace here and the echoes of history and tradition still resound.

The official Cape wine routes are Stellenbosch, Franschhoek, Paarl, Constantia (see page 286), Robertson, West Coast (Swartland and Olifantsrivier) and Worcester. The first three are by far the most popular, and they are the ones we will be discussing. If you want information on the other routes, contact *CapTour* in Cape Town or one of the associations listed below for detailed information.

Robertson Wine Trust, PO Box 550, Robertson 6705. Tel. (02351) 3167/8
Swartland Wine Route, Doornkuil, Malmesbury 7300. Tel. (0224) 2-1134
Worcester Winelands Association, PO Box 59, Worcester 6850. Tel. (0231) 2-8710

A number of companies based in Cape Town offer one day excursions to the wine country.
Vineyard Ventures. Tel. (024) 55-1620
Springbok Atlas. Tel. (021) 417-6545
Court Helicopters. Tel. (021) 25-2965
Hylton Ross Tours. Tel. (021) 438-1500
Cape Courtesy. Tel. (021) 439-5056

THE STELLENBOSCH WINE ROUTE

It is a mere 30 minute drive from Cape Town to the historic town of Stellenbosch, the second oldest European settlement in the country. The Stellenbosch wine route was the first to be established in South Africa and

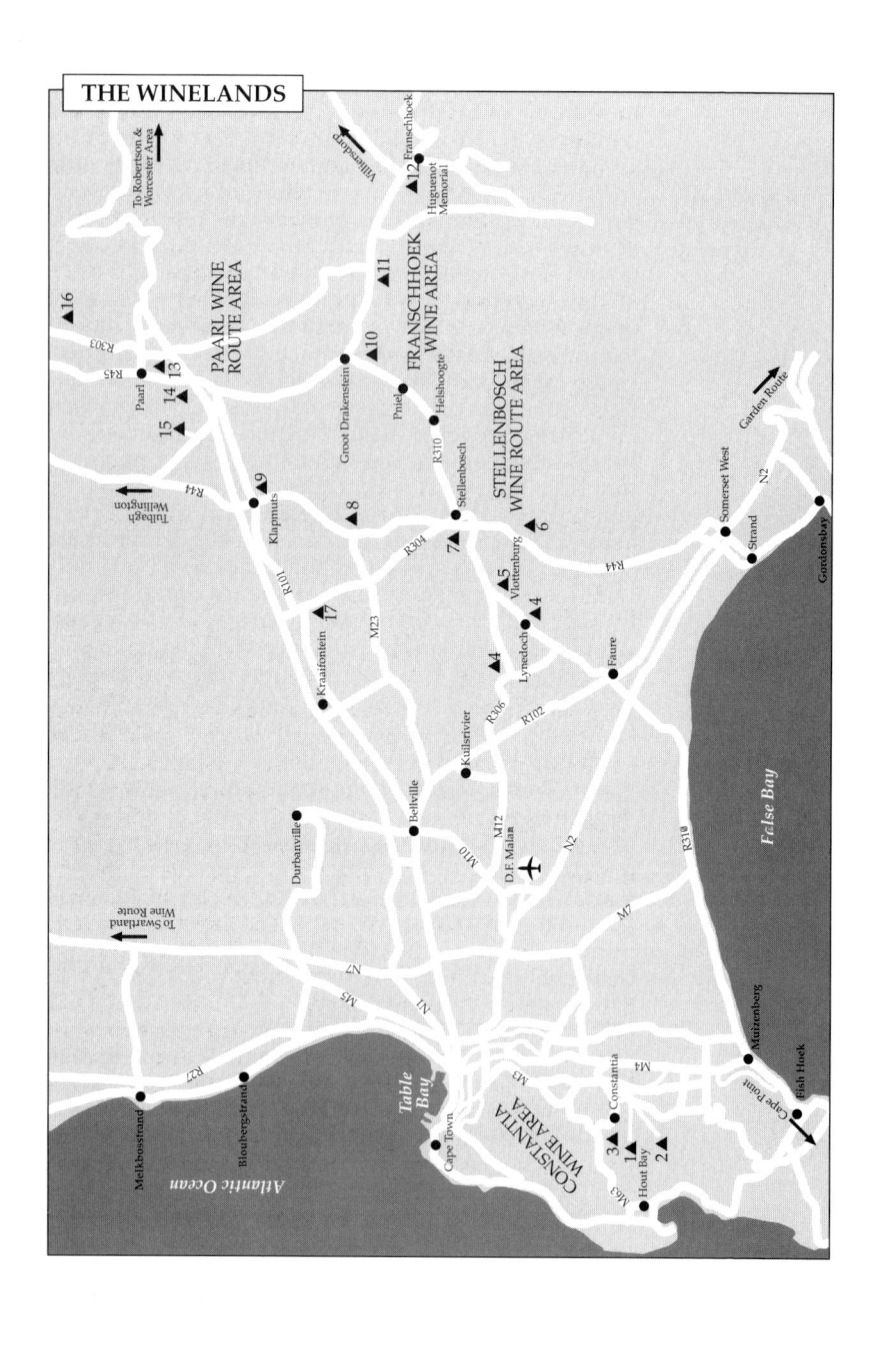

South Africa

The Winelands

The town of oaks comprises 18 private cellars and five co-operative wineries all within a 12 km radius of town. The majority of the estates produce quality wine and most of the cellars are open to the public for tastings and sales. Space does not permit a complete description of each winery so I have just listed a small selection. If you choose to explore the Stellenbosch route, do not overlook the charming town, home to one of the best universities in Africa. Known as the 'town of oaks', its shaded streets and gracious buildings are steeped in history and it is an excellent place to base yourself if you plan to devote a few days to the Winelands.

Getting There
The most direct route is via the N2 from Cape Town. Exit at the R310 North and follow the signposts into Stellenbosch. There is also daily train service from Cape Town with departures at 10h00 and 12h15; the trip takes one hour and the train departs Stellenbosch at 17h50.

Accommodation
D'Ouwe Werf Country Inn***. 30 Church St, Stellenbosch. Tel. (02231) 7-4608; fax (02231) 7-4626. Nicely situated in a quiet street in the heart of the town, **The oldest inn** this is South Africa's oldest existing inn, dating from 1802. There are 35 cozy and charmingly decorated rooms with private baths, telephones and radio. There is a very small swimming pool, lovely public rooms including a TV lounge, and a coffee house serving three meals a day.

Stellenbosch Hotel***. Corner of Dorp and Andringa St. Tel. (02231) 7-3644; fax (02231)4427. A country hotel centrally situated, with 20 rooms that exude old-world charm. The rooms are clean but tend to be on the small side, except the Victorian room. The amenities include private bathrooms, TV, telephone and radio. There is a small pool, a bar lounge and a restaurant.

Lanzerac Hotel***. Jonkershoek Rd. Tel. (02231) 7-1132; fax (02231) 7-2310. Located on the outskirts of Stellenbosch this 40-roomed historic Cape Dutch homestead has been converted into a lovely hotel. All guest rooms have private baths, TV, radio and telephone. There is a swimming pool, an art gallery and two restaurants; wine and cheese tastings are held in the wine cellars.

Devon Valley Protea Hotel**. Devon Valley Rd. Tel. (02231) 7-0211. One of the popular Protea Hotels, the Devon Valley is nestled in a quiet valley about 8 km from Stellenbosch and it boasts lovely views and grounds.

There are three categories of rooms, each with private bath, telephone, and TV with video channel. Choose from two swimming pools and dine in the a la carte restaurant that specializes in country fare.

Dorphuis Guest House. Corner of Dorp and Weidenhof St. Tel. (02231) 9-9881; fax (02231) 9-9884. Situated near the town centre, this elegant new bed and breakfast establishment has seven large rooms and five luxury suites. The bathrooms are fitted out with Italian marble, bidets and heated towel bars and the rooms have telephone, TV and bar fridge. There is a swimming pool and dining room for breakfast only.

Lord Charles Hotel***.** Corner of Faure and Stellenbosch Rd, Somerset West; Tel. (024) 51-2970; fax (024) 55-1107. This very luxurious hotel is located on the fringe of wine country, 15 km from Stellenbosch, 4 km from the sea and 43 km from Cape Town. Rooms are very large and tastefully appointed with all the amenities and services you would expect from a five star hotel.

> Five star facilities

Mountain Breeze Caravan Park. 7 km from Stellenbosch on the R44 to Somerset West. Tel. (02231) 2924. There are 50 stands with full facilities, a swimming pool, a recreation hall and a shop nearby.

Dining

Ralphs. 13 Andringa St. Tel. (02231) 3532. The atmosphere is casual but the menu is ambitious and creative and features a large selection of game and offal as well as a full range of meats and fish. This establishment is very popular with the locals and the portions are enormous. Dinner is served every night except Sunday; lunch every day except Monday. Ralph's is unlicensed so bring your own drink.

> Enormous portions

De Kelder Restaurant. 63 Dorp St. Tel. (02231) 3797. The building that houses this restaurant was once an old wine cellar and is now a national monument. The atmoshpere is cozy and charming, especially in the winter when the huge fireplace is in use. The food is continental, with an emphasis on Austrian dishes. The menu changes every few days and the food represents good value for money. Lunch and dinner are served every day except Monday.

Arizona Spur Steak Ranch. Bird St. Tel. (02231) 4511. Steak and salad in a casual, frontier setting with reasonable prices. Lunch and dinner daily till late.

De Volkskombuis. Old Strand Rd. Tel. (02231) 7-2121. This highly regarded restaurant is housed in a restored farm cottage that is now a national monument. Traditional Cape cuisine is their speciality and reservations are essential. Lunch and dinner are offered from Monday to Saturday.

Doornbosch Wine House. Strand Rd (R44). Tel. (02231) 6163. Located just outside town on the road to Somerset West, the Doornbosch specializes in Cape Dutch and Malay cuisines in addition to international selections. Lunch is served every day except Monday; dinner is available from Tuesday to Saturday. Booking is recommended.

Traditional dishes

Shopping
Oom Samie se Winkel. 84 Dorp St. Tel. (02231) 7-0797. A terrific store filled with the aroma of spices, herbs and tobacco and crammed with the memorabilia of yesteryear. You name it and they sell it, from handicrafts to jams and antiques to fine wines. If you love to browse, don't miss this unique general store. Open daily.

Jean Craig Pottery. Devon Valley Rd. Tel. (02231) 2998. A working pottery where visitors can watch all stages of production from raw clay to opening the kiln door. The entire range of products made here is for sale in the shop on the premises. Open Monday–Saturday.

Dombeya Farm. Annandale Road off R44 to Somerset West. Tel. (02231) 9-3746. Home-made woollen clothing is sold here and you can watch the spinning and dying. Open Monday–Saturday.

Dorp Street Gallery. Corner of Dorp and Ryneveld St. Tel. (02231) 7-2256. Ceramics, graphics, glassware, designer jewellery and paintings.

Goldart. 36 Plein St. Tel. (02231) 7-3047. Unique and exquisitely beautiful original jewellery designs.

Sightseeing
The very best way to explore Stellenbosch is on foot. The town is renowned for its typical Cape Dutch architecture and is one of the best preserved towns dating from the colonial era in South Africa. Look for the complimentary leaflet entitled *Discover Stellenbosch on Foot* at the Visitors' Bureau or in any hotel. It maps out a walking tour around the centre of the town and shows the location of 60 buildings that have been classified as national monuments; these are numbered on the pamphlet and have corresponding descriptions.

Walking tour

Don't miss the **Village (Dorp) Museum** which covers 5,000 square metres of the oldest part of town. The entrance is at 18 Ryneveld Street, and for a small fee you can step back in time to the earliest days of settlement.

You can visit four original houses depicting colonial

Cape Dutch, Georgian and Victorian styles, each furnished with period pieces echoing the tastes of the era. These houses illustrate the architectural development and stylistic changes which occurred between 1700 and 1870. The garden areas adjoining each house are beautifully maintained and the plants reflect the medicinal, cultural and decorative uses of the particular period. The Village Museum is open Monday–Saturday, 9.30 a.m.–5 p.m., and Sunday from 2 to 5 p.m.

One other museum of interest is the **Oude Meester Brandy Museum** at the corner of Dorp and Strand Streets. As its name suggests, the emphasis here is on the history and development of the brandy industry in the Cape. Open Monday–Saturday 9.30 a.m.–12.45 p.m. and 2 p.m.–5 p.m., Sunday 2.30 p.m.–5.30 p.m..

Crocodile farming

Out of town on the R44 north to N1 is **Le Bonheur Crocodile Farm** (tel. (02211) 63-1142). For a small entrance fee the public is entertained with a 20 minute video dealing with the ethology of crocodiles and then taken on a brief tour to see the reptiles. There are also a few ostriches at the car park area and you can buy sacks of corn to feed them. If you like ostrich or crocodile leather, the gift shop here will be of interest. They have a good selection of handbags, belts, wallets and shoes at very fair prices. Compared to the USA or Europe, they seem to be a real bargain, but it should be noted that these skins are not inexpensive anywhere in the world.

Wine Estates

Excellent wine tours given

Die Bergkelder. Near railway station. Tel. (02231) 7-3480. The cellars of Die Bergkelder have been tunnelled into a mountainside and are renowned for their 22 impressive oak wine casks that display beautifully carved ends illustrating the history of wine-making in South Africa. There are actually 19 Bergkelder estates and the wine from all of them can be tasted here, although no sales are made. Tours are given in season from December to mid-January every hour from 9 a.m. to 3 p.m., Monday–Friday; on Saturdays there are tours at 10 a.m., 11 a.m., 2 p.m. and 3 p.m.. Advance booking is essential in the high season. During the rest of the year tours are held Monday–Saturday at 10 a.m. and 3 p.m. only.

Spier. 3.7 km from Stellenbosch on the R310. Tel. (02231) 9-3808. Picturesque, historic Cape Dutch buildings grace this estate, which also has an art gallery, cellar tours, wine sales and two excellent restaurants. A wide range of white, red, sparkling and port wines are produced at Spier and both recent and older vintages are for sale.

Cellar and vineyard tours

Tours are given at the Goedgeloof Estate on weekdays only at 11 a.m.; in December and January there is an additional tour at 3 p.m.

Blaauwklippen Farm. 3.9 km from Stellenbosch on the R44. Tel. (02231) 90-0133. White, red, sparkling and port wines are produced at this enchanting 300 year old farm. In season, between November and Easter, vineyard tours are conducted by horse-drawn carriage, Monday–Friday 10 a.m.–12 noon and 2 p.m.–3.45 p.m. It has a small museum of coaches, Cape furniture and kitchen implements, and homemade jams, cheeses, pickles and chutneys are on sale as well as gifts. Wine tastings and cellar tours are available Monday–Friday and Saturday mornings.

Kanonkop Estate. 9.1 km from Stellenbosch on the R44. Tel. (02231) 9-4656. This small winery produces only red wine, with an annual production of around 15,000 cases. Its Pintotages are considered the best in the country by many people. Tours are not available but there are tastings and sales Monday–Friday 8.30 a.m.–5 p.m. and Saturday 8.30 a.m.–12 noon.

Van Ryn Brandy Cellar. On the R310 near Vlottenberg. Tel. (02231) 9-3875. Visitors are introduced to the brandy-making process with a video presentation. From here the tour progresses to the distillery, maturation cellar and cooperage, where master coopers are at work making oak vats. Tours are given at 10.30 a.m. and 2.30 p.m. on Monday–Thursday and at 10.30 a.m. on Friday.

SERVICES

TOURIST INFORMATION

Visitors' Bureau, 30 Plein St. Tel. (02231) 3584. The very helpful public relations director will help you to find accommodation in the area. A number of brochures, route guides and maps are available free of charge, and they are useful for exploring the historic places in town and the wine estates. Open Monday–Friday 9 a.m.–4.30 p.m.; Saturday 9 a.m.–12 noon.

For detailed information on the vineyards, visit the Stellenbosch Wine Route Office, situated next to the Doornbosch Restaurant on the R44; open MondayFriday, 8.30 a.m.–5 p.m.

GETTING AROUND

Car Hire
Avis. 1 Dorp St. Tel. (02231) 7-0492
Imperial. Stellenbosch Auto, Merriman Ave. Tel. (02231) 9-8140
Budget. 98 Dorp St. Tel. (02231) 9910

Taxi
Tel. (02231) 5808

Bicycle Hire
Bikes can be hired for the day or by the hour from the Visitors' Bureau in Plein Street or at the railway station. Book at (02231) 7-4279 and be sure to bring identification or passport.

Horse Riding
Devon Valley Riding School. Tel. (02231) 9-2286

THE FRANSCHHOEK WINE ROUTE

Franschhoek Valley is the French corner of South Africa, home of the Huguenots who fled to Africa to escape the religious persecution that followed the revocation of the Edict of Nantes in 1685. Between 1688 and 1690, 207 Huguenots settled in this valley, which came to be known as Le Quartier Français. Some of them had been wine-makers in France and with their knowledge the Cape wine industry took root. Even today, more than 300 years later, many of the farms and families still bear French names. The Franschhoek Wine Route comprises 14 estates and conveniently, all the valley's wine can be tasted at the Franschhoek Vineyards Co-operative in town if you don't have time to visit the individual estates. Try not to miss the Boschendal winery however, as it is a perfect picture, the showcase of the Winelands.

Le Quartier Français

Franschhoek itself is a charming little village, just a fraction of the size of Stellenbosch and much more rural. It is embraced by purple-hued, weathered mountains and the surrounding countryside is a patchwork of neatly tended orchards, vineyards and fields. Most people agree that it is one of the most beautiful valleys in the world in any season.

Getting There

From Stellenbosch, the easiest and most scenic route to Franschhoek is the R310 east. This road winds through Helshoogte (Hell's Heights) Pass and after about 14 km will bring you to Boschendal.

The Fruit Route

From Cape Town there is a marvellously scenic route called the Four Passes Fruit Route which will bring you to Franschhoek in about two hours. Take the N2 south to the Grabouw/R321 exit. This route winds through Viljoen's Pass, notable for the deep gorge of the Palmiet River and a forest reserve at the summit. The road then passes through the Vyeboom Valley, crossing the Tweewaterskloof Dam. At the junction of the R45, turn left (north) and take the Franschhoek Pass, a spectacular stretch of mountain road that was built over an old elephant trail. The summit is at 750 metres and there are superb views over the Groot Drakenstein and Franschhoek valleys from here.

Outbreak of phylloxera

All along this route are a number of fruit farms and stalls, museums, restaurants and small villages. When the vineyards of South Africa were destroyed by an outbreak of phylloxera in 1885, Cecil Rhodes established fruit orchards to revive the dying economy of the Cape until

the vineyards could again be productive. Plums, peaches, nectarines, apples, pears and apricots are grown and the fruit industry today forms a vital sector of the national economy. Fruit tours are given at a number of farms; for information and reservations contact:
Vyeboom. Tel. (0225) 4210
Villiersdorp. Tel.(0225) 3-2126
Anglo-American Farms (at Boschendal). Tel. (02211) 4-1031
Grabouw and Elgin. The Information Centre at (024) 59-2880

Accommodation
La Cotte Inn*. Huguenot Rd. Tel. (02212) 2081. La Cotte is an historic hotel located a little way outside the village with nine rooms each with en-suite bathroom, TV and radio. It has a swimming pool, an a la carte restaurant and a bar.

Hotel Huguenot**. Huguenot Rd. Tel. (02212) 2092. This hotel is in the centre of the village and is family-owned and operated. There are 12 rooms all with private baths, air conditioning and telephones, and the amenities include swimming pool, TV lounge, restaurant, bar and *braai* area.

Swiss Farm Excelsior***. Excelsior Rd. Tel. (02212)2071; fax (02212) 2177. This is a family-oriented leisure resort magnificently set in the Franschhoek/Drakenstein Mountains, 3 km from the village. There are 45 luxury guest rooms with air conditioning, telephone and TV; tennis, squash, swimming and hiking are offered. The Swiss Club Excelsior adjoins the hotel and guests may use the spa facilities. In addition to two restaurants, there is a restored wine cellar on the property called Die Binnehof that is open for light lunches and the sampling of local vintages.

Dining
Le Quartier Français. 16 Huguenot Rd. Tel. (02212) 2248. Le Quartier Francais serves delightful gourmet French cuisine and was selected as the number one restaurant in South Africa for 1991. The food is creative as well as beautifully prepared and presented, and the ambience of this restored farmhouse is charming. The restaurant is open for lunch daily and dinner is served from 7.30 to 9 p.m. Tuesday–Saturday. The winter hours may differ so it is best to phone in advance; at any rate, reservations are recommended. It is worth noting that the owners are in the process of building guest accommodation around the lovely gardens, to be called La Maison Provençal.

Creative cuisine

Undoubtedly the 15 planned rooms will be as delightful and charming as the restaurant.

Le Café. 18 Huguenot Rd. Tel. (02212) 2034. For an excellent light lunch or a pastry and espresso, try Le Café, next door to Le Quartier Francais. There is outdoor dining if the weather permits. Open daily 10 a.m.–5 p.m.

La Petite Ferme. R45 2 km east of Franschhoek. Tel. (02212) 3016. This is a highly regarded restaurant that specializes in country cooking enhanced with fresh herbs and vegetables. The views from the dining room are gorgeous and the smoked trout is delectable. Open for tea and lunch every day except Monday from 10.30 a.m. to 5 p.m.; reservations are essential at weekends.

La Fontaine. 66 Huguenot Rd.; Tel. (02212)2514
A cozy, intimate restaurant situated in an old Cape home with outdoor dining in good weather. The menu is small but changes daily and the food is good. Open for breakfast and lunch daily except Monday and Thursday; dinner service on Friday and Saturday only.

Shopping
Ron Campbell Gallery. 4 Berg St, off Dirkie Uys St. Tel. (02212) 3350. If you are enthralled by the scenic vistas of this area, call at this talented artist's gallery for a wonderful selection of landscapes in pastel and oil. Open Tuesday–Sunday from 10 a.m.–6 p.m. or by appointment. Shipping abroad is easily arranged.

Maradadi Ethnic Crafts. Huguenot Rd. Native African crafts of high quality; closed Mondays and Thursdays.

Artists' Workshop. Huguenot Rd. Original paintings.

L'Afrique. Oude Stallen Shopping Centre, Huguenot Rd. Souvenirs and curios.

Sightseeing

Huguenot Monument. This simple but elegant monument was dedicated in 1948 to commemorate the arrival of the French Huguenots 260 years earlier and to express the descendants' gratitude for their Protestant heritage.

Huguenot history

Huguenot Memorial Museum. If you are interested in the story of the French Huguenots, this is an excellent place to spend an hour. There is a visual presentation of their history dating from the Edict of Nantes to their arrival in Franschhoek. Lovely antique furniture and decorative items from the seventeenth and eighteenth centuries are on display. Open Monday–Saturday, 9 a.m.–5 p.m. and Sunday 2 p.m.–5 p.m.

Wine Estates

Boschendal Estate. R310. Tel. (02211) 4-1031. If you only visit one winery in South Africa, this should be it. The H-shaped manor house and its outlying buildings are classic Cape Dutch architecture at its best and the grounds are meticulously maintained. Boschendal wines are very highly regarded; white, red and sparkling wines are produced. Tastings are held outside on a tree shaded patio when the weather is mild, otherwise in the Taphuis where visitors are welcome to try any or all of the wines. Cellar tours and video presentations are given Monday–Friday, 8.30 a.m.–1 p.m. and 2 p.m.–5 p.m.; Saturday 8.30 a.m.–12.30 p.m. Vineyard tours are offered on weekdays only at 11 a.m.; booking is essential.

Wine tastings

The estate has two superb restaurants (Tel. (02211) 4-1252): Le Pique Nique for simple country fare under the shade of huge pine trees, or the Boschendal, which serves a sumptuous buffet lunch in a gracious setting. Le Pique Nique is open daily from November to April; the Boschendal is open all year round with one seating for lunch at 12.45. Advance bookings are essential for both. Other attractions of this estate are the restored manor house itself, now a museum open to the public, and the Waenhuis, a quaint gift shop that sells wine, produce and hand-made items.

Bellingham Winery. R45, 4.4 km from junction with R310. Tel. (02211) 4-1258. This well-respected winery was founded in 1693 and it has one of the largest outputs in the country, numbering about 350,000 cases annually. Quality whites, reds and sparkling wines are produced and the public is welcome to join the half-hour cellar and tasting tours on weekdays at 10 a.m., 2 p.m. and 3 p.m. Saturday tours are only given by prior arrangement but tastings are held at 10.30 and 11 a.m.

Franschhoek Vineyards Co-Operative. Huguenot Rd (R45). Tel. (02212) 2086. This co-operative was established in 1945 and it makes wine for six of its 122 members with their own grapes and labels. All the wines of the Franschhoek Valley vintners are available for sale here and tastings are held between 8.30 a.m. and 1 p.m. and 2 p.m. and 5.30 p.m. on weekdays; and between 9 a.m. and 1 p.m. on Saturdays. Tours are by appointment only.

THE PAARL WINE ROUTE

The Paarl Wine Route was established in 1978 and incorporates 14 cellars, all but three of which are open to the public. This region is farther from the sea than

Inland from the sea

Stellenbosch and as a result the climate is drier and warmer. Award winning red, white and port wines are produced and the most successful *méthode champenoise* winery in the country is based here. The Paarl route is my least favourite, possibly because the town itself lacks the rustic charm and beauty of Franschhoek and the historic architecture and university atmoshpere of Stellenbosch. This having been said, the estates of Paarl are very highly rated and together with Franschhoek and Stellenbosch, produce the best wines in South Africa. If you are an oenophile, you won't want to miss an excursion along this route; if not, the other two will probably suffice.

Getting There
Paarl lies 56 km from Cape Town and the most direct route is the N1 to Exit 17. If you are coming from Franschhoek, take the R45 north to the R303; from Stellenbosch follow the R44 until it joins the N1, Go east to Exit 17.

Accommodation
Mountain Shadows Manor House. Off the N1 7km north of Paarl. Tel. (02211) 62-3192; fax (02211) 62-6796. This charming Cape Dutch homestead nestled among the vines of the beautiful Klein Drakenstein Valley offers warm hospitality, ten lovely rooms and excellent food. Combined with the availability of horse riding, fishing, tennis, golf and swimming, this is a perfect spot to spend a few days enjoying the Winelands. The friendly owners will arrange a variety of outings for interested guests: fishing trips, wildlife safaris, hunting and estate tours.
Paarl Hotel*. 158 Main St. Tel. (02211) 2-3116; fax (02211) 2-3110. At the budget end of the spectrum, the Paarl Hotel offers 25 recently refurbished rooms, about half of which have en-suite bathrooms. All rooms have TV and telephone and there is an a la carte restaurant and a swimming pool.
Berg River Holiday Resort. R45 south of Paarl. Tel. (02211) 63-1650; fax (02211) 63-2583. Pleasantly situated next to the Berg River, this resort offers camping and caravan sites as well as 15 fully equipped cottages for self-catering. Facilities include a swimming pool, a laundry, petrol, mini-golf and a shop.
Grande Roche, Plantasie St., Paarl. Tel. (0211) 63-2727. Fax (02211) 63-2220. If you are looking for the ultimate in charm and luxury, seek no further. The Grand Roche is set amidst a 17th century vineyard and the stucco and thatch buildings seem to float in an undulating sea of

vines. The 29 guest suites are divine and no detail or amenity has been overlooked. There are two swimming pools, tennis courts, a fitness centre and the elegant Bosman Restaurant offers dining at its finest.

Dining
Laborie Restaurant and Wine House. Taillefert St. Tel. (02211) 63-2034. This is one of the best restaurants in the area, owned by the KWV estate and set in an historic manor house. The menu features traditional Cape Dutch cuisine and the wine list concentrates on the local products. Lunch is available daily and dinner is served Tuesday–Saturday.

Troubadour. 113 Main St. Tel. (02211) 63-3556. Continental cuisine in a charming Victorian house. Lunch is served Tuesday–Friday; dinner Tuesday–Saturday.

Sightseeing
The town of Paarl was established in 1690 as a wagon-building centre. Three massive granite rock formations shelter the town and their resemblance to glistening pearls when wet suggested the name for the village. Paarl is considered to be the headquarters of the Afrikaans language, for it was here that the Bible was translated into Afrikaans and the first newspaper in that language was published. Sightseeing opportunities are limited here, apart from the wineries and countryside, but if you are based in the vicinity for a few days you may want to visit some of the cultural monuments.

Headquarters of the Afrikaans language

Afrikaans Language (Taal) Monument. Off Main Rd, on Paarl Mountain. High on the granite domes of Paarl is the monument erected in 1975 to honour and celebrate the culture and languages of Europe, Africa and the Malays, all of which influenced the development of the Afrikaans language. Open daily 8 a.m.–5 p.m.

Jan Phillips Mountain Drive. For scenic views of the town and countryside, consider taking this 11 km drive along the eastern slope of Paarl Mountain. The route is circular and provides access to Paarl Rock and a lovely wild flower garden.

Oude Pastorie Museum. Main Rd (R45). Tel. (02211) 2-2651. This restored 1787 building now houses the Cultural History Museum which focuses on the history of Paarl. The collection includes period Cape stinkwood furniture, Imari porcelain, textiles and the work of 17 silversmiths. Open weekdays 8 a.m.–5 p.m.

Fairview Estate. 2.3 km off the R101 south in Agter Paarl Rd. Tel. (02211) 2-2367. This delightful family-run farm produces its own goats' milk cheese, yoghurts and ice creams, as well as good wines. There are cheese and wine tastings Monday–Friday, 8.30 a.m.–12.30 p.m. and 1.30 p.m.–6 p.m.; Saturday 8.30 a.m.–1 p.m. The goats are milked at 4 p.m. and the public is welcome to watch.

Safariland Game Park. 8 km south of Paarl on the R303. Tel. (02211) 64-0064. 200 hectares of open country with a number of roads allow for decent game-viewing, including cheetah. Accommodation, an amusement park, a shop and a coffee bar are also available. Open daily 8 a.m.–6 p.m. There is an admission fee.

Hot air ballooning over the vineyards

Wineland Ballooning. Tel. (02211) 4-1685; fax (02211) 2-7230. See the Berg River Valley from the air in a hot-air balloon. Flights leave at sunrise every day, weather permitting, and the price includes a champagne picnic after touchdown. Transport from Stellenbosch, Franschhoek and Cape Town can be arranged.

Wine Estates
Villiera Estate. Off the R304 to Stellenbosch. Tel. (02231) 9-2002. This is the award-winning winery producing *méthode champenoise* sparkling wines. Tours are only given by appointment but tastings and sales are conducted on weekdays from 8.30 a.m. to 5 p.m. and Saturdays from 8.30 a.m. to 1 p.m. As an added attraction, Austrian-style lunches are served on the Oak Terrace from late November to Easter every day except Sunday.

Largest wine cellar in the world

KWV. Main Street. Tel. (02231) 63-1001. KWV is the most powerful wine and spirit producer in South Africa. In fact, this company's wine and brandy cellars are the biggest in the world and with the exception of its Laborie vineyard, its wines are only sold for export. There are 11/2 hour tours on weekdays at 9.30 a.m., 11 a.m., 2.15 p.m., and 3.45 p.m. The entrance is at Gate 5 in Kohler Street .

Nederburg Winery. R303 north. Tel. (02212) 62-3104. No wine-drinking visitor to South Africa will be unfamiliar with Nederburg for long. This estate produces the largest range of quality wines in the country and has won many local and international awards. Tours are given by appointment and wine sales and tastings are offered Monday–Friday, 8.30 a.m.–4.30 p.m.

Tourist Information
Paarl Valley Publicity Association, 216 Main St., Paarl 7646.
Tel. (02211) 2-4842
Monday–Friday 9 a.m.–5 p.m.; Saturday: 10 a.m.–4 p.m.;
Sunday: 10 a.m.–4 p.m.

THE GARDEN ROUTE

INTRODUCTION.

The 230 km stretch of road that hugs the coastline from Mossel Bay to Port Elizabeth is commonly called the Garden Route. Although the name conjures up visions of parks and gardens and meadows of wildflowers, the route is only a 'garden' in comparison to the arid Karoo desert which flanks it to the north. However, there is plenty of amazing flora here of the Cape *fynbos* variety and even if the gardens aren't quite what you'd anticipated, the spectacular coastline, skirted by rugged mountains, lush valleys, vertiginous gorges and magnificent evergreen forests should more than make up for that. For most, it is the long golden beaches bathed by the warm waters of the Indian Ocean that beckon: a paradise for swimmers, surfers, fishermen and divers. The Garden Route is a kaleidoscope of images: azure sea, fine white sand, crystalline lakes and lagoons, verdant mountains, dense forests and above all, breathtaking vistas. Scenic walks, superb angling, whale watching, thriving artists' colonies, all manner of water sports, history and pristine natural beauty are among the diverse pleasures that await the visitor to the southern coast.

If your holiday is too short to explore every beach and village along the way, concentrate on the 150 km stretch between George and the Tsitsikamma National Park. This is the very heart of the Garden Route and encompasses the most magnificent scenery and the best attractions. Most travellers don't have the luxury of unlimited time, so I have outlined a Garden Route itinerary designed for three or four days which includes detours to Arniston, and Oudtshoorn (see boxes.) Neither is part of the actual Garden Route, but both merit the exploring, if possible. South Africa offers so many glorious attractions that it is impossible to see all of them in the course of a single holiday. However, the Garden Route is definitely one of the highlights of this country and it should not be missed.

Margin notes: Garden is a misnomer · Fabulous beaches · Planning your route

GETTING THERE

From Cape Town to George via the N2 is a distance of 447 km; the journey can easily be done in four hours (add 1½ hours if you are calling at Arniston).

If time is short, you might consider flying to George rather than driving. SAA has daily flights from Cape Town, Johannesburg, Port Elizabeth and Durban. Hire cars are available at the airport.

South African Transport Services also run luxury coaches daily from Cape Town to Port Elizabeth via the Garden Route and Oudtshoorn. For information ring (021) 931-8000 or (041) 39-2200.

MOSSEL BAY

Mossel Bay is the official start of the Garden Route. It also has the distinction of being the first place in South Africa where Bartholomew Dias made landfall after

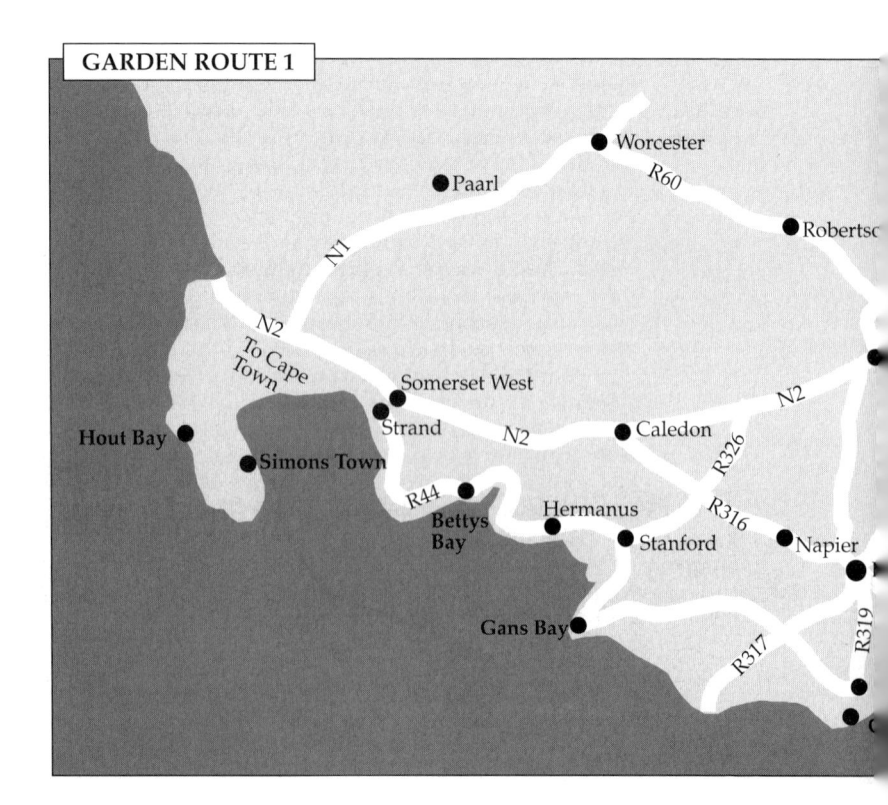

GARDEN ROUTE 1

The Garden Route

The Post Office Tree

circumnavigating the Cape of Good Hope in 1488. A perennial fresh water spring flows here and this became an important stop for ships en route to the East. Of interest is the *Post Office Tree*, believed to be at least 500 years old, which grows above this spring. The tree is beautiful and massive – as large as a house. Early sailors placed messages in old boots which they then tied to the huge milkwood tree; passing seamen from other ships would retrieve and relay the messages.

Today there is a boot-shaped post box next to the Post Office Tree in the Municipal Park and if you post a letter there it will be franked with a commemorative mark.

Bartholemew Dias

In 1988 Mossel Bay celebrated the 500th. anniversary of Dias' landing, and for the occasion, redeveloped this historic site. It now includes the spring, the Post Office Tree, a fascinating Maritime Museum with a life-size replica of Dias' ship, a Shell Museum and Granary. The *Bartholemew Dias Museum Complex*, as it is known, is open

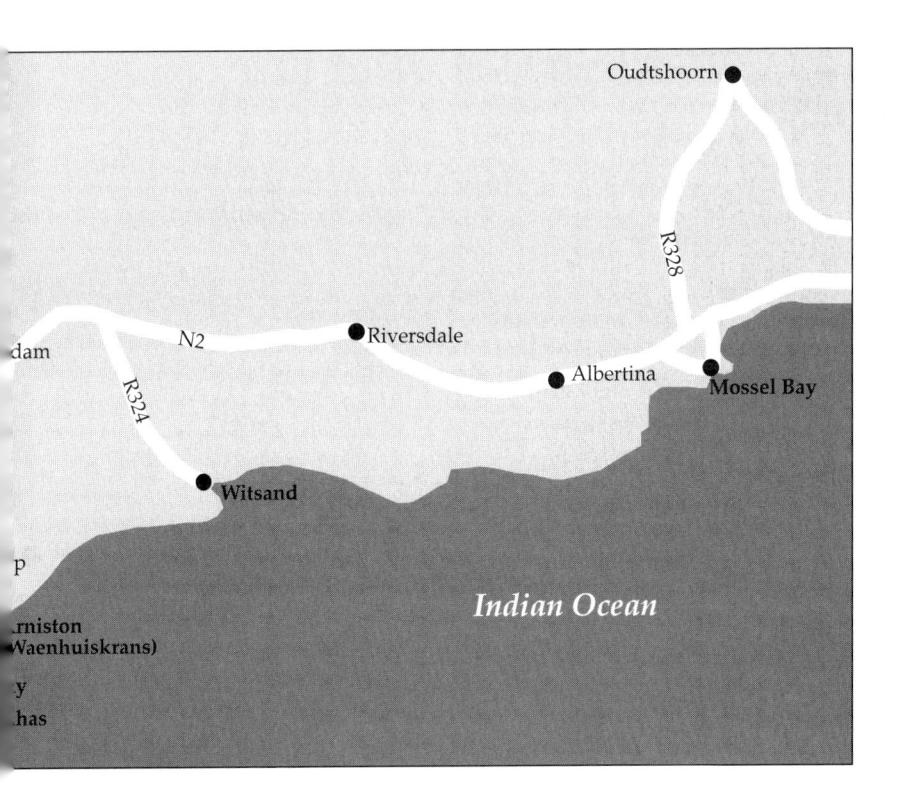

South Africa

ARNISTON

Arniston is one of the most scenic and quaint fishing villages in South Africa. White-washed cottages with thatched roofs nestle together on a windswept bluff. Below this headland a blinding white sand beach runs uninterrupted and unadorned. The long stretch of pristine shoreline sweeps out as if to embrace the azure waters, creating a small, somewhat sheltered harbour. The local fisherfolk call this town Waenhuiskrans and indeed, many maps also refer to it as such; the name, which means wagon house cliff, is a reference to the enormous cavern located nearby. To others, notably the English-speaking population, the village is known as Arniston in memory to the British troopship that foundered here on May 3, 1815 with a loss of 372 lives. To reach the village, either take the direct route along the N5, turning off along the R316 or follow the coast, using the R 44 and R 430.

Arniston is a sleepy little town that boasts only one hotel. It is a very popular summer resort however, and the several hundred homes that have been built here are usually occupied during school holidays. Itis a marvelous spotto stop off en route to the Garden Route. The place to stay is the three star **Arniston Hotel** (tel. (02847) 5-9000 on the seafront. There are 24 bright and airy, newly renovated rooms. Those in the main building have views of the sea but are equipped with showers rather than baths The courtyard rooms overlook a pool and have baths without shower facilities; the room rate is the same for either building. The hotel has an excellent restaurant which serves breakfst, lunch and dinner daily. Appropriately enough, fresh, locally caught fish is featured on the menu in addition to a good selection of meat dishes.

Another good place to eat is **Die Waenhuis Restaurant,** not far from the Arniston Hotel. This is a fun eating house which claims to serve the best steaks in town. A fresh fish of the day is offered as well as a large children's menu. This establishment is open daily from 6:00 pm til late and is unlicensed, so you must bring your own drink.

There is not a lot to do in Arniston other than relax and walk along the beach. The beach, however, is one of the most beautiful in the world and at low tide it is possible to see the remains of prehistoric fish traps. In centuries past a vanished race of people called the strandlopers, or beach walkers, built low stone-walled enclosures along the tide line. These 'traps' would submerge with high tide, leaving fish stranded within them when water levels subsided.

If the weather is pleasant and you have timed your arrival well, you might catch the fishing fleet in action. There are a dozen or so boats, each painted in gay, primary colours with loved ones' names emblazoned on the bows. Because the harbour has no pier or moorings, the boats must be hauled out of the water after each journey. It is an interesting procedure to watch: a cable is attached to each vessel and it is then dragged up a concrete slipway for safekeeping. These old-fashioned, homely woooden boats have been braving the reefs and tides of this coastline for more than 200 years. Don't forget your camera!

If you are in the mood for a walk, stroll through the historic fishing village with its humble cottages that hug the hillside. The people and dogs are friendly and life here seems untouched by time. Just outside the village is the cavern which lends the town its Afrikaans name. Check about the tides before you set out; you can only get to the cave one hour either side of low tide. From the car park it will take about five minutes to reach to the cave entrance.

Further afield, but an easy day's outing from Arniston is Cape Agulhas, the southernmost tip of the Africa. The Portuguese called this cape Agulhas, which means `needles', because at this spot a compass will point directly north. On the way you will drive through Struisbaai, a pretty fishing village with a small harbour and 16 km of beach. Continue on to Agulhas where the second oldest lighthouse in South Africa (1848) can be found along with some of the richest fishing grounds in the world. Here, where the waters of the Indian and Atlantic Oceans meet, many a sailor has encountered what Rudyard Kipling dubbed 'the dread Agulhas roll'. The coves and beaches along this stretch of shoreline are strewn with wreckage, mute testimony to the power and fury of the sea.

to the public free of charge every day. Adjacent to the Maritime Museum there is restaurant called *The Gannet* where seafood and pizzas are a speciality. Although I do not recommend staying overnight in Mossel Bay (it lacks the charm and scenic beauty of the towns further along the Garden Route), it is a good spot to interrupt your journey for an hour or two and the Dias complex definitely deserves a perusal.

GEORGE

Gateway to the Garden Route Often called the Garden City, George is the gateway, unofficial headquarters and principal town of the Garden

A whitewashed fisherman's cottage in Arniston.

Route. It sits inland on a coastal plateau wedged between the sea and a massive flank of the Outeniqua Mountains. In the early days ancient forests blanketed the mountain slopes and in the nineteenth century George became the thriving centre of the timber industry. Unchecked and rapacious exploitation quickly destroyed huge stands of exotic indigenous trees such as stinkwood, blackwood and yellow-wood, and in 1936 the government was forced to step in and issue a 200-year ban on the felling of native trees. Fortunately some tracts of indigenous forest were spared and today the forestry industry remains an important economic contributor, owing to the reforestation of large plantations.

Indigenous forests

Accommodation
Far Hills Protea Hotel**, equidistant from George and Wilderness on the N2. Tel. (0441) 4941 Perched on a hill with beautiful lawns, flowers and trees, this unpretentious hotel has great mountain views. The cottages and standard rooms in the two storey hotel are uninspired but clean, and all have telephones, TV, and hair dryers. There is a nice swimming pool and a restaurant and bar.

Fancourt Country Estate Hotel. 6 km west of George in Blanco; Tel. (0441) 70-8282; Fax (0441) 70-7605. Luxury accommodation is provided here in a tranquil setting of manicured gardens. Facilities are excellent and include 2 restaurants, a swimming pool, a health spa, a 27-hole Gary Player golf-designed course, and tennis courts. The resort has yet to be graded but it will probable receive four or five stars.

Country estate

Dining
The Copper Pot. Meade St. Tel. (0441) 74-3191 This is the best restaurant in town, serving French cuisine in an elegant and somewhat formal setting. The menu leans heavily toward seafood – always fresh – and all dishes are beautifully prepared and presented. Lunch is served on weekdays and dinner every day except Sunday.

Geronimo Spur. 126 York St.; Tel (0441) 4279 A very popular steakhouse with fast-food service in a saloon atmosphere. Open for lunch and dinner daily with reasonable prices and large portions.

Sightseeing
NG Kerk (Church), Courtenay Street. The Dutch Reformed Church is a beautiful and imposing edifice set amidst manicured lawns and flower beds. There is extensive use of indigenous woods in the church (note

The Garden Route

Steam train excursion

the dome and pulpit) and the public is welcome to visit on weekdays.
Outeniqua Choo-Tjoe.George Station; Tel. (0441)68202. If you are basing yourself in George or Wilderness for a night or two, consider taking this nostalgic steam train, which plies a narrow gauge track between George and Knysna. For incredible views of the beaches, lakes and forests of the Garden Route, this magical trip should not be missed. It leaves at 8 a.m. from George station and arrives at Knysna at 11.30 a.m.. After a 75 minute refuelling stop, the train retraces its route back to George. Allow a full day for the round trip or 3-3½ hours for a one-way journey. No food or refreshments are served on board so bring a picnic lunch or eat in Knysna. This is a very popular excursion and it is advisable to book in advance.

SERVICES

TOURIST INFORMATION

SATOUR. 124 York St. Tel. (0441) 5228
Tourist Information Bureau. Civic Centre; Tel (0441) 74-4000
For excellent advice on the area's highlights and detailed maps, make this your first stop.

GETTING AROUND

Airline
SAA: Tel.(0441) 74-3344 Airport. P.W.Botha Airport is 10 km south of George

Car Hire
The following companies have desks at the airport:
Avis (0441) 74-5082
Budget (0441) 76-9216
Imperial (0441) 6742

Coach Tours
Garden Route Tours: (0441) 70-7993; Fax (0441) 70-7569

GOLF
George Golf Course. Langenhoven Rd. Tel(0441) 2411

RIDING
The Riding Club Tel.(0441) 2672

WILDERNESS

Dolphin's Point lookout

Leaving George the road gradually descends as it winds for 15 km to the seaside resort of Wilderness. After crossing the beautiful Kaaimans River gorge via a curved bridge, look out for the scenic viewpoint at Dolphin's Point; from here you have a terrific uninterrupted view of the beach at Wilderness.

Although the village is diminutive, Wilderness is a good place to base yourself if you like to spend your day at the shore and won't miss the diversions of a town. The 18 km ribbon of golden sandy beach here is unforgettable, and as if that weren't enough, just inland is an unique national park called Wilderness Lakes. In 1983

Wilderness Lakes system

it was proclaimed the first National Lakes Area in an innovative conservation move aimed at reconciling the protection of the environment with man's utilization of it. The Lakes along the coast were coming under increasing pressure, and in a country not blessed with many wetlands it was important to save this one from the onslaught of development, with its corollaries of pollution and habitat degradation. The Wilderness Lakes system stretches for 50 km from the Touw River in the west to the Goukamma River in the east, a narrow strip of land sandwiched between the Indian Ocean and the Outeniqua Mountains.

This region has been likened to a necklace, and from the air it looks like a continuous string of glistening vlei, river and marsh, all controlled and shaped by tidal flow. The vegetation is incredibly diverse, ranging from hardwood rain forest to the reeds and rushes of the lagoons and the scrub grasses of dune barriers. Water activities such as swimming, boating, skiing, wind surfing and fishing are popular and offer an alternative to the big surf of the coastal beaches.

The village itself has a grocery shop, a chemist, a petrol station, a post office, an art gallery with a coffee bar, a curio shop and a restaurant. A tourist association recently was established; it is located at the railway station, tel. (0441) 77-0045.

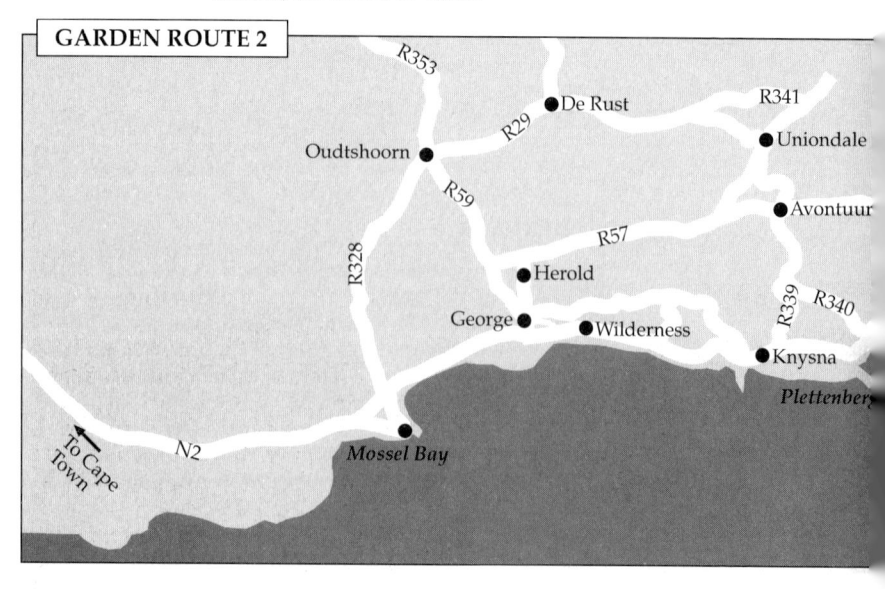

GARDEN ROUTE 2

The Garden Route

Accommodation.
Karos Wilderness Hotel***, Tel. (0441) 9-1110; Fax (0441) 90600 Situated on the northern side of the road overlooking the Touw River lagoon, this very pretty hotel has recently been doubled in size. The rooms in the new wing are spacious and pleasantly appointed; those in the older part need refurbishing. The majority of rooms do not have sea views. There are swimming pools, a playground, tennis courts, a gym, a carvery restaurant and a cocktail lounge.

Wilderness Holiday Inn***, Tel (0441) 9-1104; Fax (0441) 9-1134 Perched on a bluff high above Flat Rock Beach, this is the only hotel in Wilderness that is directly on the sea. The rooms are standard and need redecorating but you can't beat the setting. The grounds are well kept and facilities include a large swimming pool, tennis court, a playground, a volleyball and pitch and put. There are two good restaurants, a bar and a disco.

Fairy Knowe Hotel**, Dumbleton Rd. Tel. (0441) 9-1100; fax (0441) 9-3064. This resort is tucked away on the banks of the Touw River, 2 1/2 km from the village. Rooms are small but clean, and all have private baths, TV, telephone and radio. Also available are a number of de luxe thatched rondavels. Fairy Knowe caters for families and a number of activities are offered: tennis, water skiing, canoeing, paddle boats and river bathing.

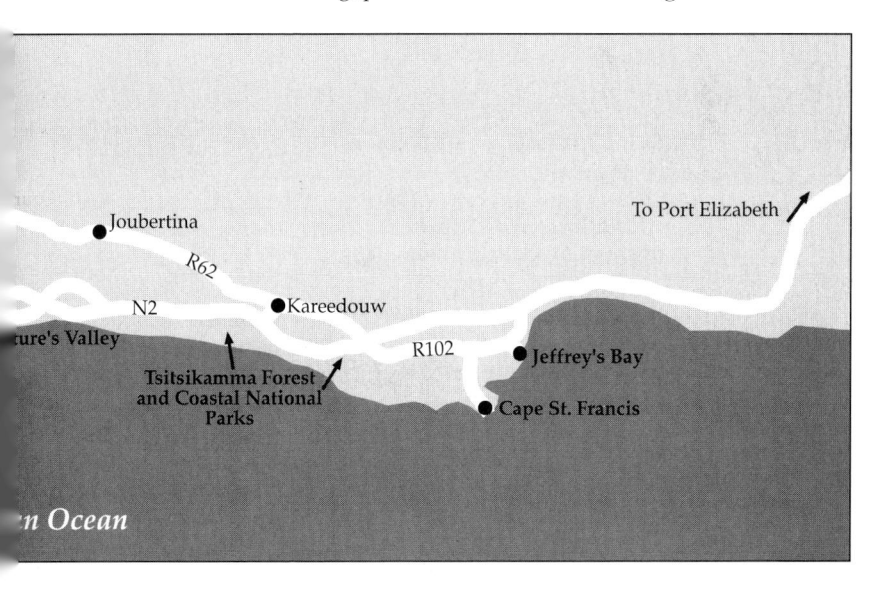

On the beach

The beach at Wilderness as seen from Dolphin's Point.

Wilderness Rest Camp. Tel. (0441) 74-6924 or contact the National Parks Board, POBox 787, Pretoria 0001; tel.(012) 343-1991; fax (0 12)343-0905. Situated on verdant banks at the confluence of the Touw River and the Serpentine Channel, this lovely camp provides both fully-equippped chalets and caravan and camp sites. Boats and caravans are also available for hire.

Dining:
There is only one separate restaurant in Wilderness: most holiday makers self-cater or eat in one of the hotel restaurants.
Uncle Tom's Tavern, Wilderness Village. A casual place with a large menu featuring pasta, pizzas and seafood; open for lunch and dinner daily.

Activities

The Kingfisher Trails

Birdwatching and Walking. The Pied Kingfisher Trail originates near the Karos Wilderness Hotel; it is so named for one of the five varieties of kingfishers which inhabit this area. To create the trail an elevated boardwalk was constructed that skirts the edge of the Touw Lagoon for 1.4 km; the boardwalk was cleverly built over the water and curves through stands of reeds. It is very scenic and the bird-watching opportunities are excellent. Four other Kingfisher Trails have also been developed to create a network of paths through the National Lakes Area. The Wilderness tourist office can

provide interested visitors with maps and details of these other walks.
Horse Riding. *Cherie's Riding Centre*, Sedgefield; tel. (04455) 3-1575.

KNYSNA
The 40 km stretch from Wilderness to Knysna on the N2 is a delightful drive which skirts the shore of pristine lakes and edges along the base of tree-covered mountain slopes. Knysna (pronounced 'nigh-znah'), is a Hottentot word meaning 'from the forest'. Girdled by ancient stands of trees and a large tidal lagoon, the town was founded in 1803 and grew to become a vital port for the timber trade. The safe anchorage afforded by the lagoon provided a perfect harbour for the docking of ships; in the 1870s some 80 ships a day moored in Knysna. Twin cliffs, called the Heads, stand guard like sentinels at the entrance to the lagoon. The passage through these imposing portals was treacherous and many a ship was lost on the rocks while crossing the bar. Today, Knysna is a popular and lively holiday resort, a charming blend of old and new with many shops, restaurants and interesting sightseeing. In additon, there are seven beautiful beaches in the area, stretching from Buffels Bay to Noetzie, although none are in Knysna proper.

The Heads

Seven beaches

Accommodation
Knysna Protea Hotel***, 51 Main St.. Tel. (0445) 2-2127. One of the ubiquitous Protea establishments, this hotel is situated right in the centre of town. There are 50 luxurious rooms with tasteful furnished as well as a pool, a restaurant and a bar.

Yellowwood Lodge. 18 Handel St. Tel. (0445) 82-5906. A charming Victorian bed and breakfast within walking distance of town, affording beautiful views across the lagoon to the Heads. The five suites all have their own sitting areas and private bathrooms and are lovingly furnished with antiques.

Bed and breakfast

Belvidere House Belvidere Estate. Tel. (0445) 87-1055; Fax (0445) 87-1059 Framed by beautiful oak and gum trees planted over a century ago, the historic Belvidere House offers gracious country house accommodation enhanced by delicious home cooking. The spacious guest cottages are individually decorated and each has an en suite bathroom, a living room with fireplace, TV, telephone and a mini- fridge. The estate is on the Knysna Lagoon; the grounds are meticulously maintained and the views are splendid. Boating, fishing, sailing and walking are all possible and there is the added bonus of a lovely swimm ing pool at the water's edge. Full English breakfasts are included in the rate and five-course dinners are served every evening; the food is delicious and highly acclaimed. If you don't feel a need to stay in the centre of town and you are not on a budget, this is my top recommendation.

Old Drift Forest Lodges. Old Drift, Old Cape Rd.. Tel. (0445) 2-1994. Seven luxurious log chalets nestled in the forest along the banks of the Knysna River, 6 km from Knysna. Each is immaculately furnished and has a fully equippped kitchen; one- two- or three-bedroomed chalets are available and all have colour TV, fireplace, braii and veranda.

Lovely setting

Lagoonside Holiday and Caravan Park. Main St. Tel. (0445) 2-1751 This pleasant resort is 1 km from town and has a view out over the lagoon. Flats and cabins are fully-equipped and self-contained. Camping and caravan sites are grassed and there is a restaurant, a laundry. a swimming pool, fishing, wind surfing and boats for hire.

Dining

Jetty Tapas. Long St, on Thesen's Jetty. Tel. (0445) 2-1927 This rustic restaurant, situated on a spit of landing jutting out into the lagoon, is the most lively place in town. Tapas are served buffet style with a heavy emphasis on seafood and the bar stays open until everyone goes home. Open for lunch every day and dinner Monday–Saturday.

Top spot for lunch

Pink Umbrella. 14 Kingsway, Leisure Isle. Tel. (0445) 2-2409 For a delightful garden setting and delicious health-conscious food, try this unusual al-fresco restaurant. Open daily for lunch and tea if the weather permits closed for the months of August, September and October. Reservations are essential.

Jolly Joe.16 Grey St. Tel. (0445) 2-3341 The best pizzeria in town with good pasta dishes as an added incentive. Open for lunch every day except Saturday; dinner is served every day.

Pelican Restaurant. Woodmill Lane. Tel. (0445) 82-5711 One of Knysna's newest restaurants., the Pelican features American 'Tex-Mex' and Cajun cuisine. The menu is innovative and extensive, the atmosphere casual and fun. Open for lunch and dinner every day except Sunday.

La Loerie. 57 Main St, Tel. (0445) 2-1616 This is an excellent spot for lunch and very good a la carte dinners are served as well at night. The restaurant is unlicensed so bring your own drink. It is advisable to book a table as the seating capacity is small.

The Heads. Tel. (0445) 82-5938 You can't beat this restaurant for setting, but unfortunately the food is

marginal and there is no atmosphere. Because of the view, however, this is a good spot for a cocktail at sunset. Open for lunch and dinner daily.
O'Pescador. At the Knysna Chalets, Belvidere. Tel. (0445) 87-1064. A very popular restaurant with a menu featuring excellent seafood, Mozambican style. Prices are reasonable and the cuisine is worth the drive from town. Dinner is served every day except Sunday.

Mozambican seafood

Shopping:
Knysna is the centre of authentic cottage-style furniture-making using indigenous timber with designs in stinkwood, yellow-wood and blackwood. This is an arty town with dozens of interesting shops selling handicrafts.
Woodmill Lane. A multitude of boutiques, antique and craft shops grace this architecturally-pleasing pedestrian precinct on the corner of Main and Long Streets.
Bitou Crafts. Thesen House, Long St. Visitors are welcome to watch spinners, weaver and potters at work. Lovely one-off handcrafts are sold.
Spring Street Gallery. 19 Spring St. Original paintings and prints.
Knysna Craft Village. 52 Main St.
Die ou Fabriek. Main St. A boutique shopping centre specializing in quality crafts.

Cottage-style furniture

Sightseeing
Millwood House Museum, Queen St. In 1885 gold was discovered inland at the town of Millwood, but it was quickly depleted. One of the original houses from the gold rush days has been rebuilt in Knysna and it is now a museum housing material relating to the history of the town. The museum is open every day except Sunday from 9.30 a.m. to 12.30 p.m.
Featherbed Nature Reserve. Tel. (0445)81-0070 or 82-5775. The Featherbed Nature Reserve is on the western-most of the Knysna Heads and has been vigorously protected as a wilderness area. Visitors may join 1 $1/2$ hour guided walking tours along the 2 $1/2$ km Bushbuck Trail. The highlight of the tour is a descent to Nature's Arch and the Honeymoon Cave at the foot of the bluff. This descent entails 111 steps which unfortunately must also be climbed on the way back. The trail is not strenuous but it is important to wear trainers as there is a bit of scrambling over rocks.

Bushbuck Trail

Featherbed Ferry

To get to the reserve catch the Featherbed Ferry at the municipal jetty near the railway station. The ferry leaves at 10.30 a.m. and 12 noon each day and as it is not possible to book in advance, it is important to arrive at the jetty about 45 minutes before departure, especially at weekends or during school holidays. The charge for this excursion, which includes the boat trip guided tour and lunch is currently R12. Lunch is served under the shade of leafy milkwood trees on rustic tables and benches. The menu features burgers, sausages and grilled fish, all served with salads. Bring a book or a bathing costume as there is some waiting involved before the ferry leaves for the return trip to Knysna.

The Heads Two enormous sandstone cliffs guard the entrance to the Knysna Lagoon, forming a narrow, treacherous channel between the estuary and the open sea. For a panoramic view over the town and lagoon, drive up to the summit of the Eastern Head. The narrow road twists and turns as it winds through a wealthy residential area. At the top there is a small car park and from here a short path leads to the edge of the cliff where you can sit and savour the shimmering sea. On the way to The Heads you will pass Leisure Isle on your right, a sandy spit of land jutting into the Knysna Lagoon. This has become a lovely residential enclave and is worth a drive through.

Holy Trinity Church, Belvidere. Across the lagoon from Knysna lies the charming and historic hamlet of Belvidere. Nestled among the oaks planted over 150 years ago is one of the most charming and picturesque stone churches imaginable. It is a beautiful example in miniature of the eleventh and twelvth century Norman style of architecture. The church is open to visitors during daylight hours and services are still held on Sundays.

Norman-style stone church

Scenic Walks. There are a number of walks, scenic spots and picnic sites east of town in the Knysna Forest, South Africa's largest indigenous forest. Excellent maps detailing each recreation area are available from the Publicity Association. The Garden of Eden, just off the N2 on the way to Plettenberg Bay, is a pleasant picnic site and there is an easy walk through an indigenous forest where all the trees are identified. The 18 km Elephant Walk is in the vicinity of the Diepwalle Forest Station; you can see by turning on to R339 from the N2, 4 km out of Knysna at the Uniondale signpost. The road is gravel and passes a number of picnic spots. The Elephant Walk starts at Big Tree (also known as King Edward's Tree), a massive yellow-wood tree believed to be 700 years old. There are a number of short walks in this vicinity as well as the 18 km trail. A family of four elephants lives in the forest here and they are occasionally seen by walkers.

The Elephant Walk

The Garden Route

Once a great many pachyderms inhabited these woods but sadly, only four are left today.

Lagoon Cruises. Tel. (0445) 2-1693. There are cruises to The Heads on the MV John Benn daily at 10 a.m., 1 p.m., 3 p.m. and 6 p.m., weather permitting. Refreshments, beer and wine are sold on board and they depart from the municipal pier. This is popular, so book in advance.

Knysna Oyster Company. Thesen's Jetty. Tel. (0445) 2-2168. The Knysna Lagoon is one of the few places on the southern coast that supports an oyster hatchery. Delicious fresh local oysters and mussels are sold and there is an oyster bar for tasting. Open weekdays from 8 a.m. to 4.30 p.m.

Noetzie Beach. About 8 km east of Knysna on the N2 you will see a signpost on the right for Noetzie. Turn off and drive 5 km down a gravelled road until you reach the car park. From here you must follow the private road on foot down to the beach; take the right hand fork. A gorgeous bay fringed with powdery white sand and azure waters is your reward. Set back from the shore there are four spectacular stone castles (private residences) which defy explanation but are wonderful nonetheless. At the far end of the beach a fresh-water river flows into the sea – great for wading. This would be a wonderful spot for a picnic lunch and a swim, so come prepared.

Stone castles

SERVICES

TOURIST INFORMATION
Knysna Publicity Association, 40 Main St.; Tel (0445) 2-1610 or 2-5510. This office is an excellent source for maps, sightseeing, restaurant and accommodation information. Open 8.15 a.m. to 4.30 p.m. on weekdays and 9 a.m. to 12 noon Saturday.
Bed & Breakfast. Tel. (0445) 2-2758. This organization acts as an accommodation service and will find rooms for visitors in private homes throughout the Garden Route.

ACTIVITIES
Camping
Knysna Camper Hire. Tel. (0445) 2-2444

Cruising Boats
Lightley's Holiday Cruisers.Tel. (0445) 87-1026; fax (0445) 87-1067
Cruise the inland waterway of Knysna Lagoon on easy-to-sail boats that sleep 2 – 8 people.

Deep Sea Fishing
Lagoon Charters, Municipal Jetty. Tel. (0445) 2-1693.

Horse Back Riding
Cherie's Riding Centre, Sedgefield. Tel. (04455) 3-1575
For lagoon, forest or beach rides; all ages levels of experience are welcome.

Scuba Diving
Diventures Knysna. Tel. (0445) 2-1441.

Walking Tours
Every Wednesday and Thursday morning at 10 a.m. a 2 1/2 hour 'Walk/Talk' is given on a Knysna Forest trail. For details ring Judith at (0445) 4788 or just turn up at the Rheenendal Post Office; tours are also possible on other days.
Windsurfers, Boats and Scuba Gear
Knysna Hire Centre, 62A Main St. Tel. (0445) 2-1342.

PLETTENBERG BAY

It is known that early in the fifteenth century Portuguese sailors called this spot Bahia Formosa, meaning 'beautiful bay'. For centuries the land stood untouched, but in the 1780s the Dutch established a settlement here, called Plettenberg Bay, to facilitate exploitation of the native forests. Over a century later, a Norwegian whaling station was built on Beacon Island but its function was short-lived; soon after that tourism became the mainstay of the community. Although the Norwegians left in 1920, the whales are still around and come into the bay every spring to calve.

Whaling station

With more than 10 km of safe beaches, Plettenberg Bay is often called the Riviera of South Africa. Warm water, golden sand, terrific fishing and the availability of every conceivable watersport combine to make it the most popular resort on the Garden Route.

Accommodation

Hunter's Country House. 10 km west of Plettenberg Bay just off the N2. Tel. (04457) 7818; fax (04457) 7878 Catering for only 20 guests, this idyllic retreat is one of the most charming and romantic spots I have ever visited. The individual thatched garden suites are set in an almond orchard and each has its own private patio, fireplace and antique furnishings. All suites have TV, telephone and radio and the manor house has a library for the guests as well as a stunning dining room where breakfast and dinner are served. Swimming, forest trails and bass fishing are available on the estate.

Romantic hideaway

The Plettenberg****. Look Out Rocks. Tel. (04457) 30-2030. Built on a rocky headland separating two beaches, this de luxe hotel has the air of a country manor. There are 26 exquisitely furnished rooms with antiques, original art and all amenities. The hotel has a very highly regarded restaurant and a beautifully situated small swimming pool next to a grassy lounging area.

Superb accommodation

The Beacon Island Hotel***. Beacon Island. Tel. (04457) 3-1120. Beacon Island is separated from the mainland at high tide by the Piesangs River. The hotel is dramatically perched on this rocky promontory and is surrounded by water on three sides. There is a wonderful beach here as well as a lagoon area ideal for small children. Run by the Southern Sun chain, this hotel, once queen of Plettenberg Bay, is now in dire need of refurbishing and updating. Hopefully that will be underway soon because the hotel's location and facilities are excellent: 200 rooms, two restaurants, indoor & outdoor pools, tennis, squash, shops and scuba diving.

Formosa Inn**. On the N2 just outside town. Tel. (04457) 3-2060. This 1850 farmhouse is one of the old inns of the Garden Route. Accommodation is in chalets set in pleasant gardens, with showers, TV, telephones and radio. Facilities include a restaurant, a bar, a disco, a swimming pool, tennis and squash courts, a *braai* pit and a playground.

Robberg Holiday Resort. Robberg Beach. Tel. (04457) 3-2571. Situated at the far end of Robberg Beach, this resort offers camping and caravan sites as well as fully equipped wooden chalets.

Dining

The Plettenberg. Tel. (04457) 3-2030. Located in the luxury hotel of the same name, this elegant restaurant serves food matched by the excellence and charm of the accommodation. The dining room is open to the general public when resident guests have not booked all the tables. The *table d'hôte* menu is ambitious but expensive for South Africa.

The Islander. 8 km west of town on the N2. Tel. (04457) 7776. A rustic restaurant specializing in 'island-style' seafood and a smoked fish buffet. The fish is caught locally and the herbs and vegetables are grown in the restaurant's organic garden. Dinner is served all year round from Wednesday to Saturday; a la carte lunches are available in the summer, December-April.

The Med. Village Square, Main St. Tel. (04457) 3-3102. A good seafood bistro with a Mediterranean decor and ambience. Open daily for lunch and dinner (closed Sunday out of season).

Elle's Restaurant. Opposite Central Beach and the Beacon Island Hotel. Tel. (04457) 3-2106. This restaurant specializes in French cuisine and seafood. Adjoining the dining room is a pizzeria and terrace coffee bar serving lighter meals. Open for breakfast, lunch and dinner.

Shopping

African Market. Look Out Centre, Main St. Curios, baskets, carvings, jewellery and authentic African crafts.

Look Out Gallery. Look Out Centre, Main St. Fine contemporary paintings, sculptures and wall hangings.

The Bundu Shop. Piesang Valley Rd. African cultural artefacts.

Gallery Plett. Village Square, Main St. Contemporary paintings and sculpture, ceramics and jewellery.

Coastal walk and rock fishing

Sightseeing.
Robberg Nature Reserve. At the western end of Plettenberg Bay there is a rocky red sandstone peninsula which juts 6 km into the sea. The rock fishing is superb here and the reserve is rich in bird and intertidal life. If you would like to explore this peninsula, obtain a permit for the Robberg Coastal Walk, a circular trail of 11 km, from the *Nature Conservation Office* in Zenon Street (8 a.m. to 10 a.m., Monday – Saturday).

SERVICES

TOURIST INFORMATION
Plettenberg Bay Publicity Association, Sewall St. Tel (04457) 3-2050.

ACTIVITIES

Boat Hire
Angling Club, Main St.. Tel. (04457) 31325.

Fishing
Chembe Charters (deep sea fishing). Tel. (04457) 3-2881

Plett Mountain Trout. Tel. (04457) 3-2885 .

Golf
Country Club, Piesang Valley Rd. Tel. (04457) 3-2132.

Horse Riding
Equitrailing. Tel. (04457)9718. Mini, half and full day trails with experienced guides.

Scuba Diving
Ocean Divers International, Beacon Island Hotel. Tel. (04457) 3-1158.

The Storms River suspension bridge at Tsitsikamma.

NATURE'S VALLEY

Leaving Plettenberg Bay the N2 crosses the Keurbooms River where there is fine boating, lagoon and sea bathing and a variety of accommodation. Sixteen kilometers past the river the road splits and travellers must choose between the Toll Road or the Groot River Pass (the R102). The Toll Road is the more direct route to the Tsitsikamma National Park, but if time permits, Nature's Valley is a pleasant diversion. It consists of a village and a beach, and is part of a nature reserve next to the heavily wooded Tsitsikamma Forest. Access is via Groot River Pass, an old road that was completed in 1885. Even by today's standards, the construction of this roadway was quite an engineering feat. At the foot of the pass the Groot River flows into the sea, creating both lagoon and sea bathing. If the river has cut through to the beach and is flowing strongly into the sea, however, the currents could make swimming dangerous. There is a small but very nicely laid out camp site at Nature's Valley called **De Vasselot,** with 45 grassy sites for tents and caravans; clean ablution blocks and *braai* pits are provided.

A pleasant diversion

TSITSIKAMMA COASTAL NATIONAL PARK

In 1964 a wild and rugged 80 km stretch of coastline running from Natures's Valley to the Groot River mouth was proclaimed a protected area with the formation of the Tsitsikamma Coastal National Park. This was the first such park to be established in Africa and the marine reserve is home to many species of birds and mammals, both land and aquatic. Nowhere along the Garden Route is the scenery more splendid or unrestrained. Nature has sculpted and carved this shoreline with extravagant abandon and its cliffs, gorges, pinnacle rocks, secret bays and ceaseless surf are awesome and primeval.

Unrestrained scenery

To experience this spectacular piece of nature's handiwork at its best, take the Storms River Mouth off the Toll Road. This is perhaps the most dramatic vantage point of the Tsitsikamma National Park. The famous Otter Trail begins here, a 46 km coastal path that traverses ravines, cliffs and the rocky foreshore to Nature's Valley. The walk takes five days and as it is one of the most popular in South Africa, it is necessary to book in advance with the *National Parks Board* (tel. (012) 4-4191). Huts are provided along the trail but trekkers must carry all their own provisions and gear.

Otter Trail

South Africa

Suspension bridge

The Parks Board maintains an information centre at Storms River which offers detailed hiking information as well as literature and video presentations dealing with the flora and fauna of the marine reserve. Don't miss the short, 2 km Mouth Trail which leads through the coastal forest to the mouth of the Storms River. An impressive suspension bridge spans the wide gap between the ravine's headlands, and halfway across the swaying catwalk there are fabulous views up the gorge. If you cross the river and feel like a stiffer challenge, a steep 1 km trail climbs from here to Lookout Point. From this high promontory the great simple spaces of sky and sea are paramount. The flora which blankets these coastal cliffs is called *fynbos*. *Fynbos* are the smallest of the six plant kingdoms and although they cover a mere 4 per cent of the earth's surface, they comprise more than 8,500 species. In springtime, when these fine-leafed evergreen plants are in simultaneous bloom, masses of colourful flowers carpet the mountain slopes high above the sea.

Fynbos

In the other direction, consider following the Otter Trail as far as the Waterfall; this walk takes just under four hours, here and back. If the weather is warm, the snorkelling and diving trails at Storms River are a great way to spend a few hours; note that it is necessary to bring your own equipment. Fishing is also permitted here within certain restricted areas and there is a sheltered cove with a sandy beach for swimming. All in all this is a delightful spot to spend a few days and the **Storms River Rest Camp** has excellent facilities: fully equipped and serviced wooden chalets, caravan and camp sites, a restaurant, a grocery shop, a laundry and a swimming pool. The camp is strung out along the shoreline to afford maximum views and privacy. It is popular, however, so reservations should be made in advance, especially at weekends and during school holidays. If you arrive without a booking and space is available, you may hire a cottage on a night-to-night basis as long as there is a vacancy. Contact the *National Parks Board* at (012) 3431991-9, (021) 419-5363 or (0441) 74-6924.

TSITSIKAMMA FOREST NATIONAL PARK

If you rejoin the Toll Road and continue east you will drive alongside the Tsitsikamma Forest National Park on the inland side of the N2. This dense indigenous forest is home to numerous ancient yellow-wood trees and the rare Knysna lourie. Look out for the turn-off into the park, and if you want to explore, there are a few short

The Garden Route

trails leading into the woods. Nearby, the **Tsitsikamma Forest Inn** (tel. (04237) 711; fax (04237) 669) provides delightful accommodation; turn right off the N2 at the Storms River Township signpost. The inn offers guests a choice of two types of accommodation: garden chalets or rooms in the 'Village'. The chalets are the more rustic of the two; the Village rooms are newer with TV, video channel, mini bar and hair dryers. The resort has a swimming pool, a tennis court, a game room, a jacuzzi, a pub and a charming restaurant that serves excellent food.

The Paul Sauer Bridge crosses the Storms River in a single graceful span just a few kilometres beyond the park. At the bridge there is a rest area (Petroport) with two restaurants, a large curio shop, a petrol station and a biltong store.

Although the Garden Route continues for another 100 km to the east, the best has now been covered. However, if you are a surfing enthusiast you might want to continue on to Cape St Francis and Jeffrey's Bay, made famous by the 1960s film, *Endless Summer*. Although the perfect wave was discovered at St. Francis Bay, the waves at Jeffrey's Bay break more consistently. Surfing is best from May to September and the beach here is also renowned for its sea shells, an impressive collection of which may be viewed in the town library on the beachfront.

The perfect wave

If you are planning to return to George or Cape Town consider an alternative route to the N2 for a change of scenery. Retrace your steps as far as the Keurboom River outside Plettenberg Bay. Turn right on to the R340, which will cross the R339 after 30 km. This route is called Prince Alfred's Pass and it is truly breathtaking. At the junction of the R62 at Avontuur, turn left and drive west for 83 km until you reach the turn-off for Herold and the Montagu Pass. Turn left here and follow the gravel road over the Outeniqua Mountains. The Montagu pass is a monument to the tenacity and ingenuity of 19th century road builders and it crosses some beautiful countryside. The pass rejoins the main road (the R29) 4 km outside George.

The return route

OUDTSHOORN

If you have time for another diversion, I strongly recommend a visit to Oudtshoorn. Instead of turning south to George at Herold, continue on the R62 until you reach the R29; from here head north for 32 km. Oudtshoorn is located in a region known as the Little Karoo. Semi-desert in climate, terrain and flora, it is an arid but serenely beautiful landscape and is the perfect

South Africa

Ostrich captial of the world

habitat for ostriches. At the turn of the century when ostrich feathers were all the rage in Europe, farmers became millionaire 'feather barons' overnight and palatial Victorian mansions were built in the region. Alas, the heyday was shortlived and with the advent of the First World War ostrich boas went out of fashion. By the 1950s business had revived but never to the extent of the golden years when there were over 750,000 birds in the region and feathers fetched R500 per kilogramme.

Despite its relative decline in fortune, Oudtshoorn is still the ostrich feather capital of the world. There are approximately 150,000 ostriches in the world and 120,000 of them live in the Little Karoo. Feathers are still prized but they are no longer the only ostrich product: skins are used for all kinds of expensive leather articles and biltong is made from the meat.

Accommodation

There are several places to stay. The **Oudtshoorn Holiday Inn*****, Van der Riet and Baron van Rheede St. Tel. (04431) 22-2201; fax (04431) 22-3003) has been refurbished recently and is ideally situated as a base for the area's attractions. There are 120 guest rooms with air conditioning, colour TV, video channel and telephone. Facilities include a swimming pool, a tennis court, a miniature golf course and a restaurant. The **Kango Protea Inn*****, Baron van Rheede St. (tel. (0443) 6161; fax (0443) 22-6772) is on the outskirts of town on the road to the Cango Caves. The atmosphere is rural and guests are accommodated in clean, modestly furnished thatched-roof rondavels and motel-style rooms (complete with air conditioning). It has an excellent restaurant and swimming pool, and riding can be arranged. The **Kleinplaas Holiday Resort**, 171 Baron van Rheede St. (tel. (04431) 5811) is a lovely resort for campers and self-caterers offering electric hook up points, a laundry, a pool, a shop, a restaurant and fully-equipped chalets.

Sightseeing

In Oudtshoorn itself, you might like to visit the **C.P. Nel Museum,** 146 High Street. This building was originally erected during the boom days as a Boys' High School. Of special note is the fine sandstone masonry, the product of Irish stone masons who were brought to Oudtshoorn to build fancy mansions for the 'feather barons'. Today the building houses a small museum that focuses on the history of the town during the ostrich boom. It is open from 9.30 a.m. - 1 p.m. and 2 p.m.- 5 p.m., Monday –

The Garden Route

Saturday and from 2.30 p.m. to 5 p.m. Sunday.

Safari and Highgate Ostrich Show Farms
Two commercial ostrich farms are open to the public, the *Safari* and *Highgates*. Both are about 8 km south-west of Oudtshoorn on the R358 (signposted to Mossel Bay).

Ride an ostrich!

Fascinating and informative two hour guided tours are offered throughout the day and adventurous visitors can even try their hand at riding an ostrich!

I highly recommend either of these show farms for an unforgettable and unique outing. The gift shops at the farms sell a wide variety of ostrich leather goods, boas and shell articles and the prices are the best in the country. As an added attraction, at the **Safari Show Farm** the public is welcome to tour one of the original feather palaces dating from the golden days. They are open daily from 7.30 a.m. to 5 p.m. (tel. (04431) 7311 and (04431) 7115 respectively)

Cango Caves
About 26 km north of Oudtshoorn on the R328 in the foothills of the Swartberg Mountains, there is an extensive network of 80 caverns that extends for 3 km underground. The **Cango Caves** are the second largest in South Africa and two hour guided tours allow you a partial glimpse of this fabulous underworld. The calcite caves were originally used for shelter by the Bushmen in the Later Stone Age as evidenced by the rock paintings near the entrance. Today, for purposes of drama and tourism, music and coloured lights are used to highlight an amazing array of stalagmites and stalactites in grotesque and fanatastic shapes. For the truly brave there is an opportunity to leave the standard tour and do a bit of exploring without the benefit of guide or light. This necessitates crawling on your stomach through a maze of tight passageways and chutes to reach the **Devil's Chimney**. This little bit of caving is definitely not for the faint-hearted, overweight or claustrophobic! Guided tours are given every hour on the hour, December – April from 9 a.m. to 5 p.m.. The rest of the year the caves are open from 9 a.m. to 3 p.m. and tours leave at 9 a.m., 11 a.m., 1 p.m. and 3 p.m..

Guided cave tours

Cango Crocodile Ranch and Cheetahland

Crocodiles and cheetahs

Just 3 km outside Oudtshoorn on your way to the Cango Caves you will pass the **Cango Crocodile Ranch**, a commercial concern that is open to the public. Here you can learn all you ever wanted to know, and more, about these ancient reptiles during a 30 minute guided tour. In addition to the crocodiles, part of the property is devoted to an attraction called **Cheetahland**. A raised walkway meanders through the bushveld; you can observe and photograph Africa's big cats (lion, leopard and cheetah) in a restricted version of their natural environment. Added attractions include a curio shop, a tea garden, a reptile museum, a children's playground, a snake park and a farmyard with tame animals for petting. Tours are given every hour daily except during school holidays when they are every half-hour. The park is open from 8 a.m.to 4.15 p.m. (5 p.m. in summer).

KALAHARI GEMSBOK PARK

INTRODUCTION

In 1931 close to a million hectares were proclaimed a national park by the South African government in response to rampant game poaching in the Kalahari Desert. When an additional 1.8 million hectares of Bechuanaland (Botswana) territory was granted in 1938, the Kalahari Gemsbok Park became one of the largest sanctuaries in Southern Africa. Today it is under the control of the South African National Parks Board and is only accessible from South Africa, despite its common border with Namibia and Botswana. Although the territory includes an international border, there is no fence dividing the Kalahari Gemsbok Park and the adjoining Gemsbok National Park in Botswana. The very survival of the game depends on their ability to migrate freely throughout this region, especially during the not uncommon drought periods. The two parks form a self-regulating ecosystem with rainfall the main driving force. Consequently, the variety and numbers of species that you may see will fluctuate according to the time of year and the annual rainfall.

<small>Unfenced border with Botswana</small>

The Kalahari Gemsbok Park is really off the beaten path for the majority of visitors to South Africa. It is not near any city or area of tourist interest so a visit there has to be specially planned. Its appeal is not always readily apparent to first-time visitors. This is an arid, semi-desert region that suffers from a perennial shortage of water. As such, the vegetation is restricted to hardy acacia and shepherd trees, scrub grasses and drought-adapted plants. However, when it does rain, usually between December and March, an amazing variety of seeds germinate and the Kalahari's harsh aspect is softened by

<small>Off-the-beaten path</small>

the pale green of new grass and leaf. This is when the park is at its most beautiful, although it is also the hottest time of the year, with temperatures often reaching 48°C.

Fluctuating animal populations

Despite the fact that the Kalahari has no permanent natural water, a great many animals thrive here. However, it must be said that this park in no way compares to the Kruger in terms of game viewing; the game is much more difficult to find and there is less of it than in the Kruger National Park. Nevertheless, there is great beauty here and the rationale for a journey to the Kalahari Gemsbok Park should be the opportunity to experience the limitless space and the serenity of desert landscapes with the added bonus of observing some game.

Chronic shortage of water

As I have said, water is the critical variable in the Kalahari. The more or less chronic shortage of rainfall in this region prompted the Parks Board to establish a system of windmills to provide surface water during times of serious drought, for both humanitarian and tourism reasons. When the rains failed in 1979 there were over 150,000 blue wildebeest alone migrating through the Park in search of water. In 1985 there was another migration, this time a herd of 3,000 eland. One of the animals was so thirsty that it drank from a container held by a park official. Two year old eland did not know how to drink water and were observed trying to bite it; in all likelihood, they had never seen open water in their young lives. To some, the windmills are a symbol of man's interference with and manipulation of nature. Without this emergency source of water, however, the very survival of tens of thousands of animals as well as an entire ecosystem would be at risk.

The Kalahari Gemsbok Park is home to 58 species of mammals, of which 19 are predators. Most animals are encountered in the dry riverbeds adjacent to the two main roads that traverse the park. Those most frequently seen are gemsbok (oryx), springbok, eland, red hartebeest and blue wildebeest. Kalahari lions, distinguished by their dark manes, number about 250 and if you are lucky you might spot leopard, cheetah and brown hyena. Ostriches are numerous and 215 species of birds have been recorded. The best time for game viewing are August to October and March to May.

The red Kalahari sand

The sands of the Kalahari Desert are unmistakable. They occur north of the Orange River through eastern Namibia and Botswana and continue into Angola and Zaire. The colour of the sand is a deep, rusty red and is due to the presence of iron oxide which has been deposited by the wind on the grains of sand. The sight of these gently undulating, orange-red dunes boldly outlined against the backdrop of an intensely blue and cloudless sky is unique and unforgettable.

Another distinctive Kalahari feature is the massive communal nests of the sociable weaver *(Philetairus socius)*.

Gregarious sociable weavers

These birds are consummate thatchers and most camel thorn trees and telephone poles bear testimony to their industriousness. The nests can accommodate 2 – 500 birds and some measure as much as 4 metres in height and 7 metres in length! The nests contain a number of separate round chambers, each with its own entrance tunnel. The thick layers of straw provide excellent insulation from both heat and cold. The sociable weavers are as gregarious as their name suggests, for they are known to share their homes with several other species of birds.

GETTING THERE
From Cape Town and Johannesburg there are SAA flights to Upington, the closest town, four or five times weekly. Cars can be hired from Avis at the airport or in Upington itself. From Upington it takes about $3\ ^1/_2$ hours to drive to the Kalahari Gemsbok Park; the roads are mostly gravel but are in the process of being tarred. It is also possible to charter a plane from Upington directly into the Park. For details contact Walker Flying Services at (054) 2-3283. Cars and mini buses may then be hired at Twee Rivieren Camp.

Upington is served by passenger train and Mainliner coaches from Johannesburg and Cape Town, a less expensive alternative to flying.

ACCOMMODATION

Upington

Upington is the main centre of the north-western Cape and Kalahari region. A vast irrigation system taps into the perennial Orange River and allows the town literally to bloom in the heart of the desert. A pleasant town, it is 330 km from the Twee Rivieren gate of the Kalahari Gemsbok Park. If you decide to stay here the brand new **Oasis Protea Lodge***** is your best bet. Bedrooms are spacious and attractively furnished; all are air conditioned with TV, video channel and radio. Atriums, palm trees, cool colours and lots of water contribute to the oasis feeling.

Kalahari Gemsbok Park

The Oasis Lodge was built adjacent to the **Upington Protea Hotel***** which offers standard and de luxe rooms with private baths, telephones, TV, video channel and air conditioning. The rooms and public areas were worn and shabby at the time of writing and it is likely that this hotel will close for refurbishing at some future date. Both hotels are at 26 Schroder St. Upington 8800. Tel. and fax (054) 2-5414.

Just outside the park

Another option is to stay at the **Molopo Motel***, just 60 km south of the Kalahari Gemsbok Park on the R360. Accommodation is offered in pretty thatched rondavels or chalets, each with private bath. There is a lovely pool as well as a restaurant, a lounge, a TV room and a bottle store. Game viewing and trophy hunting safaris are also organized by the owner at her private 7,000 hectare game farm nearby.

Park Accommodation

Main camp

Twee Rivieren is the official entry point to the Kalahari Gemsbok Park. The rest camp here is first class with a swimming pool, a licensed restaurant, a well-stocked shop, car hire and a petrol station. The 22 fully equipped bungalows are attractively constructed of local stone, wood and thatch and each has a private bath, air conditioning and a kitchen with fridge and hot-plate. There are also a number of caravan and camp sites.

Self-catering rest camp

Mata Mata. Only five huts are available at this small camp on the western (Namibian) boundary of the Park, 138 km from Twee Rivieren. Bedding is supplied and kitchens are fully-equipped but there is no air conditioning. There is also no restaurant at this camp and the shop does not sell meat, perishables, or alcohol, so it is very important to come prepared for self-catering! A camp site with ablution facilities is also provided.

Nossob. This camp has nine fully-equipped huts (no air conditioning) and there are caravan and camp sites with ablution blocks as well. There is no restaurant here and the shop sells only sweets, cigarettes, dry groceries and soft drinks. Petrol is available and Nossob has an excellent information centre where literature on the flora and fauna of the Park may be obtained.

Reservations for any of the three rest camps should be made through *National Parks Board*, PO Box 787, Pretoria 0001. Tel. (012) 441191 or (021) 419-5365. Incidentally, a new rest camp is planned at Veertiende Boorgat and it could well have been built by the time you read this.

Driving in the Park
Access to the Kalahari Gemsbok Park is through the gate at Twee Rivieren Camp. An entrance permit must be purchased upon arrival; at the time of writing the fee is R10,00 per vehicle. The park is open between sunrise and sunset only. After completing the entrance formalities, it is advisable to check in at the shop to discuss your intended route. Your name, vehicle number, route and departure time will be logged, so that if you do not arrive at your destination or return on schedule, a search party can be mounted!

The Auob and Nossob Rivers

The two main roads in the park diverge just past Twee Rivieren. One follows the bed of the Auob River and the other the Nossob River. The Auob River tends to flood every two or three years, whereas the Nossob has been dry since 1963. In the rainy season the river beds are an important habitat and the game concentrate here in large numbers. The Auob route leads to the rest camp at Mata Mata, a distance of 138 km. This river bed is fairly narrow and supports a large number of camel thorn trees. The Nossob valley is wide and sandy and stretches a total distance of 295 km; it is only 161 km to the Nossob Camp, however. In between these two rivers there is a vast area of red Kalahari sand dunes known as the inner veld. If you are based at Twee Rivieren it is possible to drive a circular route by cutting across the park through this scenic dune belt. At present visitors are restricted to these three roads because the sand is too deep for safe off-road travelling.

SECTION 4: SWAZILAND

BACKGROUND INFORMATION
Travel Facts

Country File
AROUND SWAZILAND
Ezulwini Valley

Mbabane

Pigg's Peak

BACKGROUND INFORMATION

INTRODUCTION

The Kingdom of Swaziland is a small enclave encircled on three sides by South Africa and bordered on the fourth side by Mozambique. It has long served as a playground for South Africans, first, because it is within convenient reach of both Johannesburg and Durban, and second and most importantly, because gambling is legal. Most overseas travellers to Southern Africa, however, simply don't have the time to squeeze a visit in Swaziland into their itinerary.

Although the country does have several game sanctuaries, they don't compare with those in neighbouring countries, and tourist attractions are few. However, if you have time and interest, a few days in Swaziland can be rewarding and relaxing. The landscape is varied, a patchwork quilt of mountain peaks, rolling grasslands, pineapple and sugar plantations, and arid bush; with the exception of desert, nearly every example of African terrain can be found here. The Swazi people are extremely gracious and friendly and they cling proudly to their traditions and heritage. There is a successful blending of the old and new faces of Africa in this country that is quite enchanting.

Visitors may choose from a number of excellent resorts that offer a full spectrum of activities. The western region of the country is the main tourist centre and also boasts the most spectacular scenery, and that is the area we shall be concentrating on.

TRAVEL FACTS

ENTRY REQUIREMENTS

All visitors require valid passports or travel documents. Visas are not necessary for citizens of Great Britain and the Commonwealth, Liechtenstein, Finland, Norway, Sweden, Belgium, Denmark, Greece, Portugal, Italy, Iceland, Israel, Luxembourg, the Netherlands, South Africa and the United States. Citizens of other countries require visas and should contact British consular offices or the Swaziland trade missions.

CUSTOMS REGULATIONS

Swaziland falls under the South African customs area and normal formalities and duties are applicable.

CURRENCY

The *Lilangeni* (*emalangeni* in the plural form) is the currency of Swaziland; it is divided into 100 cents. One *Lilangeni* is interchangeable and equal in value

Travel Facts

> **QUICK FACTS**
>
> **TOTAL AREA:** At 17,364 sq km Swaziland is roughly the size of Wales.
>
> **NEIGHBOURS:** Swaziland is bordered by Mozambique on the east and South Africa on all remaining sides.
>
> **POPULATION:** 750,000 (1990 estimate)
>
> **ETHNIC GROUPS:** The majority of inhabitants are Swazi (84 per cent); Zulus form the next largest group (10 per cent)
>
> **LANGUAGES:** SiSwati and English
>
> **CAPITALS:** Mbabane is the administrative capital and Lobamba is the legislative and royal capital.
>
> **RELIGION:** About 60 per cent of the population is Christian.
>
> **INDEPENDENCE:** 1968
>
> **CURRENCY:** The lilangeni (plural: emalangeni) and the South African Rand are the legal tenders; they are interchangeable and equal in value.
>
> **ELECTRICITY:** 220/230 volts AC at 50 cycles per second
>
> **TIME:** GMT plus 2 hours

to one South African Rand. Most hotels and shops will accept either currency and the major credit cards may be used throughout Swaziland. If you do convert your money to *emalangeni*, remember to reconvert it before you leave as it is not negotiable or convertible outside Swaziland.

GETTING THERE AND GETTING AROUND

Air: There are scheduled services to Matsapha Airport, Manzini, from Johannesburg with *Royal Swazi Airways* and *Comair*; connections are also possible from Durban with *Link Air*. To get to Swaziland by air from other cities in South Africa it is necessary to go through either Johannesburg or Durban. The easiest way to arrange a trip to Swaziland is by contacting *Royal Swazi Airways*; they offer a number of air/hotel packages that generally work out to be less expensive than planning an itinerary piecemeal.

From Gaborone, Harare and Maseru (Lesotho) there are weekly flights; more frequent service connect Swaziland with Maputo (Mozambique) and Lusaka.

Road: The major roads linking Swaziland with South Africa are tarred and well-maintained. There is an entrance fee of E1 per vehicle. Access from Johannesburg or Durban is relatively easy. From Johannesburg the quickest route (371 km) to the Oshoek border post is via Ogies, Bethel and Ermelo; there are a number of options for travellers from Durban (635 km) depending on where you want to get to.

Road conditions within Swaziland vary. Main roads are tarred; other

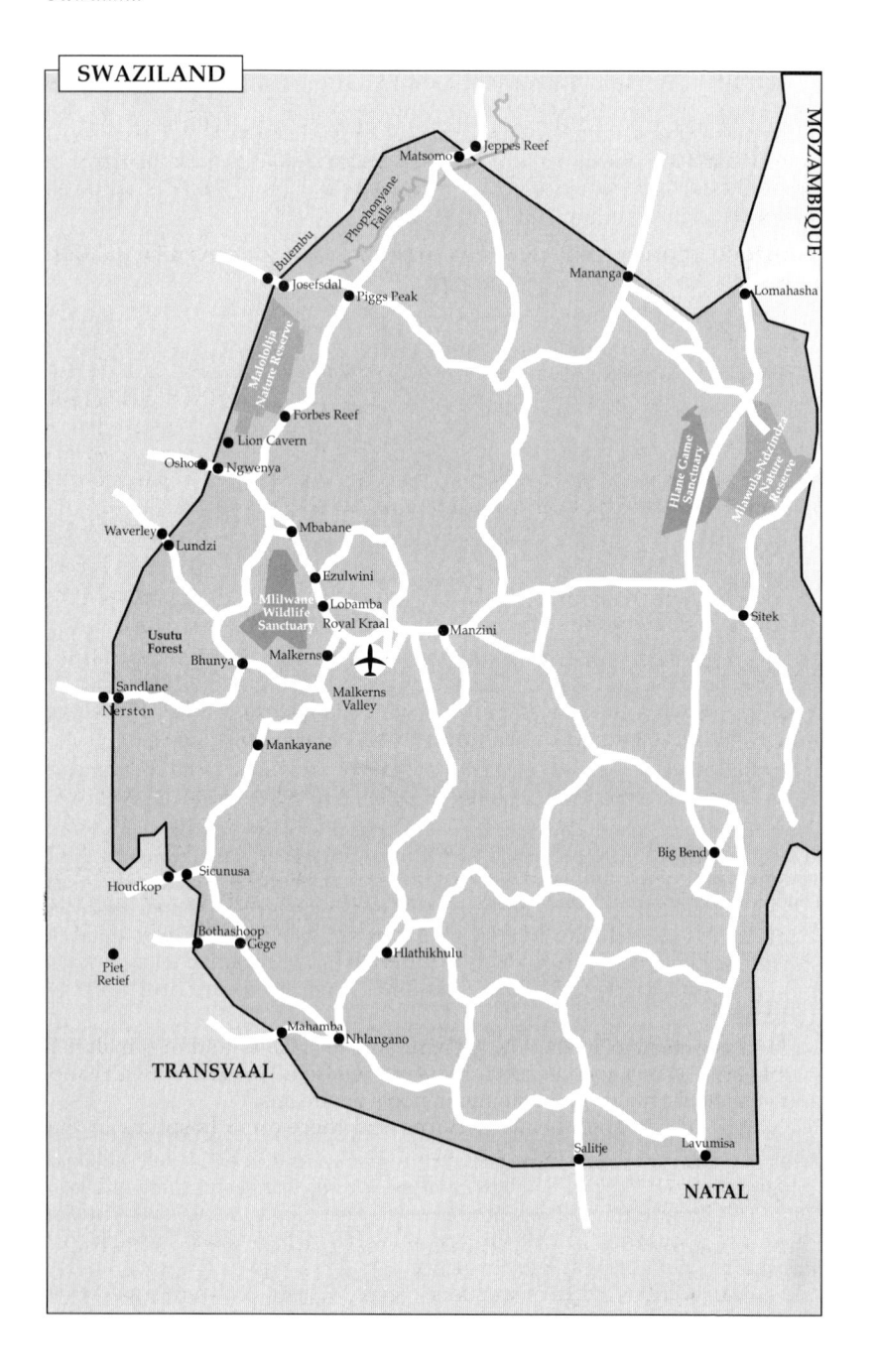

Swaziland

SWAZILAND

roads are gravel and range from good to poor. During the rainy season (November–March) conditions can deteriorate rapidly so it is best to discuss your itinerary with someone at the car hire firm when you arrive. There is a general speed limit of 80 kph and seatbelts are compulsory; petrol is generally available from 7 a.m. to 7 p.m. daily and many garages are open 24 hours.

Coach: If you want to travel to Swaziland by coach you must join a tour; refer to the list of tour companies on page 342.

CAR HIRE

Avis and Imperial both have desks at the airport. If you book an air/hotel package with *Royal Swazi Airways*, hired cars are sometimes included. Otherwise, it is prudent to reserve a car before you arrive as the supply is limited. The best map of the country is published by the AA of South Africa and is called *Motoring in Swaziland*. If you are a member of an international affiliate, it is obtainable free of charge at any AA office in South Africa.

TAXES

There is a 10 per cent general sales tax levied on accommodation, food in restaurants or take away shops, and on non-food items.

CLIMATE

Although Swaziland is a small country it has a very varied climate. In the western section, where most visitors are concentrated, the land is mountainous and the terrain ranges from highveld to middleveld. The climate here is temperate with rainfall in the summer months (November–March). Summer temperatures are warm and pleasant ranging from 21 to 30°C; winter nights and early mornings on the other hand, can be chilly in the highveld so if your travels fall within this season, pack accordingly. The eastern and southern lowveld area, in contrast, is warm all through the year, leaning toward unpleasantly hot in the summer. In this subtropical region malaria is endemic so precautions should be taken.

HEALTH

Malaria is prevalent in the lowveld areas of Swaziland and anti-malarial prophylactics are recommended. Bilharzia is also a concern in Swaziland and you should not swim in mountain pools or streams.

Swaziland has good health services and there are 6 hospitals in the kingdom. Tap water is safe to drink in all areas.

SHOPPING

Arts and crafts are the best things to buy in Swaziland and there are dozens of shops, kiosks and co-operative markets in and around all the major towns and tourist hotels. There is a flourishing handicraft industry in

Swaziland

Swaziland producing good quality and reasonably priced souvenirs. Dolls, ethnic cloth, baskets, mats, soapstone and wood carvings, decorative glassware and tapestries are some of the notable cottage crafts. If you are in need of more mundane items or necessities, there are two modern shopping centres in Mbabane: the Mall and the Swazi Plaza. The following is a selection of some of the better places to shop:

Arts & Crafts
Tishweshwe Crafts, Malkerns
Art Industries, Ezulwini Valley
Tintsaba Crafts, Pigg's Peak
Indingilizi Art Gallery, 112 Johnson St, Mbabane
Swazi Candles, Malkerns
Ngwenya Glass, Motshane
Phumulanga Tapestries, Motshane

Markets:
Mbabane Handicraft Market, Allister Miller St, Mbabane
Mantegna Craft, near entrance to Mlilwane Game Sanctuary

ACCOMMODATION

There is no hotel grading system in Swaziland; those mentioned in the following section are all recommended, however. Brochures on most of the hotels in Swaziland are available from the Swaziland Tourist Office. It is always advisable to book in advance, especially for weekday stays, as Swaziland caters for many businessmen and conventions. School holiday periods are likewise very busy as many South Africans take their holidays here.

TOURIST INFORMATION

Visit the bureau in the Swazi Plaza, Mbabane. Tel. 42531. The *Swaziland Tourist Board* also has offices at 132 Jan Smuts Ave., Parkwood, Johannesburg. Tel. (011) 788-0742.

FOOD

Most travellers tend to eat in their hotels but there is a small assortment of very good independent restaurants for those who want to change from hotel food. All the restaurants listed in the sections to follow serve lunch and dinner.

COUNTRY FILE

HISTORY

The Swazi people are relative newcomers to Southern Africa; they were part of a widespread migratory movement from East and Central Africa in the seventeenth century. They gradually moved down along the Mozambique coast and then veered inland; by 1750 they were settled in an area between the Indian Ocean and the Lubombo Mountains (now the eastern border of Swaziland). The land was fertile and teemed with game but it was not unoccupied. Under the leadership of the ruling Nkosi-Dlamini clan, the Swazis absorbed or subjugated their rivals and thus gradually extended their domain. They advanced westward and crossed the Lubombo Mountains; as the Zulu madness known as the *Mfecane* swept across the subcontinent, the Swazis then moved north, absorbing the Sotho, Nguni and Tsonga chiefdoms. Rather than suffer an uncertain fate at the hands of the notorious Shaka, the leader of the Swazi people, Sobhuza I, gave two of his daughters in marriage to the Zulu king. As a result the Swazis were basically untouched by the upheaval and were able to assimilate many of the people fleeing the *Mfecane*.

Sobhuza I was succeeded upon his death by his son, Mswazi, who assembled a formidable army to expand his realm of authority. So great was the Swazi power that in 1863 the army was able to defeat a Portuguese garrison at Lourenco Marques (now Maputo) Mozambique, and maintain control in the area for 15 years. During Mswazi's reign, a nation called Swaziland was forged, named in tribute to the King.

In 1875 Mswazi was succeeded by Mbandzeni and troubles began to brew. The Boers had their eye on the country's grazing land and more seriously, they coveted Swaziland because it blocked their access to the Indian Ocean. Then, gold was discovered in 1879 in the vicinity of Pigg's Peak and the country was suddenly swamped with prospectors, traders and opportunists. There was a great clamour for mineral, grazing and trade concessions and King Mbandzeni, in an effort to maintain this country's independence, gave away large parcels of the country in an attempt to avoid losing it to the Boer republic of the Transvaal.

Swaziland became a pawn to the interests of the British and the Boers, and when the northern, western and southern borders were defined it was to the detriment of the Swazis. Joint administration of Swaziland by the British and the Boers was attempted for several years, but the experiment was not a success; after the South African War Swaziland became a British high commission territory. Under the protection of the British crown, the Swazis spent six decades trying to repurchase the land they had bartered away to the companies and individuals who had been concessionaires; by 1968 they had been successful in regaining about half of it.

During these years the South African government on several occasions attempted to bring Swaziland into the Union; the Swazis and the British both vehemently resisted the notion, and Swaziland gained its independence in 1968. Today Swaziland is one of the world's smallest sovereign states and is ruled by a hereditary monarchy directly descended from the ancient Dlamini clan.

THE ECONOMY

Swazi society is basically agrarian; there are more cattle than people in this country and overgrazing is a serious problem. The combination of a temperate climate, adequate rainfall and fertile land allow for successful farming, although this is predominantly done on a peasant scale rather than as a commercial enterprise. Major agricultural products include sugar, maize, cotton, tobacco and citrus fruit. Asbestos, iron, coal and tin are mined and extensive afforestation has created an export timber market.

Many of the Swazi men work as migrant labourers in South Africa where jobs are more plentiful and the pay higher. As the birth rate soars and the land becomes increasingly impoverished, more and more Swazis are forced to seek employment outside their country or to become dependent on the tourist trade. In recent years the Government has sponsored the development of an handicraft industry as a means of stimulating the economy; already the country has quite a reputation for its cottage industries and the handicraft markets are one of the major tourist attractions in Swaziland.

THE PEOPLE

Although the majority of Swazis have adapted to modern ways, their belief in tradition, culture and ancestral rituals is still strong. Two major ceremonies are held each year: the *Umhlanga* or reed dance and the *Ncwala* first fruits ritual. The exact dates vary from year to year but the *Umhlanga* is held at the end of August or in early September and the *Ncwala* during late December or early January. Both ceremonies are staged at Royal Residence in the Ezulwini Valley outside Mbabane. The *Umhlanga* honours the Queen Mother: colourfully dressed young maidens gather reeds and dance and sing for two days before Her Majesty. At the end of the week-long ceremony, the King chooses one of the maidens as his new bride, a tradition that is maintained until the King's death.

The *Ncwala* ritual, a mystical ceremony of kingship, is a four-day affair culminating when the King, in full ceremonial dress, joins his warriors in a traditional dance. Both ceremonies foster unity and promote a sense of national loyalty, especially among the young Swazis. The public is welcome to attend both of these ceremonies and descriptive brochures are available from the Tourist Office; please note that no video cameras are allowed and certain parts of the *Ncwala* ceremony may not be photographed.

AROUND SWAZILAND

EZULWINI VALLEY

Valley of Heaven

Known as the Valley of Heaven, Ezulwini is the tourist playground of Swaziland. Its most famous attractions are the Mlilwane Wildlife Sanctuary and the Swazi Sun hotel complex.

ACCOMMODATION

Royal Swazi Sun Hotel. Private Bag, Ezulwini. Tel. 61001/9; fax 61606. A Sun International resort, this hotel is Swaziland's most luxurious and glamorous. It boasts a spa, an 18-hole championship golf course, riding, squash, tennis, bowls, shops and the Sun International trademark: a casino. The rooms are spacious and attractively decorated with first-rate amenities, service and facilities. The hotel offers three restaurants and bars, an enormous swimming pool, boutiques, a tour desk, and a bank. Current films are shown in the plush cinema and the casino, which is open to the public, is where it all happens in Swaziland!

Where the action is

Ezulwini Sun. PO Box 123, Ezulwini. Tel. 61201; fax 61201. Situated just down the road from its sister hotel, the Ezulwini Sun caters for business travellers. Of the three Sun hotels here it is my least favourite. The rooms are spacious but uninspired with air conditioning, telephones, radio, TV and en-suite bathrooms. The hotel has a restaurant, a bar, a large swimming pool, a boutique and adjoining riding stable; free transport is offered to the cinema and a casino.

Lugogo Sun. Private Bag, Ezulwini. Tel. 61101; fax 61111. This is the third of the Sun International group and it is also the largest hotel in the country. Set in the grounds of the valley's golf course, the hotel is modern and boasts manicured grounds. Rooms are very nicely appointed and all amenities are offered. The hotel promotes a number of special events, competitions and theme evenings to ensure that guests have plenty to keep them busy! Complimentary transport runs between the Sun hotels on a continuous basis so that guests may use the facilities of all three venues.

Timbali Caravan Park. PO Box 1, Ezulwini. Tel. 61156. Located 10 km south of Mbabane, this pretty caravan

park offers terraced camp sites, huts and rondavels. Facilities include a shop, a bottle store, a restaurant, a TV lounge, a laundry and a swimming pool.
Mlilwane Wildlife Sanctuary Rest Camp. Tel. 61037. This rest camp is inside the reserve and offers camp sites, log cabins and traditional Swazi beehive huts. There are modern ablution blocks, and a communal kitchen is provided as well as braai sites and a restaurant.

DINING

Calabash. Tel. 61187. One of Swaziland's finest restaurants with a huge menu featuring Austrian, German and Swiss cuisine; bookings essential.
1st Horse Restaurant. Tel. 61137. Curries are the speciality but there is also a full range of continental dishes; booking is essential.

EXCURSIONS

Mlilwane Wildlife Sanctuary

Ringed by mountains and picturesquely sited in the Valley of Heaven, the Mlilwane Wildlife Sanctuary is a privately run 4,500 hectare reserve that protects 28 species of animal. Half a century ago the Ezulwini Valley was teeming with wildlife, but by 1955 most of it was gone. Largely through the efforts of one man, Swaziland's most famous conservationist, Ted Reilly, a sanctuary was created and gradually restocked with game. Today there are once again healthy herds of wildebeest, buffalo, zebra and impala; the predator population is very small and does not include any of the large cat family. Bird life is prolific and game-viewing is easy because the terrain is mainly open grassland. Visitors can traverse the park on a network of roads by car, on self-guided trails by foot, or on horseback with guides. For those who like to walk and commune with nature, the main trunk of the Macobane Trail system is perfect for a three or four hour stroll and encompasses two excellent viewing points. In addition, Umhlanga Tours offers special night game drives in open Land Rovers when the sanctuary is closed to the public.

At the southern end of Mlilwane a rest camp for self-caterers has been developed (see *Accommodation* above). The restaurant is a charming and comfortable log structure called the Hippo Haunt, which overhangs a pool inhabited by these engaging animals. For some curious reason the hippos are fed daily at 3 p.m., which

Marginal notes: Twenty eight animal species; Hippo Haunt

Swazi woman trudging home with scavenged firewood.

Young maidens of Swaziland performing the annual Reed Dance.

Elephants at play.

President F. W. DeKlerk visiting King Mswati III of Swaziland.

Swazi child collecting glass bottles for recycling at Ngwenya Glassworks.

Ezulwini Valley

tends to give one the impression that this park is more like a zoo than the wild African bush. Nonetheless, the Hippo Haunt is a great spot for sundowners with a close-up view of the hippos, crocodiles and numerous birds.

Organised game viewing

Visitors can use the swimming pool at the camp and there is a convenient shop selling provisions, film and curios. Horse riding, guided trails and night game drives are also organized from the rest camp and one does not need to be a guest to partake in these activities. The south gate is near to the rest camp and can be used as an exit point after 6 p.m.; obtain a permit for this at the camp shop.

To get to the Mlilwane Wildlife Sanctuary, take the turn-off signposted off the Mbabane–Manzini road. At the entrance gate visitors must pay an entry fee and maps of the reserve are available for purchase.

Mantegna Crafts

Arts and crafts market

Just before the turn-off to the Mlilwane Wildlife Sanctuary there is a signpost for Mantegna Crafts, located next to the Mantegna Falls Hotel. Here there is a collection of ten privately run shops within a U-shaped building. Baskets, pottery and weavings comprise the bulk of the items for sale. Nearby lie the Mantegna Falls which were once a popular scenic attraction. Access to the falls is at present exceedingly difficult and dangerous because the road has deteriorated. There is talk of plans to repair the road and improve access to this site, but when this will be accomplished is anybody's guess!

MBABANE

Bustling city

Situated in the highveld at 1,200 metres, Mbabane is the bustling administrative capital of Swaziland. It is a pleasant first-world city with numerous restaurants, shops and modern office buildings. There are several hotels in the budget price range for visitors who want to be in or near a town rather than at a country resort.

ACCOMMODATION

Tavern Hotel. PO Box 25, Mbabane. Tel. 42361. The Tavern is in the centre of Mbabane and strives for an Olde Englishe Tudor look. It is a modestly priced hostelry with clean if basic rooms, two restaurants, a nightclub, a squash court and a swimming pool.

Mountain Inn. PO Box 223, Mbabane. Tel. 42781; fax

45393. Located 1.6 km out of town, this recently renovated hotel sits on a forested escarpment, giving a panoramic view of the Valley of Heaven. The 60 clean and comfortable rooms, each with en-suite bathroom, telephone, radio and TV, overlook the pool and grounds. There is a traditional Swazi kraal on the premises where cultural dancing is presented and guests can dine at the Friar Tuck restaurant.

Swazi Inn. PO Box 121, Mbabane. Tel. 42235; fax 46465. This picturesque inn is only 3.3 km from Mbabane and yet it has a wonderful country feeling, enhanced no doubt by the charming thatched roofs of the cottages and the tree-shaded grounds. The entire hotel has just been refurbished and all rooms are en-suite with TV, telephones and radio. There is a pool and a good restaurant.

Forester's Arms. PO Box 14, Mhlambanyati. Tel. 74177; fax 74051. The Forester's Arms is a delightful country inn 30 km outside Mbabane in the beautiful Usutu Forest. The 24 rooms are situated in a motel-style building and overlook the pool and lawns. All rooms are individually decorated and have en-suite bath rooms, telephones, radio and TV. There are a number of nature trails in the forest that can be explored on foot or horseback from the hotel, and the sporting facilities of the nearby Usutu Country Club (golf, tennis and squash) are available to residents. The trout and bass fishing are excellent at any of the six stocked dams on the estate. Note, however, that the gravel road from the hotel to Mbabane is under major construction, making it difficult to go out a restaurant or casino at night.

A country retreat

DINING

Lourenco Marques (LM) Restaurant. Gilfillan St. Tel. 43097. Continental dishes and Portuguese specialities.

Marco's Trattoria. Allister Miller St. Tel. 45029. Pasta and pizza.

La Casserole. The Mall. Tel. 46426. German and cosmopolitan cuisine

NATIONAL MUSEUM

Lobamba is the royal capital of Swaziland and the seat of government. Next to the Houses of Parliament is the National Museum which is devoted to Swazi history and culture. There are a number of displays and artefacts that are of interest. Next to the Museum you will find the Swazi Homestead, a cluster of beehive huts; a guide will

The royal capital of Lobamba

explain their significance. The National Museum is open weekdays from 9 a.m. to 4.30 p.m.

EXCURSIONS
Malkerns Valley Scenic Tour
Adjoining Ezulwini there is a pretty valley called Malkerns where citrus trees and fields of pineapples dot the undulating landscape. Starting in either Mbabane or Ezulwini, it is quite easy to complete a 105 km loop through the Malkern Valley that is both pleasant and extremely scenic. From the Mbabane–Manzini road watch for signposts advertising Swazican and Tishweshwe Crafts; from this turn-off it is 6 km to the small village of Malkerns. Don't miss an opportunity to stop at the charming cottages of **Tishweshwe** (open 9 a.m.–5 p.m. daily). The items sold are of top quality and I think this establishment has the best collection of crafts in the country. Behind the shop there are three traditional beehive huts you can examine.

Next door to Tishweshwe there is a country pub and restaurant called **Malandelas** that serves lunch every day except Monday. All dishes are homemade and vegetables

Traditional beehive huts in Swaziland.

are grown on the premises. Fish, chicken and pork are featured and desserts are especially good here. Try the fresh-squeezed pineapple juice: it was the best I've ever tasted!

After the village of Malkerns the road continues on to **Bhunya,** following the winding course of the Great Usutu River. The land is lush and fertile with many small farms, pineapple fields and cattle. With each passing mile the terrain steepens as you leave the valley and ascend the highveld. At Bhunya the centrepiece of the town is the modern pulp mill which has tours on Thursdays at 10 a.m.; contact the Training Manager, *Usutu Pulp Company*, tel. 74331.

From Bhunya turn north following signposts for **Mhlambanyatsi.** The 15 km stretch to the town of Mhlambanyatsi runs through the Usutu forests, an enormous tract of land that forms the heart of Swaziland's timber industry. A number of paths and streams bisect the forest and the fishing in the stocked dams is purported to be excellent. The Usutu forests are totally man-made and are among the largest in the world; more than 70 million pine trees have been planted here since 1949 covering some 65,000 hectares. Just before the charming colonial town of Mhlambanyatsi you will see a signpost for the **Foresters Arms Hotel.** This is a good spot for lunch or tea or a ride, otherwise continue on to Mhlambanyatsi. From here it is 30 km to Mbabane, 20 km of which is on a gravel road in the process of being upgraded and tarred. The route takes you past **Meikles Mount** and the **Luphohlo Dam**; some maps indicate that there are Bushman paintings in this vicinity but it would take a knowledgeable guide to find them.

Ngwenya Glassworks & Phumulanga Tapestries

The region to the north of Mbabane is highveld country characterized by rocky mountains, green fields, forested slopes and splendid vistas. A scenic one hour drive through this area will bring you to Pigg's Peak, but you can also visit these two handicraft centres on the way. The road is fully tarred. From Mbabane take the road signposted to Ermelo.

Fourteen kilometres north of Mbabane, at the hamlet of **Motshane** continue straight on rather than turning right for Pigg's Peak. Just 1 km from this junction turn right at the sign for *Ngwenya Glass*. This is the only enterprise in Africa specializing in hand-made glass; you can watch glassblowers at work and see the foundry. There is a large selection of individually fashioned pieces on sale at factory prices in the shop, including vases, wine goblets and animal figures. Every item is made from recycled clear glass and children all over Swaziland regularly collect and salvage bottles for this purpose. In addition, a percentage of each sale is contributed to the "Save the Rhino" fund. The factory does not ship but will pack all items so that you can easily handle this yourself. It is open from 9 a.m. to 4 p.m.

One kilometre down the road you will come to the *Endlotane Studios/Phumulanga Tapestries*. Here the world-famous tapestries of Swaziland are designed and made. Visitors may watch the entire process, from the carding of the wool, to the spinning, dyeing and weaving. Custom orders are taken and shipping is easily arranged. Original paintings, graphics and hand-crafted wood items are sold in the shop as well; the studio is open daily.

Malolotja Nature Reserve

Pristine mountain wilderness

If you have been to the handicraft factories, it will be necessary to retrace your route to the junction at Motshane; take a left here on to the road leading to Pigg's Peak. Once on this road it is approximately 20 km to the entrance gate to the Malolotja Nature Reserve. This reserve encompasses seven waterfalls, two of Swaziland's highest peaks, river gorges and open grasslands; it is Swaziland's last unspoilt mountain wilderness. Malolotja does not boast a large number of animals although one can commonly see zebra, impala, wildebeest, blesbok and red hartebeest. The reserve is home to 250 species of birds however, and one of its big attractions is the diverse array of flora found here, including cycads and proteas.

Ancient mine workings

In the extreme south-western corner of the Malolotja Nature Reserve lies the **Lion Cavern**, an ancient excavation dating back to the year 41,000 BC; the workings here are considered to be the oldest in the world. Haematite and specularite were mined for cosmetic and ritual uses. In more modern times this same area was extensively mined for iron, and if you are interested in seeing the pits, you can arrange for a guide at the entrance gate to accompany you to this remote spot.

Malolotja is primarily designed for hiking; there are only 20 km of road in the entire sanctuary and in the rainy summer season, these are often impassable or closed. If you are interested in walking, pick up a map at the entrance gate. There are a number of scenic day walks including one to **Malolotja Falls,** the highest in the country (100 metres). There is also an extensive network of wilderness trails for backpackers that traverse the reserve. Overnight camps are available *en route* (no facilities); obtain a permit for these trails from the ranger at the main gate. There is a small rest camp near the entrance to Malolotja: five fully furnished log cabins that sleep six and a campsite with braai sites and an ablution block are available. To book contact SNTC, PO Box 100, Lobamba; tel. 61179.

SERVICES

Car Hire
Avis. Tel. 52137 (Manzini); 52651 (airport)
Imperial. Tel. 43486 (Mbabane); 84393 (airport)

Airlines
Royal Swazi Airways. Tel. 443433 or (011) 331-9467 (South Africa)
Comair. Tel. (011) 31-5001 (South Africa)
Link Air. Tel. (031) 42-0629 or (011) 973-3841 (both South Africa)
The Matsapha Airport is 8 km west of Manzini and **taxis** are available in front of the arrivals hall. Taxi fares are not metered in Swaziland so you should agree on a price in advance. Guests of the Sun hotels are met by a minibus upon arrival at the airport.

Charter Airline
Scan Air Charter Ltd. Tel. 84474; fax 84331

Tour Companies
From South Africa:
Connex. Tel. (011) 744-4504
Springbok Atlas. Tel. (011) 493-3780
Local
Umhlanga Tours. Tel. 61431; fax 44246
Eco-Africa Safaris. Tel. 71319; fax 44246
African Camping Safaris. Tel. 44522

PIGG'S PEAK

From gold to timber

Pigg's Peak was named in honour of William Pigg who discovered gold nearby in 1872. The town was the centre of the gold-mining industry in Swaziland until 1954 when the mine was shut, owing to unprofitability. Today the hills and valleys in this region have been extensively planted with pine and eucalyptus plantations and the timber industry has replaced mining as the economic mainstay of the town. If you still haven't seen enough Swazi crafts, call at Tintsaba Crafts (open every day). The owner has been promoting a non-profit project to encourage local women to produce high quality baskets; the emphasis is on dyed and woven grass and sisal products. However, a wide variety of other crafts is also on display.

ACCOMMODATION
Protea Pigg's Peak Hotel. PO Box 385, Pigg's Peak. Tel.

71104; fax 71104. Ten km north of the village of Pigg's Peak lies Swaziland's newest luxury hotel. It is dramatically positioned, flanked by towering hills and overlooking a scenic valley. The 106 rooms all have valley views and are beautifully decorated; all amenities consistent with a luxury-class establishment are provided. Tennis, squash, horse riding, bowls, a sauna, a swimming pool, a gym and forest trails are offered for the energetic. There are two restaurants, regular live entertainment, an excellent boutique and a small casino; tours to the nearby Phophonyane Falls and the Malolotja Nature Reserve are arranged from the hotel. This resort draws a young South African crowd and many families with small children. The weekend I was there the pool was the scene of a serious drinking party and it was difficult to ignore the revelry. Furthermore, the pool is on the small side and there are not enough lounge chairs for the number of guests.

Prophonyane Lodge and Nature Reserve. PO Box 199, Pigg's Peak. Tel. 71319; fax 44246. If a more natural and idyllic retreat appeals to you, consider spending a night or two at this rural resort, tucked away in a small nature reserve near the waterfall of the same name. You can choose between two styles of accommodation: luxury thatched cottages or a tented safari camp. The tents are spacious, boast carpeting and electricity, and are nestled in the indigenous forest by the banks of the Phophonyane River. There is a stone and thatch kitchen and a lounge with fireplace. The cottages can accommodate five guests and are fully equipped for self-catering; each has its own private garden. There is a licensed a la carte restaurant serving lunch and dinner if you don't want to cook for yourself.

Choice of lodging

Prophonyane Lodge is 3 km from the Protea Hotel where tennis, riding and a casino are available. Activities in the nature reserve are centred on walking and bird-watching. A well-maintained path leads from the cottages down the mountain slopes to the base of the Prophonyane Falls; here a refreshing pool (free of bilharzia) awaits you. The path is very steep and involves negotiating several hundred steps on the return climb. More conveniently situated is a man-made rock swimming pool ingeniously fed by water diverted from the waterfall. Guests may walk through the reserve with one of the resident guides for no charge. Land rover excursions are also offered to Bushman painting sites, game reserves and even the Kruger National Park.

Don't miss the waterfall

INDEX

A
Adventure safaris
  in Botswana 119
  in Namibia 19, 61
  in South Africa 175
Ai-Ais Hot Springs 18, 88
Arniston 299-300, 302-303

B
Baines Baobabs 148
Bechuanaland Protectorate 105-106
Berlin Falls 216
Bloubergstrand 263, 275
Blue Train 169, 199, 208, 260, 283
Blyde River Canyon 213, 217, 220-221
Boschendal 292-293, 295
Bourke's Luck Potholes 216, 221
Brandberg Mountain 73
Bridal Veil Falls 219
Burnt Mountain 73-74

C
Cango Caves 320-321
Cao, Diego 23
Cape Agulhas 277, 303
Cape Cross Seal Reserve 55
Cape of Good Hope Nature Reserve 276-277
Cape Town 14-15, 17, 24, 37, 40, 112, 166-171, 176-177, 185, 195, 197, 199, 206, 243, 245, 259-275, 277-285, 287 288, 292, 296, 298, 300, 319, 324
  access 260-261
  accommodation 261-263
  activities 281-282
  dining 263-265
  map 268
  sightseeing 268-274
  shopping 265-268
Caprivi Strip 14, 18, 35, 94, 115, 134
  access 76-77
  accommodation 77-78
  background 75-76
  dining services 79
Cathedral Peak 236-237
Causeway 85
Central Kalahari Game Reserve 149-150
Champagne Castle 237

Chapman's Peak Drive 278
Chobe National Park 97, 109, 118, 133 139, 141-142, 146
  access 134
  accommodation 137, 140
  background 133-134
  campsites 133-136, 142
Consolidated Diamond Mines 34, 81
Constantia 19, 174, 262-264, 267, 273-275, 284-285
  wine estates 274-275
  wine route 274
Cullinan 174, 209

D
Daan Viljoen Game Park 46
Damaraland 9, 16, 36, 61, 71-73, 75
Dias, Bartholomew 23, 277, 300
Directorate of Nature Conservation 19, 48, 61
  booking office 19
Drakensberg Mountains 211, 234, 240
  Natal region
    access 234-235
    accommodation 236-237
    activities 235
  Panorama route
    access 216
    accommodation 213
    activities 217-221
  Southern region 218
Durban 168-169, 171, 197, 199, 223, 234, 238-253, 255-257, 259-260, 300, 328-329
  access 241
  accommodation 243-244
  activities 246-247, 251-253
  background 238
  dining 244-245
  map 242
  sightseeing 247-251

E
Elephant safari 6, 101, 120
Etosha Fly-in Safari 12, 64, 69
Etosha National Park 9, 11-12, 18, 25, 32, 64-67, 69, 75
  access 64

accommodation	67
game viewing	64
map	66
Ezulwini Valley	327, 332, 334-337

F

| Featherbed Nature Reserve | 11 |
| Fish River Canyon | 9, 19, 49, 86-89 |

Fishing
in Botswana	97, 101-102, 114, 118, 120-121, 126, 129-132, 134, 137-138, 141-144
in Namibia	19-20, 29, 33-34, 47, 56, 59-60, 76-80, 85, 89
in South Africa	174, 193, 213-214, 234, 238, 247, 251-252, 255-257, 273, 276, 278, 281, 296, 302-303, 306, 309-310, 313-314, 316, 318
in Swaziland	338, 340
Francistown	91, 94-95, 97, 115, 154, 156, 158-160
access	158
accommodation	158
background	158
Franschhoek	284-285, 292-296, 298
access	292
accommodation	293
dining	293
wine estates	295
wine route	292

G

Gaborone	91, 93-94, 97, 99, 103, 106-107, 111-112, 115, 136, 143, 150, 153-157, 160, 329
access	153-154
accommodation	154-155
background	153
dining	155
Garden Route	161, 170, 174, 260, 299-303, 305-307, 311, 313-315, 317, 319, 321
access	300
accommodation	304
map	300-301
George	303-305
Gemsbok Park	88-89, 150, 161, 322-326
Giant's Castle Game Reserve	234, 237-238
God's Window	216
Gold Reef City	174, 207
Gross Barmen	47

H

Halali	67
Hardap Dam	32, 47
Hluhluwe Game reserve	258
Hobatere	75
Horseshoe Falls	219
Hot spring	18, 38, 47, 87-88
Hout Bay	263, 278-279
Huguenot Memorial	294

Hunting
in Botswana	100-103, 119-121
in Namibia	24, 47-49, 69, 72, 75
in South Africa	172, 174, 192, 213, 257, 264, 296, 325

J

Johannesburg	14-15, 17, 37, 40, 73, 78, 94, 112, 119, 152-154, 161, 167-171, 174, 176, 197-210, 212, 219, 223, 231, 234, 238, 240, 243, 245, 260, 300, 324, 328-329, 332
access	199
accommodation	199
background	197
dining	201
entertainment	203
map	198
shopping	203
sightseeing	205

K

Kalahari Gemsbok Park
access from Botswana	150
access from Namibia	88-89
access from South Africa	161, 322-326
Kasane	15, 77, 94-95, 97, 113, 115, 134, 136-138, 143, 152, 154, 158
access	136
accommodation	137
Katima Mulilo	14-16, 38, 76-79
Keetmanshoop	15-16, 38, 40, 82, 87-89
accommodation	88
Khorixas	73-75
Kirstenbosch Botanic Gardens	273
Kokerboom Forest	88
Kolmanskop	81, 85-86
Kruger, Paul	184, 221, 223-224, 231
Kruger National Park	161, 171, 192, 196, 212-213, 219, 221-223, 225-231, 233, 323, 343
Kudiakam Pan	148
Kutse Game Reserve	149-150

L

Lesotho 105, 107, 175, 187, 239-240, 329
Lion Cavern 341
Lisbon Falls 216
Llandudno 279
Londolozi 213, 231-232
Lone Creek Fall 219
Luderitz, Adolf 80, 85
Luderitz 9, 15-16, 23-24, 38, 40, 46, 49, 80-88
   access 81
   accommodation 83
   background 80
   map 82
   sightseeing 84

M

Mababe depression 139-141
Mabuasehube Game Reserve 150
Mac Mac Falls 218
Mac Mac Pools 218
Malkerns Valley 339
Malolotja Nature Reserve 341, 343
Mashatu Game Reserve 99, 151-152
Mata Mata 89, 325-326
Maun 14, 19, 91, 94-95, 97, 101, 103, 113-122, 125-126, 128-134, 136, 142-144, 147, 152, 154, 158
   access 115
   accommodation 115
   dining 116
   safari companies 118
Mbabane 327, 329, 332, 334-335, 337-342
   accommodation
Mfecane 104, 182, 195, 333
Mkuzi Game Reserve 259
Mont aux Sources 235-236
Moremi Wildlife Reserve 97, 99, 114, 125-126, 128-129, 131-133, 146
Mossel Bay 179, 299-301, 303, 321
Mt. Etjo Safari Lodge 47-48
Muizenberg 275-276

N

Namib Desert 11-12, 17, 32-33, 50, 57-58, 60, 62, 71, 83-84, 86, 192
   tours 57
Namib-Naukluft Park 12, 50-51, 57
Namutoni 25, 67-69
Natal Game Reserve 234, 255, 257-259
   Hluhluwe 256
Mkuzi 257
St. Lucia 255
Umfolozi 257
Natal Sharks Board 249
Nature's Valley 316-317
Ngwezumba 134, 139
Noetzie Beach 313
Nossob 325-326
Nujoma, Sam 26, 31
Nxai Pan National Park 148

O

Okaukuejo 16, 67-68
Okavango Delta 5, 91-92, 97, 99-101, 109, 113-115, 118-125, 127-129, 131-133, 136, 138, 142, 144, 146
   access 122, 126
   accommodation 128
   background 121
   camping 129
   ecology 127
Ostrich farms 172, 320-321
Otter Trail 317-318
Oudtshoorn 282, 299-300, 319-321
   access 319
   accommodation 320
   sightseeing 320

P

Paarl 285, 295-299
   access 296
   accommodation 296
   wine estates 295
   wine route 298
Panhandle 91, 101, 121, 126, 131, 142-144
   access 142
   accommodation 143
Petrified Forest 73-74
Pigg's Peak 327, 332-333, 340-343
Pilgrim's Rest 212-216, 218, 220-221
Plettenberg Bay 312, 314-316
   accommodation 314
Pony trekking 240
Popa Falls 78-79
Premier Diamond Mine 174, 209
Pretoria 28-31, 166, 169, 173, 186, 199, 208-209, 212, 221, 308, 325
Prophonyane Nature Reserve 343

Q

Quiver Tree Forest 88

R

Rhodes, Cecil John 105, 183-184, 269, 273, 276, 292
    Cottage 276
    Memorial 273
Rossing Mine 34, 55
Rovos Rail 169, 221
Royal Natal National Park 234-236

S

Sabi Sabi Game Reserve 221, 232
Sabie 213-214, 219, 225, 227
Safaris 5-6, 11-12, 16, 19-20, 22, 36, 40, 44, 47-49, 57-59, 61, 63-64, 69, 75, 78, 79, 86, 89, 93-94, 98, 100-103, 113, 114, 116-120, 122, 125-126, 128-129, 131-134, 137, 141, 143, 147, 151-152, 170, 172, 174-175, 207-209, 221, 223, 228, 230, 232-233, 250, 253, 258-259, 281-282, 296, 298, 321, 325, 342-343
Safaris, adventure
    in Botswana 119
    in Namibia 19, 61
    in South Africa 175
Safaris, hunting
    in Botswana 101, 119-120
    in Namibia 47-49, 75
    in South Africa 296, 325
Sani Pass 239-240
Sandwich Harbour 56-57, 59
Savuti 95, 109, 113, 115, 118, 134, 138-142, 146, 155
    accommodation 141
    Channel 140
    ecology 139-140
Schloss Duwisib 83
Sea point 263, 265, 267, 280-281
Serondella 134-138, 146
    Camp 138
    region 134
Sesriem Canyon 58
Skeleton Coast Park 9, 12, 19, 50, 57-58, 64, 71
    fly-in safaris 59
Skukuza 223-225, 228, 231-232, 241
Sossusvlei 49, 58-59, 61, 83
Soweto 190, 206-208
Spitzkoppe 60-61, 74
St. Francis Bay 319
St. Lucia Game Reserve 255-256
Stellenbosch 260, 285, 287-292, 296, 298
    access 287
    accommodation 287
    dining 288
    sightseeing 289
    wine estates 290
    wine route 285
Storms River Rest Camp 318
Sudwala Caves 220
Sun City 42, 161, 210-211, 215, 217, 219
Swakopmund 9, 11-12, 15-16, 31, 38, 40, 46, 50-61, 74-75, 82-83
    access 50
    accommodation 51
    dining 53
    map 52
    sightseeing 54
    tours 55

T

Table Mountain Causeway 259-262, 271-275, 279
Terrace Bay 19, 58-59
Timbatavi 225, 232-233
Tjinga campsite
Torra Bay 58
Transkei 251
Tsitsikamma 299, 316-319
    Coastal National Park 317
    Forest National Park 318
Tsodilo Hills 91, 143-145
Tuli Block 151
Twee Rivieren 89, 324-326
Twyfelfontein 49, 71-75

U

Umfolozi Game Reserve 257
Upington 14, 199, 260, 324-325

V

Valley of a Thousand Hills 250
van der Post, Sir Laurens 36, 144
Victoria & Alfred Waterfront 261-262, 264-267, 272-273, 281
Victoria Falls 64, 78. 94, 115, 134, 136
Victoria Street Market 246
von Bach Dam 46

W

Waenhuiskrans (see also Arniston) 302
Walvis Bay 16, 24, 29, 40, 50-51, 53, 56-57, 59

Discovery Guide to Southern Africa

Waterberg Plateau	32, 70	access	38
ecology	69	accommodation	40
wilderness trail	70	dining	42
Welwitschia mirabilis	32-33, 57, 60, 73	map	39
Wild Coast	251	sightseeing	45
Wilderness	304-308	Wine routes	
access	305	Constantia	285
accommodation	307	Paarl	285
Windhoek	9, 11-22, 24, 28, 32, 37-41,	Stellenbosch	285
	43, 45-51, 53, 58, 64, 67-68, 70,	Franschhoek	285
	74, 77-79, 83, 88-89, 115, 168	map	286